D0083225

Modelling Fixed Income Securities and Interest Rate Options

McGraw-Hill Series in Finance

Archer and Kerr: *Readings and Cases in Coporate Finance*
Ball and Kothari: *Financial Statement Analysis*
Beaver and Parker: *Risk Management: Problems and Solutions*
Bergfield: *California Real Estate Law*
Blake: *Financial Market Analysis*
Bowlin, Martin and Scott: *Guide to Financial Analysis*
Brealey and Meyers: *Principles of Corporate Finance*
Brealey, Meyers and Marcus: *Fundamentals of Corporate Finance*
Chew: *The New Corporate Finance*
Coates: *Investment Strategy*
Cottle, Murray and Block: *Security Analysis*
Doherty: *Corporate Risk Management: A Financial Exposition*
Dubofsky: *Options and Financial Futures: Valuation and Uses*
Edmister: *Fianancial Institutions: Markets and Management*
Edwards and Ma: *Futures and Options*
Farrell: *Systematic Portfolio Management*
Francis: *Investments: Analysis and Management*
Francis: *Management of Investments*
Garbade: *Securities Markets*
Gibson: *Options Valuation: Analyzing and Pricing Standardized Option Contracts*
Hayes and Habbard: *Investment Banking*
Heck: *The McGraw-Hill Finance Literature Index*
Ibbotson and Brinson: *Investments Markets: Gaining the Performance Edge*
James and Smith: *Studies in Financial Institutions: Commercial Banks*
Jarrow: *Modelling Fixed Income Securities and Interest Rate Options*
Johnson: *Financial Institutions and Markets: A Global Perspective*
Kau and Sirmans: *Real Estate*
Kester and Luehrman: *Case Problems in International Finance*
Kohn: *Financial Institutions and Markets*
Lang: *Strategy for Personal Finance*
Levi: International Finance: *The Markets and Financial Management of Multinational Business*
McLoughlin: *Principles of Real Estate Law*
Martin, Petty and Klock: *Personal Financial Management*
Parker and Beaver: *Risk Management: Challenges and Solutions*
Peterson: *Financial Management and Analysis*
Riehl and Rodriguez: *Foreign Exchange and Money Market*
Robertson and Wrightsman: *Financial Markets*

Rothstein: *The Handbook of Financial Futures*
Schall and Haley: *Introduction to Financial Management*
Silverman: *Corporate Real Estate Handbook*
Sirmans: *Real Estate Finance*
Smith: *The Modern Theory of Corporate Finance*
Williams, Smith and Young: *Risk Management and Insurance*

Modelling Fixed Income Securities and Interest Rate Options

Robert A. Jarrow

Cornell University

THE McGRAW-HILL COMPANIES, INC.

New York St. Louis San Francisco Auckland Bogotá Caracas
Lisbon London Madrid Mexico City Milan Montreal New Delhi
San Juan Singapore Sydney Tokyo Toronto

McGraw-Hill

A Division of The **McGraw-Hill** *Companies*

*This book was set in Times Roman by Publications Services, Inc.
The editors were Michelle E. Cox and Judy Howarth;
the production supervisor was Kathryn Porzio.
The cover was designed by Janice Noto-Helmers.
Project supervision was done by Publications Services, Inc.
R. R. Donnelley & Sons Company was printer and binder.*

MODELLING FIXED INCOME SECURITIES
AND INTEREST RATE OPTIONS

This book is printed on acid-free paper.

5 6 7 8 9 0 DOC DOC 9 0 9 8 7

P/N 032373-9
PART OF
ISBN 0-07-912253-1

Library of Congress Cataloging-in-Publication Data

Jarrow, Robert A.
Modelling fixed income securities and interest rate options /
Robert A. Jarrow
p. cm.—(McGraw-Hill series in finance)
Includes bibliographical references and index.
ISBN 0-07-912253-1 (text w/software).
1. Interest rate futures—Econometric models. 2. Options (Finance)—Econometric models. 3. Fixed-income securities—Econometric Models. 4. Interest rate futures—Econmetric models—Computer-assisted instruction. 5. Options (Finance)—Econometric models–Computer-assisted instruction. 6. Fixed-income securities—Econometric models—Computer-assisted instruction. I. Title.
II. Series.
HG6024.5.J37 1996
332.63′23—cd20 95-38518

ABOUT THE AUTHOR

ROBERT A. JARROW is the Ronald P. and Susan E. Lynch Professor of Investment Management at the Johnson Graduate School of Management, Cornell University. He is a graduate of Duke University, Dartmouth College, and the Massachusetts Institute of Technology. Professor Jarrow is renowned for his pioneering work on the Heath-Jarrow-Morton model for pricing interest rate derivatives. His current research interests include the pricing of exotic interest rate options and other derivative securities as well as investment management theory. His publications include three books, *Options Pricing, Finance Theory,* and *Derivative Securities* as well as over 50 publications in leading finance and economic journals. Professor Jarrow is currently coeditor of *Mathematical Finance* and an associate editor of *Review of Financial Studies, Journal of Financial and Quantitative Analysis,* and *Review of Derivatives Research.* He is also a managing director and the director of research at Kamakura Corporation.

This book is dedicated to my family:
my wife Gail,
and my children, Kyle, Tate, and Heather.

CONTENTS

PREFACE

This book is entitled *Modelling Fixed-Income Securities and Interest Rate Options*. Its primary purpose is to teach students the basics of fixed-income securities, but not in the fashion of traditional courses and texts in this area. Traditional fixed-income courses and texts emphasize institutional details, with theories included at various points. In contrast, this book teaches fixed-income basics from a unified theoretical framework. This framework is that of the arbitrage-free option pricing methodology. This textbook is therefore more abstract than some of the traditional textbooks in this area. This is the reason for the word *modelling* in the title. It is the hope (and belief) of this author, however, that this material is the approach of the future.

As a secondary purpose, this textbook explains the arbitrage-free term structure models used for pricing interest rate derivatives with particular emphasis on the Heath-Jarrow-Morton model and its applications. It is designed to make this material accessible to MBAs and advanced undergraduates, with a minimum of course prerequisites. This textbook has already been used many times for a class at Cornell's Johnson Graduate School of Management on fixed-income securities with no prerequisites other than a basic core finance course and a core quantitative methods course.

The textbook is integrated with computer software both to facilitate the student's understanding and to familiarize the student with the types of professional software used "on the street."

Contrary to what a quick skimming of this text might suggest, this book is appropriate for MBA electives. The organization of the text facilitates various levels of presentation, either at the MBA or the Ph.D. level.

For an MBA-level course, all proofs can be omitted. This is facilitated by the book's layout, as proofs are separated from the text and distinguished by smaller fonts. The instructor may want to emphasize the examples for each chapter for an MBA course. The format of the text facilitates this option as the examples are accentuated via boldface subheadings.

For a Ph.D.-level course, the text could be read word for word. Proofs can be emphasized, and the suggested references at the end of each chapter can become assigned readings.

This manuscript's organization and content was greatly influenced by the careful reading by and comments from reviewers, friends, and students. Thanks are especially extended to Arkadev Chatterjea, Raoul Davie, William Dimm, Blair Kanbar, David Lando, Bill Margrabe, Tal Schwartz, and Stuart Turnbull. Thanks are also extended to George Catsiapis, Columbia University; Andrew Chen, Southern Methodist University; Robert Bruce Cochran, San Jose State University; Bradford Cornell, University of

California, Los Angeles; Ayman Hindy, Stanford University; William A. Kracaw, Purdue University; Nelson Lacey, University of Massachusetts; John S. Strong, College of William and Mary; Bruce Tuckman, New York University; and Adel Turki, Purdue University. The author would also like to thank Chuck Jones and Joachim Rebholz of BARRA, Inc., for their suggestions and improvements to the C^{++} version of the HJM code. Thanks are also expressed to the careful and patient word processing provided by Barb Drake.

Robert A. Jarrow

CHAPTER 1

Introduction

This book provides an introduction to fixed-income securities and interest rate options. The focus of this textbook is on *risk management,* i.e., the pricing and hedging of fixed-income securities and interest rate options. This is in contrast to the focus of traditional textbooks in this area. Traditional textbooks study the institutional setting of these markets. This book provides a self-contained study of a new approach for pricing and hedging fixed-income securities and interest rate options. The new approach utilizes option pricing theory and was developed in a sequence of papers by Heath, Jarrow, and Morton [4, 5, 6]. It was motivated by the earlier work of Ho and Lee [7] on this same topic and by the martingale methods of Harrison and Pliska [3].

This flexible, new approach is already being employed on Wall Street to price and hedge numerous types of fixed-income securities and interest rate options. It has the added advantage that it is easily extendible, and with additional structure it can handle the pricing of foreign currency derivatives, commodity derivatives, and credit derivatives (see Chapter 15).

The approach taken in this text to study the pricing and hedging of fixed-income securities and interest rate options follows the standard binomial approach so often used to analyze the pricing and hedging of equity options. This basic approach, used in Chapters 1–11, is independent of the Heath, Jarrow, and Morton (HJM) model. It can, in fact, be used to approximate any arbitrage-free term structure model, e.g., that of Black, Derman, and Toy [1], Cox, Ingersoll, and Ross [2], Hull and White [8], or Vasicek [9]. Chapter 14, on these spot rate models, is included to illustrate this point.

The first chapter in this text that takes the HJM forward rate perspective is Chapter 12, where the binomial model's parameters are specialized to approximate an HJM limit economy. Other parameter specifications would generate different limit economies and different models. Chapter 13 discusses how to estimate these parameters, but similar techniques apply in other contexts as well. Consequently, a study of the techniques used to estimate the HJM parameters will be useful elsewhere. Only two chapters out of fifteen, Chapters 12 and 13, are specific to the HJM model. The competing spot rate models are discussed in Chapter 14. Thus, this textbook should be relevant to those interested in other term structure models as well.

SECTION A
THE METHODOLOGY

As mentioned earlier, we use the standard binomial option pricing methodology for our study of the pricing and hedging of fixed-income securities and interest rate options. The binomial approach is easy to understand and widely used in practice. As shown in Chapter 3, the only difference between this application and that used for equity options is in the construction of the binomial tree. Here, an array of bond prices must be considered, rather than a single stock's price as in the case of equity options. Otherwise, the analysis is identical.

The binomial approach determines the arbitrage-free prices of the relevant security, in a frictionless and competitive market, where there is no counterparty risk (these terms are explained later in the text). It does this by constructing a synthetic security, using some underlying asset and a money market account. The synthetic security's cost of construction is the theoretical value of the security. If the traded security's price differs from the theoretical value, an arbitrage opportunity is implied. The identification of arbitrage opportunities is one of the most popular uses of these techniques. Other uses will become apparent as the techniques are mastered.

SECTION B
AN OVERVIEW

This book is divided into two parts. Part I is the textbook, and Part II describes the computer software. Part I contains fifteen chapters. Chapter 1 is the introduction. Chapter 2 gives a brief description of the actually traded fixed-income securities and interest rate options studied in this text. As the financial markets continue to expand, the collection of relevant instruments to which these models apply will also increase.

Chapter 3 introduces the notation, terminology, and assumptions used in the remainder of the text. For the sake of understanding, many of the actually traded financial securities are simplified here.

Chapter 4 sets up the binomial tree for the entire term structure of zero-coupon bonds. A one-factor model is emphasized in Chapter 4 and throughout the remainder of the text. Economies of two and more factors are also considered. Because of its subsequent relevance, the traditional expectations hypothesis is also discussed.

Chapter 5 contains an abstract analysis of trading strategies, arbitrage opportunities, and market completeness. It can be omitted on a first reading of this material.

Chapter 6 applies the material of Chapters 1–5 to the pricing of zero-coupon bonds.

Chapter 7 discusses option pricing theory in the context of the term structure of interest rates. Chapters 8–11 are just applications of this technology.

Chapter 8 studies the pricing of coupon bonds and the pricing of options on bonds (both European and American). The traditional risk measures of duration and convexity are discussed here, and their limitations clarified.

Chapter 9 studies the pricing and hedging of forwards, futures, and options on futures.

Chapter 10 analyzes swaps, caps, floors, and swaptions.

Chapter 11 prices various interest rate exotic options including digitals, range notes, and index-amortizing swaps.

Chapter 12 studies a continuous-time limit of the discrete time model, the HJM economy.

Chapter 13 shows how to estimate the parameters needed as inputs to the previous model.

Chapter 14 is a discussion of the class of spot rate models, providing an alternative perspective to that contained in the HJM Chapters 12 and 13.

Chapter 15 completes part I with a discussion of various extensions and a list of suggested references regarding extensions.

Part II of the book contains two chapters, 16 and 17. Chapter 16 discusses the Trees software available with the book. Chapter 17 demonstrates a studentized version of professional software used in this area. Chapter 17 emphasizes the practicality of the techniques for pricing and hedging fixed-income securities and interest rate options as they are used in actual practice.

SECTION C
REFERENCES TO CHAPTER 1

1. Black, F., E. Derman, and W. Toy, 1990. "A One-Factor Model of Interest Rates and Its Application to Treasury Bond Options." *Financial Analyst Journal* 46, 33–39.
2. Cox, J., J. Ingersoll, and S. Ross, 1985. "A Theory of the Term Structure of Interest Rates." *Econometrica* 53, 385–407.
3. Harrison, J. M., and S. Pliska, 1981. "Martingales and Stochastic Integrals in the Theory of Continuous Trading." *Stochastic Processes and Their Applications* 11, 215–260.

4. Heath, D., R. Jarrow, and A. Morton, 1990. "Bond Pricing and the Term Structure of Interest Rates: A Discrete Time Approximation." *Journal of Financial and Quantitative Analysis* 25, 419–440.
5. Heath, D., R. Jarrow, and A. Morton, 1991. "Contingent Claim Valuation with a Random Evolution of Interest Rates." *Review of Futures Markets* 9 (1), 54–76.
6. Heath, D., R. Jarrow, and A. Morton, 1992. "Bond Pricing and the Term Structure of Interest Rates: A New Methodology for Contingent Claims Valuation." *Econometrica* 60 (1), 77–105.
7. Ho, T. S., and S. Lee, 1986. "Term Structure Movements and Pricing Interest Rate Contingent Claims." *Journal of Finance* 41, 1011–1028.
8. Hull, J., and A. White, 1990. "Pricing Interest Rate Derivative Securities." *Review of Financial Studies* 3 (4), 573–592.
9. Vasicek, O., 1977. "An Equilibrium Characterization of the Term Structure." *Journal of Financial Economics* 5, 177–188.

PART I

The Textbook

CHAPTER 2

Traded Securities

This chapter provides the institutional background on the financial securities studied in this book. These securities include Treasury bonds, notes, bills, Treasury futures, and interest rate options. In subsequent chapters, some of these institutional features are simplified. This is done to facilitate understanding, and it is especially true for Treasury futures contracts (see Chapter 9). The more complicated contractual provisions can be mastered once the simplified versions are well understood.

The presentation in this chapter is brief, as the emphasis in this book is on models and not institutional considerations. More complete institutional references are suggested (at the appropriate places) for the interested reader.

SECTION A
TREASURY SECURITIES

United States Treasury securities (bonds, notes, and bills) are debt obligations of the U.S. government, and their payment (coupons plus principal) is guaranteed by the taxing authority of the United States. As such, they are generally considered to be default free. These securities are used to finance the cumulative U.S. government spending deficits, and in 1990, Treasury securities outstanding had a face value of over 1.97 trillion dollars (Edwards and Ma [1, p. 275]). There are over 245 distinct issues of Treasury bonds, notes, and bills outstanding.

Treasury securities are issued in two basic types: *(i)* coupon-bearing instruments paying interest every six months[1] with a principal amount (or face value) paid at maturity, called *coupon bonds*, and *(ii)* discount securities bearing no coupons and paying only a principal amount at maturity, called *zero-coupon bonds*. By historic convention, the Treasury issues all securities with maturities of one year or less as zero-coupon bonds, and all securities with maturities greater than a year as coupon bonds.[2]

The zero-coupon Treasury securities are called *bills*. The coupon Treasury securities are called *notes* or *bonds* depending upon whether the maturity at issuance is from 2 to 10 years or greater than 10 years, respectively.

There are some old Treasury bonds outstanding and selling at lower yields that are redeemable at face value in the event of the owner's death, called *flower bonds*. These are the February 1995 and November 1998 bonds. See Stigum [5, p. 427].

Treasury bonds issued prior to February 1985 are callable by the Treasury Department anytime within the last five years of the bond's life (see Fabozzi and Fabozzi [2, p. 81]). This *call provision* reduces the value of the bond to its owner. This value differential is significant, and it is discussed further in Chapter 8.

The bonds, notes, and bills currently issued are listed in Fig. 2.1. This figure is taken from *The Wall Street Journal* of Friday, December 2, 1994. It reports the prices on transactions that took place on the preceding day, Thursday, December 1. Under government bonds and notes, the first column provides the coupon rate (as a percentage). The second column provides the month and year in which the bond or the note matures. Notes are indicated by an *n* after the year. The particular day within each month when the bond or note matures is determined by the following conventions (see Fabozzi and Fabozzi [2, p. 84]):

1. Three-, five-, 10-, and 30-year securities mature on February 15, May 15, August 15, and November 15.
2. Seven-year securities mature on January 15, April 15, July 15, and October 15.
3. Two-year (monthly) and four-year (March, June, September, December) securities mature on the last business day of the month.

For example, the first row in Fig. 2.1 is a $4\frac{5}{8}$ coupon rate Treasury note that was to mature on December 30, 1994. Callable Treasury bonds are indicated

[1]Some Treasury securities issued to foreign investors pay interest annually as opposed to semi-annually (see Fabozzi and Fabozzi [2, p. 81]).

[2]Since January 1, 1983, all Treasury securities issued are in book entry form at the Federal Reserve Bank, with the owner receiving a receipt of ownership.

TREASURY BONDS, NOTES & BILLS

Thursday, December 1, 1994

Representative Over-the-Counter quotations based on transactions of $1 million or more.

Treasury bond, note and bill quotes are as of mid-afternoon. Colons in bid-and-asked quotes represent 32nds; 101:01 means 101 1/32. Net changes in 32nds. n-Treasury note. Treasury bill quotes in hundredths, quoted on terms of a rate of discount. Days to maturity calculated from settlement date. All yields are to maturity and based on the asked quote. Latest 13-week and 26-week bills are boldfaced. For bonds callable prior to maturity, yields are computed to the earliest call date for issues quoted above par and to the maturity date for issues below par. *-When issued.

Source: Federal Reserve Bank of New York.

U.S. Treasury strips as of 3 p.m. Eastern time, also based on transactions of $1 million or more. Colons in bid-and-asked quotes represent 32nds; 101:01 means 101 1/32. Net changes in 32nds. Yields calculated on the asked quotation. ci-stripped coupon interest. bp-Treasury bond, stripped principal. np-Treasury note, stripped principal. For bonds callable prior to maturity, yields are computed to the earliest call date for issues quoted above par and to the maturity date for issues below par.

Source: Bear, Stearns & Co. via Street Software Technology Inc.

GOVT. BONDS & NOTES

Rate	Maturity Mo/Yr	Bid	Asked	Chg.	Ask Yld.
4 5/8	Dec 94n	99:29	99:31	+ 1	4.97
7 5/8	Dec 94n	100:04	100:06	....	4.80
8 5/8	Jan 95n	100:11	100:13	....	4.80
4 1/4	Jan 95n	99:24	99:26	....	5.39
3	Feb 95	99:02	100:02	....	2.65
5 1/2	Feb 95n	99:30	100:00	....	5.41
7 3/4	Feb 95n	100:12	100:14	....	5.36
7 7/8	Feb 95-00	100:13	100:17	....	5.01
10 1/2	Feb 95	100:30	101:00	- 1	5.17
11 1/4	Feb 95n	101:03	101:05	....	5.11
3 7/8	Feb 95n	99:17	99:19	....	5.57
3 7/8	Mar 95n	99:12	99:14	....	5.63
8 3/8	Apr 95n	100:25	100:27	- 1	5.91
3 7/8	Apr 95n	99:02	99:04	- 1	6.07
5 7/8	May 95n	99:27	99:29	- 1	6.07
8 1/2	May 95n	100:31	101:01	- 3	6.09
10 3/8	May 95	101:26	101:28	- 1	6.01
11 1/4	May 95n	102:06	102:08	- 1	6.02
12 5/8	May 95	103:03	103:07	....	5.18
4 1/8	May 95n	98:31	99:01	....	6.17
4 1/8	Jun 95n	98:24	98:26	- 1	6.27
8 7/8	Jul 95n	101:11	101:13	- 1	6.50
4 1/4	Jul 95n	98:16	98:18	- 1	6.52
4 5/8	Aug 95n	98:19	98:21	- 1	6.63
8 1/2	Aug 95n	101:07	101:09	- 1	6.59
10 1/2	Aug 95n	102:19	102:21	- 1	6.54
3 7/8	Aug 95n	97:31	98:01	- 2	6.66
3 7/8	Sep 95n	97:21	97:23	- 2	6.78
8 5/8	Oct 95n	101:13	101:15	- 1	6.84
3 7/8	Oct 95n	97:11	97:13	- 2	6.88
5 1/8	Nov 95n	98:12	98:14	- 1	6.86
8 1/2	Nov 95n	101:12	101:14	- 3	6.90
9 1/2	Nov 95n	102:14	102:16	- 2	6.73
11 1/2	Nov 95	104:05	104:09	- 4	6.75
4 1/4	Nov 95n	97:13	97:15	....	6.95
4 1/4	Dec 95n	97:04	97:06	- 2	7.02
9 1/4	Jan 96n	102:08	102:10	- 3	7.05
4	Jan 96n	96:18	96:20	- 2	7.09
7 1/2	Jan 96n	100:14	100:16	- 1	7.04
4 5/8	Feb 96n	97:03	97:05	- 3	7.14
7 7/8	Feb 96n	100:25	100:27	- 3	7.13
8 7/8	Feb 96n	101:30	102:00	- 3	7.10
4 5/8	Feb 96n	97:01	97:03	- 3	7.12
7 1/2	Feb 96n	100:12	100:14	- 3	7.12
5 1/8	Mar 96n	97:12	97:14	- 3	7.19
5 1/8	Mar 98n	92:17	92:19	....	7.69
7 7/8	Apr 98n	100:15	100:17	- 1	7.69
5 1/8	Apr 98n	92:11	92:13	- 1	7.70
9	May 98n	103:26	103:28	- 1	7.70
5 3/8	May 98n	92:28	92:30	- 1	7.72
5 1/8	Jun 98n	91:30	92:00	- 1	7.73
8 1/4	Jul 98n	101:18	101:20	- 2	7.73
5 1/4	Jul 98n	92:05	92:07	....	7.73
9 1/4	Aug 98n	104:24	104:26	- 3	7.73
4 3/4	Aug 98n	90:13	90:15	- 1	7.74
4 3/4	Sep 98n	90:07	90:09	- 1	7.74
7 1/8	Oct 98n	98:01	98:03	- 3	7.71
4 3/4	Oct 98n	90:00	90:02	- 1	7.75
3 1/2	Nov 98	91:05	92:05	....	5.75
8 7/8	Nov 98n	103:23	103:25	- 3	7.74
5 1/8	Nov 98n	91:02	91:04	- 2	7.76
5 1/8	Dec 98n	90:28	90:30	- 2	7.76
6 3/8	Jan 99n	95:05	95:07	- 2	7.75
5	Jan 99n	90:09	90:11	- 2	7.76
8 7/8	Feb 99n	103:28	103:30	- 2	7.76
5 1/2	Feb 99n	92:01	92:03	- 1	7.72
5 7/8	Mar 99n	93:04	93:06	- 2	7.76
7	Apr 99n	97:04	97:06	- 3	7.77
6 1/2	Apr 99n	95:07	95:09	- 1	7.79
9 1/8	May 99n	104:30	105:00	- 2	7.77
6 3/4	May 99n	96:02	96:04	- 2	7.79
6 3/4	Jun 99n	96:00	96:02	- 2	7.79
6 3/8	Jul 99n	94:19	94:21	- 2	7.78
6 7/8	Jul 99n	96:13	96:15	- 2	7.79
8	Aug 99n	100:27	100:29	- 3	7.77
6 7/8	Aug 99n	96:11	96:13	- 3	7.80
7 1/8	Sep 99n	97:08	97:10	- 3	7.80
6	Oct 99n	92:26	92:28	- 3	7.79
7 1/2	Oct 99n	98:24	98:26	- 1	7.80
7 7/8	Nov 99n	100:10	100:12	- 2	7.78
7 3/4	Nov 99n	99:26	99:28	- 1	7.78
6 3/8	Jan 00n	93:31	94:01	- 4	7.81
8 1/2	Feb 00n	102:31	103:01	- 1	7.76
5 1/2	Apr 00n	90:01	90:03	- 2	7.80
8 7/8	May 00n	104:25	104:27	....	7.77
8 3/8	Aug 95-00	100:22	100:26	- 3	7.16
8 3/4	Aug 00n	104:07	104:09	- 2	7.80
8 1/2	Nov 00n	103:06	103:08	- 1	7.81
7 3/4	Feb 01n	99:19	99:21	....	7.82
11 3/4	Feb 01	119:04	119:08	- 6	7.78

Rate	Maturity Mo/Yr	Bid	Asked	Chg.	Ask Yld.
9 1/8	May 18	110:09	110:11	- 8	8.13
9	Nov 18	109:01	109:03	- 10	8.13
8 7/8	Feb 19	107:24	107:26	- 9	8.13
8 1/8	Aug 19	99:29	99:31	- 9	8.13
8 1/2	Feb 20	103:29	103:31	- 9	8.13
8 3/4	May 20	106:20	106:22	- 9	8.12
8 3/4	Aug 20	106:21	106:23	- 10	8.12
7 7/8	Feb 21	97:09	97:11	- 10	8.12
8 1/8	May 21	100:02	100:04	- 9	8.11
8 1/8	Aug 21	100:04	100:06	- 9	8.11
8	Nov 21	98:27	98:29	- 9	8.10
7 1/4	Aug 22	90:26	90:28	- 8	8.08
7 5/8	Nov 22	94:30	95:00	- 9	8.08
7 1/8	Feb 23	89:16	89:18	- 9	8.07
6 1/4	Aug 23	79:28	79:30	- 8	8.05
7 1/2	Nov 24	94:05	94:07	- 9	8.01

TREASURY BILLS

Maturity	Days to Mat.	Bid	Asked	Chg.	Ask Yld.
Dec 08 '94	3	4.64	4.54	+ 0.03	4.60

U.S. Treasury strips

Mat.	Type	Bid	Asked	Chg.	Ask Yld.
Nov 96	np	86:23	86:24	- 1	7.43
Feb 97	ci	85:04	85:05	- 1	7.45
May 97	ci	83:13	83:15	....	7.53
May 97	np	83:11	83:13	....	7.56
Aug 97	ci	81:26	81:28	+ 1	7.56
Aug 97	np	81:23	81:25	....	7.60
Nov 97	ci	80:03	80:05	....	7.65
Nov 97	np	80:03	80:05	....	7.66
Feb 98	ci	78:17	78:19	....	7.68
Feb 98	np	78:16	78:18	+ 1	7.69
May 98	ci	76:31	77:01	....	7.72
May 98	np	76:29	76:31	....	7.74
Aug 98	ci	75:14	75:17	+ 1	7.74
Aug 98	np	75:14	75:16	+ 2	7.75
Nov 98	ci	73:31	74:02	+ 1	7.76
Nov 98	np	73:30	74:01	+ 1	7.77
Feb 99	ci	72:16	72:19	- 1	7.78
Feb 99	np	72:14	72:17	- 1	7.80
May 99	ci	71:03	71:06	- 1	7.79
May 99	np	71:01	71:04	- 1	7.81
Aug 99	ci	69:26	69:29	- 1	7.77
Aug 99	np	69:22	69:26	- 1	7.81
Nov 99	ci	68:21	68:25	- 1	7.72
Nov 07	ci	35:14	35:18	- 4	8.15
Feb 08	ci	34:23	34:27	- 4	8.15
May 08	ci	33:31	34:04	- 4	8.16
Aug 08	ci	33:08	33:12	- 4	8.17
Nov 08	ci	32:18	32:23	- 4	8.18
Feb 09	ci	31:28	32:00	- 4	8.19
May 09	ci	31:07	31:11	- 4	8.19
Aug 09	ci	30:19	30:23	- 4	8.20
Nov 09	ci	29:30	30:03	- 4	8.20
Nov 09	bp	29:22	29:26	- 4	8.26
Feb 10	ci	29:10	29:14	- 4	8.21
May 10	ci	28:22	28:27	- 4	8.22
Aug 10	ci	28:03	28:07	- 4	8.22
Nov 10	ci	27:17	27:21	- 4	8.23
Feb 11	ci	26:30	27:02	- 4	8.23
May 11	ci	26:13	26:17	- 4	8.23
Aug 11	ci	25:28	26:00	- 5	8.24
Nov 11	ci	25:11	25:15	- 4	8.24
Feb 12	ci	24:26	24:30	- 5	8.24
May 12	ci	24:10	24:14	- 5	8.24
Aug 12	ci	23:26	23:30	- 5	8.24
Nov 12	ci	23:11	23:15	- 5	8.24
Feb 13	ci	22:28	23:00	- 5	8.24
May 13	ci	22:14	22:17	- 5	8.24
Aug 13	ci	21:31	22:03	- 5	8.24
Nov 13	ci	21:17	21:21	- 5	8.24
Feb 14	ci	21:03	21:07	- 5	8.24
May 14	ci	20:22	20:25	- 5	8.24
Aug 14	ci	20:08	20:12	- 5	8.24
Nov 14	ci	19:27	19:31	- 5	8.24
Feb 15	ci	19:15	19:18	- 5	8.24
Feb 15	bp	19:17	19:21	- 5	8.22
May 15	ci	19:02	19:06	- 5	8.24
Aug 15	ci	18:22	18:25	- 5	8.24
Aug 15	bp	18:24	18:28	- 5	8.22
Nov 15	ci	18:10	18:14	- 5	8.24
Nov 15	bp	18:12	18:16	- 5	8.22
Feb 16	ci	17:30	18:02	- 5	8.24
Feb 16	bp	18:00	18:04	- 5	8.22
May 16	ci	17:19	17:22	- 5	8.24
May 16	bp	17:29	18:01	- 5	8.15
Aug 16	ci	17:07	17:11	- 5	8.24
Nov 16	ci	16:28	17:00	- 5	8.24
Nov 16	bp	17:04	17:08	- 5	8.17
Feb 17	ci	16:17	16:21	- 5	8.24

FIGURE 2.1

7 3/4	Mar 96n	100:20	100:22	− 4	7.20
9 3/8	Apr 96n	102:22	102:24	− 4	7.22
5 1/2	Apr 96n	97:20	97:22	− 2	7.26
7 5/8	Apr 96n	100:15	100:17	− 4	7.22
4 1/4	May 96n	95:27	95:29	− 2	7.28
7 3/8	May 96n	100:03	100:05	....	7.26
5 7/8	May 96n	98:00	98:02	− 2	7.27
7 5/8	May 96n	100:16	100:18	− 2	7.22
6	Jun 96n	98:01	98:03	− 2	7.31
7 7/8	Jun 96n	100:24	100:26	− 5	7.32
7 7/8	Jul 96n	100:25	100:27	− 4	7.31
6 1/8	Jul 96n	98:02	98:04	− 2	7.35
7 7/8	Jul 96n	100:26	100:28	− 4	7.30
4 3/8	Aug 96n	95:09	95:11	− 2	7.34
6 1/4	Aug 96n	98:05	98:07	− 2	7.36
7 1/4	Aug 96n	99:25	99:27	− 3	7.35
6 1/2	Sep 96n	98:15	98:17	− 3	7.38
7	Sep 96n	99:12	99:14	− 2	7.34
8	Oct 96n	101:01	101:03	− 1	7.36
6 7/8	Oct 96n	99:02	99:04	− 3	7.38
4 3/8	Nov 96n	94:16	94:18	− 2	7.43
7 1/4	Nov 96n	99:21	99:23	− 2	7.41
6 1/2	Nov 96n	98:10	98:12	− 2	7.39
7 1/4	Nov 96n	99:22	99:24	− 1	7.39
6 1/8	Dec 96n	97:18	97:20	− 3	7.38
8	Jan 97n	101:00	101:02	− 1	7.45
6 1/4	Jan 97n	97:19	97:21	− 1	7.45
4 3/4	Feb 97n	94:14	94:16	− 1	7.51
6 3/4	Feb 97n	98:13	98:15	− 2	7.51
6 7/8	Mar 97n	98:20	98:22	− 2	7.50
8 1/2	Apr 97n	102:01	102:03	− 2	7.52
6 7/8	Apr 97n	98:17	98:19	− 2	7.53
6 1/2	May 97n	97:21	97:23	− 2	7.54
8 1/2	May 97n	102:02	102:04	− 1	7.53
6 3/4	May 97n	98:05	98:07	− 2	7.55
6 3/8	Jun 97n	97:09	97:11	− 2	7.53
8 1/2	Jul 97n	102:05	102:07	....	7.55
5 1/2	Jul 97n	95:01	95:03	− 1	7.57
6 1/2	Aug 97n	97:12	97:14	− 1	7.57
8 5/8	Aug 97n	102:16	102:18	− 1	7.56
5 5/8	Aug 97n	95:05	95:07	− 1	7.59
5 1/2	Sep 97n	94:23	94:25	....	7.59
8 3/4	Oct 97n	102:25	102:27	− 2	7.63
5 3/4	Oct 97n	95:04	95:06	− 1	7.63
7 3/8	Nov 97n	99:11	99:13	− 1	7.60
8 7/8	Nov 97n	103:05	103:07	− 2	7.63
6	Nov 97n	95:20	95:22	− 1	7.64
6	Dec 97n	95:16	95:18	− 1	7.65
7 7/8	Jan 98n	100:16	100:18	− 1	7.67
5 5/8	Jan 98n	94:08	94:10	− 1	7.69
8 1/8	Feb 98n	101:06	101:08	− 1	7.68
5 1/8	Feb 98n	92:23	92:25	− 1	7.69
8	May 01n	100:24	100:26	− 4	7.84
13 1/8	May 01	126:22	126:26	....	7.76
7 7/8	Aug 01n	100:07	100:09	− 3	7.82
8	Aug 96-01	100:22	100:26	− 2	7.48
13 3/8	Aug 01	128:22	128:26	....	7.78
7 1/2	Nov 01n	98:02	98:04	− 5	7.86
15 3/4	Nov 01	142:10	142:14	+ 2	7.74
14 1/4	Feb 02	135:04	135:08	+ 2	7.77
7 1/2	May 02n	98:00	98:02	− 6	7.85
6 3/8	Aug 02n	91:11	91:13	− 5	7.89
11 5/8	Nov 02	121:30	122:02	− 2	7.84
6 1/4	Feb 03n	90:03	90:05	− 4	7.90
10 3/4	Feb 03	117:03	117:07	− 2	7.86
10 3/4	May 03	117:10	117:14	− 3	7.88
5 3/4	Aug 03n	86:15	86:17	− 5	7.92
11 1/8	Aug 03	119:29	120:01	− 4	7.90
11 7/8	Nov 03	124:29	125:01	− 3	7.92
5 7/8	Feb 04n	86:22	86:24	− 5	7.93
7 1/4	May 04n	95:14	95:16	− 4	7.94
12 3/8	May 04	129:02	129:06	− 2	7.93
7 1/4	Aug 04n	95:11	95:13	− 5	7.94
13 3/4	Aug 04	138:21	138:25	+ 5	7.94
7 7/8	Nov 04n	99:22	99:24	− 3	7.91
11 5/8	Nov 04	124:23	124:27	− 4	7.96
8 1/4	May 00-05	101:15	101:19	− 1	7.88
12	May 05	128:04	128:08	− 5	7.97
10 3/4	Aug 05	119:16	119:20	− 4	7.99
9 3/8	Feb 06	110:12	110:16	− 4	7.94
7 5/8	Feb 02-07	96:15	96:19	− 6	8.07
7 7/8	Nov 02-07	98:30	99:02	− 8	7.99
8 3/8	Aug 03-08	101:17	101:21	− 7	8.11
8 3/4	Nov 03-08	103:30	104:02	− 6	8.10
9 1/8	May 04-09	106:20	106:24	− 8	8.09
10 3/8	Nov 04-09	115:15	115:19	− 7	8.07
11 3/4	Feb 05-10	125:14	125:18	− 9	8.03
10	May 05-10	113:11	113:15	− 5	8.07
12 3/4	Nov 05-10	133:22	133:26	− 4	8.05
13 7/8	May 06-11	142:29	143:01	− 7	8.05
14	Nov 06-11	144:30	145:02	− 9	8.06
10 3/8	Nov 07-12	117:25	117:29	− 8	8.11
12	Aug 08-13	131:24	131:28	− 6	8.10
13 1/4	May 09-14	143:06	143:10	− 12	8.11
12 1/2	Aug 09-14	137:03	137:07	− 10	8.12
11 3/4	Nov 09-14	131:03	131:07	− 10	8.11
11 1/4	Feb 15	130:25	130:27	− 11	8.12
10 5/8	Aug 15	124:27	124:29	− 11	8.12
9 7/8	Nov 15	117:14	117:16	− 10	8.12
9 1/4	Feb 16	111:07	111:09	− 10	8.13
7 1/4	May 16	91:08	91:10	− 9	8.11
7 1/2	Nov 16	93:20	93:22	− 10	8.12
8 3/4	May 17	106:09	106:11	− 8	8.13
8 7/8	Aug 17	107:18	107:20	− 9	8.13

Dec 15 '94	10	4.70	4.60	− 0.13	4.67
Dec 22 '94	**17**	**5.37**	**5.27**	**− 0.04**	**5.36**
Dec 22 '94	**17**	**5.37**	**5.27**	**− 0.08**	**5.36**
Dec 29 '94	24	4.45	4.35	− 0.08	4.42
Jan 05 '95	31	4.85	4.81	− 0.04	4.90
Jan 12 '95	38	5.05	5.01	− 0.07	5.11
Jan 19 '95	45	5.07	5.03	− 0.11	5.13
Jan 26 '95	52	5.19	5.15	− 0.07	5.26
Feb 02 '95	59	5.36	5.34	− 0.02	5.46
Feb 09 '95	66	5.40	5.38	− 0.01	5.51
Feb 16 '95	73	5.42	5.40	− 0.03	5.54
Feb 23 '95	80	5.51	5.49	− 0.01	5.63
Mar 02 '95	**87**	**5.55**	**5.53**	**− 0.01**	**5.68**
Mar 09 '95	94	5.62	5.60	+ 0.04	5.76
Mar 16 '95	101	5.59	5.57	− 0.02	5.74
Mar 23 '95	108	5.60	5.58	− 0.01	5.75
Mar 30 '95	115	5.58	5.56	− 0.02	5.74
Apr 06 '95	122	5.71	5.69		5.88
Apr 13 '95	129	5.74	5.72	0.01	5.92
Apr 20 '95	136	5.78	5.76	− 0.01	5.97
Apr 27 '95	143	5.85	5.83	+ 0.02	6.05
May 04 '95	150	5.91	5.89	+ 0.01	6.12
May 11 '95	157	5.95	5.93	+ 0.03	6.17
May 18 '95	164	5.98	5.96	+ 0.04	6.21
May 25 '95	171	5.99	5.97	+ 0.03	6.23
Jun 01 '95	**178**	**5.99**	**5.97**	**+ 0.03**	**6.24**
Jun 29 '95	206	6.03	6.01	+ 0.03	6.29
Jul 27 '95	234	6.13	6.11	0.02	6.41
Aug 24 '95	262	6.23	6.21	+ 0.02	6.53
Sep 21 '95	290	6.27	6.25	0.01	6.59
Oct 19 '95	318	6.42	6.40	+ 0.04	6.78
Nov 16 '95	346	6.49	6.47	+ 0.03	6.83

U.S. TREASURY STRIPS

Mat.	Type	Bid	Asked	Chg.	Ask Yld.
Feb 95	ci	98:29	98:29	+ 1	5.68
Feb 95	np	98:28	98:29	+ 1	5.72
May 95	ci	97:10	97:10	+ 1	6.18
May 95	np	97:09	97:10	+ 1	6.24
Aug 95	ci	95:20	95:21	+ 1	6.50
Aug 95	np	95:18	95:18	....	6.62
Nov 95	ci	93:27	93:28	....	6.81
Nov 95	np	93:26	93:27	....	6.85
Feb 96	ci	91:31	92:00	− 1	7.09
Feb 96	np	91:29	91:30	[illegible]	7.17
May 96	ci	90:06	90:07	− 1	7.26
May 96	np	90:04	90:05	− 1	7.30
Aug 96	ci	88:19	88:20	− 1	7.25
Nov 96	ci	86:24	86:26	− 1	7.11
Nov 99	np	68:12	68:15	− 1	7.81
Feb 00	ci	67:02	67:05	− 2	7.81
Feb 00	np	67:00	67:04	− 1	7.82
May 00	ci	65:29	66:01	− 1	7.77
May 00	np	65:26	65:30	− 1	7.80
Aug 00	ci	64:15	64:19	− 3	7.82
Aug 00	np	64:14	64:17	− 3	7.84
Nov 00	ci	63:08	63:12	− 2	7.82
Nov 00	np	63:06	63:10	− 2	7.84
Feb 01	ci	61:31	62:02	− 3	7.85
Feb 01	np	61:30	62:02	− 3	7.85
May 01	ci	60:23	60:27	− 3	7.86
May 01	np	60:23	60:27	− 3	7.86
Aug 01	ci	59:16	59:20	− 3	7.88
Aug 01	np	59:17	59:21	− 3	7.87
Nov 01	ci	58:10	58:13	− 3	7.89
Nov 01	np	58:10	58:14	− 3	7.89
Feb 02	ci	57:03	57:07	− 3	7.91
May 02	ci	56:06	56:10	− 3	7.86
May 02	np	56:04	56:08	− 3	7.88
Aug 02	ci	54:27	54:31	− 3	7.93
Aug 02	np	54:30	55:02	− 3	7.91
Nov 02	ci	53:23	53:27	− 2	7.95
Feb 03	ci	52:20	52:24	− 3	7.96
Feb 03	np	52:24	52:28	− 3	7.93
May 03	ci	51:17	51:21	− 4	7.98
Aug 03	ci	50:15	50:20	− 4	7.99
Aug 03	np	50:22	50:26	− 3	7.94
Nov 03	ci	49:16	49:20	− 3	7.99
Feb 04	ci	48:15	48:19	− 3	8.00
Feb 04	np	48:23	48:27	− 3	7.95
May 04	ci	47:15	47:19	− 3	8.02
May 04	np	47:23	47:27	− 3	7.96
Aug 04	ci	46:16	46:20	− 3	8.03
Aug 04	np	46:26	46:30	− 4	7.96
Nov 04	ci	45:18	45:22	− 3	8.03
Nov 04	bp	45:17	45:22	− 4	8.04
Nov 04	np	45:31	46:04	− 4	7.94
Feb 05	ci	44:19	44:23	− 4	8.05
May 05	ci	43:21	43:26	− 4	8.06
May 05	bp	43:22	43:26	− 4	8.06
Aug 05	ci	42:24	42:29	− 4	8.07
Aug 05	bp	42:24	42:29	− 4	8.07
Nov 05	ci	41:28	42:00	− 4	8.08
Feb 06	ci	41:01	41:05	− 4	8.09
Feb 06	bp	41:17	41:21	− 4	7.98
May 06	ci	40:07	40:11	− 4	8.09
Aug 06	ci	39:13	39:17	− 4	8.09
Nov 06	ci	38:18	38:22	− 4	8.11
Feb 07	ci	37:24	37:29	− 4	8.12
May 07	ci	36:31	37:03	− 4	8.13
Aug 07	ci	36:06	36:10	− 4	8.14
May 17	ci	16:07	16:10	− 4	8.24
May 17	bp	16:10	16:13	− 5	8.22
Aug 17	ci	15:28	16:00	− 4	8.24
Aug 17	bp	15:31	16:03	− 4	8.22
Nov 17	ci	15:19	15:22	− 4	8.24
Feb 18	ci	15:09	15:12	− 4	8.24
May 18	ci	14:31	15:02	− 4	8.24
May 18	bp	15:02	15:05	− 4	8.21
Aug 18	ci	14:21	14:25	− 4	8.24
Nov 18	ci	14:13	14:16	− 4	8.23
Nov 18	bp	14:15	14:18	− 4	8.21
Feb 19	ci	14:04	14:07	− 4	8.23
Feb 19	bp	14:06	14:10	− 4	8.20
May 19	ci	13:27	13:30	− 4	8.22
Aug 19	ci	13:18	13:22	− 4	8.22
Aug 19	bp	13:23	13:26	− 5	8.18
Nov 19	ci	13:10	13:13	− 4	8.22
Feb 20	ci	13:02	13:05	− 4	8.22
Feb 20	bp	13:05	13:08	− 4	8.18
May 20	ci	12:25	12:28	− 4	8.22
May 20	bp	12:29	13:00	− 4	8.18
Aug 20	ci	12:18	12:21	− 4	8.21
Aug 20	bp	12:22	12:25	− 4	8.17
Nov 20	ci	12:11	12:14	− 4	8.20
Feb 21	ci	12:05	12:08	− 4	8.18
Feb 21	bp	12:09	12:12	− 4	8.14
May 21	ci	11:29	12:00	− 4	8.18
May 21	bp	12:02	12:05	− 3	8.13
Aug 21	ci	11:25	11:28	− 4	8.15
Aug 21	bp	11:29	12:00	− 4	8.11
Nov 21	ci	11:20	11:23	− 4	8.12
Nov 21	bp	11:24	11:27	− 4	8.08
Feb 22	ci	11:13	11:16	− 4	8.11
May 22	ci	11:09	11:12	− 4	8.08
Aug 22	ci	11:06	11:08	− 4	8.04
Aug 22	bp	11:09	11:12	− 4	8.00
Nov 22	ci	11:01	11:04	− 4	8.02
Nov 22	bp	11:03	11:06	− 4	7.99
Feb 23	ci	10:30	11:01	− 4	7.98
Feb 23	bp	10:31	11:02	− 4	7.96
May 23	ci	10:23	10:25	− 4	7.98
Aug 23	ci	10:19	10:22	− 4	7.95
Aug 23	bp	10:22	10:25	− 4	7.91
Nov 23	ci	10:16	10:19	− 4	7.91
May 24	ci	10:19	10:22	− 4	7.74
Nov 24	ci	10:01	10:04	− 4	7.80
Nov 24	bp	10:04	10:07	− 4	7.76

FIGURE 2.1 *(continued)*

by a five-year span in the maturity date. For example, the security in the eighth row is a callable $7\frac{7}{8}$ coupon rate Treasury bond, first callable on February 15, 1995. The bond matures on February 15, 2000.

For the Treasury bills, the first column gives the maturity date and the second column gives the days to maturity. The remaining columns in Fig. 2.1 will be discussed in the next section.

In addition to bills, notes, and bonds, Treasury securities called STRIPS (separate trading of registered interest and principal of securities) have traded since August 1985. These are the coupons or principal amounts of Treasury bonds trading separately through the Federal Reserve's book-entry system. They are, in effect, *synthetically* created zero-coupon bonds of longer maturities than a year. They were created in response to investor demands, and STRIPS of various maturities of up to 30 years are currently available (see Fig. 2.1).

New Treasury securities are issued in an auction market on a regular basis. The auction uses competitive bids, although noncompetitive bids are accepted and tendered at the average yield of the competitive bids. See Fabozzi and Fabozzi [2, p. 83] or Stigum [5, p. 431] for further details. Ninety-one-day and 182-day Treasury bills are auctioned every Monday for issuance the following Thursday. They mature 91 and 182 days after issuance, respectively. Fifty-two-week Treasury bills are auctioned every fourth Thursday, to be issued the following Thursday. Treasury notes and bonds are issued on a monthly or quarterly basis.

SECTION B
TREASURY SECURITY MARKETS

The majority of Treasury securities are traded in the over-the-counter market, where U.S. government securities dealers provide bid/ask quotes. (The New York Stock Exchange lists some issues, but the trading volume is small.) Treasury notes and bonds are quoted in units of one 32d on a 100-dollar par basis. For example, again referring to Fig. 2.1, the $4\frac{5}{8}$ coupon rate Treasury note maturing December 1994 has a bid price of 99 and $\frac{29}{32}$ and an ask price of 99 and $\frac{31}{32}$. The change in column 5 is the change from the previous day's bid price. Finally, the ask yield in column 6 is calculated as follows. The ask yield solves the following equation:

$$\text{ask price} = \left(\sum_{t=1}^{2T} \frac{\text{coupon}/2}{(1+\text{ask yield}/2)^{(t-1+\tau)}}\right) + \frac{\text{face value}}{(1+\text{ask yield}/2)^{(2T-1+\tau)}}$$

where[3]

$$T = \text{number of years to maturity from the settlement date}$$

$$\tau = \frac{\text{number of days from settlement until the next coupon payment}}{\text{number of days in the coupon period}}$$

The quotes given in Fig. 2.1 are without accrued interest. The price the buyer actually pays (or receives) when transacting in the bonds or notes is the quoted price *plus accrued interest,* which is calculated as follows:

accrued interest

$$= \left(\frac{\text{coupon}}{2}\right)\left[\frac{\text{number of days since the last coupon date from settlement}}{\text{number of days in the coupon period}}\right]$$

Treasury STRIPS are quoted on the same basis as notes and bonds. These bid and asked quotes are given in the third and fourth columns. The second column, "type," refers to whether the STRIPS is a coupon interest (ci), note principal (np), or bond principal (bp). Columns 1, 5, and 6 are similar to those given for the Treasury bonds and notes. They represent the maturity date, the change in the bid price, and the bid yield, respectively.

Finally, the Treasury bills bid/ask quotes are also contained in Fig. 2.1. However, for Treasury bills, the quotes are provided on a *banker's-discount* basis. The *banker's-discount yield* (ask or bid) is calculated as follows:

banker's discount yield

$$= \left(\frac{\text{face value} - \text{price}}{\text{face value}}\right)\left(\frac{360}{\text{number of days from settlement until maturity}}\right)$$

The bid/ask banker's discount yields are provided in columns 4 and 5 of Fig. 2.1. Column 6 is the change in the bid yield from the previous day's quote. Column 7 is the ask yield, calculated as follows:

ask yield

$$= \left(\frac{\text{face value} - \text{ask price}}{\text{ask price}}\right)\left(\frac{365}{\text{number of days from settlement until maturity}}\right)$$

The difference between the ask yield and the banker's discount yield is twofold. First, the denominator in the banker's discount yield is the face value,

---

[3]The days to maturity are measured from the settlement day. The settlement day is the day when the actual cash flows are exchanged for the Treasury security transaction. Settlement for institutional traders in Treasury securities is usually the next business day.

while in the ask yield it is the ask price. Second, the banker's discount yield annualizes on a 360-day basis, while the ask yield annualizes on a 365-day basis.

EXAMPLE: COMPUTATION OF THE ASK YIELD. To illustrate these computations, consider the Treasury bill maturing December 15, 1994. Its banker's discount ask yield in column 4 is 4.60. To compute the ask price, we substitute the relevant information into the banker's discount yield formula. For simplicity, we let the face value be one dollar. There are 10 days from settlement until maturity. According to these quotes, entering a transaction on Thursday, December 1, has settlement on Monday, December 5, which is 10 days prior to Thursday, December 15. Then

$$0.0460 = \left(\frac{1 - \text{ask price}}{1}\right)\frac{360}{10}$$

Algebra yields

$$\text{ask price} = 1 - 0.0460\left(\tfrac{10}{360}\right) = 0.998722$$

We can check the ask yield in column 7. Substitution in the ask yield's formula gives

$$\text{ask yield} = \left(\frac{1 - 0.998722}{0.998722}\right)\frac{365}{10} = 0.0467$$

which matches the number provided. ■

For the subsequent analysis we are primarily interested in the prices (ask/bid) quoted for the various Treasury securities. The banker's discount yield is meaningful only to the extent that it is the necessary input to a transformation (given above) that yields the Treasury bill's price. We will have no use for it otherwise.

SECTION C
REPO MARKETS

In addition to trading in the Treasury securities themselves, there is an active repo market for Treasury securities, both overnight and term (more than one day). (For more details, see Stigum [5, chapter 12].) From the dealer's perspective, a *repo*, or *repurchase agreement,* is a transaction in which a dealer sells a Treasury security to an investor and simultaneously promises to buy it back at a fixed future date and at a fixed future price. The price at which the Treasury security is repurchased is larger than the selling price, the difference being interest, called the *repo rate*. The investor in the above transaction is said to have entered a *reverse repo*. A repurchase agreement is equivalent to the dealer's borrowing funds from the investor and using the Treasury security as collateral.

Alternatively, a repurchase agreement is simply a forward contract on a Treasury security, having a zero initial value (the Treasury security is exchanged for its fair value in cash), and with a forward price equal to the repurchase price. The repo rate is then nothing more than a specific maturity, *forward interest rate,* as subsequently defined in Chapter 3.

SECTION D
TREASURY FUTURES MARKETS

There are basically three markets in which to buy or sell a Treasury security: *(i)* the spot market, *(ii)* the forward market, and *(iii)* the futures market.

The first method by which to buy or sell a Treasury security is in the *spot* or *cash* market for immediate delivery. These markets were discussed in Section 2.B. The price at which the exchange takes place is called the *spot* or *cash* price.

The second method is by entering a *forward contract.* A forward contract is an agreement made in the present (today) between a buyer and seller of a commodity to exchange the commodity for cash at a predetermined future date, but at a price agreed upon today. The agreed upon price is called the *forward price*. For Treasury securities, the repo markets discussed in Section 2.C are examples of a forward market.

Finally, the third method is by entering a *futures contract.* A *futures contract* is a standardized financial security, issued by an organized exchange, for future purchase/sale of a commodity at a predetermined future date and at an agreed upon price. The agreed upon price is called the *futures price*, and it is paid via a sequence of "daily installments" over the contract's life. These "daily installments" were instituted by the futures exchange to guarantee that the purchaser/seller of a futures contract would fulfill his or her obligations. It is this daily settlement procedure that differentiates forward contracts from futures contracts and forward prices from futures prices. See Jarrow and Oldfield [3].

Daily settlement is called *marking to market.* The procedure is as follows. When a buyer/seller of a futures contract opens a position, a margin account is required. The margin account is usually an interest-earning account consisting of an initial cash deposit. The margin account's magnitude is set by the exchange so as to ensure (with reasonable probability) that the buyer/seller's obligation of the futures contract will be fulfilled. Marking to market occurs when the daily change to the futures price is added or subtracted from the margin account. For example, the purchaser of a futures contract would have the margin account's balance decreased if the futures price falls. This adjustment resets the value of the futures contract to zero at the end of each trading day. Marking to market is discussed in greater detail in Chapter 3.

For Treasury securities, the following futures contracts are available: 90-day Treasury bills on the Chicago Mercantile Exchange (CME) and on the MidAmerica Commodity Exchange (MCE), two-year Treasury notes on the Chicago Board of Trade (CBT), five-year Treasury notes on the CBT, $6\frac{1}{2}$- to 10-year Treasury notes on the CBT, and 15-year Treasury bonds on the CBT and the MCE. Of these markets, the Chicago Board of Trade's 15-year Treasury Bond futures market is the most actively traded in the world. See Edwards and Ma [1].

Futures contracts on Treasury securities are standardized in terms of the contract size, the delivery months, the deliverable securities, and the delivery procedure. In fact, for Treasury notes and bonds this contract specification is quite complicated, involving various imbedded options known as *(i)* the delivery option, *(ii)* the wildcard option, and *(iii)* the quality option. For the details of the contract specifications and an explanation of these imbedded options, see Edwards and Ma [1, pp. 284 and 312] or Kolb [4, chapter 7].

SECTION E
INTEREST RATE OPTION MARKETS

The phrase *interest rate options* is a catchall that includes all contingent claims, not already considered, whose payoffs depend on the evolution of the zero-coupon bond price curve or, as it is more commonly called, the *term structure of interest rates*.

These contingent claims include the 30-day interest rate futures traded on the CBT and the three-month Eurodollar futures on the Chicago Mercantile Exchange. They include the Chicago Board Options Exchange's (CBOE) options on short-term interest rates and options on long-term interest rates; the CBT's options on T-bond futures, 10-year T-note futures, and five-year Treasury note futures; and the CME's options on Eurodollar futures and Treasury bills. (For details, see Edwards and Ma [1, pp. 502, 508, and 560].) They also include swaps, caps, floors, collars, swaptions, digital options, range notes, and index-amortizing swaps that are traded in an over-the-counter market among large commercial and investment banks. These contracts are described in more detail in subsequent chapters.

The purpose of this book is to provide a general procedure for pricing and hedging these interest rate options.

SECTION F
REFERENCES TO CHAPTER 2

1. Edwards, F. R., and C. W. Ma, 1992. *Futures and Options*. McGraw-Hill, New York.

2. Fabozzi, F. J., and T. D. Fabozzi, 1989. *Bond Markets, Analysis and Strategies.* Prentice Hall, Englewood Cliffs, N.J.
3. Jarrow, R., and G. Oldfield, 1981. "Forward Contracts and Futures Contracts." *Journal of Financial Economics* 9 (4), 373–382.
4. Kolb, R. W., 1991. *Understanding Futures Markets*, 3d ed. Kolb Publishing, Miami, Fla.
5. Stigum, M., 1989. *The Money Market*, 3d ed. Dow Jones–Irwin, Homewood, Ill.

CHAPTER 3

The Term Structure of Interest Rates

This chapter presents the preliminaries of the model. The model selected for analysis and presentation is an abstraction from reality. It is an abstraction because it is a simplification. It is simplified in order to facilitate understanding and analysis. Of course, the hope is that the simplified model is still a good approximation to the actual economy. The approximation needs to be good enough to provide both *(i)* accurate valuation of interest rate options and *(ii)* accurate synthetic replication of the cash flows to interest rate options using the traded Treasury securities. How accurate the valuation and the synthetic replication need to be is determined in each application. Our experience, however, is that this model and its extensions are accurate enough to have proven quite useful in actual practice.

SECTION A
THE ECONOMY

We consider a *frictionless, competitive,* and *discrete trading* economy. By frictionless we mean that there are no transaction costs in buying and selling financial securities, there are no bid/ask spreads, there are no restrictions on trade (legal or otherwise) such as margin requirements or short sale restrictions, and there are no taxes. The frictionless markets assumption can be justified on two grounds. First, very large institutional traders approximate frictionless markets since their transaction costs are minimal. If these traders determine prices, this model may approximate actual pricing and hedging well. The second argument is that understanding frictionless markets is a necessary prelude to understanding friction-filled markets. Only by understanding the ideal case can we hope to understand the more complicated friction-filled economy. Both arguments have merit, and either provides us with sufficient motivation to continue with the analysis.

The markets are assumed to be *competitive;* i.e., each trader believes that she can buy/sell as many shares of a traded security as she desires without influencing its price. This implies, of course, that the market for any financial security is perfectly (infinitely) liquid. This is an idealization of the actual security markets. It is more nearly satisfied by large volume trading on organized exchanges than it is in the over-the-counter markets. Nonetheless, it is a reasonable starting hypothesis, from which we will proceed. The modification of the subsequent theory for a relaxation of this competitive markets assumption is a fruitful area for future research. (For some work along these lines, see Back [1], Gastineau and Jarrow [2], Jarrow [3, 4].)

Last, we consider a *discrete trading* economy with trading dates $\{0, 1, 2, \ldots, \tau\}$. This assumption is not very restrictive because it is a reasonable approximation to actual security markets, especially if τ is large and the time interval between trading periods is small. The alternative, continuous trading, provides similar results but with significantly more complicated mathematics.

SECTION B
THE TRADED SECURITIES

Traded in this economy are zero-coupon bonds of all maturities $\{0, \ldots, \tau\}$ and a *money market account*. The price of a zero-coupon bond at time t that pays a sure dollar at time $T \geq t$ is denoted $P(t, T)$. All zero-coupon bonds are assumed to be default free and have strictly positive prices. Table 3.1 provides three different hypothetical zero-coupon bond price curves. Panel A gives these prices for a flat term structure, panel B is for a downward sloping term structure, and panel C is for an upward sloping term structure. The numbers are constructed so that each time period corresponds to half a year.

The money market account is initialized at time 0 with a dollar investment, and its time t value is denoted $B(t)$. Thus, by convention, $B(0) = 1$. More will be said about the money market account in the next section.

SECTION C
INTEREST RATES

Various different interest rates will play significant roles in the subsequent analysis. This section defines the most important of these: yields, forward rates, and spot rates. As a convention in this book, for simplicity of notation and exposition, *all rates will be denoted as one plus a percentage* (these are sometimes

TABLE 3.1

Hypothetical zero-coupon bond prices, forward rates, and yields for various term structures

Time to maturity (T)	Zero-coupon bond prices $P(O,T)$	Forward rates $f(O,T)$	Yields $y(O,T)$
Panel A: Flat term structure			
0	1.	1.02	
1	0.980392	1.02	1.02
2	0.961168	1.02	1.02
3	0.942322	1.02	1.02
4	0.923845	1.02	1.02
5	0.905730	1.02	1.02
6	0.887971	1.02	1.02
7	0.870560	1.02	1.02
8	0.853490	1.02	1.02
9	0.836755		1.02
Panel B: Downward sloping term structure			
0	1.	1.024431	
1	0.976151	1.023342	1.024431
2	0.953885	1.022701	1.023886
3	0.932711	1.022319	1.023491
4	0.912347	1.022025	1.023198
5	0.892686	1.021794	1.022963
6	0.873645	1.021627	1.022768
7	0.855150	1.021544	1.022605
8	0.837115	1.020748	1.022472
9	0.820099		1.022281
Panel C: Upward sloping term structure			
0	1.	1.016027	
1	0.984225	1.016939	1.016027
2	0.967831	1.017498	1.016483
3	0.951187	1.017836	1.016821
4	0.934518	1.018102	1.017075
5	0.917901	1.018312	1.017280
6	0.901395	1.018465	1.017452
7	0.885052	1.018542	1.017597
8	0.868939	1.019267	1.017715
9	0.852514		1.017887

called dollar returns). This convention greatly simplifies all the subsequent formulas.

The *yield* at time t on a T-maturity zero-coupon bond, denoted $y(t,T)$, is defined by expression (3.1):

$$y(t,T) \equiv \left[\frac{1}{P(t,T)}\right]^{1/(T-t)} \tag{3.1}$$

The yield is one plus the percentage return earned per period by holding the T-maturity bond from time t until its maturity. It is often called the *holding period return.* Alternatively written, expression (3.1) implies

$$P(t,T) = \frac{1}{[y(t,T)]^{(T-t)}} \tag{3.2}$$

The time t *forward rate* for the period $[T,T+1]$, denoted $f(t,T)$, is defined by

$$f(t,T) \equiv \frac{P(t,T)}{P(t,T+1)} \tag{3.3}$$

This corresponds to the rate contracted at time t for a riskless loan over the time period $[T,T+1]$.

To see this interpretation, consider forming the following portfolio at time t: *(i)* buy one zero-coupon bond maturing at time T, and *(ii)* sell $P(t,T)/P(t,T+1)$ zero-coupon bonds maturing at time $T+1$. Hold each zero-coupon bond until maturity. The cash flows to this portfolio are given in Table 3.2. The initial cash flow from forming this portfolio at time t is zero. Indeed, the cash outflow is $P(t,T)$ dollars, but the cash inflow is $[P(t,T)/P(t,T+1)]P(t,T+1) = P(t,T)$ dollars. These net to zero. The first cash flow of one dollar occurs at time T. It is an inflow. In addition, there is a cash outflow of $P(t,T)/P(t,T+1)$ dollars at time $T+1$.

TABLE 3.2

Cash flows to a portfolio generating a cash flow equal to the time t forward rate for date T, $f(t,T)$

Time	t	T	$T+1$
Buy bond with maturity T	$-P(t,T)$	$+1$	
Sell $P(t,T)/P(t,T+1)$ bonds with maturity $T+1$	$+\frac{P(t,T)}{P(t,T+1)}P(t,T+1)$		$-\frac{P(t,T)}{P(t,T+1)}$
Total cash flow	0	$+1$	$-\frac{P(t,T)}{P(t,T+1)}$

This pattern of cash flows is the same as that obtained from a dollar loan over $[T, T+1]$, contracted at time t. The implicit rate on this loan is $P(t,T)/P(t,T+1)$, the forward rate. This completes the argument.

From expression (3.3) we can derive an expression for the bond's price in terms of the various maturity forward rates:

$$P(t,T) = \frac{1}{\prod_{j=t}^{T-1} f(t,j)} \tag{3.4}$$

DERIVATION OF EXPRESSION (3.4)

Step 1

$$f(t,t) = \frac{P(t,t)}{P(t,t+1)}$$

$$= \frac{1}{P(t,t+1)}$$

since $P(t,t) = 1$. So

$$P(t,t+1) = \frac{1}{f(t,t)}$$

Step 2. Next,

$$f(t,t+1) = \frac{P(t,t+1)}{P(t,t+2)}$$

So,

$$P(t,t+2) = \frac{P(t,t+1)}{f(t,t+1)}$$

Substitution yields

$$P(t,t+2) = \frac{1}{f(t,t)f(t,t+1)}$$

Continuing, we get

$$P(t,t+j) = \frac{1}{f(t,t)f(t,t+1)f(t,t+2)\cdots f(t,t+j-1)} \quad \blacksquare$$

Expression (3.4) shows that the bond's price is equal to a dollar received at time T and discounted by the different maturity forward rates.[1]

EXAMPLE: COMPUTING FORWARD RATES AND BOND PRICES USING TABLE 3.1. In Table 3.1, panel A gives the forward rates for a flat term structure, panel B those for a downward sloping term structure, and panel C for an upward

[1]The symbol $\prod_{j=t}^{T-1} f(t,j) = f(t,t)\cdot f(t,t+1)\cdots f(t,T-1)$ means the result obtained from multiplying together the terms arising when the index j runs from t to $T-1$.

sloping term structure. The shape of the term structure is defined by the slope of the graph of the forward rate versus time to maturity. To illustrate the use of the definitions, from panel A we have, in symbols,

$$f(0,3) \equiv \frac{P(0,3)}{P(0,4)}$$

or, in numbers,

$$1.020000 = \frac{0.942322}{0.923845}$$

For this example the forward rate is $f(0,3) = 1.02$, and it is the rate one can contract at time 0 for borrowing starting at time 3 and ending at time 4.

Conversely, given the forward rates, we can determine the bond prices. Using expression (3.4), the calculation is

$$P(0,3) = \frac{1}{f(0,0)f(0,1)f(0,2)}$$

or, in numbers,

$$0.942322 = \frac{1}{(1.02)^3}$$

This shows that the three-period zero-coupon bond's price is equal to a discounted dollar at 2 percent for three periods. This completes the example. ■

Last, the *spot rate*, denoted $r(t)$, is defined as the rate contracted at time t on a one-period riskless loan starting immediately. By definition, therefore,

$$r(t) \equiv f(t,t) \tag{3.5}$$

From Table 3.1 we see that the spot rate $r(0) = f(0,0)$ is 1.02 for the flat term structure, 1.024431 for the downward sloping term structure, and 1.016027 for the upward sloping term structure.

Alternatively, using expressions (3.1) and (3.3), the spot rate is seen to be the holding period return on the shortest maturity bond, i.e.,

$$r(t) = y(t,t+1) \tag{3.6}$$

We can now return to clarify the return on the money market account. By construction,

$$B(t) = B(t-1)r(t-1) = \prod_{j=0}^{t-1} r(j) \tag{3.7}$$

The money market account invests its entire fund in the shortest maturity bond each period, thereby obtaining the spot rate over each subsequent period. From Table 3.1 we see that for the flat term structure in panel A, $B(1) = B(0)r(0) = 1.02$. The money market account earns 2 percent over the first interval. The data in Table 3.1 do not enable us to determine the money market account's value at any future date beyond time 1 because the future spot rates are not available.

SECTION D
FORWARD PRICES

A *forward contract* is a financial security obligating the purchaser to buy a commodity at a prespecified price (determined at the time the contract is written) and at a prespecified date. At the time the contract is initiated, no cash changes hands. The contract has zero value. The prespecified purchase price is called the *forward price*. The prespecified date is called the *delivery* or *expiration* date. We are interested in forward contracts on zero-coupon bonds.

There are three dates of importance for forward contracts on zero-coupon bonds: the date the contract is written (t), the date the zero-coupon bond is purchased or delivered (T_1), and the maturity date of the zero-coupon bond (T_2). The dates must necessarily line up as $t \leq T_1 \leq T_2$. We denote the time t forward price of a contract with expiration date T_1 on the T_2-maturity zero-coupon bond as $F(t, T_1 : T_2)$.

By definition, therefore, the forward price on a contract with immediate delivery is the *spot price* of the zero-coupon bond; i.e.,

$$F(T_1, T_1 : T_2) = P(T_1, T_2) \tag{3.8}$$

SECTION E
FUTURES PRICES

A futures contract,[2] like a forward contract, is an agreement to purchase the commodity at a prespecified date, called the *delivery* or *expiration* date, and for a given price, called the *futures price*. The futures price is paid via a sequence of installments over the contract's life. At the time the contract is initiated, no cash changes hands. The contract has zero value at initiation. A cash payment, however, is made at the end of each trading interval, and it is equal to the change in the futures price over that interval. This cash payment resets the value of the futures contract to zero. To see how this process works, let us denote the time t futures price on a contract with delivery date T_1 on a T_2-maturity zero-coupon bond as $\mathcal{F}(t, T_1 : T_2)$. By definition, the futures price for a contract with immediate delivery of the T_2-maturity zero-coupon bond is

---

[2]This section discusses a hypothetical futures contract, devoid of the imbedded options associated with actual market traded futures contracts; see Chapter 2, Section 2.D.

TABLE 3.3
Cash flow comparison of a forward contract and a futures contract

Time	Forward contract	Futures contract
t	0	0
$t+1$	0	$\mathcal{F}(t+1, T_1 : T_2) - \mathcal{F}(t, T_1 : T_2)$
$t+2$	0	$\mathcal{F}(t+2, T_1 : T_2) - \mathcal{F}(t+1, T_1 : T_2)$
$\vdots$	$\vdots$	$\vdots$
$T_1 - 1$	0	$\mathcal{F}(T_1 - 1, T_1 : T_2) - \mathcal{F}(T_1 - 2, T_1 : T_2)$
T_1	$P(T_1, T_2) - F(t, T_1 : T_2)$	$P(T_1, T_2) - \mathcal{F}(T_1 - 1, T_1 : T_2)$
Sum	$P(T_1, T_2) - F(t, T_1 : T_2)$	$P(T_1, T_2) - \mathcal{F}(t, T_1 : T_2)$

the bond's price; i.e.,

$$\mathcal{F}(T_1, T_1 : T_2) = P(T_1, T_2) \tag{3.9}$$

Table 3.3 compares the cash flows of a forward contract and a futures contract. The forward contract has a cash flow only at the expiration date T_1. The futures contract has a cash flow at the end of each intermediate trading date equal to the change in the futures price on that day. The total (undiscounted) sum of all the cash flows paid is the spot price of the T_2-maturity bond less the forward price (futures price) for the forward contract (futures contract). The difference between the two contracts, therefore, is solely in the timing of the cash flows. The forward contract receives one cash flow at the end of the contract, and the futures contract receives a cash flow at the end of each trading date. This cash payment to the futures contract is called *marking to the market*.

SECTION F
SUMMARY

The basic assumptions and traded securities introduced in this chapter are used throughout the remainder of the book.

The assumptions are that the economy is frictionless and competitive and has only discrete trading. The discrete trading assumption is relaxed in Chapter 12.

The traded securities are zero-coupon bonds of all maturities ($P(t, T)$) and a money market account ($B(t)$). From these traded securities, we define the bond's yield ($y(t, T)$), forward rates ($f(t, T)$), and spot rates ($r(t)$). By convention, all these rates are given as one plus a percentage. The relations among these rates are provided.

Last, forward contracts and futures contracts on zero-coupon bonds have been defined in this chapter. The forward price of a contract with delivery date time T_1 on a zero-coupon bond maturing at time T_2 is denoted $F(t, T_1 : T_2)$. The futures price of a contract with delivery date time T_1 on a zero-coupon bond maturing at time T_2 is denoted $\mathcal{F}(t, T_1 : T_2)$. The difference between futures and forward contracts is that futures contracts are marked to market, whereas forward contracts are not.

SECTION G
COMPUTER EXAMPLE

The following exercise using the Trees software (Chapter 16) will help the reader understand the relations among zero-coupon bond prices, yields, and forward rates.

EXAMPLE. Using the Trees software, enter the following initial forward rate structure:

$$f(0,0) = 1.07$$
$$f(0,1) = 1.065$$
$$f(0,2) = 1.06$$
$$f(0,3) = 1.055$$
$$f(0,4) = 1.06$$
$$f(0,5) = 1.065$$
$$f(0,6) = 1.07$$
$$f(0,7) = 1.075$$
$$f(0,8) = 1.08$$
$$f(0,9) = 1.085$$
$$f(0,10) = 1.09$$

Compute the zero-coupon bond prices and yields.

Solution. Enter Trees software, select "model" from the menu, and select "initial term structure." Input the new forward rates by deleting the current numbers and replacing them with the new numbers. Next, go to the "display" menu, and select "term structure." Change the description to "pure discount bond prices." Then go to the first node and click on it. The following vector of zero-coupon bond prices will appear:

$$P(0,1) = 0.93458$$
$$P(0,2) = 0.87754$$
$$P(0,3) = 0.82787$$
$$P(0,4) = 0.78471$$
$$P(0,5) = 0.74029$$
$$P(0,6) = 0.69511$$
$$P(0,7) = 0.64963$$

$$P(0,8) = 0.60431$$
$$P(0,9) = 0.55955$$
$$P(0,10) = 0.51571$$
$$P(0,11) = 0.47313$$

Then go to "display," select "term structure," and change the description to "pure discount bond yields." Then go to the first node and click on it.

The following yields appear:

$$y(0,1) = 1.07$$
$$y(0,2) = 1.067497$$
$$y(0,3) = 1.064992$$
$$y(0,4) = 1.062485$$
$$y(0,5) = 1.061988$$
$$y(0,6) = 1.062489$$
$$y(0,7) = 1.063559$$
$$y(0,8) = 1.064982$$
$$y(0,9) = 1.066641$$
$$y(0,10) = 1.068463$$
$$y(0,11) = 1.070403$$

These are the answers. Notice how the yields change much more slowly than do forward rates. ■

SECTION H EXERCISES

a. Repeat the above example with

$$f(0,1) = 1.05$$
$$f(0,2) = 1.05$$
$$f(0,3) = 1.05$$
$$f(0,4) = 1.07$$
$$f(0,5) = 1.07$$
$$f(0,6) = 1.07$$
$$f(0,7) = 1.09$$
$$f(0,8) = 1.09$$
$$f(0,9) = 1.09$$
$$f(0,10) = 1.09$$

Check these computations by hand using expressions (3.1)–(3.3).

b. What happens to the zero-coupon bond prices and yields if you input forward rates that are less than 1, e.g., $f(0,1) = f(0,2) = \cdots = f(0,10) = 0.9$? Remember that forward rates less than one imply negative percentage returns.

SECTION I
REFERENCES TO CHAPTER 3

1. Back, K., 1993. "Asymmetric Information and Options." *Review of Financial Studies* 6 (3), 435–472.
2. Gastineau, G., and R. Jarrow, 1991. "Large Trader Impact and Market Regulation." *Financial Analysts Journal* 47 (4), 40–51.
3. Jarrow, R., 1992. "Market Manipulation, Bubbles, Corners and Short Squeezes." *Journal of Financial and Quantitative Analysis* 27 (3), 311–336.
4. Jarrow, R., 1994. "Derivative Security Markets, Market Manipulation, and Option Pricing Theory." *Journal of Financial and Quantitative Analysis* 29 (2), 241–261.

CHAPTER 4

The Evolution of the Term Structure of Interest Rates

Arbitrage pricing theory is often called a *relative pricing theory.* It is called a relative pricing theory because it takes the prices of a primary set of traded assets as given, as well as their stochastic evolution, and then it prices a secondary set of traded assets. It prices a secondary traded asset by constructing a portfolio of the primary assets, dynamically rebalanced across time, such that the portfolio's cash flows and value replicate the cash flows and value of the traded secondary asset. To prevent riskless profit opportunities, or *arbitrage,* the cost of this replicating portfolio and the price of the traded secondary asset must be identical. Of course, the cost of the replicating portfolio is known, since the prices of the primary traded assets are given. The given stochastic evolution of the primary traded assets determines whether this synthetic replication is possible (whether markets are complete).

For this text, the primary set of traded assets comprises zero-coupon bonds and the money market account. The secondary set of traded assets comprises either other zero-coupon bonds (Chapter 6) or interest rate options (Chapters 7–11). The basic inputs to this relative pricing theory are the prices of the zero-coupon bonds and their stochastic evolution through time.

This chapter introduces the stochastic evolution for the zero-coupon bond price curve. The stochastic structure is introduced sequentially, starting with a one-factor model, then presenting a two-factor model, and so forth. Starting with the simplest stochastic structure (one factor) facilitates understanding. After this one-factor model is mastered, additional factors can be added in a straightforward fashion. The next chapter formalizes the meaning of arbitrage opportunities and market completeness.

SECTION A
THE ONE-FACTOR ECONOMY

The uncertainty in the economy is best visualized by utilizing a *tree diagram* as given in Fig. 4.1. The next section explains this figure.

1 The State Space Process

At time 0, one of two possible outcomes can occur over the next time interval: "up," denoted by u, and "down," denoted by d. The up state occurs with probability $q_0 > 0$, and the down state occurs with probability $1 - q_0 > 0$. At this point, the states up and down have no real economic interpretation. They are just an abstraction formulated to characterize the only uncertainties influencing the term structure of interest rates. At time 1, one of two possible states exists: $\{u, d\}$. We denote the generic state at time 1, s_1. Thus, $s_1 \in \{u, d\}$.

Over the next time interval, one of two possible outcomes can occur again: up, denoted by u, or down, denoted by d. The resulting state at time 2 is $s_1 u$ or $s_1 d$. The up state occurs with probability $q_1(s_1) > 0$, and the down state occurs

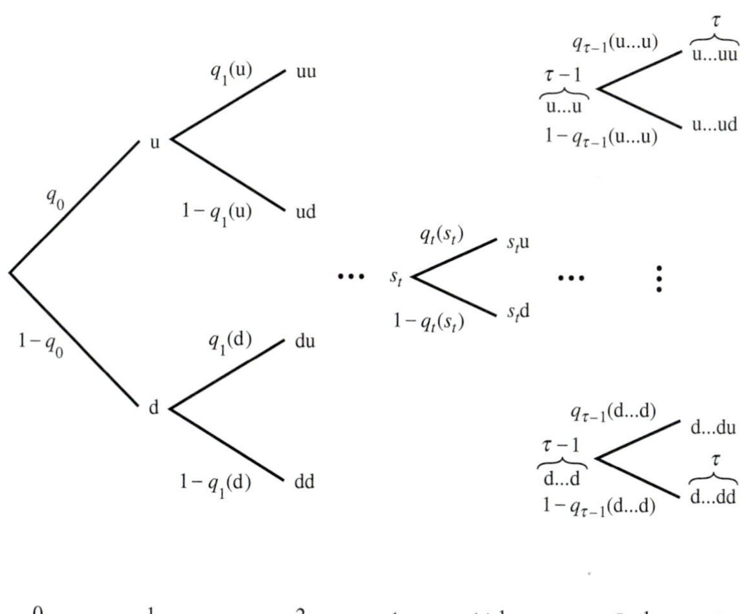

FIGURE 4.1
One-factor state space tree diagram.

with probability $1 - q_1(s_1) > 0$. At time 2, therefore, there are four possible states (s_1u, s_1d for each $s_1 \in \{u, d\}$), namely, uu, ud, du, and dd. The ordering in which the ups and downs occur is important; ud is considered distinct from du.

The process continues in this up-and-down fashion until time τ. For an arbitrary time t, there are 2^t possible states. The possible states at time t correspond to all possible t-sequences of u and d.[1] We let s_t denote a generic state at time t, so $s_t \in$ {all possible t-sequences of u's and d's}.

Over the next time period $[t, t+1]$, one of two possible outcomes can occur, up and down. The resulting state at time $t+1$ is s_tu or s_td. The up outcome occurs with probability $q_t(s_t) > 0$, and the down outcome occurs with probability $1 - q_t(s_t) > 0$. At time $t+1$, therefore, there are 2^{t+1} possible states (s_tu, s_td for each $s_t \in$ {all possible t-sequences of u's and d's}), namely, all possible $t+1$–sequences of u's and d's. The ordering within the sequence of the u's and d's is important, as distinct orderings are considered different *states*. Note that this specification of a state provides the complete history of the process.

At the last date τ all uncertainty is resolved, and the state s_τ is some τ-sequence of u's and d's. The *state space* consists of all possible τ-sequences of u's and d's, where ordering is important.

As the state space process is constructed, the entire history at any node may be important in determining the probabilities of the next outcome in the tree. This is indicated by making the probabilities at each date t dependent on the state s_t, i.e., $q_t(s_t)$. Thus, the state process is said to be *path dependent* and the tree is often called *bushy*. Such a tree ensures the most flexibility for modeling term structure evolutions.

EXAMPLE: ONE-FACTOR STATE SPACE PROCESS. An example of a one-factor state space tree diagram is given in Fig. 4.2. The tree starts at time 0 and terminates at time 3. The initial probability of jumping up is $\frac{3}{4}$, and the initial probability of jumping down is $\frac{1}{4}$. If a u occurs, the probabilities of jumping up and down remain the same: $\frac{3}{4}$ and $\frac{1}{4}$, respectively. This pattern repeats itself throughout the tree. This completes the example. ■

The state space process in Fig. 4.1 or Fig. 4.2 is called a *one-factor model* because at each node in the tree, only one of *two* possibilities can happen (up or down). Each branch also occurs with strictly positive probability. One can conceptualize the tree's being constructed by tossing *one coin* (one-factor).[2]

If, instead, at each node of the tree there were three branches, each with strictly positive probability, it would be called a *two-factor model*. It would be

---

[1]There are t empty slots, and each slot can take a u or d. Therefore, there are $2 \cdot 2 \cdots 2$ possibilities, where 2 is multiplied by itself t times. This totals 2^t.

[2]The coin would not be fair, however, because the probability of coming up heads at time t would be $q_{t-1}(s_{t-1})$, which need not be $\frac{1}{2}$, as in Figure 4.2.

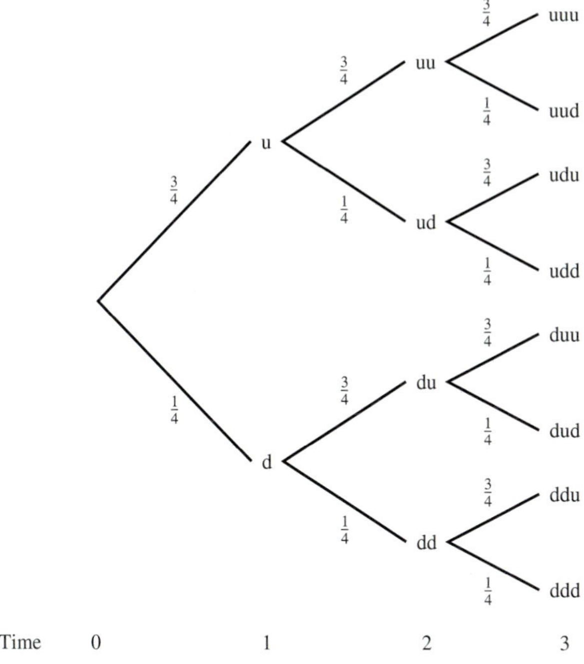

FIGURE 4.2
A one-factor state space tree diagram.

a two-factor model because it would take *two coins* to construct the tree.[3] The first coin would decide between the up branch, on the one hand, and the middle and down branches, on the other hand. The second coin would determine the splitting of the last two branches into middle and down. Conceptually, the analytics of describing the evolution of the state space process is no more difficult in multiple-factor models than it is in a one-factor model. Multiple-factor models will be discussed in subsequent sections.

2 The Bond Price Process

The state space process describes the uncertainty underlying and generating the evolution of all the zero-coupon bond prices. The evolution of the zero-coupon bond prices, in turn, determines the evolution of the forward rates and the spot rates. We now describe these stochastic processes.

---

[3]As in the case of a one-factor model, in general these coins will not be fair.

Formally, we indicate this state process's influence on the zero-coupon bond prices by expanding the notation, letting $P(t,T;s_t)$ be the T-maturity zero-coupon bond's price at time t under state s_t. Similarly, we expand the notation for yields, forward rates, spot rates, and so on.

We assume that $P(T,T;s_T) = 1$ for all T and s_T. This assumption formalizes the statement that zero-coupon bonds are default-free, i.e., that they are worth a dollar at maturity under all possible states. In addition, we assume that $P(t,T;s_t) > 0$ for all $t \le T$ and s_t. This ensures that one cannot get something for nothing, i.e., that a sure dollar costs something.

The zero-coupon bond price process tree is depicted in Fig. 4.3. To understand this figure, we first introduce a new notation for the returns on the zero-coupon bond in the up state and in the down state:

$$u(t,T;s_t) \equiv \frac{P(t+1,T;s_t u)}{P(t,T;s_t)} \qquad \text{for } t+1 \le T \qquad (4.1a)$$

and

$$d(t,T;s_t) \equiv \frac{P(t+1,T;s_t d)}{P(t,T;s_t)} \qquad \text{for } t+1 \le T \qquad (4.1b)$$

where $u(t,T;s_t) > d(t,T;s_t)$ for all $t < T-1$ and s_t. Expression (4.1a) defines $u(t,T;s_t)$ as the return at time t on the T-maturity zero-coupon bond in the up state. Similarly, expression (4.1b) defines $d(t,T;s_t)$ as the return at time t on the T-maturity bond in the down state. The up and down terminology is given economic meaning by these expressions, for they are seen to describe the relative changes in the magnitudes of the zero-coupon bond prices as[4] $u(t,T;s_t) > d(t,T;s_t)$. This strict inequality only holds for $t < T-1$ because at time T, its maturity date, the zero-coupon bond pays a sure dollar, i.e.; $P(T,T;s_T) = 1$ for all s_T. Therefore, expression (4.1) implies the following:

$$u(t,t+1;s_t) = d(t,t+1;s_t) = \frac{1}{P(t,t+1;s_t)} \equiv r(t;s_t) \qquad \text{for all } t \text{ and } s_t \qquad (4.2)$$

Over the last interval in the bond's life, the returns in the up and down states are identical, nonrandom, and equal to the spot rate (see expression (3.5)).

Expression (4.2) implies an important fact regarding the money market account's value at any time t. Since $B(t) = B(t-1)r(t-1)$, we see that the money market account's value at time t depends only on state s_{t-1} of the process at time $t-1$, and not time t's state. Hence, we write $B(t;s_{t-1})$ as the money market account's time t value.

Although Fig. 4.3 looks complicated, it is in fact quite simple. The first observation to make is that Fig. 4.3 depicts the evolution of the entire zero-coupon

[4]This restriction is somewhat stronger than that which is actually needed. For the subsequent analysis, we need only require that $u(t,T;s_t) \ne d(t,T;s_t)$ for all $t < T-1$ and s_t.

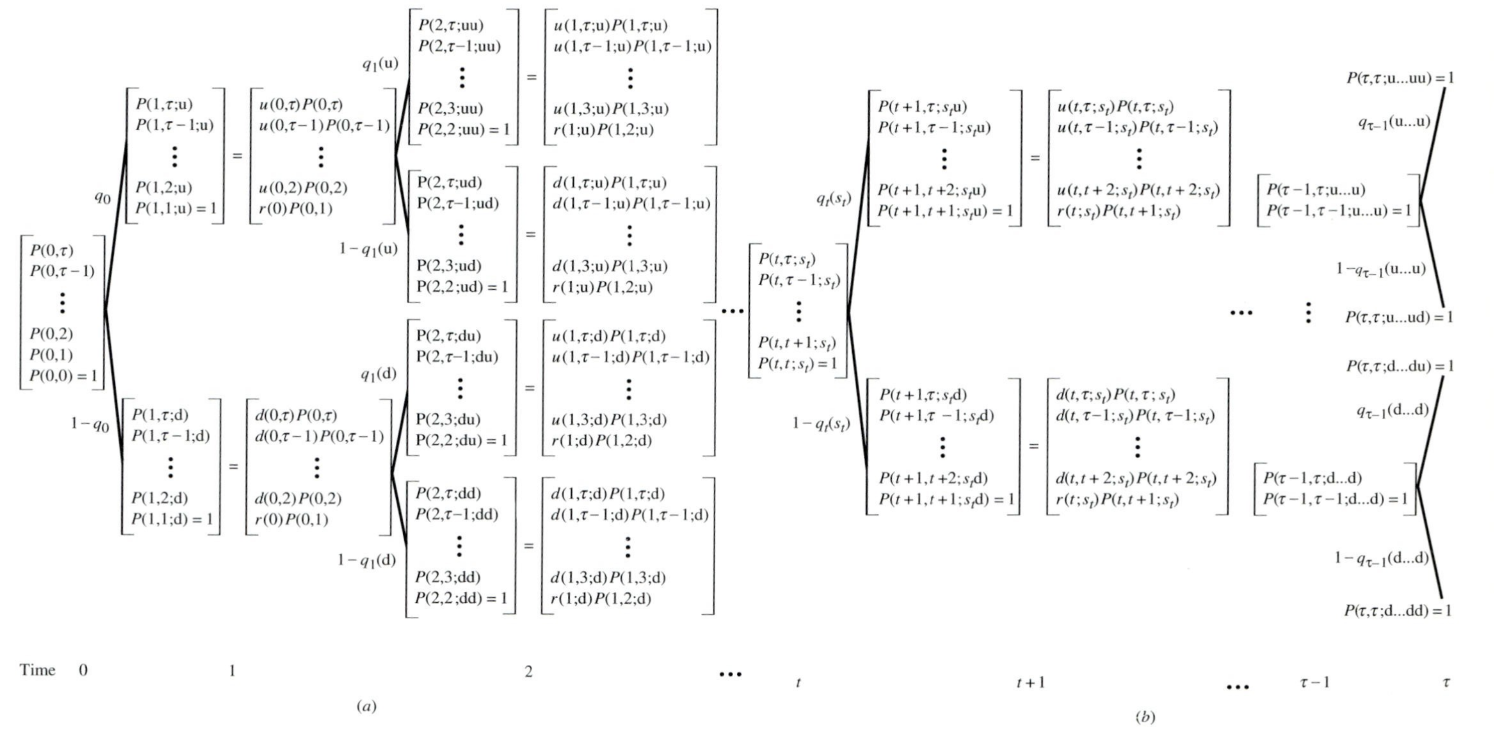

FIGURE 4.3
One-factor bond price curve evolution.

bond price curve (a vector). Hence, at each node there is a vector of zero-coupon bond prices, and not just a single point as in Fig. 4.1.

At time 0 we start with the initial zero-coupon bond price curve ($P(0,\tau)$, $P(0,\tau-1),\ldots,P(0,1),P(0,0)=1$). There are $(\tau+1)$ elements in this vector. For consistency, the price of the bond maturing at time 0 ($P(0,0)$) with a price of unity is included as the last element in this vector.

Over the time interval between 0 and time 1, the zero-coupon bond price curve moves up to $(P(t,\tau;u),\ldots,P(1,2;u),1)$ with probability $q_0>0$ or down to $(P(1,\tau;d),\ldots,P(1,2;d),1)$ with probability $1-q_0>0$. These zero-coupon bond price curves, however, consist of only τ elements, because the one-period zero-coupon bond at time 0 matures at time 1 and pays a sure dollar. After that date, it no longer trades. For convenience, these new price vectors are alternatively written in Fig. 4.3 as the zero-coupon bond price curve at time 0 multiplied by the return over the period 0 to 1. For the up state the new vector is $(u(0,\tau)P(0,\tau),\ldots,u(0,2)P(0,2),r(0)P(0,1))$ and the down vector is $((d(0,\tau)P(0,\tau),\ldots,d(0,2)P(0,2),r(0)P(0,1))$. At time 1, therefore, there are two possible zero-bond price curves as determined by the returns.

Between time 1 and time 2, given the state at time 1 (either u or d), the entire curve again shifts up or down. For example, if the state at time 1 is $s_1 = u$, then with probability $q_1(u)>0$ the curve moves up to $(P(2,\tau;uu),\ldots,1)$, or with probability $1-q_1(u)>0$ the curve moves down to $(P(2,\tau;ud),\ldots,1)$. In return form this is $(u(1,\tau;u)\times P(1,\tau;u),\ldots,r(1;u)P(1,2;u))$ or $(d(1,\tau;u)\times P(1,\tau;u),\ldots,r(1;u)P(1,2;u))$. At time 2 four possible zero-coupon bond price curves are possible. Each curve now has only $\tau-1$ elements.

Starting from an arbitrary curve $(P(t,\tau;s_t),\ldots,P(t,t;s_t)=1)$ at time t under state s_t, the curve moves up with probability $q_t(s_t)>0$ to $(P(t+1,\tau;s_tu),\ldots,P(t+1,t+1;s_tu)=1)$ or down with probability $1-q_t(s_t)>0$ to $(P(t+1,\tau;s_td),\ldots,P(t+1,t+1;s_td)=1)$. In return form these can be written as $(u(t,\tau;s_t)P(t,\tau;s_t),\ \ldots,\ r(t;s_t)P(t,t+1;s_t))$ and $(d(t,\tau;s_t)P(t,\tau;s_t),\ \ldots,r(t;s_t)P(t,t+1;s_t))$, respectively.

The evolution of the zero-coupon bond price curve continues in this fashion until time τ. Over the last interval in the model, time $\tau-1$ to time τ, there is only one zero-coupon bond trading, the bond that matures at time τ. This bond pays a sure dollar at time τ regardless of the state, and after time τ the model ends.

It is important to point out that the traded zero-coupon bonds do not span the relevant uncertainty over this last time interval. For any history $s_{\tau-1}$ at time $\tau-1$, the state space process tree branches up or down. However, the single traded zero-coupon bond pays a certain amount, a dollar, regardless of the state. Hence, this zero-coupon bond's payoff does not differentiate the up and down states at time τ. This is the only time period in the model that has this property. Indeed, we will later show that in all other time intervals the market is complete with enough zero-coupon bonds trading to span all the relevant states or histories.

We can summarize the evolution of the one-factor zero-coupon bond price curve analytically as in expression (4.3):

$$P(t+1,T;s_{t+1})$$
$$= \begin{cases} u(t,T;s_t)P(t,T;s_t) & \text{if } s_{t+1} = s_t\text{u (with probability } q_t(s_t) > 0) \\ d(t,T;s_t)P(t,T;s_t) & \text{if } s_{t+1} = s_t\text{d (with probability } 1 - q_t(s_t) > 0) \end{cases} \tag{4.3}$$

where

$$u(t,T;s_t) > d(t,T;s_t) \qquad \text{for } t < T-1$$
$$u(t,t+1;s_t)P(t,t+1;s_t) = d(t,t+1;s_t)P(t,t+1;s_t) = 1$$

For simplicity of presentation, we have constructed the economy so that at each trading date, a zero-coupon bond matures and it is removed from trading. In addition, no new zero-coupon bonds are issued. It is an easy adjustment to introduce a *newly* issued τ-maturity zero-coupon bond at each trading date. In this situation, the zero-coupon bond price vector would be of constant size containing τ-elements at every date. Expression (4.3) is simply expanded to accommodate these newly issued bonds.

EXAMPLE: ONE-FACTOR ZERO-COUPON BOND CURVE EVOLUTION. Figure 4.4 contains an example of a one-factor bond price curve evolution. The state space process is that contained in Fig. 4.2. The initial bond price curve is at

$$\begin{bmatrix} P(0,4) \\ P(0,3) \\ P(0,2) \\ P(0,1) \\ P(0,0) \end{bmatrix} = \begin{bmatrix} 0.923845 \\ 0.942322 \\ 0.961169 \\ 0.980392 \\ 1 \end{bmatrix}$$

With probability $\frac{3}{4}$ this curve jumps up to

$$\begin{bmatrix} P(1,4;\text{u}) \\ P(1,3;\text{u}) \\ P(1,2;\text{u}) \\ P(1,1;\text{u}) \end{bmatrix} = \begin{bmatrix} 0.947497 \\ 0.965127 \\ 0.982699 \\ 1 \end{bmatrix}$$

and with probability $\frac{1}{4}$ it jumps down to

$$\begin{bmatrix} P(1,4;\text{d}) \\ P(1,3;\text{d}) \\ P(1,2;\text{d}) \\ P(1,1;\text{d}) \end{bmatrix} = \begin{bmatrix} 0.937148 \\ 0.957211 \\ 0.978085 \\ 1 \end{bmatrix}$$

The returns in the up state are

$$\begin{bmatrix} u(0,4) \\ u(0,3) \\ u(0,2) \\ u(0,1) \end{bmatrix} = \begin{bmatrix} 0.947497/0.923845 \\ 0.965127/0.942322 \\ 0.982699/0.961169 \\ 1/0.0980392 \end{bmatrix} = \begin{bmatrix} 1.025601 \\ 1.024201 \\ 1.022400 \\ 1.02 \end{bmatrix}$$

These returns are greater than the returns in the down state, which are

$$\begin{bmatrix} d(0,4) \\ d(0,3) \\ d(0,2) \\ d(0,1) \end{bmatrix} = \begin{bmatrix} 0.937148/0.923845 \\ 0.957211/0.942322 \\ 0.978085/0.961169 \\ 1/0.980392 \end{bmatrix} = \begin{bmatrix} 1.014399 \\ 1.015800 \\ 1.017600 \\ 1.02 \end{bmatrix}$$

The zero-coupon bond price curve evolution given in Fig. 4.4 continues in a similar fashion until time 4, when the tree ends. We see that as each period occurs, the shortest maturity bond matures and then disappears from the tree. The trick for constructing trees such as that given in Fig. 4.4 will be explained in Chapter 12. This completes the example. ■

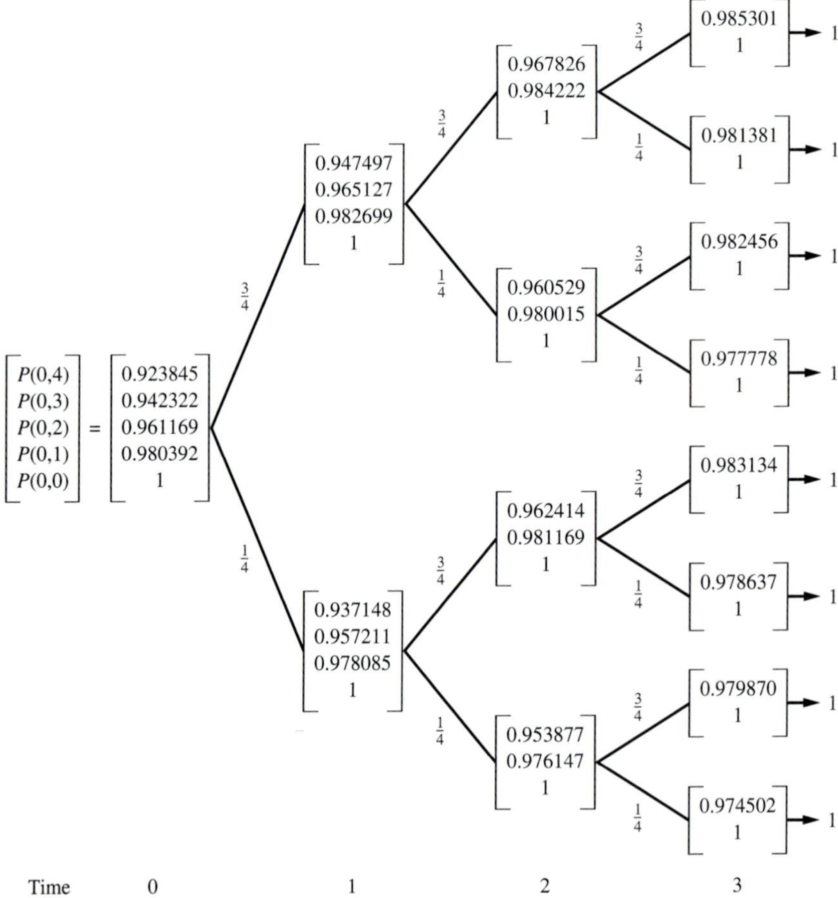

FIGURE 4.4
A one-factor bond price curve evolution. Actual probabilities lie along the tree's branches.

3 The Forward Rate Process

The forward rate curve evolution is given in Fig. 4.5. To understand this figure, we introduce a new notation for the rate of change in the forward rate over any interval of time $[t, t + 1]$ conditional upon the history at time t; i.e.,

$$\alpha(t, T; s_t) \equiv \frac{f(t + 1, T; s_t\mathrm{u})}{f(t, T; s_t)} \qquad \text{for } t + 1 \leq T \leq \tau - 1 \qquad (4.4a)$$

and

$$\beta(t, T; s_t) \equiv \frac{f(t + 1, T; s_t\mathrm{d})}{f(t, T; s_t)} \qquad \text{for } t + 1 \leq T \leq \tau - 1 \qquad (4.4b)$$

Expression (4.4a) defines the rate of change in the T-maturity forward rate over $[t, t + 1]$ to be $\alpha(t, T; s_t)$ in the up state and to be $\beta(t, T; s_t)$ in the down state. These rates of change depend on the history s_t.

Like the preceding figures, Fig. 4.5 describes the stochastic evolution of an entire vector of forward rates. At time 0 the tree starts with the initial vector of forward rates $(f(0, \tau - 1), \ldots, f(0, 0) = r(0))$. There are τ elements in this vector, the last element being the spot rate.

This forward rate curve jumps at time 1 to the vector $(f(1, \tau - 1; \mathrm{u}), \ldots, f(1, 1; \mathrm{u}))$ in the up state and $(f(1, \tau - 1; \mathrm{d}), \ldots, f(1, 1; \mathrm{d}))$ in the down state. These can alternatively be written in return form as $(\alpha(0, \tau - 1)f(0, \tau - 1), \ldots, \alpha(0, 1)f(0, 1))$ and $(\beta(0, \tau - 1)f(0, \tau - 1), \ldots, \beta(0, 1)f(0, 1))$, respectively. Each new vector has only $\tau - 1$ elements, its size being reduced by one as the time 0, one-period zero-coupon bond matures.

Consider an arbitrary time t and state s_t, where the forward rate curve is at $(f(t, \tau - 1; s_t), \ldots, f(t, t; s_t))$. It moves with probability $q_t(s_t) > 0$ to $(f(t + 1, \tau - 1; s_t\mathrm{u}), \ldots, f(t + 1, t + 1; s_t\mathrm{u}))$ and with probability $(1 - q_t(s_t)) > 0$ to $(f(t+1, \tau-1; s_t\mathrm{d}), \ldots, f(t+1, t+1; s_t\mathrm{d}))$. In return form, these can be written as $(\alpha(t, \tau - 1; s_t)f(t, \tau - 1; s_t), \ldots, \alpha(t, t + 1; s_t)f(t, t + 1; s_t))$ and $(\beta(t, \tau - 1; s_t)f(t, \tau - 1; s_t), \ldots, \beta(t, t + 1; s_t)f(t, t + 1; s_t))$, respectively. The forward rate curve starts at time t with $\tau - t$ elements and is reduced to $\tau - t - 1$ elements at time $t + 1$.

We can summarize this evolution for an arbitrary time t as in expression (4.5):

$$f(t + 1, T; s_{t+1}) = \begin{cases} \alpha(t, T; s_t)f(t, T; s_t) & \text{if } s_{t+1} = s_t\mathrm{u} \text{ (with probability } q_t(s_t) > 0) \\ \beta(t, T; s_t)f(t, T; s_t) & \text{if } s_{t+1} = s_t\mathrm{d} \text{ (with probability } 1 - q_t(s_t) > 0) \end{cases} \qquad (4.5)$$

where $\tau - 1 \geq T \geq t + 1$.

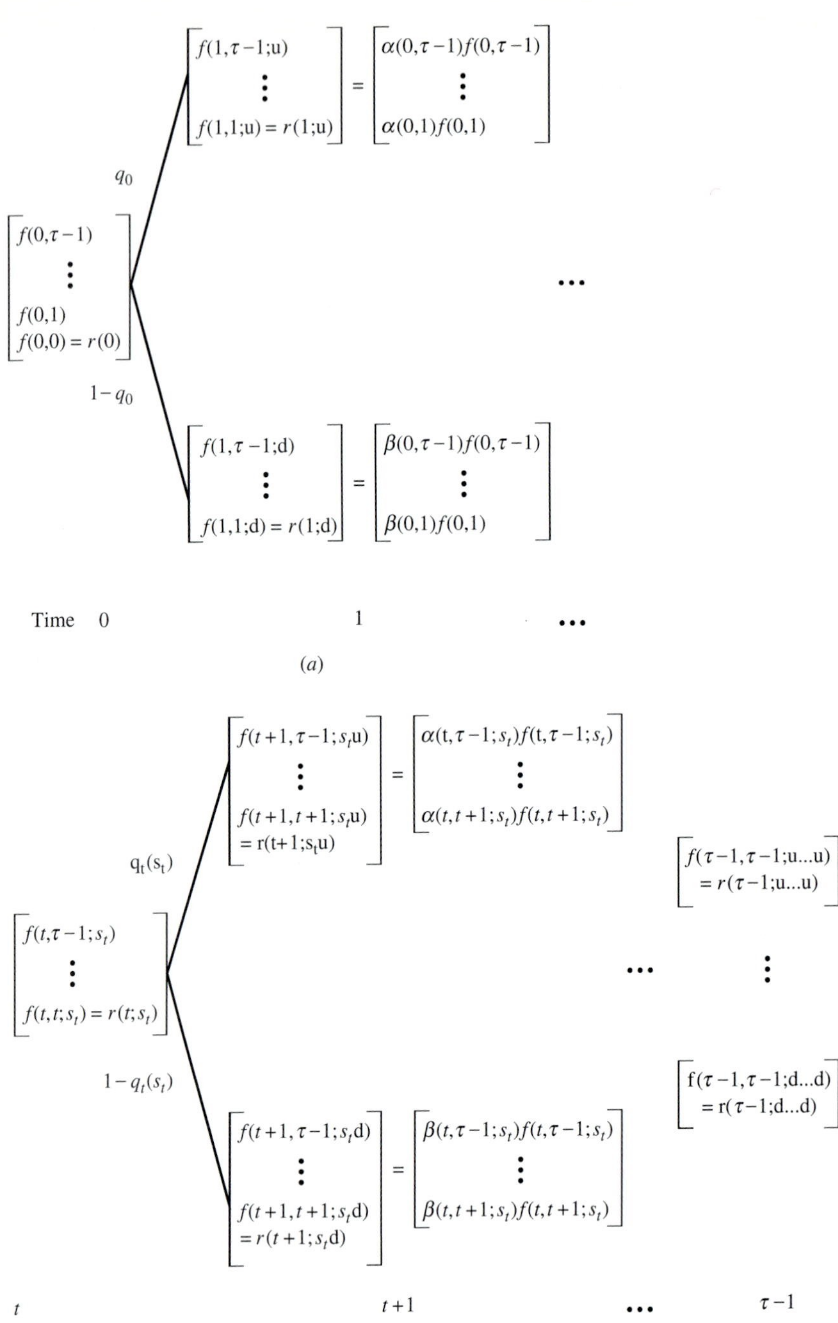

FIGURE 4.5
One-factor forward rate curve evolution.

Finally, at time $\tau - 1$ only one zero-coupon bond remains in the market and only one forward rate exists, the spot rate. At time τ, when the last zero-coupon bond matures, no additional forward rates can be defined, and the model is terminated.

EXAMPLE: ONE-FACTOR FORWARD RATE CURVE EVOLUTION. Figure 4.6 gives the one-factor forward rate curve evolution implied by the zero-coupon bond price curve evolution example in Fig. 4.4. The process starts with a flat term structure with forward rates given by

$$\begin{bmatrix} f(0,3) \\ f(0,2) \\ f(0,1) \\ f(0,0) \end{bmatrix} = \begin{bmatrix} 1.02 \\ 1.02 \\ 1.02 \\ 1.02 \end{bmatrix}$$

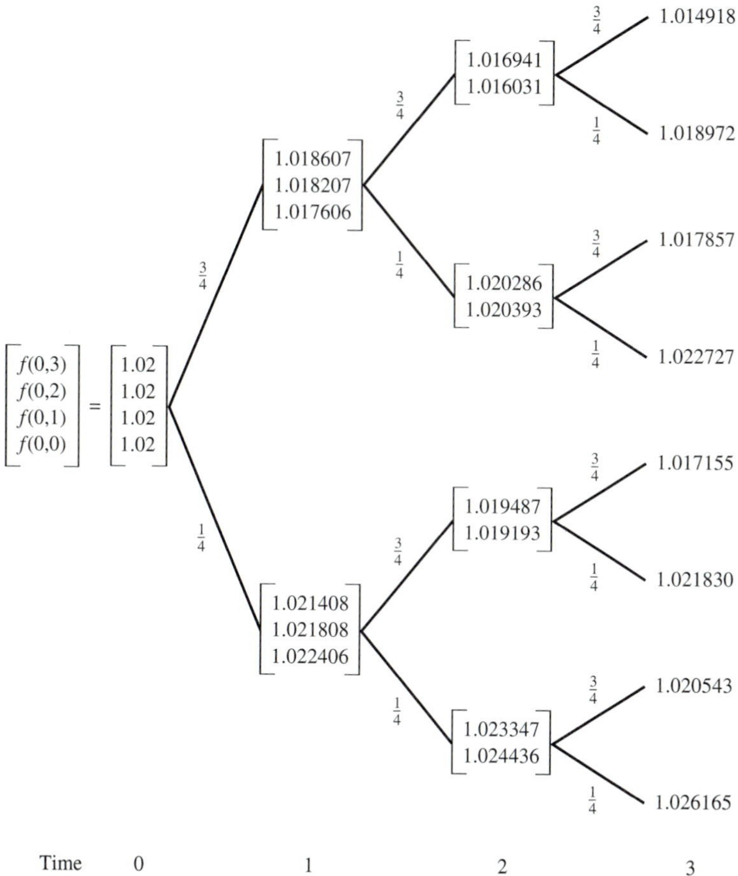

FIGURE 4.6
One-factor forward rate curve.

With probability $\frac{3}{4}$, the forward rate curve shifts up to

$$\begin{bmatrix} f(1,3;\mathrm{u}) \\ f(1,2;\mathrm{u}) \\ f(1,1;\mathrm{u}) \end{bmatrix} = \begin{bmatrix} 1.018607 \\ 1.018207 \\ 1.017606 \end{bmatrix}$$

The term up corresponds to bond prices. Because rates move inversely to prices, the forward rate curve actually moves down.

With probability $\frac{1}{4}$, the forward rate curve shifts down to

$$\begin{bmatrix} f(1,3;\mathrm{d}) \\ f(1,2;\mathrm{d}) \\ f(1,1;\mathrm{d}) \end{bmatrix} = \begin{bmatrix} 1.021408 \\ 1.021808 \\ 1.022406 \end{bmatrix}$$

The rates of change in the forward rate curve in the up and down states are given by

$$\begin{bmatrix} \alpha(0,3) \\ \alpha(0,2) \\ \alpha(0,1) \end{bmatrix} = \begin{bmatrix} 1.018607/1.02 \\ 1.018207/1.02 \\ 1.017606/1.02 \end{bmatrix} = \begin{bmatrix} 0.998634 \\ 0.998242 \\ 0.997653 \end{bmatrix}$$

and

$$\begin{bmatrix} \beta(0,3) \\ \beta(0,2) \\ \beta(0,1) \end{bmatrix} = \begin{bmatrix} 1.021408/1.02 \\ 1.021808/1.02 \\ 1.022406/1.02 \end{bmatrix} = \begin{bmatrix} 1.001380 \\ 1.001773 \\ 1.002359 \end{bmatrix}$$

Given the evolution of the forward rate curve, we can deduce the evolution of the bond price curve. For example, at time 1, the up node in the forward rate curve enables us to generate the bond price vector in Fig. 4.4 as follows:

$$\begin{bmatrix} P(1,4;\mathrm{u}) \\ P(1,3;\mathrm{u}) \\ P(1,2;\mathrm{u}) \\ P(1,1;\mathrm{u}) \end{bmatrix} = \begin{bmatrix} 1/[(1.018607)(1.018207)(1.0176066)] \\ 1/[(1.018207)(1.017606)] \\ 1/1.017606 \\ 1 \end{bmatrix} = \begin{bmatrix} 0.947497 \\ 0.965127 \\ 0.982699 \\ 1 \end{bmatrix}$$

The remainder of the forward rate process in Fig. 4.6 continues in a similar fashion. ■

As seen in the example, the relation between the zero-coupon bond price process and the forward rate process can be easily deduced. First, by the definition of a forward rate (expression (3.3)),

$$\frac{P(t+1,T;s_{t+1})}{P(t+1,T+1;s_{t+1})} = f(t+1,T;s_{t+1}) \tag{4.6}$$

Letting $s_{t+1} = s_t\mathrm{u}$, we can rewrite expression (4.6) in return form:

$$\frac{P(t,T;s_t)u(t,T;s_t)}{P(t,T+1,s_t)u(t,T+1,s_t)} = f(t+1,T;s_t\mathrm{u}) \tag{4.7}$$

Using the definition of a forward rate, expression (3.3), again yields

$$f(t,T;s_t)\frac{u(t,T;s_t)}{u(t,T+1;s_t)} = f(t+1,T;s_t u) \tag{4.8a}$$

A similar analysis for $s_{t+1} = s_t\text{d}$ yields

$$f(t,T;s_t)\frac{d(t,T;s_t)}{d(t,T+1;s_t)} = f(t+1,T;s_t\text{d}) \tag{4.8b}$$

Comparison with expression (4.5) gives the final result:

$$\alpha(t,T;s_t) = \frac{u(t,T;s_t)}{u(t,T+1;s_t)} \qquad \text{for } \tau - 1 \geq T \geq t+1 \tag{4.9a}$$

and

$$\beta(t,T;s_t) = \frac{d(t,T;s_t)}{d(t,T+1;s_t)} \qquad \text{for } \tau - 1 \geq T \geq t+1 \tag{4.9b}$$

Expression (4.9) relates the forward rate's rate of change parameters to the zero-coupon bond price process's rate of return parameters in the up (4.9a) and down (4.9b) states, respectively. *Expression (4.9) is useful when one parameterizes the bond price process first and then wants to deduce the forward rate process from it.*

The parameterization can also work in the reverse direction. Given the forward rate process parameters as in Fig. 4.5, one can alternatively deduce the zero-coupon bond price process's rate of return parameters in the up and down states. These relations are given in expression (4.10). The proof follows.

$$u(t,T;s_t) = \frac{r(t;s_t)}{\Pi_{j=t+1}^{T-1}\alpha(t,j;s_t)} \qquad \text{for } \tau - 1 \geq T \geq t+2 \tag{4.10a}$$

and

$$d(t,T;s_t) = \frac{r(t;s_t)}{\Pi_{j=t+1}^{T-1}\beta(t,j;s_t)} \qquad \text{for } \tau - 1 \geq T \geq t+2 \tag{4.10b}$$

DERIVATION OF EXPRESSION (4.10). From (4.9a) we have that $u(t,t+1;s_t)/\alpha(t,t+1;s_t) = u(t,t+2;s_t)$. But $u(t,t+1;s_t) = r(t;s_t)$, so substitution generates

$$\frac{r(t;s_t)}{\alpha(t,t+1;s_t)} = u(t,t+2;s_t) \tag{$*$}$$

Similarly, from (4.9a) we have that

$$\frac{u(t,t+2;s_t)}{\alpha(t,t+2;s_t)} = u(t,t+3;s_t)$$

Substituting in ($*$) gives

$$r(t;s_t)/\alpha(t,t+1;s_t)\alpha(t,t+2;s_t) = u(t,t+3;s_t)$$

Proceeding inductively gives the result (4.10a). Finally, (4.10b) follows in a similar fashion. ■

Expression (4.10) is useful when one parameterizes the forward rate process first and then wants to deduce the bond price process from it. This is the focal point of the analysis, for example, in Heath, Jarrow, and Morton [1, 2, 3]. This perspective is detailed in Chapter 12 of this text.

In summary, the evolution of the zero-coupon bond price curve can be specified in one of two ways. First, one can directly specify the changes in the zero-coupon bond price curve itself as in Fig. 4.3 or expression (4.3). Alternatively, one can specify the changes in the forward rate curve as given in Fig. 4.5 or expression (4.5) and then use the relation between the changes in forward rates and zero-coupon bond prices as given in expression (4.10) to deduce the bond price curve evolution. For reasons based on the stability of empirical estimates of the various parameters, the latter approach may be preferred (see Heath, Jarrow, and Morton [2]).

4 The Spot Rate Process

The stochastic process for the spot rate can be deduced from the zero-coupon bond price process's evolution in Fig. 4.3. Indeed, as each one-period zero-coupon bond matures, its return determines the spot rate. This spot-rate process is given in Fig. 4.7.

The spot rate curve starts at $r(0)$, and it moves "up" to $r(1; \mathrm{u})$ with probability $q_0 > 0$ and "down" to $r(1; \mathrm{d})$ with probability $1 - q_0 > 0$. Quotes are placed around "up" and "down" because the spot rate actually moves inversely to the zero-coupon bond price curve movement. So, in fact, u indicates that spot rates move down and d indicates that spot rates move up. The spot-rate process's parameters are deduced from Fig. 4.3 (expression 4.3)) as $u(1, 2; \mathrm{u})$ or $d(1, 2; \mathrm{d})$.

The spot rate process continues in this branching fashion. At time t, under state s_t, the spot rate $r(t; s_t)$ again moves down to $r(t + 1; s_t\mathrm{u}) = u(t + 1, t + 2; s_t\mathrm{u})$ with probability $q_t(s_t) > 0$ and up to $r(t + 1; s_t\mathrm{d}) = d(t + 1, t + 2; s_t\mathrm{d})$ with probability $1 - q_t(s_t) > 0$.

The last period's spot rate is determined at time $\tau - 1$: it is $r(\tau - 1; s_{\tau-1})$, and it is either $u(\tau - 1, \tau; s_{\tau-2}\mathrm{u})$ with probability $q_{\tau-2}(s_{\tau-2}) > 0$ or $d(\tau - 1, \tau; s_{\tau-2}\mathrm{d})$ with probability $1 - q_{\tau-2}(s_{\tau-2}) > 0$. We can summarize the spot rate's stochastic process as

$$r(t + 1; s_{t+1}) = \begin{cases} u(t + 1, t + 2; s_t\mathrm{u}) & \text{with probability } q_t(s_t) > 0 \\ d(t + 1, t + 2; s_t\mathrm{d}) & \text{with probability } 1 - q_t(s_t) > 0 \end{cases} \tag{4.11}$$

for all s_t and $t + 1 \leq T - 1$.

It is in fact possible to go in the opposite direction. In later sections, using the risk-neutral valuation methodology, we will show that Fig. 4.7 is sufficient (given additional information) to deduce the evolution of the zero-coupon bond price curve as given in Fig. 4.3.

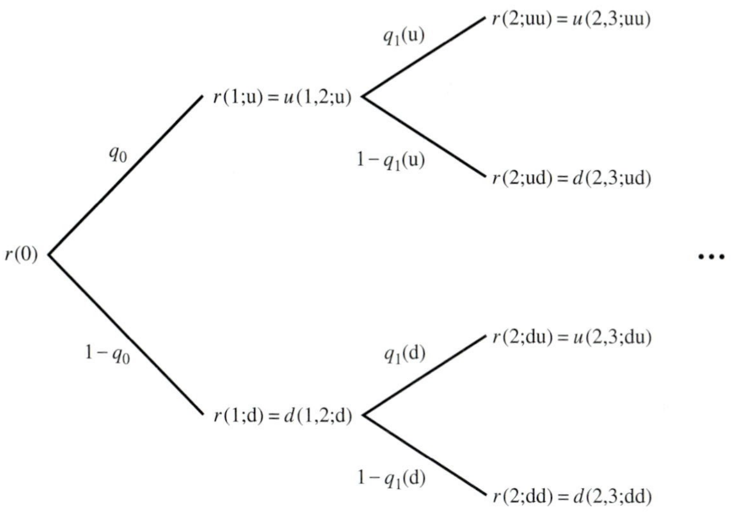

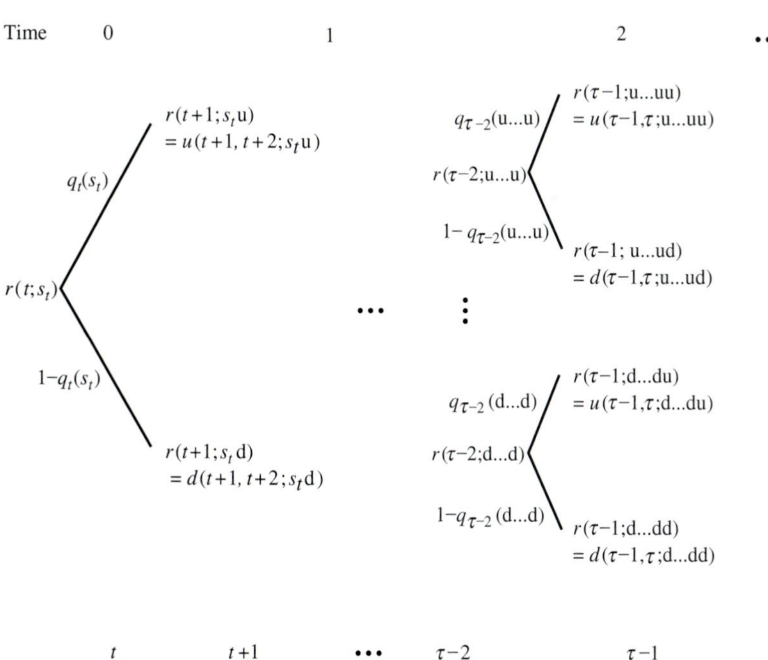

FIGURE 4.7
One-factor spot rate process.

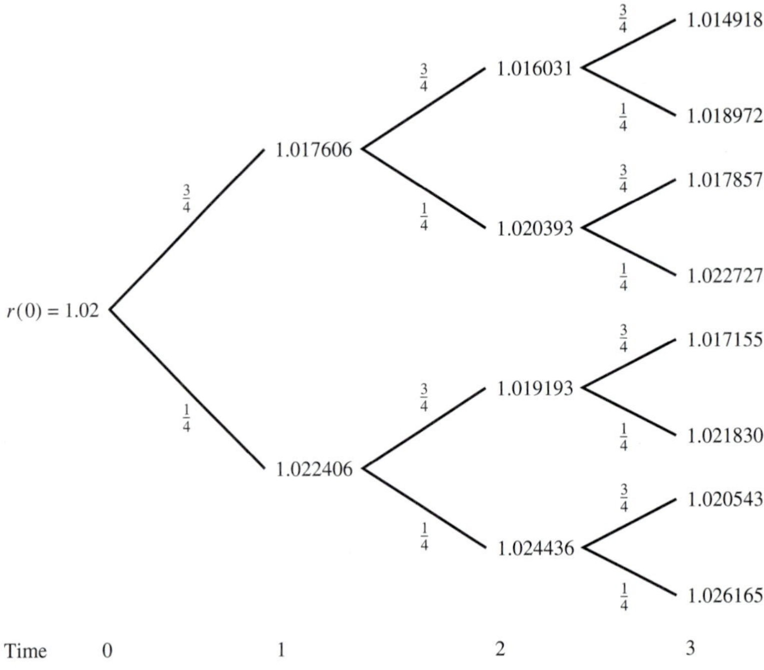

FIGURE 4.8
A one-factor spot rate process.

EXAMPLE: ONE-FACTOR SPOT RATE PROCESS EVOLUTION. The spot rate process evolution implied by the example in Fig. 4.4 is given in Fig. 4.8. This curve can be read off Fig. 4.6, because it corresponds to the last entry in every vector. ■

SECTION B THE TWO-FACTOR ECONOMY

Given the analysis for a one-factor economy, the extension to a two-factor economy is straightforward. For brevity, the presentation proceeds using only the analytic representation.

1 The State Space Process

Between time 0 and time 1, one of three possible outcomes can occur: up, denoted by u; middle, denoted by m; and down, denoted by d; i.e., $s_1 \in \{u, m, d\}$.

The probability that $s_1 = \text{u}$ is $q_0^{\text{u}} > 0$, the probability that $s_1 = \text{m}$ is $q_0^{\text{m}} > 0$, and the probability that $s_1 = \text{d}$ is $1 - q_0^{\text{u}} - q_0^{\text{m}} > 0$.

At time $t \in \{1, 2, \ldots, \tau\}$, the generic initial state is labeled $s_t \in$ {all possible t sequences of u's, m's, and d's}. There exist 3^t possible histories at time t. Over the time interval $[t, t+1]$, the new state s_{t+1} is generated according to expression (4.12):

$$s_{t+1} = \begin{cases} s_t\text{u} & \text{with probability } q_t^{\text{u}}(s_t) > 0 \\ s_t\text{m} & \text{with probability } q_t^{\text{m}}(s_t) > 0 \\ s_t\text{d} & \text{with probability } 1 - q_t^{\text{u}}(s_t) - q_t^{\text{m}}(s_t) > 0 \end{cases} \tag{4.12}$$

The state space at time τ contains 3^τ possible histories and is {all possible ordered τ sequences of u's, m's, and d's}.

2 The Bond Price Process

The notation for the return on a zero-coupon bond is expanded to include the middle state as in expression (4.13):

$$u(t, T; s_t) \equiv \frac{P(t+1, T; s_t\text{u})}{P(t, T; s_t)} \qquad \text{for } t+1 \le T \tag{4.13a}$$

$$m(t, T; s_t) \equiv \frac{P(t+1, T; s_t\text{m})}{P(t, T; s_t)} \qquad \text{for } t+1 \le T \tag{4.13b}$$

and

$$d(t, T; s_t) \equiv \frac{P(t+1, T; s_t\text{d})}{P(t, T; s_t)} \qquad \text{for } t+1 \le T \tag{4.13c}$$

where $u(t, T; s_t) > m(t, T; s_t) > d(t, T; s_t)$ for $t < T - 1$ and s_t, and

$$\begin{bmatrix} 1 & u(t, T; s_t) & u(t, T^*; s_t) \\ 1 & m(t, T; s_t) & m(t, T^*; s_t) \\ 1 & d(t, T; s_t) & d(t, T^*; s_t) \end{bmatrix}$$

is nonsingular for $T \ne T^*$, $t + 1 < \min(T, T^*)$, and s_t. By construction,

$$\begin{aligned} u(t, t+1; s_t) &= m(t, t+1; s_t) \\ &= d(t, t+1; s_t) = \frac{1}{P(t, t+1; s_t)} \equiv r(t; s_t) \end{aligned} \tag{4.14}$$

Expressions (4.13) and (4.14) are a straightforward extension of the one-factor model with the exception of the nonsingularity condition on the matrix in expression (4.13c). This is included so that different maturity bonds ($T \ne T^*$) are not identical in their return structure either to each other or to the money market account. (As in the one-factor case, we do not need the restriction that

$u(t,T;s_t) > m(t,T;s_t) > d(t,T;s_t)$ for all $t < T - 1$ and s_t. It is imposed for clarity of the exposition.)

The evolution of the zero-coupon bond price curve is described by expression (4.15):

$$P(t+1,T;s_{t+1}) = \begin{cases} u(t,T;s_t)P(t,T;s_t) & \text{if } s_{t+1} = s_t\text{u (with probability } q_t^{\text{u}}(s_t) > 0) \\ m(t,T;s_t)P(t,T;s_t) & \text{if } s_{t+1} = s_t\text{m (with probability } q_t^{\text{m}}(s_t) > 0) \\ d(t,T;s_t)P(t,T;s_t) & \text{if } s_{t+1} = s_t\text{d (with probability } \\ & \qquad 1 - q_t^{\text{u}}(s_t) - q_t^{\text{m}}(s_t) > 0) \end{cases} \tag{4.15}$$

for all $t \leq T - 1 \leq \tau - 1$ and s_t.

This completes the description of the zero-coupon bond price evolution.

3 The Forward Rate Process

The new notation for the rate of change of the forward rate is given in expression (4.16):

$$\alpha(t,T;s_t) \equiv \frac{f(t+1,T;s_t\text{u})}{f(t,T;s_t)} \qquad \text{for } t+1 \leq T \leq \tau - 1 \tag{4.16a}$$

$$\gamma(t,T;s_t) \equiv \frac{f(t+1,T;s_t\text{m})}{f(t,T;s_t)} \qquad \text{for } t+1 \leq T \leq \tau - 1 \tag{4.16b}$$

and

$$\beta(t,T;s_t) \equiv \frac{f(t+1,T;s_t\text{d})}{f(t,T;s_t)} \qquad \text{for } t+1 \leq T \leq \tau - 1 \tag{4.16c}$$

The evolution of the forward rate curve is described by expression (4.17):

$$f(t+1,T;s_{t+1}) = \begin{cases} \alpha(t,T;s_t)f(t,T;s_t) & \text{if } s_{t+1} = s_t\text{u (with probability } q_t^{\text{u}}(s_t) > 0) \\ \gamma(t,T;s_t)f(t,T;s_t) & \text{if } s_{t+1} = s_t\text{m (with probability } q_t^{\text{m}}(s_t) > 0) \\ \beta(t,T;s_t)f(t,T;s_t) & \text{if } s_{t+1} = s_t\text{d (with probability } \\ & \qquad 1 - q_t^{\text{u}}(s_t) - q_t^{\text{m}}(s_t) > 0) \end{cases} \tag{4.17}$$

where $\tau - 1 \geq T \geq t + 1$.

The same derivation that generates expressions (4.9) and (4.10) generates expressions (4.18) and (4.19). We can derive the forward rate process from the bond price process:

$$\alpha(t,T;s_t) = \frac{u(t,T;s_t)}{u(t,T+1;s_t)} \qquad \text{for } \tau - 1 \geq T \geq t+1 \tag{4.18a}$$

$$\gamma(t,T;s_t) = \frac{m(t,T;s_t)}{m(t,T+1;s_t)} \qquad \text{for } \tau - 1 \geq T \geq t+1 \qquad (4.18b)$$

$$\beta(t,T;s_t) = \frac{d(t,T;s_t)}{d(t,T+1;s_t)} \qquad \text{for } \tau - 1 \geq T \geq t+1 \qquad (4.18c)$$

We can derive the bond price process from the forward rate process:

$$u(t,T;s_t) = \frac{r(t;s_t)}{\Pi_{j=t+1}^{T-1}\alpha(t,j;s_t)} \qquad \text{for } \tau - 1 \geq T \geq t+2 \quad (4.19a)$$

$$m(t,T;s_t) = \frac{r(t;s_t)}{\Pi_{j=t+1}^{T-1}\gamma(t,j;s_t)} \qquad \text{for } \tau - 1 \geq T \geq t+2 \quad (4.19b)$$

and

$$d(t,T;s_t) = \frac{r(t;s_t)}{\Pi_{j=t+1}^{T-1}\beta(t,j;s_t)} \qquad \text{for } \tau - 1 \geq T \geq t+2 \quad (4.19c)$$

This completes the description of the forward rate process evolution.

4 The Spot Rate Process

The spot rate process evolution is described by expression (4.20):

$$r(t+1,s_{t+1}) = \begin{cases} u(t+1,t+2;s_t\text{u}) & \text{with probability } q_t^{\text{u}}(s_t) > 0 \\ m(t+1,t+2;s_t\text{m}) & \text{with probability } q_t^{\text{m}}(s_t) > 0 \\ d(t+1,t+2;s_t\text{d}) & \text{with probability } 1 - q^{\text{u}}(s_t) - q_t^{\text{m}}(s_t) > 0 \end{cases} \qquad (4.20)$$

This completes the description of the spot rate process evolution.

SECTION C
$N \geq$ 3-FACTOR ECONOMIES

The extension in Section 4.B from a one-factor economy to a two-factor economy is straightforward. It just corresponds to adding an additional branch on every node in the appropriate tree (or analytic expression). This procedure for extending the economy to three factors, four factors, and so on is similar and is left to the reader's imagination. This procedure is, in fact, a blueprint for the design of a computer program for generating these evolutions.

SECTION D
EXPECTATIONS HYPOTHESIS

The traditional literature studying the term structure of interest rates emphasized an economic theory called the *expectations hypothesis* for zero-coupon bond price determination. Two different versions of this hypothesis can be found in the literature; see Jarrow [4]. They are the equivalent expected returns form and the unbiased forward rate form of the expectations hypothesis. Each of these is discussed below. The equivalent expected returns form of the expectations hypothesis will be used, *in a modified form,* as the basis of the risk-neutral valuation procedure introduced in subsequent chapters.

1 Equivalent Expected Returns

The first version of the expectations hypothesis involves the expected returns on zero-coupon bonds of different maturities. To characterize this hypothesis, we first define a *liquidity premium* (sometimes called a *term premium* or *risk premium*), $L_1(t,T;s_t)$, as

$$L_1(t,T;s_t) \equiv \frac{E_t(P(t+1,T;s_{t+1}))}{P(t,T;s_t)} - r(t;s_t) \tag{4.21}$$

for $1 \leq t+1 < T \leq \tau$ and for all s_t. $E_t(\bullet)$ is the time t expected value using the actual probabilities as given in Fig. 4.1 for a one-factor economy or expression (4.12) for a two-factor economy. The liquidity premium $L_1(t,T;s_t)$ represents the excess expected return that the T-maturity zero-coupon bond earns above the spot rate. In various equilibrium asset pricing models, this excess expected return is the compensation that risk-averse traders require for bearing risk; see Jarrow [5]. If traders are risk-neutral, they value assets only via expected returns, and in equilibrium, the excess expected return on all assets, including bonds, is zero.

The *equivalent expected returns form of the expectations hypothesis* is that

$$L_1(t,T;s_t) \equiv 0 \qquad \text{for } 1 \leq t+1 < T \leq \tau \text{ and for all } s_t$$

This implies that the time t value of a T-maturity zero-coupon bond is its time $t+1$ expected value, discounted at the spot rate; i.e.,

$$P(t,T;s_t) = \frac{E_t(P(t+1,T;s_{t+1}))}{r(t;s_t)} \tag{4.22}$$

This is the value that a bond would have in an economy populated by risk-neutral investors.

EXAMPLE: EXPECTATIONS HYPOTHESIS—EQUIVALENT EXPECTED RETURNS. For the one-factor example given in Fig. 4.4, we see that the expected returns on the bonds are given by the following:

$$\begin{bmatrix} E(P(1,4;s_1)/P(0,4)) \\ E(P(1,3;s_1)/P(0,3)) \\ E(P(1,2;s_1)/P(0,2)) \\ 1/P(0,1) \end{bmatrix} = \begin{bmatrix} (\frac{3}{4})1.025601 + (\frac{1}{4})1.014399 \\ (\frac{3}{4})1.024201 + (\frac{1}{4})1.015800 \\ (\frac{3}{4})1.022400 + (\frac{1}{4})1.017600 \\ (\frac{3}{4})1.02 + (\frac{1}{4})1.02 \end{bmatrix} = \begin{bmatrix} 1.022801 \\ 1.022101 \\ 1.021200 \\ 1.02 \end{bmatrix}$$

where $E(\bullet)$ stands for the expectation operator based on the actual probabilities $q_t(s_t)$ in Fig. 4.2.

We see that the longer-maturity zero-coupon bonds are expected to earn more than the spot rate. This difference is consistent with the existence of a liquidity premium. Alternatively stated, the equivalent expected returns form of the expectations hypothesis does not hold for this example because the discounted, expected bond prices are not equal to the current zero-coupon bond prices. Indeed,

$$\begin{bmatrix} E(P(1,4;s_1)/r(0)) \\ E(P(1,3;s_1)/r(0)) \\ E(P(1,2;s_1)/r(0)) \\ P(1,1;s_1)/r(0) \end{bmatrix} = \begin{bmatrix} [(\frac{3}{4})0.947496 + (\frac{1}{4})0.937148]/1.02 \\ [(\frac{3}{4})0.965127 + (\frac{1}{4})0.957211]/1.02 \\ [(\frac{3}{4})0.982699 + (\frac{1}{4})0.978085]/1.02 \\ 1/1.02 \end{bmatrix} = \begin{bmatrix} 0.926381 \\ 0.944262 \\ 0.962299 \\ 0.980392 \end{bmatrix}$$

does not equal the initial bond price vector in Fig. 4.4.

$$\begin{bmatrix} 0.923845 \\ 0.942322 \\ 0.961169 \\ 0.980392 \end{bmatrix}$$

■

2 Unbiased Forward Rates

The second version of the expectations hypothesis involves the different maturity forward rates. To characterize this hypothesis, we define a second *liquidity premium*, $L_2(t,T;s_t)$, as

$$L_2(t,T;s_t) \equiv f(t,T;s_t) - E_t(r(T;s_t)) \tag{4.23}$$

for $0 \leq t \leq T \leq \tau - 1$ and for all s_t. The liquidity premium $L_2(t,T;s_t)$ represents the bias in using the forward rate as an estimate of the expected future spot rate at time T.

It is common belief among traders that the forward rate is a good forecast of the spot rate expected to hold in the future. This belief is formalized as the second version of the expectations hypothesis.

The *unbiased forward rate form of the expectations hypothesis* is that

$$L_2(t,T;s_t) \equiv 0 \qquad \text{for } 0 \leq t \leq T \leq \tau - 1 \text{ and for all } s_t$$

This hypothesis implies that forward rates are unbiased predictors of future spot rates.

It is also common belief among traders that the slope of the forward rate curve predicts the future evolution of spot rates. For example, if the forward rate slope is positive, traders expect spot rates to increase over time.

Contrary to common belief, the slope of the forward rate curve has no simple relation to the expected increase or decrease in future spot rates. Indeed, let the slope of the forward rate curve be fixed and given as in Fig. 4.5. We can alter the expected future spot rates for this fixed curve simply by decreasing or increasing the probabilities $q_t(s_t)$. For example, it could be that the slope of the forward rate curve is positive but the spot rates are expected to decline. We clarify this argument through an example.

EXAMPLE: EXPECTATIONS HYPOTHESIS—UNBIASED FORWARD RATES. Consider the example contained in Fig. 4.6. First, the forward rate process in Fig. 4.6 does not satisfy this version of the expectations hypothesis, because forward rates do not give an unbiased estimate of the future spot rates. Indeed, at time 0, all forward rates are 1.02. The expected spot rates are

$$E(r(1)) = \left(\tfrac{3}{4}\right)1.017606 + \left(\tfrac{1}{4}\right)1.022406 = 1.018806$$

$$\begin{aligned} E(r(2)) &= \left(\tfrac{3}{4}\right)^2 1.016031 + \left(\tfrac{3}{4}\right)\left(\tfrac{1}{4}\right)1.020393 \\ &\quad + \left(\tfrac{1}{4}\right)\left(\tfrac{3}{4}\right)1.019193 + \left(\tfrac{1}{4}\right)^2 1.024436 = 1.017967 \end{aligned}$$

$$\begin{aligned} E(r(3)) &= \left(\tfrac{3}{4}\right)^3 1.014918 + \left(\tfrac{3}{4}\right)^2\left(\tfrac{1}{4}\right)1.018972 \\ &\quad + \left(\tfrac{3}{4}\right)\left(\tfrac{1}{4}\right)\left(\tfrac{3}{4}\right)1.017857 + \left(\tfrac{3}{4}\right)\left(\tfrac{1}{4}\right)^2 1.022727 \\ &\quad + \left(\tfrac{1}{4}\right)\left(\tfrac{3}{4}\right)^2 1.017155 + \left(\tfrac{1}{4}\right)\left(\tfrac{3}{4}\right)\left(\tfrac{1}{4}\right)1.021830 \\ &\quad + \left(\tfrac{1}{4}\right)^2\left(\tfrac{3}{4}\right)1.020543 + \left(\tfrac{1}{4}\right)^3 1.026165 = 1.017345 \end{aligned}$$

Second, the forward rate curve is flat, but spot rates are expected to decline from time 0 to time 1 to time 2 to time 3 (1.02 to 1.018806 to 1.017967 to 1.017345). By changing the probabilities in the tree, we can get the expected spot rate to increase or decrease in any period, leaving the forward rate curve's slope unchanged from that contained in Fig. 4.6. This demonstrates the absence of any simple relation between the future course of interest rates and the slope of the forward rate curve. ■

3 Relation between the Two Versions of the Expectations Hypothesis

This section examines the relation between the two versions of the expectations hypothesis. It is more abstract than the previous two sections, and it can be skipped, as it is not subsequently used in the text.

The two versions of the expectations hypothesis are not equivalent; i.e., $L_1(t, T; s_t) = 0$ does not imply, nor is it implied by, $L_2(t, T; s_t) = 0$. The easiest way to prove this statement is to rewrite expressions (4.21) and (4.23) in an equivalent form. These are given by expressions (4.24) and (4.25):

$$P(t,T;s_t) = E_t\left(\frac{1}{\Pi_{j=t}^{T-1}\left[L_1(j,T;s_j) + r(j;s_j)\right]}\right) \tag{4.24}$$

$$P(t,T;s_t) = \frac{1}{\Pi_{j=t}^{T-1}E_t\left[L_2(t,j;s_t) + r(j;s_t)\right]} \tag{4.25}$$

For general random processes, $L_1(t,T;s_t) \equiv 0$ does not imply that $L_2(t,T;s_t) \equiv 0$ (and conversely), because the expected value of the inverse of a product does not equal the inverse of the products of the expected values.

DERIVATION OF EXPRESSIONS (4.24) AND (4.25). From (4.21) we have

$$P(t,T;s_t) = \frac{E_t(P(t+1,T;s_{t+1}))}{L_1(t,T;s_t) + r(t;s_t)}$$

This also holds true for time $t+1$ and state s_{t+1}. Successive substitution for $P(t,T;s_t)$ and the law of iterated expectations, $E_t(E_{t+1}(\bullet)) = E_t(\bullet)$, give (4.24).

From (4.23), substituting in the definition of $f(t,T;s_t) \equiv P(t,T;s_t)/P(t,T+1;s_t)$ yields

$$P(t,T+1;s_t) = \frac{P(t,T;s_t)}{L_2(t,T;s_t) + E_t(r(T;s_T))}$$

This holds for maturity T as well. Successive substitution for $P(t,T;s_t)$ yields

$$P(t,T+1;s_t) = \frac{1}{\Pi_{j=t}^{T}\left[L_2(t,j;s_t) + E_t(r(j;s;))\right]}$$

A change of maturity from $T+1$ to T gives (4.25). ■

EXAMPLE: COMPARISON OF THE TWO LIQUIDITY PREMIUMS. The example of Figs. 4.4 and 4.5 illustrates the fact that there is no simple relation between $L_1(t,T;s_t)$ and $L_2(t,T;s_t)$. This can be seen by examining Table 4.1, which contains the two liquidity premiums for time 0. ■

TABLE 4.1
Liquidity premiums $L_1(0,T)$ and $L_2(0,T)$ for the example of Fig. 4.4

T	$L_1(0,T)$	$L_2(0,T)$
0	Not defined	0.
1	0.	0.001194
2	0.001200	0.002033
3	0.002101	0.002655
4	0.002801	Not defined

SECTION E
CONSISTENCY WITH EQUILIBRIUM

The preceding material in Chapter 4 exogenously imposes a stochastic structure on the evolution of the zero-coupon bond price curve. The evolution, except for the number of factors, is almost completely unrestricted. But a moment's reflection reveals that this cannot be the case. A T-maturity zero-coupon bond is, of course, a close substitute (for investment purposes) to a $T-1$ or a $T+1$ maturity zero-coupon bond. Therefore, in an economic *equilibrium*, the returns on these similar-maturity zero-coupon bonds cannot be too different. If they were too different, no investor would hold the bond with the smaller return. This difference could not persist in an economic equilibrium.

Furthermore, the entire zero-coupon bond curve is pairwise linked in this manner to adjacent-maturity zero-coupon bonds. Consequently, to be consistent with an economic equilibrium, there must be some additional explicit structure required on the parameters of the evolution of the zero-coupon bond price curve. But what are these restrictions? The next chapter introduces these restrictions by studying the meaning and existence of *arbitrage opportunities*.

SECTION F
COMPUTER EXAMPLE

This example and the following set of exercises using the Trees software (Chapter 16) should help the reader understand the evolution of the term structure of interest rates given different inputs.

EXAMPLE. Using the Trees software, change the initial term structure of forward rates to one that is upward sloping, and see how the evolution of interest rates changes. Use the following as a new term structure:

$$
\begin{aligned}
f(0,0) &= 1.02\\
f(0,1) &= 1.03\\
f(0,2) &= 1.04\\
f(0,3) &= 1.05\\
f(0,4) &= 1.06\\
f(0,5) &= 1.07\\
f(0,6) &= 1.08\\
f(0,7) &= 1.09\\
f(0,8) &= 1.10\\
f(0,9) &= 1.11\\
f(0,10) &= 1.12
\end{aligned}
$$

Solution. Enter Trees software, select "Model," select "initial term structure," and input the new forward rates. The new spot rates appear. We list the spot rates for the first two time periods:

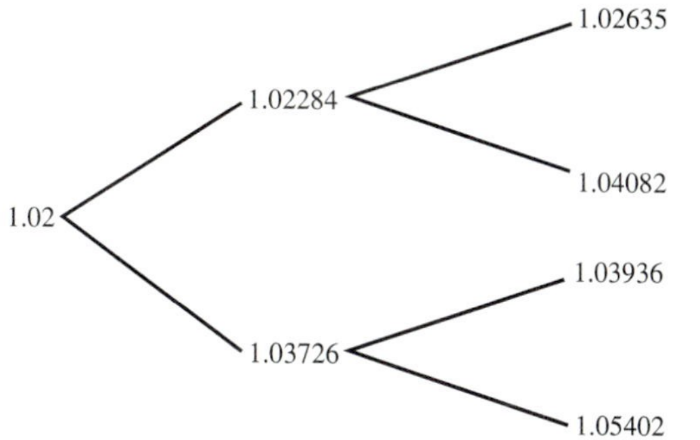

■

SECTION G EXERCISES

a. For the previous example, suppose the probability of up is $\frac{9}{10}$ and the probability of down is $\frac{1}{10}$. What is $E_0(r(2))$? Is the forward rate an unbiased predictor of the future spot rate in this case?

b. Change the forward rate structure to downward sloping from $f(0, 1) = 1.12, \ldots, f(0, 10) = 1.02$. Find the evolution of spot rates and repeat exercise (*a*).

SECTION H REFERENCES TO CHAPTER 4

1. Heath, D., R. Jarrow, and A. Morton, 1990. "Bond Pricing and the Term Structure of Interest Rates: A Discrete Time Approximation." *Journal of Financial and Quantitative Analysis* 25 (4), 419–440.
2. Heath, D., R. Jarrow, and A. Morton, 1991. "Contingent Claim Valuation with a Random Evolution of Interest Rates." *Review of Futures Markets* 9 (1), 54–76.
3. Heath, D., R. Jarrow, and A. Morton, 1992. "Bond Pricing and the Term Structure of Interest Rates: A New Methodology for Contingent Claims Valuation." *Econometrica* 60 (1), 77–105.
4. Jarrow, R., 1981. "Liquidity Premiums and the Expectations Hypothesis." *Journal of Banking and Finance* 5 (4), 539–546.
5. Jarrow, R., 1988. *Finance Theory,* Prentice Hall, Englewood Cliffs, N.J.

CHAPTER 5

Trading Strategies, Arbitrage Opportunities, and Complete Markets

This chapter studies trading strategies, arbitrage opportunities, and the meaning of complete markets. As previously mentioned, the basic idea underlying the arbitrage pricing methodology is that given the initial prices and the evolution of a set of zero-coupon bonds, we construct a portfolio of these bonds, perhaps rebalancing it across time (called a *trading strategy*), such that the portfolio's cash flows and value match the cash flows and value of a secondary traded asset, say an interest rate option. Then, to avoid riskless profit opportunities (called *arbitrage opportunities*), the cost of constructing this portfolio must equal the market price of the traded interest rate option. This argument only works, however, if a portfolio can be found that replicates the cash flows and value of the interest rate option (called *complete markets*). Such a replicating portfolio, if it exists, is called a *synthetic interest rate option*. These ideas (trading strategies, arbitrage opportunities, and complete markets) are the building blocks for the risk-neutral valuation procedure applied in subsequent chapters. This chapter formalizes these ideas in a mathematical fashion so that specific results relating to prices and trading strategies can be derived.

This chapter is more abstract than the preceding chapters, and the material it contains may be skimmed at first reading. The material is illustrated more concretely via an example in Chapter 6, Section 6.A. After reading that example, the reader may want to return to this chapter.

SECTION A
TRADING STRATEGIES

Intuitively, a trading strategy is a dynamic investment portfolio involving some or possibly all of the traded zero-coupon bonds. Portfolio revisions can occur within the investment horizon, and they are based on information available at the time the portfolio is revised.

We now formalize this intuitive definition. First, fix a particular zero-coupon bond with maturity date τ_1, where $0 < \tau_1 \leq \tau$. The simplest *trading strategy* is a pair of security holdings

$$(n_0(t; s_t), n_1(t; s_t)) \quad \text{for all } s_t \text{ and } t \in \{0, 1, \ldots, \min(\tau_1, \tau - 1) - 1\}$$

such that

$n_0(t; s_t)$ is the number of units of the money market account held at time t under state s_t.

$n_1(t; s_t)$ is the number of shares of the τ_1-maturity zero-coupon bond held at time t under state s_t.

This portfolio is initially formed at time 0, and it is liquidated at the horizon date $\tau^* = \min(\tau_1, \tau - 1)$. The horizon date is the smaller of the zero-coupon bond's maturity, τ_1, or the last relevant date in the model, $\tau - 1$. The last relevant date in the model is time $\tau - 1$ because over the last period in the model, the remaining traded τ-maturity zero-coupon bond does not span the relevant uncertainties; see Fig. 4.3. Consequently, this period is not useful for analysis, and it is omitted from the trading strategy horizon.

The fact that these time t portfolio holdings $(n_0(t; s_t), n_1(t; s_t))$ depend only on the past history s_t implies that the information requirement discussed earlier is satisfied.

The initial value of this trading strategy at time 0 is

$$n_0(0) \cdot 1 + n_1(0)P(0, \tau_1) \tag{5.1}$$

At an intermediate time t its value is

$$n_0(t; s_t)B(t; s_{t-1}) + n_1(t; s_t)P(t, \tau_1; s_t) \tag{5.2}$$

At the horizon date, $\tau^* = \min(\tau_1, \tau - 1)$, its value is

$$n_0(\tau^* - 1; s_{\tau^*})B(\tau^*; s_{\tau^*-1}) + n_1(\tau^* - 1; s_{\tau^*})P(\tau^*, \tau_1; s_{\tau^*}) \tag{5.3}$$

This is the value of the portfolio entering time τ^*. The portfolio is then liquidated at time τ^* before any rebalancing occurs.

This trading strategy is said to be *self-financing* if at every intermediate trading date $t \in \{1, 2, \ldots, \tau^* - 1\}$ the value of the portfolio entering time t equals its value after portfolio rebalancing; i.e.,

$$\begin{aligned} &n_0(t-1; s_{t-1})B(t; s_{t-1}) + n_1(t-1; s_{t-1})P(t, \tau_1; s_t) \\ &\qquad = n_0(t; s_t)B(t; s_{t-1}) + n_1(t; s_t)P(t, \tau_1; s_t) \end{aligned} \tag{5.4}$$

We will only be interested in self-financing trading strategies. For convenience, define the set Φ_1 by

$$\Phi_1 \equiv \{\text{all self-financing trading strategies involving only the money market account and the } \tau_1\text{-maturity zero-coupon bond}\}$$

Note that these trading strategies are only defined on the time horizon $\tau^* - 1 = \min(\tau_1, \tau - 1) - 1$ determined by the τ_1-maturity bond. After time τ_1, the τ_1-maturity bond no longer trades.

Similarly, one could investigate a self-financing trading strategy involving three securities: two distinct zero-coupon bonds with maturities τ_1, τ_2 where $0 < \tau_1 < \tau_2 \leq \tau$, and the money market account. This would be represented by a triplet $(n_0(t; s_t), n_1(t; s_t), n_2(t; s_t))$ for all s_t and $t \in \{0, 1, \ldots, \tau_1 - 1\}$ such that

$n_0(t; s_t)$ and $n_1(t; s_t)$ are as defined before.
$n_2(t; s_t)$ is the number of shares of the τ_2-maturity zero-coupon bond held at time t under state s_t.

We assume that the self-financing condition, condition (5.5), is also satisfied:

$$\begin{aligned} n_0(t-1; s_{t-1})B(t; s_{t-1}) &+ n_1(t-1; s_{t-1})P(t, \tau_1; s_t) \\ &+ n_2(t-1; s_{t-1})P(t, \tau_2; s_t) = n_0(t; s_t)B(t; s_{t-1}) \quad (5.5) \\ &+ n_1(t; s_t)P(t, \tau_1; s_t) + n_2(t; s_t)P(t, \tau_2; s_t) \end{aligned}$$

for $t \in \{1, 2, \ldots, \tau_1 - 1\}$. This portfolio is liquidated at time τ_1 with value

$$n_0(\tau_1 - 1; s_{\tau_1-1})B(\tau_1; s_{\tau_1-1}) + n_1(\tau_1 - 1; s_{\tau_1-1})1 + n_2(\tau_1 - 1; s_{\tau_1-1})P(\tau_1, \tau_2; s_{\tau_1}) \quad (5.6)$$

In an analogous manner, we define the set Φ_2 by

$\Phi_2 \equiv$ {all self-financing trading strategies involving only the money market account, the τ_1-maturity zero-coupon bond, and the τ_2-maturity zero-coupon bond}

For convenience, we have defined the trading strategy over the time horizon determined by the shortest maturity bond τ_1. We could have, however, equivalently defined it over the longer time period determined by the longest maturity bond, $[0, \tau_2]$. This would have required that we set the position in the τ_1-maturity zero-coupon bond to be identically zero over the later part of this horizon; i.e., $n_1(t; s_t) \equiv 0$ for $t \in [\tau_1, \tau_2]$. This later restriction would be necessary because the τ_1-maturity bond does not trade after time τ_1. When convenient, we will utilize this definition without additional comment.

The set of self-financing trading strategies Φ_1 is a subset of Φ_2. It is the subset in which the holdings of the τ_2-maturity bond in Φ_2 are identically equal to zero.

In a straightforward fashion, given any $K < \tau$ bonds with maturities $\tau_1 < \tau_2 < \cdots < \tau_K$, we could define analogous sets of self-financing trading strategies Φ_K. The relation $\Phi_1 \subset \Phi_2 \subset \Phi_3 \subset \cdots \subset \Phi K$ holds.[1]

[1]Formally, we are imbedding Φ_1 into Φ_2, Φ_2 into Φ_3, etc., because they are not strict subsets but only isomorphic to a strict subset.

One last set of self-financing trading strategies needs to be defined. This is the set simultaneously utilizing all the zero-coupon bonds of different maturities. Formally, consider the self-financing trading strategy $(n_1(t; s_t), n_2(t; s_t), \ldots, n_\tau(t; s_t))$ for all s_t and $t \in \{0, 1, \ldots, \tau - 2\}$ such that

$n_j(t; s_t)$ is the number of units of the jth-maturity zero-coupon bond purchased at time t under state s_t for $j = 1, 2, \ldots, \tau$.
$n_j(t; s_t) \equiv 0$ for $t \geq j$.

The self-financing condition (5.7) is satisfied; i.e.,

$$\sum_{j=1}^{\tau} n_j(t-1; s_{t-1})P(t, j; s_t) = \sum_{j=1}^{\tau} n_j(t; s_t)P(t, j; s_t) \tag{5.7}$$

for all s_t and $t \in \{0, 1, 2, \ldots, \tau - 2\}$.

The value of this portfolio at liquidation, time $\tau - 1$, is

$$\sum_{j=1}^{\tau} n_j(\tau - 2; s_{\tau-2})P(\tau - 1, j; s_{\tau-1}) \\ = n_{\tau-1}(\tau - 2; s_{\tau-2})1 - n_\tau(\tau - 2; s_{\tau-2})P(\tau - 1, \tau; s_{\tau-1}) \tag{5.8}$$

This is because the only bonds still trading are those with maturities $\tau - 1$ and τ.

Define the set Φ_τ by

$$\Phi_\tau \equiv \{\text{all self-financing trading strategies involving all the different maturity zero-coupon bonds}\}$$

There are a couple of subtle observations to make about this set of trading strategies. First, the horizon for this class of trading strategies is the whole trading interval less one period: $[0, \tau - 1]$. This is because over the last period in the model, the traded zero-coupon bonds cannot span the relevant uncertainties; e.g., see Fig. 4.3. The last period in the model is a vestige that has no real economic purpose and is therefore omitted from the trading strategy horizon. Second, after any zero-coupon bond matures, the holdings in this bond must be set to be identically zero. This is because the bond no longer exists after it matures. This fact is captured by the condition that $n_j(t; s_t) \equiv 0$ for $t \geq j$.

Third, this class of trading strategies takes no explicit position in the money market account, because the money market account can be created within this class of trading strategies. Indeed, the money market account is obtainable (by itself or in conjunction with additional holdings of the zero-coupon bonds) with the following self-financing trading strategy. First, purchase $1/P(0, 1)$ units of the one-period zero-coupon bond at time 0. The cost of this purchase is $(1/P(0, 1))P(0, 1) = 1$ dollar. This cost equals the money market account's value at time 0, i.e., $B(0) = 1$. This position then pays off $1/P(0, 1) = r(0) = B(1)$ dollars at time 1. Next, reinvest this $B(1)$ dollars at time 1 into the zero-coupon bond that matures at time 2 (i.e., purchase

$B(1)/P(1,2;s_1)$ of these bonds). The time 2 value of this position is then $B(1)r(1;s_1) = B(2;s_1)$. Continuing in this fashion generates the money market account $B(t;s_{t-1})$ for any t, s_{t-1}.

For this reason, and for consistency of the notation with the previously defined sets Φ_j for $j < \tau$, we can without loss of generality redefine Φ_τ to be the class of all self-financing trading strategies

$$(n_0(t;s_t), n_1(t;s_t), \ldots, n_\tau(t;s_t)) \quad \text{for all } s_t \text{ and } t \in \{0, 1, \ldots, \tau - 2\}$$

where

$n_j(t;s_t)$ for $j = 1, \ldots, \tau$ are defined as before.
$n_0(t;s_t)$ is the number of units of the money market account $B(t;s_{t-1})$ held at time t under state s_t.

The self-financing condition holds; i.e.,

$$n_0(t-1;s_{t-1})B(t,s_{t-1}) + \sum_{j=1}^{\tau} n_j(t-1;s_{t-1})P(t,j;s_t)$$
$$= n_0(t;s_t)B(t,s_{t-1}) + \sum_{j=1}^{\tau} n_j(t;s_t)P(t,j;s_t) \tag{5.9}$$
$$\text{for all } s_t \text{ and } t \in \{0, 1, 2, \ldots, \tau - 2\}.$$

The value of this portfolio at liquidation, time $\tau - 1$, is

$$n_0(\tau-2;s_{\tau-2})B(\tau-1;s_{\tau-2}) + n_{\tau-1}(\tau-2;s_{\tau-2})1 + n_\tau(\tau-2;s_{\tau-2})P(\tau-1,\tau;s_{\tau-1}) \tag{5.10}$$

SECTION B
ARBITRAGE OPPORTUNITIES

One type of self-financing trading strategy is of special interest. It is the self-financing trading strategy that provides positive or zero returns at no risk of a loss, called an *arbitrage opportunity.* Formally, an arbitrage opportunity is defined with respect to a specific class of self-financing trading strategies. In particular, an *arbitrage opportunity* with respect to Φ_K for $K = 1, 2, \ldots, \tau$ is a self-financing trading strategy[2] $(n_0(t;s_t), n_1(t;s_t), \ldots, n_K(t;s_t)) \in \Phi_K$ such that

$$n_0(0)B(0) + \sum_{j=1}^{K} n_j(0)P(0,\tau_j) = 0 \tag{5.11a}$$

[2]One might argue that an arbitrage opportunity not covered by (5.11) occurs when (5.11*a*) is strictly negative and (5.11*b*) is identically zero. This type of arbitrage opportunity can be transformed into one of the form in (5.11) by investing the initial cash flow in the money market account and rolling it over until time τ_1.

and

$$n_0(\tau_1 - 1; s_{\tau_1 - 1})B(\tau_1; s_{\tau_1 - 1}) + \sum_{j=1}^{K} n_j(\tau_1 - 1; s_{\tau_1 - 1})P(\tau_1, \tau_j; s_{\tau_1}) \begin{cases} \geq 0 \text{ for all } s_{\tau_1} \\ > 0 \text{ for some } s_{\tau_1} \end{cases} \tag{5.11b}$$

Condition (5.11a) states that the initial cost of the arbitrage portfolio is zero; i.e., the portfolio is self-financing at time 0. The portfolio is liquidated[3] at time τ_1. Condition (5.11b) states that at liquidation, the arbitrage portfolio's value is nonnegative for all states s_{τ_1} and strictly positive for some states. An arbitrage opportunity offers the possibility of turning nothing into something, with no chance of a loss. That is a money pump! Obviously, we would not expect to find many of these opportunities in well-functioning markets.

To illustrate the meaning of an arbitrage opportunity, suppose the τ_1-maturity bond had a zero price at time 0; i.e., $P(0, \tau_1) = 0$. This implies that there exists an arbitrage opportunity. An arbitrage opportunity in the smallest class of trading strategies Φ_1 would be holding the τ_1-maturity bond until time τ_1. Indeed, the initial cost is 0, satisfying expression (5.11a). At maturity, it is worth a sure dollar, satisfying expression (5.11b). Consequently, in well-functioning markets, we would expect $P(0, \tau_1) > 0$ for all τ_1. This is the reason we imposed this strict positivity condition earlier, in Chapter 4.

In closing, note that because the trading strategies are subsets of each other, i.e., $\Phi_1 \subset \Phi_2 \subset \cdots \subset \Phi_\tau$, an arbitrage opportunity with respect to a trading strategy set Φ_j is an arbitrage opportunity with respect to a larger trading strategy set Φ_K for $j \leq K \leq \tau$. Thus, if there are no arbitrage opportunities in the larger trading strategy set Φ_K, there are no arbitrage opportunities in the smaller trading strategy set Φ_j for $j \leq K$. The converse is, of course, not true.

SECTION C
COMPLETE MARKETS

The concept of a complete market is the last issue we need to introduce before studying risk-neutral valuation. Roughly, a complete market is one in which any cash flow pattern desired can be obtained via a self-financing trading strategy. To formalize this concept, we must first define a simple contingent claim. Simple contingent claims will be shown to be the building blocks for all possible derivative securities issued against the term structure of interest rates. This includes forward and futures contracts, call and put options both European and American, as well as other interest rate options, exotic or otherwise.

A *simple contingent claim* with maturity date τ^* for $0 \leq \tau^* \leq \tau - 1$ is defined to be a cash flow $x(\tau^*; s_{\tau^*})$ dependent on time τ^* and state s_{τ^*}. We can

---

[3] For $K = \tau$ we make the following identification for the indices: $\tau_1 \equiv 1, \tau_2 \equiv 1, \ldots, \tau_\tau \equiv \tau$. In this case, the portfolio's liquidation date is $\tau - 1$, not τ_1 as in expression (5.11b).

now define what we mean by a complete market. A market is said to be *complete with respect to the trading strategies* Φ_K for $K \in \{1, 2, 3, \ldots, \tau\}$ if given any simple contingent claim with maturity date[4] $\tau^* \le \tau_1 - 1$, there exists a self-financing trading strategy $(n_0(t; s_t), n_1(t; s_1), \ldots, n_K(t; s_K)) \in \Phi_K$ such that at time τ^*,

$$n_0(\tau^* - 1; s_{\tau^*-1})B(\tau^*; s_{\tau^*-1}) + \sum_{j=1}^{K} n_j(\tau^* - 1; s_{\tau^*-1})P(\tau^*, \tau_j; s_{\tau^*}) = x(\tau^*; s_{\tau^*}) \tag{5.12}$$

for all s_{τ^*}. Condition (5.12) states that the trading strategy's value at time τ^* replicates the contingent claim's time τ^* cash flow at each state s_{τ^*}. Explicit in expression (5.12) is the condition that only the money market account and the zero-coupon bonds with maturities $\tau_1, \tau_2, \ldots, \tau_K$ are utilized in this trading strategy. We will call the trading strategy in expression (5.12) that replicates the simple contingent claim's time τ^* cash flow the *synthetic simple contingent claim x*.

Note that if the market is complete with respect to the trading strategy set Φ_K, it is also complete with respect to a larger set trading strategy set Φ_j for any $j \ge K$. This follows because the smaller trading strategy set Φ_K is contained in the larger trading strategy set Φ_j for $j \ge K$. So any portfolio obtainable in the smaller set is obtainable in the larger set. This observation will prove useful in subsequent chapters.

We define the *arbitrage-free price of the simple contingent claim with maturity date* τ^* to be the initial cost of constructing the synthetic contingent claim, i.e.,

$$n_o(0)B(0) + \sum_{j=1}^{K} n_j(0)P(0, \tau_j) \tag{5.13}$$

The idea behind this definition is that if the simple contingent claim x traded, its price would have to be that given by expression (5.13). Otherwise, it would be possible to construct an arbitrage opportunity involving the τ_1-, τ_2-, …, τ_K-maturity zero-coupon bonds and the traded contingent claim. This logic will be further clarified in subsequent chapters.

We now show that all other derivative securities issued against the term structure of interest rates can be constructed from simple contingent claims. Consider a more complex contingent claim than that defined above, namely,

---

[4]The convention followed for the remainder of the text is that when $K = \tau$, the following identifications hold:

1. $\tau_1 = 1, \tau_2 = 2, \ldots, \tau_\tau = \tau$.
2. The trading horizon is $[0, \tau - 1]$.
3. All holdings in bonds that have already matured must be identically zero.

one having multiple random cash flows at the different dates $\{0, 1, \ldots, \tau^*\}$, the cash flows being denoted $x(t; s_t)$ for each $t \in \{0, 1, \ldots, \tau^*\}$. This *complex contingent claim,* however, is nothing more than a collection of τ^* simple contingent claims each with a different maturity date. The self-financing trading strategy that duplicates the complex contingent claim is consequently *defined* to be the sum of the self-financing trading strategies that generate each simple contingent claim composing the complex contingent claim. The holdings in each underlying zero-coupon bond are merely summed to get the aggregate holdings of each zero-coupon bond in the complex contingent claim. Correspondingly, the arbitrage-free price of this complex contingent claim having multiple cash flows is the sum of the arbitrage-free prices of the simple contingent claims of which it is composed. The motivation for this definition is that if both the simple contingent claims and the complex contingent claim traded simultaneously, this would be the only price consistent with the absence of arbitrage opportunities.

The previous two types of contingent claims are of the *European* type, because the cash flows are independent of any active decision made by the investors holding the claim. Contingent claims in which the cash flows depend on an active decision of the investors holding the claim are of the *American* type.[5] These contingent claims can also be analyzed using an extension of the above procedure.

Let us denote the cash flows to an American-type, complex contingent claim at time $t \in \{0, 1, \ldots, \tau - 1\}$ given a decision choice $a \in A$ of the investor by $x(t, a; s_t)$ where A represents the set of possible decisions. Given an arbitrary decision $a^* \in A$, the cash flow to the claim is $x(t, a^*; s_t)$ for each $t \in \{0, 1, \ldots, \tau - 1\}$. Now the cash flow no longer depends on the investor making a choice, for it is already determined by a^*. Given $a^* \in A$, the claim is now a European-type claim (sometimes called *pseudo-American*). Both the self-financing trading strategy in Φ_K that duplicates the European complex contingent claim under a^* and its arbitrage-free price are determined as discussed previously. Finally, to get the American claim's replicating trading strategy and arbitrage-free price, we choose that $\tilde{a} \in A$ such that the arbitrage-free price is maximized for the investor holding the claim. The replicating trading strategy for $x(t, \tilde{a}; s_t)$ for every t replicates the American claim's cash flows, and the arbitrage-free price of $x(t, \tilde{a}; s_t)$ is the arbitrage-free price for the American claim.

---

[5]A European call option's payoff at maturity is considered to be a *passive* decision, because it is always exercised if it is in the money.

CHAPTER 6

Bond Trading Strategies

This chapter shows how to use the concepts of the preceding chapters to investigate the existence of arbitrage opportunities within the yield curve. Taken as given in this chapter are the stochastic processes for a few zero-coupon bonds (that is, one bond for the one-factor model, two bonds for the two-factor model, and so forth), the stochastic process for the spot rate, and the assumption that there are no arbitrage opportunities (for a particular class of trading strategies). The purpose is to find the arbitrage-free prices of all the remaining zero-coupon bonds. If the market prices for the remaining zero-coupon bonds differ from these arbitrage-free prices, then arbitrage opportunities have been discovered.

This is the modern analogue of arbitraging the yield curve. Prior to the development of these techniques, traders would plot bond prices versus maturity, fitting a smooth curve to the graph (perhaps using spline techniques), and would buy or sell outliers from the curve. In the following procedure, these outliers are analogous to the arbitrage opportunities.

This is one of the longest chapters in the book. We first do the analysis for the one-factor economy, then for the two-factor economy, and then for the $N \geq 3$–factor economy. The analysis differs between the one- and two-factor cases, but for two or more factors the analysis is very similar. In the first reading of this chapter, we recommend only studying the one-factor case. The two-factor economy can be read after the remaining chapters in the text have been studied.

SECTION A
THE ONE-FACTOR ECONOMY

Consider the one-factor economy as described in Chapter 4, Section 4.A. We assume that there are no arbitrage opportunities with respect to the smallest class of trading strategies Φ_1. In this class of trading strategies, we choose a particular τ_1-maturity zero-coupon bond and all trades take place with respect to it and the money market account.

Taken as given (exogenous) are the stochastic process for the τ_1-maturity zero-coupon bond, $P(0, \tau_1)$ and $(u(t, \tau_1; s_t), d(t, \tau_1; s_t))$, and the stochastic process for the spot rate, $r(0)$, and $(u(t, t+1; s_t))$. The purpose is to price all the remaining zero-coupon bonds in the market. Because the processes for the τ_1-maturity bond and the money market account are exogenously supplied, we need to discuss whether these specifications are consistent with some economic equilibrium. This is also pursued below.

1 Complete Markets

First, we want to show that the market is complete with respect to the trading strategies Φ_1. To introduce the arguments, we first illustrate the analysis through an example, and then we provide the general (and more abstract) theory.

EXAMPLE: CONSTRUCTION OF SYNTHETIC SECURITIES. To illustrate the procedure for creating synthetic securities, we consider a four-period example using the state space process as given in Fig. 4.2. The trading strategy set Φ_1 will

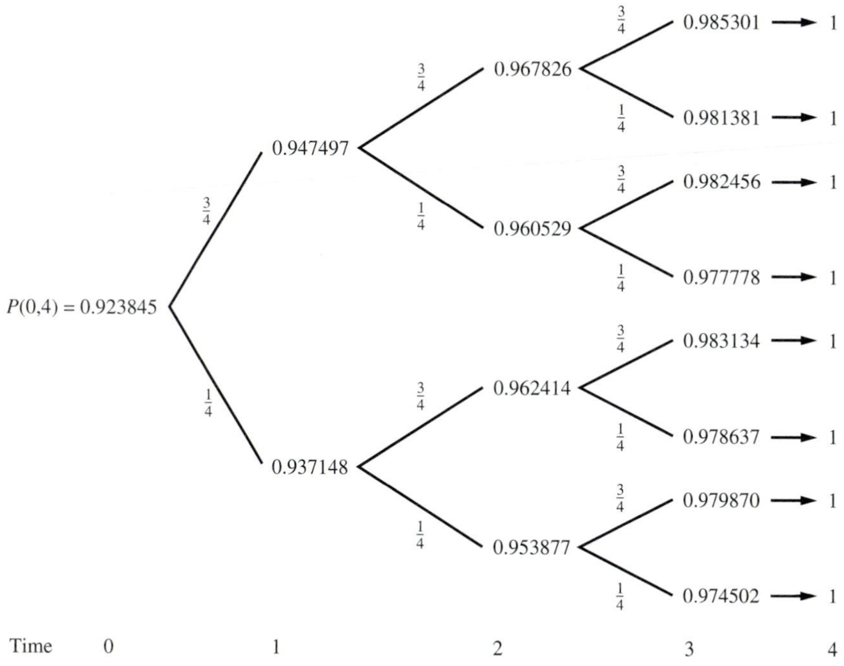

FIGURE 6.1
A four-period zero-coupon bond price process.

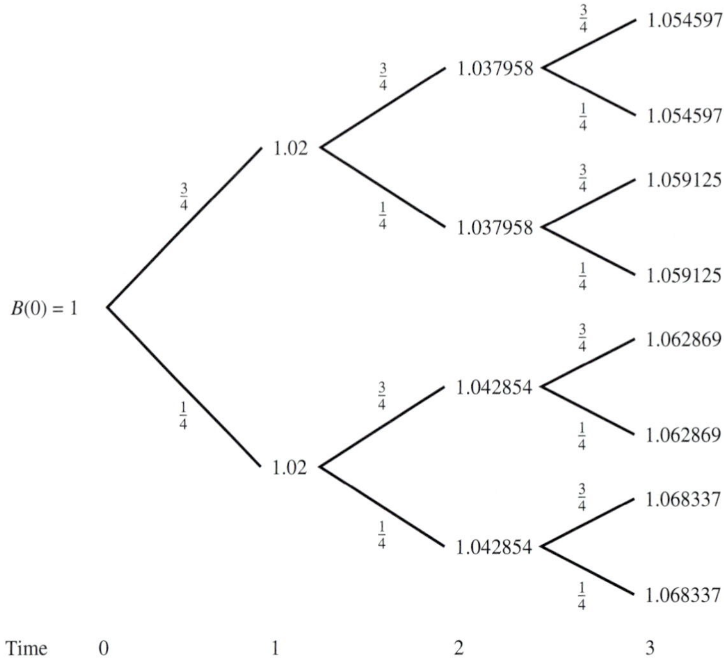

FIGURE 6.2
A stochastic money market account's value.

consist of a four-period zero-coupon bond ($P(t, 4)$) with the stochastic process as given in Fig. 6.1 and a money market account ($B(t)$) with the stochastic process as given in Fig. 6.2 (these processes are obtained from Fig. 4.4). These are the exogenously supplied data.

From Fig. 6.1 we can easily calculate the corresponding return processes ($u(t, 4), d(t, 4)$) for the four-period zero-coupon bond. These are shown in Fig. 6.5. We see that in all states and times $t \leq 3, u(t, 4) > d(t, 4)$. This will be proven to be a sufficient condition for market completeness. The reason for the sufficiency of this condition will be further clarified by actually constructing synthetic contingent claims for this example.

First, let us construct a synthetic *two-period zero-coupon bond*. The payoff to this contingent claim is one dollar at time 2 across all states (uu, ud, du, dd). To construct this contingent claim, we work backwards through the tree, starting at time 1. We form a state-dependent portfolio first at time 1, state u, and then at time 1, state d, to duplicate the two-period zero-coupon bond's payoff at time 2. Then we move back to time 0 and create a portfolio that duplicates the previous portfolio values needed at time 1, state u, and at time 1, state *d*. This procedure will result in a dynamic, self-financing trading strategy that duplicates the payoff to a two-period zero-coupon bond.

Let $n_0(1;\text{u})$ and $n_1(1;\text{u})$ be the number of units of the money market account and number of units of the four-period bond, respectively, held at time 1 under state u, such that the portfolio's resulting time 2 value equals one dollar in both states; i.e.,

$$n_0(1;\mathrm{u})B(2;\mathrm{u}) + n_1(1;\mathrm{u})P(2,4;\mathrm{uu}) = n_0(1;\mathrm{u})1.037958 + n_1(1;\mathrm{u})0.967826 = 1 \quad (6.1a)$$

$$n_0(1;\mathrm{u})B(2;\mathrm{u}) + n_1(1;\mathrm{u})P(2,4;\mathrm{ud}) = n_0(1;\mathrm{u})1.037958 + n_1(1;\mathrm{u})0.960529 = 1 \quad (6.1b)$$

The solution to this system of equations is obtained by subtracting expression (6.1*b*) from (6.1*a*) and first solving for $n_1(1;\mathrm{u})$. Then, we substitute the value for $n_1(1;\mathrm{u})$ into (6.1*a*) and solve for $n_0(1;\mathrm{u})$. The solution is

$$n_0(1;\mathrm{u}) = \frac{1}{1.037958} = 0.963430 \quad (6.2a)$$

$$n_1(1;\mathrm{u}) = 0 \quad (6.2b)$$

The duplicating portfolio at time 1 under state u is to hold 0.963430 units of the money market account and zero units of the four-period zero-coupon bond. This makes sense, because the payoff at time 1 must be certain, and the four-period zero-coupon bond's payout is risky.

The time 1 cost at state u of constructing this portfolio is

$$n_0(1;\mathrm{u})B(1) + n_1(1;\mathrm{u})P(1,4;\mathrm{u}) = n_0(1;\mathrm{u})1.02 + n_1(1;\mathrm{u})0.947947 = 0.982699 \quad (6.3)$$

To prevent arbitrage, therefore, this must be the arbitrage-free value of a two-period zero-coupon bond; i.e.,

$$P(1,2;\mathrm{u}) \stackrel{a}{=} 0.982699 \quad (6.4)$$

The symbol $\stackrel{a}{=}$ indicates that this is an arbitrage-free pricing condition.

A similar construction at time 1 under state d necessitates the time 2 payoff to the portfolio to be

$$n_0(1;\mathrm{d})B(2;\mathrm{d}) + n_1(1;\mathrm{d})P(2,4;\mathrm{du}) = n_0(1;\mathrm{d})1.042854 + n_1(1;\mathrm{d})0.962414 = 1 \quad (6.5a)$$

$$n_0(1;\mathrm{d})B(2;\mathrm{d}) + n_1(1;\mathrm{d})P(2,4;\mathrm{dd}) = n_0(1;\mathrm{d})1.042854 + n_1(1;\mathrm{d})0.953877 = 1 \quad (6.5b)$$

The solution to this system is

$$n_0(1;\mathrm{d}) = \frac{1}{1.042854} = 0.958907 \quad (6.6a)$$

$$n_1(1;\mathrm{d}) = 0 \quad (6.6b)$$

The synthetic two-period zero-coupon bond at time 1 under state d consists of 0.958907 unit of the money market account and 0 unit of the four-period zero-coupon bond. Its time 1, state d, arbitrage-free value must be

$$\begin{aligned} P(1,2;\mathrm{d}) &\stackrel{a}{=} n_0(1;\mathrm{d})B(1) + n_1(1;\mathrm{d})P(1,4;\mathrm{d}) \\ &= n_0(1;\mathrm{d})1.02 + n_1(1;\mathrm{d})0.937148 = 0.978085 \end{aligned} \quad (6.7)$$

Now, moving backward in the tree to time 0, the values in expressions (6.4) and (6.7) become the new payoffs we need to duplicate at time 1. Let $n_0(0)$ and $n_1(0)$ be the number of units of the money market account and of the four-period zero-coupon bond, respectively, needed at time 0 such that

$$n_0(0)B(1) + n_1(0)P(1,4;\mathrm{u}) = n_0(0)1.02 + n_1(0)0.947497$$
$$= 0.982699 \overset{a}{=} P(1,2;\mathrm{u}) \qquad (6.8a)$$
$$n_0(0)B(1) + n_1(0)P(1,4;\mathrm{d}) = n_0(0)1.02 + n_1(0)0.937148$$
$$= 0.978085 \overset{a}{=} P(1,2;\mathrm{d}) \qquad (6.8b)$$

A solution to this system exists because

$$\mathrm{u}(0,4) = 0.947497/0.923845$$
$$= 1.025602 > d(0,4) = 0.937148/0.923845 = 1.014399$$

The solution is

$$n_0(0) = 0.549286 \qquad (6.9a)$$
$$n_1(0) = 0.445835 \qquad (6.9b)$$

The synthetic two-period zero-coupon bond consists of 0.549286 unit of the money market account and 0.445835 unit of the four-period zero-coupon bond. Its time 0 arbitrage-free value is the cost of constructing this portfolio, i.e.,

$$P(0,2) \overset{a}{=} n_0(0)B(0) + n_1(0)P(0,4) = n_0(0)1 + n_1(0)0.923845 = 0.961169 \qquad (6.10)$$

These values and portfolio positions are summarized in Fig. 6.3.

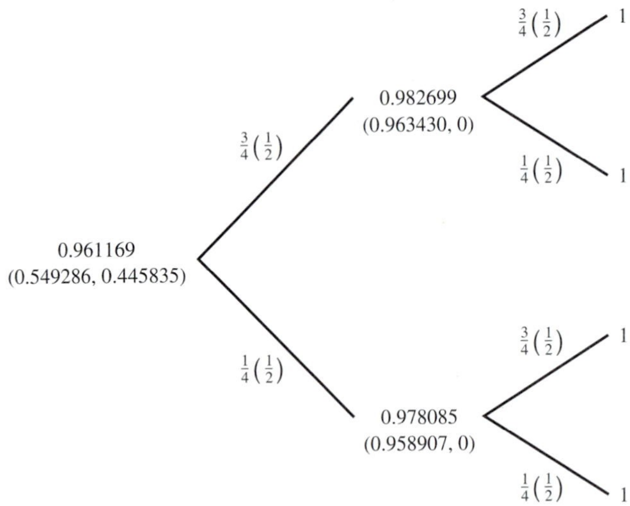

FIGURE 6.3

Arbitrage-free values ($P(t,2;s_t)$) and synthetic portfolio positions ($n_0(t;s_t)$, $n_1(t;s_t)$) for the two-period zero-coupon bond; the pseudo probabilities are in parentheses beside the actual probabilities along the branches of the tree.

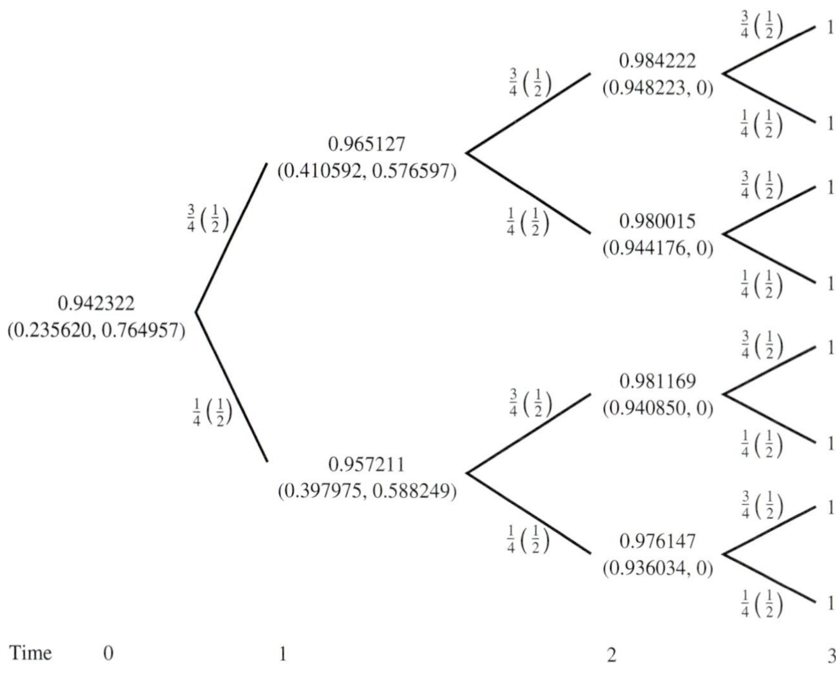

FIGURE 6.4
Arbitrage-free values ($P(t, 3; s_t)$) and synthetic portfolio positions ($n_0(t; s_t)$, $n_q(t; s_t)$, $n_1(t; s_t)$) for the three-period zero-coupon bond.

Figure 6.4 presents the arbitrage-free values $P(t, 3; s_t)$ and the synthetic portfolio positions $n_0(t; s_t)$ in the money market account and $n_1(t; s_t)$ in the four-period zero-coupon bond that are needed to construct the three-period zero-coupon bond. These values and positions are obtained similarly to those in Fig. 6.3. The verification of these numbers is left to the reader as an exercise. ■

We now show that the market is complete with respect to the trading strategies Φ_1. To do this, consider any arbitrary simple contingent claim with maturity date $\tau_1 - 1$, denoted $x(\tau_1 - 1; s_{\tau_1 - 1})$. In the example, the two-period zero-coupon bond was such a simple contingent claim. We need to construct a synthetic contingent claim that replicates the cash flows to x at time $\tau_1 - 1$ under all states $s_{\tau_1 - 1}$. The easiest way to do this is to first pretend we are at time $\tau_1 - 2$, and form the synthetic contingent claim there, to replicate x's cash flows over the last trading period $[\tau_1 - 2, \tau_1 - 1]$.

In this case, we need to choose the number of units of the money market account $n_0(\tau_1 - 2; s_{\tau_1 - 2})$ and the number of τ_1-maturity bonds purchased $n_1(\tau_1 - 2; s_{\tau_1 - 2})$ at time $\tau_1 - 2$ such that

$$n_0(\tau_1 - 2; s_{\tau_1 - 2})B(\tau_1 - 2; s_{\tau_1 - 3})r(\tau_1 - 2; s_{\tau_1 - 2}) + n_1(\tau_1 - 2; s_{\tau_1 - 2})P(\tau_1 - 2, \tau_1; s_{\tau_1 - 2})u(\tau_1 - 2, \tau_1; s_{\tau_1 - 2}) = x(\tau_1 - 1; s_{\tau_1 - 2}\mathrm{u}) \quad (6.11a)$$

$$n_0(\tau_1 - 2; s_{\tau_1 - 2})B(\tau_1 - 2; s_{\tau_1 - 3})r(\tau_1 - 2; s_{\tau_1 - 2}) + n_1(\tau_1 - 2; s_{\tau_1 - 2})P(\tau_1 - 2, \tau_1; s_{\tau_1 - 2})d(\tau_1 - 2, \tau_1; s_{\tau_1 - 2}) = x(\tau_1 - 1; s_{\tau_1 - 2}\mathrm{d}) \quad (6.11b)$$

Expression (6.11a) states that if the τ_1-maturity zero-coupon bond's price goes up, the portfolio's time $\tau_1 - 1$ value matches x. Expression (6.11b) states that if the τ_1-maturity zero-coupon bond's price goes down, the portfolio's time $\tau_1 - 1$ value also matches x. This is a linear system of two equations in two unknowns. The solution can be computed by elementary methods, and it exists because $u(\tau_1 - 2, \tau_1; s_{\tau_1 - 2}) > d(\tau_1 - 2, \tau_1; s_{\tau_1 - 2})$. The solution is given by

$$n_0(\tau_1 - 2; s_{\tau_1 - 2}) = \frac{x(\tau_1 - 1; s_{\tau_1 - 2}d)u(\tau_1 - 2, \tau_1; s_{\tau_1 - 2}) - x(\tau_1 - 1; s_{\tau_1 - 2}\mathrm{u})d(\tau_1 - 2, \tau_1; s_{\tau_1 - 2})}{B(\tau_1 - 2; s_{\tau_1 - 3})r(\tau_1 - 2; s_{\tau_1 - 2})[u(\tau_1 - 2, \tau_1; s_{\tau_1 - 2}) - d(\tau_1 - 2, \tau_1; s_{\tau_1 - 2})]} \quad (6.12a)$$

$$n_1(\tau_1 - 2; s_{\tau_1 - 2}) = \frac{x(\tau_1 - 1; s_{\tau_1 - 2}u) - x(\tau_1 - 1; s_{\tau_1 - 2}d)}{P(\tau_1 - 2, \tau_1; s_{\tau_1 - 2})[u(\tau_1 - 2, \tau_1; s_{\tau_1 - 2}) - d(\tau_1 - 2, \tau_1; s_{\tau_1 - 2})]} \quad (6.12b)$$

As expression (6.12) makes clear, this time $\tau_1 - 2$ portfolio choice only utilizes information available at time $\tau_1 - 2$ (because all the terms in expression (6.12) are known at time $\tau_1 - 2$).

DERIVATION OF EXPRESSION (6.12). First solve expression (6.11a) for $n_0(\tau_1 - 2; s_{\tau_1 - 2})$:

$$n_0(\tau_1 - 2; s_{\tau_1 - 2}) = \frac{x(\tau_1 - 1; s_{\tau_1 - 2}\mathrm{u})}{B(\tau_1 - 2; s_{\tau_1 - 3})r(\tau_1 - 2; s_{\tau_1 - 2})} - n_1(\tau_1 - 2; s_{\tau_1 - 2})\frac{P(\tau_1 - 2, \tau_1; s_{\tau_1 - 2})}{B(\tau_1 - 2; s_{\tau_1 - 3})r(\tau_1 - 2; s_{\tau_1 - 2})}u(\tau_1 - 2, \tau_1; s_{\tau_1 - 2}) \quad (*)$$

Substitute this expression for $n_0(\tau_1 - 2; s_{\tau_1 - 2})$ into (6.11b) to obtain

$$x(\tau_1 - 1; s_{\tau_1 - 2}\mathrm{u}) - n_1(\tau_1 - 2; s_{\tau_1 - 2})P(\tau_1 - 2, \tau_1; s_{\tau_1 - 2})u(\tau_1 - 2, \tau_1; s_{\tau_1 - 2}) + n_1(\tau_1 - 2; s_{\tau_1 - 2})P(\tau_1 - 2, \tau_1; s_{\tau_1 - 2})d(\tau_1 - 2, \tau_1; s_{\tau_1 - 2}) = x(\tau_1 - 1; s_{\tau_1 - 2}\mathrm{d})$$

Next, solve for $n_1(\tau_1 - 2; s_{\tau_1 - 2})$, giving expression (6.12b).

Substitution of (6.12b) into (∗) gives (6.12a). ■

The cost of constructing this portfolio at time $\tau_1 - 2$ is given by expression (6.13) and is defined to be $x(\tau_1 - 2; s_{\tau_1-2})$,

$$\begin{aligned} x(\tau_1 - 2; s_{\tau_1-2}) \equiv\ & n_0(\tau_1 - 2; s_{\tau_1-2})B(\tau_1 - 2; s_{\tau_1-3}) \\ & + n_1(\tau_1 - 2; s_{\tau_1-2})P(\tau_1 - 2, \tau_1; s_{\tau_1-2}) \end{aligned} \tag{6.13}$$

Next, we move back to time $\tau_1 - 3$ and form a portfolio to replicate expression (6.13) at time $\tau_1 - 2$. That is, we need to choose holdings in the money market account, $n_0(\tau_1 - 3; s_{\tau_1-3})$, and holdings in the τ_1-maturity zero-coupon bond, $n_1(\tau_1 - 3; s_{\tau_1-3})$, such that

$$\begin{aligned} & n_0(\tau_1 - 3; s_{\tau_1-3})B(\tau_1 - 3; s_{\tau_1-4})r(\tau_1 - 3; s_{\tau_1-3}) \\ & \quad + n_1(\tau_1 - 3; s_{\tau_1-3})P(\tau_1 - 3, \tau_1; s_{\tau_1-3})u(\tau_1 - 3, \tau_1; s_{\tau_1-3}) \\ & \quad = x(\tau_1 - 2; s_{\tau_1-3}\mathrm{u}) \end{aligned} \tag{6.14a}$$

$$\begin{aligned} & n_0(\tau_1 - 3; s_{\tau_1-3})B(\tau_1 - 3; s_{\tau_1-4})r(\tau_1 - 3; s_{\tau_1-3}) \\ & \quad + n_1(\tau_1 - 3; s_{\tau_1-3})P(\tau_1 - 3, \tau_1; s_{\tau_1-3})d(\tau_1 - 3, \tau_1; s_{\tau_1-3}) \\ & \quad = x(\tau_1 - 2; s_{\tau_1-3}\mathrm{d}) \end{aligned} \tag{6.14b}$$

Expression (6.14*a*) duplicates (6.13) in the up outcome and expression (6.14*b*) duplicates (6.13) in the down outcome. Again, this is a system of two linear equations in two unknowns. A comparison with expression (6.11) reveals that it is the identical system except that all the time and state subscripts are reduced by one. Consequently, the solution is given by expression (6.12) with the corresponding reduction in the time and state subscripts, i.e.,

$$\begin{aligned} & n_0(\tau_1 - 3; s_{\tau_1-3}) \\ & = \frac{[x(\tau_1 - 2; s_{\tau_1-3}\mathrm{d})u(\tau_1 - 3, \tau_1; s_{\tau_1-3}) - x(\tau_1 - 2; s_{\tau_1-3}\mathrm{u})d(\tau_1 - 3, \tau_1; s_{\tau_1-3})]}{B(\tau_1 - 3; s_{\tau_1-4})r(\tau_1 - 3; s_{\tau_1-3})[u(\tau_1 - 3, \tau_1; s_{\tau_1-3}) - d(\tau_1 - 3, \tau_1; s_{\tau_1-3}]} \end{aligned} \tag{6.15a}$$

$$\begin{aligned} & n_1(\tau_1 - 3; s_{\tau_1-3}) \\ & = \frac{x(\tau_1 - 2; s_{\tau_1-3}u) - x(\tau_1 - 2; s_{\tau_1-3}\mathrm{d})}{P(\tau_1 - 3, \tau_1; s_{\tau_1-3})[u(\tau_1 - 3, \tau_1; s_{\tau_1-3}) - d(\tau_1 - 3, \tau_1; s_{\tau_1-3})]} \end{aligned} \tag{6.15b}$$

The cost of constructing this portfolio at time $\tau_1 - 3$, defined to be $x(\tau_1 - 3; s_{\tau_1-3})$, is given in the next expression:

$$\begin{aligned} & x(\tau_1 - 3; s_{\tau_1-3}) \\ & \quad \equiv n_0(\tau_1 - 3; s_{\tau_1-3})B(\tau_1 - 3; s_{\tau_1-4}) + n_1(\tau_1 - 3; s_{\tau_1-3})P(\tau_1 - 3, \tau_1; s_{\tau_1-3}) \end{aligned} \tag{6.16}$$

A pattern is emerging. The next step is to construct a portfolio at time $\tau_1 - 4$ to duplicate expression (6.16) at time $\tau_1 - 3$. This portfolio is formulated as before. This process continues backward in time until we reach time 0. At time 0, we choose holdings in the money market account $n_0(0)$ and holdings in the τ_1-maturity zero-coupon bond $n_1(0)$ to duplicate $x(1; s_1)$ at time 1. The solution is given by

$$n_0(0) = \frac{x(1; \mathrm{d})u(0, \tau_1) - x(1; \mathrm{u})d(0, \tau_1)}{r(0)[u(0, \tau_1) - d(0, \tau_1)]} \tag{6.17a}$$

$$n_1(0) = \frac{x(1; \mathrm{u}) - x(1; \mathrm{d})}{P(0, \tau_1)[u(0, \tau_1) - d(0, \tau_1)]} \tag{6.17b}$$

with an initial cost of

$$x(0) \equiv n_0(0) \cdot 1 + n_1(0)P(0, \tau_1) \tag{6.18}$$

The trading strategy $(n_0(\mathrm{t}; s_\mathrm{t}), n_1(\mathrm{t}; s_\mathrm{t}))$ for all s_t and $0 \leq t \leq \tau_1 - 2$ constructed above is easily seen to be self-financing. At the start of each period, enough value is generated by the entering portfolio position so that the rebalanced holdings can be obtained without any excess cash flows (either plus or minus). This follows at time $\tau_1 - 2$, for example, from comparing expressions (6.13) and (6.14). Expression (6.13) is the value needed at time $\tau_1 - 2$, and expression (6.14) is the value of the portfolio entering time $\tau_1 - 2$. It also follows at time $\tau_1 - 3$ by similar logic; and so forth.

Thus, this portfolio represents the synthetic contingent claim $x(\tau_1 - 1; s_{\tau_1 - 1})$. As the contingent claim $x(\tau_1 - 1; s_{\tau_1 - 1})$ was an arbitrary contingent claim, we have just finished our demonstration that the market is complete with respect to the trading strategy set Φ_1. Obviously, therefore, it is complete with respect to the larger sets of trading strategies Φ_K for $K > 1$ as well.

The time 0 arbitrage-free price for the contingent claim $x(\tau_1 - 1; s_{\tau_1 - 1})$ is defined to be that value given in expression (6.18). We will return to this observation later on in the section.

2 Risk-Neutral Probabilities

Arbitrage opportunities with respect to the trading strategies in Φ_1 are assumed to be nonexistent in this economy. This section explores the implication of this assumption for the stochastic processes exogenously imposed on the zero-coupon bond price $P(t, \tau_1; s_t)$ and the spot rate process $r(t; s_t)$. These processes' parameters are not completely arbitrary, as seen below. These restrictions are the ones necessary and sufficient to make these processes consistent with some economic equilibrium.[1]

---

[1]This follows when we give this economy the interpretation of being risk-neutral, with equilibrium prices being determined by discounted expected values; see Harrison and Kreps [2] for a formal discussion of these issues.

Given that the relevant trading strategies in Φ_1 only involve the money market account and the τ_1-maturity zero-coupon bond, no arbitrage implies that neither security dominates the other, i.e.,

$$u(t, \tau_1; s_t) > r(t; s_t) > d(t, \tau_1; s_t) \qquad \text{for all } s_t \text{ and } t < \tau_1 - 1 \quad (6.19)$$

Indeed, suppose expression (6.19) were not true. That is, suppose $r(t; s_t) \geq u(t, \tau_1; s_t)$ for some s_t and $t < \tau_1 - 1$. An arbitrage opportunity with respect to Φ_1 can easily be constructed because the money market account pays off more than the τ_1-maturity bond at time $t + 1$ given state s_t at time t. The construction is as follows: hold no position until time t. If state s_t does not occur, do nothing. If state s_t occurs, buy $1/B(t; s_t)$ units of the money market account and finance it by selling $1/P(t, \tau_1; s_t)$ units of the τ_1-maturity bond. Liquidate the position at time $t + 1$. This portfolio satisfies expression (5.11*a*) because it has an initial value of zero. It is self-financing, and it satisfies expression (5.11*b*) because $r(t; s_t) \geq u(t, \tau_1; s_t) > d(t, \tau_1; s_t)$. This contradiction implies that $u(t, \tau_1; s_t) > r(t; s_t)$ for all s_t and $t < \tau_1 - 1$. The argument that $r(t; s_t) > d(t, \tau_1; s_t)$ for all s_t and $t < \tau_1 - 1$ is similar and is left to the reader as an exercise.

Expression (6.19) implies that there exists a unique, strictly positive number less than one, $\pi(t; s_t)$, such that

$$r(t; s_t) = \pi(t; s_t)u(t, \tau_1; s_t) + (1 - \pi(t; s_t))d(t, \tau_1; s_t) \quad (6.20)$$

To interpret the significance of this expression, we need to perform some algebra. First, divide both sides of expression (6.20) by $r(t; s_t)$ to get

$$1 = \pi(t; s_t)\frac{u(t, \tau_1; s_t)}{r(t; s_t)} - (1 - \pi(t; s_t))\frac{d(t, \tau_1; s_t)}{r(t; s_t)} \quad (6.21)$$

Next, multiply both sides of expression (6.21) by $P(t, \tau_1; s_t)/B(t; s_{t-1})$ and use expressions (4.1) and (3.7). The resulting expression is

$$\frac{P(t, \tau_1; s_t)}{B(t; s_{t-1})} = \pi(t; s_t)\frac{P(t + 1, \tau_1; s_t\text{u})}{B(t + 1; s_t)} + (1 - \pi(t; s_t))\frac{P(t + 1, \tau_1; s_t\text{d})}{B(t + 1; s_t)} \quad (6.22)$$

This is true for all s_t and $t < \tau_1 - 1$.

To understand expression (6.22), first note that the number $\pi(t; s_t)$ can be interpreted as a probability of the up outcomes occurring at time t. Indeed, it is a strictly positive number less than one. Correspondingly, $1 - \pi(t; s_t)$ can be interpreted as a probability of the down outcomes occurring at time t. Because the true probabilities are $q(t; s_t)$ and $1 - q(t; s_t)$, we call the $\pi(t; s_t)$ *pseudo probabilities*. With this interpretation, expression (6.22) can be written as

$$\frac{P(t, \tau_1; s_t)}{B(t; s_{t-1})} = \tilde{E}_t\left(\frac{P(t + 1, \tau_1; s_{t+1})}{B(t + 1; s_t)}\right) \quad (6.23)$$

where $\tilde{E}_t(\bullet)$ is the time t expected value under the pseudo probabilities $\pi(t; s_t)$.

Expression (6.23) states that the τ_1-maturity zero-coupon bond price at time t, discounted by the money market account's value, is equal to its discounted expected value at time $t+1$. Expression (6.23) also states that the ratio of the τ_1-maturity zero-coupon's bond price to the money market account's value $(P(t,\tau_1)/B(t))$ is a *martingale* under the pseudo probabilities. (A martingale (for a discrete time- discrete state space process) is a stochastic process whose current value equals its expected future value, as in expression (6.23).) This provides us with the second name often used for the pseudo probabilities, *martingale probabilities*.

It is instructive to rewrite expression (6.23) in an alternative form. Multiplying both sides of this expression by $B(t; s_{t-1})$ and recognizing that $B(t; s_{t-1})/B(t+1; s_t) = 1/r(t; s_t)$ gives

$$P(t,\tau_1; s_t) = \frac{\tilde{E}_t(P(t+1,\tau_1; s_{t+1}))}{r(t; s_t)} \tag{6.24a}$$

Expression (6.24a) shows that the price of the τ_1-maturity zero-coupon bond at time t is its expected value at time $t+1$ (under the pseudo probabilities) discounted at the spot rate of interest. This form of expression (6.23) is the version most easily programmed on a computer or used in hand calculations.

Expression (6.24a) is the value that the τ_1-maturity zero-coupon bond would have in a *risk-neutral economy* in which the actual beliefs of all investors are the pseudo probabilities. This is verified by referring back to expression (4.22) in Chapter 4, where the expectations hypothesis was defined. There, expression (6.24) appears as expression (4.22), but with the actual probabilities used in the expectations operator. Consequently, the pseudo probabilities are also called *risk-neutral probabilities*. We can rewrite expression (6.24a) only in terms of spot interest rates:

$$P(t,\tau_1; s_t) = \tilde{E}_t\left(\frac{1}{\prod_{j=t}^{\tau_1-1} r(j; s_j)}\right) \tag{6.24b}$$

Expression (6.24b) makes clear the statement that the τ_1-maturity zero-coupon bond's price is its time τ_1 expected value (one dollar) discounted by the spot interest rates over the intermediate periods.[2]

DERIVATION OF EXPRESSION (6.24*b*). From expression (6.24a) at time $\tau_1 - 1$, we have

$$P(\tau_1 - 1, \tau_1; s_t - 1) = \tilde{E}_{\tau_1 - 1}\left(\frac{1}{r(\tau_1 - 1; s_{\tau_1 - 1})}\right) \tag{*}$$

[2]One class of interest rate option models uses expression (6.24) as the starting point. These are called *spot rate* models. Exogenously given are the pseudo probabilities $\pi(t; s_t)$ and the stochastic process for the spot rate $(r(0), (u(t, t+1; s_t))$. The approach followed in this chapter differs from the spot rate model approach by using the bond price process $P(0,\tau_1), (u(t,\tau_1; s_t), d(t,\tau_1; s_t))$ and the absence of arbitrage to determine $\pi(t; s_t)$; see Chapter 14 for an elaboration of these ideas.

Continuing backward from (6.24a) at time $\tau_1 - 2$ and using (*), we have

$$P(\tau_1 - 2, \tau_1; s_{\tau_1 - 2}) = \tilde{E}_{\tau_1 - 2}\left(\tilde{E}_{\tau_1 - 1}\left(\frac{1}{r(\tau_1 - 1; s_{\tau_1 - 1})}\right)\frac{1}{r(\tau_1 - 2; s_{\tau_1 - 2})}\right)$$

Using the fact that $\tilde{E}_{\tau_1 - 2}(\tilde{E}_{\tau_1 - 1}(\bullet)) = \tilde{E}_{\tau_1 - 2}(\bullet)$, we get

$$P(\tau_1 - 2, \tau_1; s_{\tau_1 - 2}) = \tilde{E}_{\tau_1 - 2}\left(\frac{1}{r(\tau_1 - 1; s_{\tau_1 - 1})r(\tau_1 - 2; s_{\tau_1 - 2})}\right)$$

which is (6.24b) at $\tau_1 - 2$. Continuing backward until time t gives the desired result. ■

For future reference, from expression (6.20) we can explicitly write down an expression for the pseudo probabilities in terms of the τ_1-maturity zero-coupon bond's and the spot rate processes' parameters,

$$\pi(t; s_t) = \frac{r(t; s_t) - d(t, \tau_1; s_t)}{u(t, \tau_1; s_t) - d(t, \tau_1; s_t)} \tag{6.25a}$$

$$1 - \pi(t; s_t) = \frac{u(t, \tau_1; s_t) - r(t; s_t)}{u(t, \tau_1; s_t) - d(t, \tau_1; s_t)} \tag{6.25b}$$

The no-arbitrage condition, expression (6.19), guarantees that each of these probabilities is strictly positive and less than one.

In summary, no arbitrage with respect to the trading strategy set Φ_1 implies the existence of these pseudo probabilities $\pi(t; s_t)$ satisfying expression (6.23). The converse of this statement is also true. The existence of pseudo probabilities $\pi(t; s_t)$ satisfying expression (6.23) implies that there are no arbitrage opportunities with respect to the trading strategy set Φ_1 (the proof of this assertion is contained in the appendix to this chapter). Therefore, the existence of pseudo probabilities $\pi(t; s_t)$ satisfying expression (6.23) is both necessary and sufficient for the absence of arbitrage opportunities with respect to the trading strategy set Φ_1. This is an important observation and is especially useful when constructing stochastic processes for the evolution of the zero-coupon bond price curve.

EXAMPLE: RISK-NEUTRAL PROBABILITIES. Using the bond and money market account processes of Figs. 6.1 and 6.2, we can calculate the one-period rate of return processes. These are provided in Fig. 6.5. We see that for all states and times,

$$u(t, 4; s_t) > r(t; s_t) > d(t, 4; s_t)$$

The four-period bond does not dominate nor is it dominated by the money market. This guarantees the existence of the pseudo probabilities. The pseudo probabilities for this example are easily calculated using expression (6.25):

$$\pi(0) = \frac{1.02 - 1.014400}{1.025602 - 1.014400} = 0.5$$

$$\pi(1;\mathrm{u}) = \frac{1.017606 - 1.013754}{1.021455 - 1.013754} = 0.5$$

$$\pi(1;\mathrm{d}) = \frac{1.022406 - 1.017851}{1.026961 - 1.017851} = 0.5$$

$$\pi(2;\mathrm{uu}) = \frac{1.016031 - 1.014006}{1.018056 - 1.014006} = 0.5$$

$$\pi(2;\mathrm{ud}) = \frac{1.020393 - 1.017958}{1.022828 - 1.017958} = 0.5$$

$$\pi(2;\mathrm{du}) = \frac{1.019193 - 1.016857}{1.021529 - 1.016857} = 0.5$$

$$\pi(2;\mathrm{dd}) = \frac{1.024436 - 1.021622}{1.027250 - 1.021622} = 0.5$$

The pseudo probabilities are all equal to 0.5. This is not a general rule, but just a special result in this example. We will explore an additional use of these pseudo probabilities in Section 4 below.

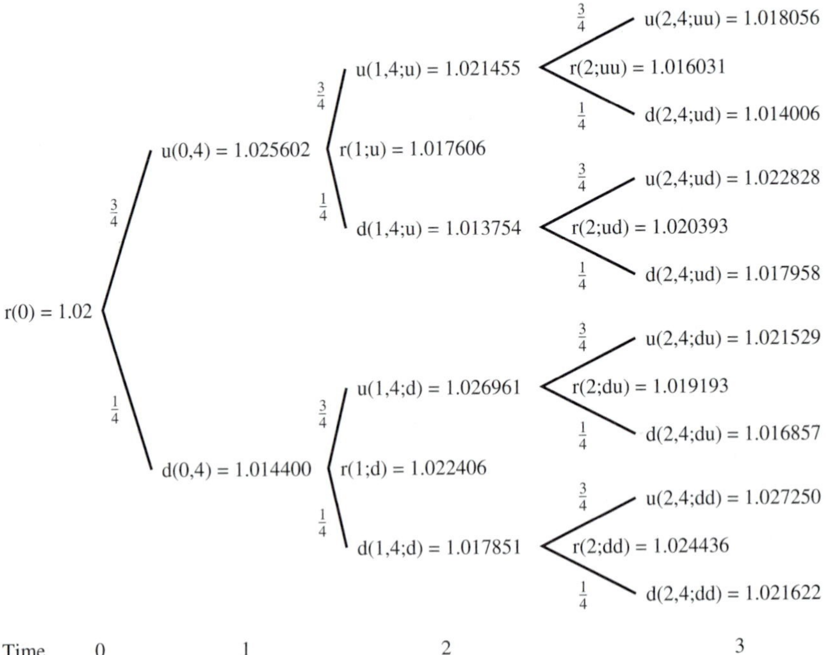

FIGURE 6.5
The rate of return processes for the four-period zero-coupon bond in Fig. 6.1 and the money market account in Fig. 6.2.

We can now verify that expression (6.24) is satisfied in this example. Referring back to Fig. 6.1, we get

$$
\begin{aligned}
P(2,4;\mathrm{uu}) &= \frac{\tilde{E}_2(P(3,4;s_t))}{r(2;\mathrm{uu})} \\
&= \frac{(1/2)0.985301 + (1/2)0.981381}{1.016031} = 0.967826 \\
P(2,4;\mathrm{ud}) &= \frac{\tilde{E}_2(P(3,4;s_3))}{r(2;\mathrm{ud})} \\
&= \frac{(1/2)0.982456 + (1/2)0.977778}{1.020393} = 0.960529 \\
P(2,4;\mathrm{du}) &= \frac{\tilde{E}_2(P(3,4;s_3))}{r(2;\mathrm{du})} \\
&= \frac{(1/2)0.983134 + (1/2)0.978637}{1.019193} = 0.962414 \\
P(2,4;\mathrm{dd}) &= \frac{\tilde{E}_2(P(3,4;s_3))}{r(2;\mathrm{dd})} \\
&= \frac{(1/2)0.979870 + (1/2)0.974502}{1.024436} = 0.953877 \\
P(1,4;\mathrm{u}) &= \frac{\tilde{E}_1(P(2,4;s_2))}{r(1;\mathrm{u})} \\
&= \frac{(1/2)0.967826 + (1/2)0.960529}{1.017606} = 0.947497 \\
P(1,4;\mathrm{d}) &= \frac{\tilde{E}_1(P(2,4;s_2))}{r(1;\mathrm{d})} \\
&= \frac{(1/2)0.962414 + (1/2)0.953877}{1.022406} = 0.937148 \\
P(0,4) &= \frac{\tilde{E}_0(P(1,4;s_1))}{r(0)} \\
&= \frac{(1/2)0.947497 + (1/2)0.937148}{1.02} = 0.923845
\end{aligned}
$$

■

3 Risk-Neutral Valuation

Given a simple contingent claim $x(\tau_1 - 1; s_{\tau_1 - 1})$ with maturity date $\tau_1 - 1$, we showed in Section 6.A.1 that its arbitrage-free price, denoted $x(0)$, is

$$x(0) = n_0(0) + n_1(0)P(0, \tau_1) \tag{6.26}$$

where $(n_0(t; s_t), n_1(t; s_t)) \in \Phi_1$ is the self-financing trading strategy that creates the synthetic contingent claim.

Using the risk-neutral probabilities, we can rewrite this expression in an alternative but equivalent form. Using a backward inductive argument, it can be shown that expression (6.27*a*) holds:

$$x(0) = \tilde{E}_0\left(\frac{x(\tau_1 - 1; s_{\tau_1-1})}{B(\tau_1 - 1; s_{\tau_1-2})}\right)B(0) \tag{6.27a}$$

where $\tilde{E}_0(\bullet)$ is the time 0 expected value using the pseudo probabilities $\pi(t; s_t)$. This is the *risk-neutral valuation* procedure for calculating current values. The arbitrage-free price of the contingent claim x is seen to be its discounted expected value using the risk-neutral probabilities $\pi(t; s_t)$ as given in expression (6.25). This is the equilibrium value that would obtain in an economy identical to the one studied except that all investors are risk-neutral and hold the pseudo probabilities as their beliefs (and not $q_t(s_t)$).

DERIVATION OF EXPRESSION (6.27*a*). Expression (6.13) states that

$$x(\tau_1 - 2; s_{\tau_1-2}) = n_0(\tau_1 - 2; s_{\tau_1-2})B(\tau_1 - 2; s_{\tau_1-3}) + n_1(\tau_1 - 2; s_{\tau_1-2})P(\tau_1 - 2, \tau_1; s_{\tau_1-2})$$

Substitution of (6.12) into this expression yields

$$x(\tau_1 - 2; s_{\tau_1-2}) = \frac{x(\tau_1 - 1; s_{\tau_1-2}\mathrm{d})u(\tau_1 - 2, \tau_1; s_{\tau_1-2}) - x(\tau_1 - 1; s_{\tau_1-2}\mathrm{u})d(\tau_1 - 2, \tau_1; s_{\tau_1-2})}{r(\tau_1 - 2; s_{\tau_1-2})[u(\tau_1 - 2, \tau_1; s_{\tau_1-2}) - d(\tau_1 - 2, \tau_1; s_{\tau_1-2})]} + \frac{x(\tau_1 - 1; s_{\tau_1-2}\mathrm{u}) - x(\tau_1 - 1; s_{\tau_1-2}\mathrm{d})}{u(\tau_1 - 2, \tau_1; s_{\tau_1-2}) - d(\tau_1 - 2, \tau_1; s_{\tau_1-2})}$$

Rearranging terms yields

$$x(\tau_1 - 2; s_{\tau_1-2}) = \left\{ x(\tau_1 - 1; s_{\tau_1-2}\mathrm{u})\frac{r(\tau_1 - 2; s_{\tau_1-2}) - d(\tau_1 - 2, \tau_1; s_{\tau_1-2})}{u(\tau_1 - 2, \tau_1; s_{\tau_1-2}) - d(\tau_1 - 2, \tau_1; s_{\tau_1-2})} + x(\tau_1 - 1; s_{\tau_1-2}\mathrm{d})\frac{u(\tau_1 - 2, \tau_1; s_{\tau_1-2}) - r(\tau_1 - 2; s_{\tau_1-2})}{u(\tau_1 - 2, \tau_1; s_{\tau_1-2}) - d(\tau_1 - 2, \tau_1; s_{\tau_1-2})}\right\} \times \frac{1}{r(\tau_1 - 2; s_{\tau_1-2})}$$

Using (6.25) and the definition of $B(t; s_{t-1})$ yields

$$x(\tau_1 - 2; s_{\tau_1-2}) = \{x(\tau_1 - 1; s_{\tau_1-2}\mathrm{u})\pi(\tau_1 - 2; s_{\tau_1-2}) + x(\tau_1 - 1; s_{\tau_1-2}\mathrm{d})(1 - \pi(\tau_1 - 2; s_{\tau_1-2}))\}\frac{B(\tau_1 - 2; s_{\tau_1-3})}{B(\tau_1 - 1; s_{\tau_1-2})}$$

Using the expectation notation gives

$$x(\tau_1 - 2; s_{\tau_1-2}) = \tilde{E}_{\tau_1-2}\left(\frac{x(\tau_1 - 1; s_{\tau_1-1})}{B(\tau_1 - 1; s_{\tau_1-2})}\right)B(\tau_1 - 2; s_{\tau_1-3}) \tag{*}$$

This is expression (6.27*a*) at time $\tau_1 - 2$.

Next, using the identical algebra as above, but expression (6.16) instead of (6.13), we get

$$x(\tau_1 - 3; s_{\tau_1-3}) = \tilde{E}_{\tau_1-3}\left(\frac{x(\tau_1 - 2; s_{\tau_1-2})}{B(\tau_1 - 2; s_{\tau_1-3})}\right)B(\tau_1 - 3; s_{\tau_1-4})$$

Substitution of (*) into this expression gives

$$x(\tau_1 - 3; s_{\tau_1-3}) = \tilde{E}_{\tau_1-3}\left(\tilde{E}_{\tau_1-2}\left(\frac{x(\tau_1 - 1; s_{\tau_1-1})}{B(\tau_1 - 1; s_{\tau_1-2})}\right)\right)B(\tau_1 - 3; s_{\tau_1-4})$$

because the $B(\tau_1 - 2; s_{\tau_1-3})$ terms cancel. Using the well-known law of iterated expectations that $\tilde{E}_{\tau_1-3}(\tilde{E}_{\tau_1-2}(\bullet)) = \tilde{E}_{\tau_1-3}(\bullet)$, we get

$$x(\tau_1 - 3; s_{\tau_1-3}) = \tilde{E}_{\tau_1-3}\left(\frac{x(\tau_1 - 1; s_{\tau_1-1})}{B(\tau_1 - 1; s_{\tau_1-2})}\right)B(\tau_1 - 3; s_{\tau_1-4})$$

This is expression (6.27*a*) at time $\tau_1 - 3$. Continuing backward in this fashion until time 0 generates expression (6.27*a*) as written. ■

For computations, either by hand or on a computer, one normally employs the backward induction procedure underlying the proof of expression (6.27*a*). For these computations, an equivalent form of expression (6.27*a*) is needed, i.e.,

$$x(t; s_t) = \frac{1}{r(t; s_t)}[\pi(t; s_t)x(t + 1; s_t\text{u}) + (1 - \pi(t; s_t))x(t + 1; s_t\text{d})] \qquad (6.27b)$$

for all s_t where $0 \leq t \leq \tau_1 - 2$. The proof that this expression is equivalent to (6.27*a*) is contained in the derivation of expression (6.27*a*).

From expressions (6.27) and (6.25) it is easily seen that one can determine the arbitrage-free price of any simple contingent claim using only the current price of the τ_1-maturity zero-coupon bond, its stochastic process, the current spot rate, and the current spot rate's stochastic process, i.e., (*i*) $P(0, \tau_1)$ and $(u(t, \tau_1; s_t), d(t, \tau_1; s_t))$ and (*ii*) $r(0)$ and $(u(t, t + 1; s_t))$. These processes, however, need to satisfy the no-arbitrage restriction given in expression (6.19). We do not need to know the prices of the other zero-coupon bonds nor their stochastic processes. These, in fact, can be determined from expression (6.27); that analysis is the content of the next section.

It is important to note that the actual probabilities $q_t(s_t)$ do not enter the valuation formula for the simple contingent claim x. This is seen by examining expression (6.27), which can be calculated using only the data (*i*) $P(0, \tau_1)$ and $(u(t, \tau_1; s_t), d(t, \tau_1; s_t))$, and (*ii*) $r(0)$ and $(u(t, t + 1; s_t))$. This independence of the actual probabilities $q_t(s_t)$ follows because deviations from formula (6.27) can be arbitraged no matter which state occurs. Consequently, the likelihood of a state's occurrence is irrelevant to the procedure. This independence implies that two traders who differ in their beliefs about future probabilities $(q_t(s_t))$, but who agree with the data concerning (*i*) $P(0, \tau_1)$ and $(u(t, \tau_1; s_t), d(t, \tau_1; s_t))$ and (*ii*) $r(0)$ and $(u(t, t + 1; s_t))$ will agree upon all the remaining zero-coupon bond prices.

We need to pause and review the valuation of contingent claims more complex than those previously defined. The simple contingent claim x with maturity $\tau_1 - 1$ defined above consists of a single, random cash flow $x(\tau_1 - 1; s_{\tau_1 - 1})$ at time $\tau_1 - 1$. Consider a complex contingent claim having multiple random cash flows at the different dates $\{0, 1, \ldots, \tau^*\}$ over its life, each denoted $x(t; s_t)$ for $t \in \{0, 1, \ldots, \tau^*\}$. This claim is nothing more than a collection of τ^* separate simple contingent claims each with a different maturity date. The arbitrage-free value of this complex contingent claim is defined to be the sum of the arbitrage-free values of the simple contingent claims into which it can be decomposed; therefore, using expression (6.27) gives

$$\sum_{j=0}^{\tau^*} \tilde{E}_0 \left(\frac{x(j; s_j)}{B(j; s_{j-1})} \right) B(0) \tag{6.28}$$

Finally, consider an American-type contingent claim with cash flows $x(t, a; s_t)$ at time $t \in \{0, 1, \ldots, \tau^*\}$ given decision choice $a \in A$. Now, if we arbitrarily fix a decision $a^* \in A$, the cash flows to this claim for each t are $x(t, a^*; s_t)$. Using expression (6.28), its arbitrage-free price at time 0 is then

$$\sum_{j=0}^{\tau^*} \tilde{E} \left(\frac{x(j, a^*; s_j)}{B(j; s_{j-1})} \right) B(0) \tag{6.29}$$

But a^* might not be the best action for the person making the decision. This person, if holding the American contingent claim, would obviously want to select $a^* \in A$ to maximize expression (6.29). This maximum value is defined to be the *arbitrage-free price of the American contingent claim*. This is the standard approach used in the option pricing literature for pricing American-type contingent claims. For more discussion, we refer the reader to Jarrow and Rudd [3] or Cox and Rubinstein [1]. We will see an example of this procedure in Chapter 8.[3]

4 Bond Trading Strategies

The purpose of this chapter is to develop a procedure for valuing the entire zero-coupon bond price curve given (*i*) the price of one zero-coupon bond $P(0, \tau_1)$ and its stochastic process $(u(t, \tau_1; s_t), d(t, \tau_1; s_t))$, (*ii*) the current spot rate $r(0)$ and its stochastic process $(u(t, t+1; s_t))$, and (*iii*) the assumption of no arbitrage opportunities in the trading strategy set Φ_1. We are now in a position to do just this.

All the distinct zero-coupon bonds maturing at times $T \leq \tau_1 - 1$ can be viewed as contingent claims (of the simple, European type) and valued using

---

[3]The standard approach for solving $\max_{a^* \in A} \sum_{j=0}^{\tau^*} \tilde{E}(x(j, a^*; s_j)/B(j; s_{\tau_1 - 1}))B(0)$ is by using stochastic dynamic programming. This is the approach taken to solve this problem in Chapter 8.

either of the expressions (6.18) or (6.24). Formally, however, the procedure was only derived for contingent claims maturing at or prior to time $\tau_1 - 1$. To value the zero-coupon bonds with maturities greater than $\tau_1 - 1$, we need to specify their state-contingent payoffs at time $\tau_1 - 1$. Alternatively, we could define $\tau \equiv \tau$, so that no bonds mature after time τ_1.

In this context the arbitrage-free price of the T-maturity discount bonds with $T < \tau_1$ are given by

$$P(t,T;s_t) = \tilde{E}_t\left(\frac{1}{\Pi_{j=t}^{T-1} r(j;s_j)}\right) \tag{6.30a}$$

or, equivalently,

$$P(t,T;s_t) = \frac{\tilde{E}_t(P(t+1,T;s_{t+1}))}{r(t;s_t)} \tag{6.30b}$$

where $\tilde{E}_t(\bullet)$ is the time t expectation using the pseudo probabilities $\pi(t;s_t)$ given in expression (6.25).

The procedure given in expressions (6.12) and (6.15)–(6.18) enables us to construct a synthetic T-maturity zero-coupon bond using a self-financing trading strategy involving the τ_1-maturity bond and the money market account. The initial cost of this synthetic T-maturity zero-coupon bond gives its arbitrage-free price. This price does not need to equal the traded price. If the traded price of a T-maturity bond differs from the arbitrage-free price given in expression (6.30), an arbitrage opportunity exists. Indeed, suppose the traded price exceeds (6.30). Then, sell the traded T-maturity zero-coupon bond short, and create the T-maturity zero-coupon bond synthetically. The combined position yields an arbitrage opportunity. It is important to emphasize that expression (6.30) is independent of the actual probabilities $q_t(s_t)$.

EXAMPLE: RISK-NEUTRAL VALUATION. To illustrate this risk-neutral valuation procedure, consider the example analyzed in Figs. 6.1 and 6.2. Our goal is to compute the prices of the two- and three-period zero-coupon bonds using expression (6.30). The simplest way to do this is to start at time 3 and work backward to time 0, calculating expected values and discounting according to expression (6.30*b*).

For the two-period bond, the calculations are as follows:

$$P(1,2;\mathrm{u}) = \frac{\tilde{E}_1(P(2,2;s_2))}{r(1;\mathrm{u})} = \frac{(1/2)1 + (1/2)1}{1.017606} = 0.982699$$

$$P(1,2;\mathrm{d}) = \frac{\tilde{E}_1(P(2,2;s_2))}{r(1;\mathrm{d})} = \frac{(1/2)1 + (1/2)1}{1.022406} = 0.978085$$

$$P(0,2) = \frac{\tilde{E}_0(P(1,2;s_1))}{r(0)} = \frac{(1/2)0.982699 + (1/2)0.978085}{1.02} = 0.961169$$

These values generate the nodes of the tree in Fig. 6.3 with less effort than the technique utilized before.

From the above calculations, the price of the two-period bond at time zero is $P(0,2) = 0.961169$. Suppose that the actual price quoted in the market was 0.970000. An arbitrage opportunity exists. To create this arbitrage opportunity, we need to determine the portfolio that generates the synthetic two-period zero-coupon bond. This can be obtained using the procedure from Section 1. Alternatively, it can be obtained using only expression (6.30) and Figs. 6.1 and 6.2. This alternative approach calculates the *delta*. The delta is the change in the value of a derivative security with respect to the change in value of some underlying asset. The delta for the two-period bond at time 1, state u, denoted $n_1(1;\mathrm{u})$, is

$$\begin{aligned} n_1(1;\mathrm{u}) &= \frac{\Delta P(2,2;s_2)}{\Delta P(2,4;s_2)} \\ &= \frac{P(2,2;\mathrm{uu}) - P(2,2;\mathrm{ud})}{P(2,4;\mathrm{uu}) - P(2,4;\mathrm{ud})} = \frac{1-1}{0.967826 - 0.960529} = 0 \end{aligned}$$

This represents the change in the two-period zero-coupon bond's price relative to that of the four-period zero-coupon bond. This gives the position in the four-period zero-coupon bond, i.e., $n_1(1;\mathrm{u})$. To get the number of units in the money market account, we use

$$\begin{aligned} n_0(1;\mathrm{u}) &= \frac{P(1,2;\mathrm{u}) - n_1(1;\mathrm{u})P(1,4;\mathrm{u})}{B(1)} \\ &= \frac{0.982699 - 0(0.947497)}{1.02} = 0.963430 \end{aligned}$$

This last relation is obtained from the self-financing constraint (6.14). The price $P(1,2;\mathrm{u})$ used in this formula is that calculated using expression (6.30).

Continuing,

$$\begin{aligned} n_1(1;\mathrm{d}) &= \frac{\Delta P(2,2;s_2)}{\Delta P(2,4;s_2)} \\ &= \frac{P(2,2;\mathrm{du}) - P(2,2;\mathrm{dd})}{P(2,4;\mathrm{du}) - P(2,4;\mathrm{dd})} = \frac{1-1}{0.962414 - 0.953877} = 0 \end{aligned}$$

and

$$\begin{aligned} n_0(1;\mathrm{d}) &= \frac{P(1,2;\mathrm{d}) - n_1(1;\mathrm{d})P(1,4;\mathrm{d})}{B(1)} \\ &= \frac{0.978085 - 0(0.937148)}{1.02} = 0.958907 \end{aligned}$$

Finally,

$$\begin{aligned} n_1(0) &= \frac{\Delta P(1,2;s_1)}{\Delta P(1,4;s_1)} \\ &= \frac{P(1,2;\mathrm{u}) - P(1,2;\mathrm{d})}{P(1,4;\mathrm{u}) - P(1,4;\mathrm{d})} = \frac{0.982699 - 0.978085}{0.947497 - 0.937148} = 0.445835 \end{aligned}$$

and

$$n_0(0) = \frac{P(0,2) - n_1(0)P(0,4)}{B(0)}$$

$$= \frac{0.961169 - 0.445835(0.923845)}{1} = 0.549286$$

To create the arbitrage opportunity, sell the two-period bond at time 0. This brings in +0.97000 dollar in cash. Invest $n_0(0) = 0.549286$ dollar of this in a money market account and buy $n_1(0) = 0.445835$ unit of $P(0,4) = 0.923845$, at a total cost of 0.961169 dollar. This leaves $0.97000 - 0.961169 = 0.008831$ dollar in excess cash available at time 0.

At time 1, if state u occurs, we rebalance our money market account and four-period bond holdings to $n_0(1; \mathrm{u})$ and $n_1(1; \mathrm{u})$. No excess cash is generated. This follows from the self-financing constraint. At time 1, if state d occurs, we rebalance our money market account and four-period bond holdings to $n_0(1; \mathrm{d})$ and $n_1(1; \mathrm{d})$. No excess cash is generated. At time 2, our long position in the money market account and four-period bond exactly offsets our short position in the two-period bond. This completes the illustration for the two-period bond.

The use of expression (6.30) to obtain the numbers in Fig. 6.4 is left to the reader as an exercise. ■

SECTION B THE TWO-FACTOR ECONOMY

Having illustrated the procedure for pricing the zero-coupon bond price curve in the one-factor economy, we can proceed more swiftly in the two-factor case. Consider the two-factor economy described in Chapter 4, Section 4.B. We assume that there are no arbitrage opportunities with respect to the trading strategy set Φ_2. In this class of trading strategies, we fix two zero-coupon bonds with maturities τ_1 and τ_2, and all trades take place with respect to these bonds and the money market account.

Taken as given (exogenous) are the stochastic processes for the τ_1- and τ_2-maturity zero-coupon bonds, i.e., $\{P(0,\tau_1), (u(t,\tau_1;s_t), m(t,\tau_1;s_t), d(t,\tau_1;s)t))\}$ and $\{P(0,\tau_2), (u(t,\tau_2;s_t), m(t,\tau_2;s_t)), d(t,\tau_2;s_2))\}$; and the stochastic process for the spot rate $r(0), (u(t, t+1; s_t))$. The purpose is to price all the remaining zero-coupon bonds in the market. Because the τ_1- and τ_2-maturity zero-coupon bonds and the money market account processes are exogenously supplied, we need to discuss the restrictions implied by there being no arbitrage opportunities in the trading strategy set Φ_2. We proceed as we did for the one-factor economy.

1 Complete Markets

This economy is complete with respect to the trading strategy set Φ_2. To prove this, consider an arbitrary simple contingent claim with maturity date

$\tau_1 - 1, x(\tau_1 - 1; s_{\tau_1 - 1})$. To duplicate x's cash flows over $[\tau_1 - 2, \tau_1 - 1]$, we need to choose $n_0(\tau_1 - 2; s_{\tau_1 - 2}), n_1(\tau_1 - 2; s_{\tau_1 - 2})$, and $n_2(\tau_1 - 2; s_{\tau_1 - 2})$ at time $\tau_1 - 2$ such that the portfolio's payoff at time $\tau_1 - 1$ duplicates the contingent claim's payoffs:

$$\begin{aligned} n_0(\tau_1 - 2; s_{\tau_1 - 2})&B(\tau_1 - 2; s_{\tau_1 - 3})r(\tau_1 - 2; s_{\tau_1 - 2}) \\ &+ n_1(\tau_1 - 2; s_{\tau_1 - 2})P(\tau_1 - 2; s_{\tau_1 - 2})u(\tau_1 - 2, \tau_1; s_{\tau_1 - 2}) \\ &+ n_2(\tau_1 - 2; s_{\tau_1 - 2})P(\tau_1 - 2, \tau_2; s_{\tau_1 - 2})u(\tau_1 - 2, \tau_2; s_{\tau_1 - 2}) \\ &= x(\tau_1 - 1; s_{\tau_1 - 2}\mathrm{u}) \end{aligned} \tag{6.31a}$$

$$\begin{aligned} n_0(\tau_1 - 2; s_{\tau_1 - 2})&B(\tau_1 - 2; s_{\tau_1 - 3})r(\tau_1 - 2; s_{\tau_1 - 2}) \\ &+ n_1(\tau_1 - 2; s_{\tau_1 - 2})P(\tau_1 - 2, \tau_1; s_{\tau_1 - 2})m(\tau_1 - 2, \tau_1; s_{\tau_1 - 2}) \\ &+ n_2(\tau_1 - 2; s_{\tau_1 - 2})P(\tau_1 - 2, \tau_2; s_{\tau_1 - 2})m(\tau_1 - 2, \tau_2; s_{\tau_1 - 2}) \\ &= x(\tau_1 - 1; s_{\tau_1 - 2}\mathrm{m}) \end{aligned} \tag{6.31b}$$

$$\begin{aligned} n_0(\tau_1 - 2; s_{\tau_1 - 2})&B(\tau_1 - 2; s_{\tau_1 - 3})r(\tau_1 - 2; s_{\tau_1 - 2}) \\ &+ n_1(\tau_1 - 2; s_{\tau_1 - 2})P(\tau_1 - 2, \tau_1; s_{\tau_1 - 2})d(\tau_1 - 2, \tau_1; s_{\tau_1 - 2}) \\ &+ n_2(\tau_1 - 2; s_{\tau_1 - 2})P(\tau_1 - 2, \tau_2; s_{\tau_1 - 2})d(\tau_1 - 2, \tau_2; s_{\tau_1 - 2}) \\ &= x(\tau_1 - 1; s_{\tau_1 - 2}\mathrm{d}) \end{aligned} \tag{6.31c}$$

This is a linear system of three equations in three unknowns. Because of condition (4.13), this system has a unique solution given by

$$\begin{aligned} n_2(\tau_1 - 2; s_{\tau_1 - 2}) = \\ &\frac{(x(\tau_1 - 1; s_{\tau_1 - 2}\mathrm{m}) - x(\tau_1 - 1; s_{\tau_1 - 2}\mathrm{d}))(u(\tau_1 - 2, \tau_1; s_{\tau_1 - 2})}{\mathrm{DENOM}} \\ &\frac{-m(\tau_1 - 2, \tau_1; s_{\tau_1 - 2})) - (x(\tau_1 - 1; s_{\tau_1 - 2}\mathrm{u})}{\mathrm{DENOM}} \\ &\frac{-x(\tau_1 - 1; s_{\tau_1 - 2}\mathrm{m}))(m(\tau_1 - 2, \tau_1; s_{\tau_1 - 2}) - d(\tau_1 - 2, \tau_1; s_{\tau_1 - 2}))}{\mathrm{DENOM}} \end{aligned} \tag{6.32a}$$

where

$$\begin{aligned} \mathrm{DENOM} \equiv P(\tau_1 - 2, \tau_2; s_{\tau_1 - 2})&(u(\tau_1 - 2, \tau_1; s_{\tau_1 - 2}) - m(\tau_1 - 2, \tau_1; s_{\tau_1 - 2})) \\ &\times (m(\tau_1 - 2, \tau_2; s_{\tau_1 - 2}) - d(\tau_1 - 2, \tau_2; s_{\tau_1 - 2})) \\ &- (u(\tau_1 - 2, \tau_2; s_{\tau_1 - 2}) - m(\tau_1 - 2, \tau_2; s_{\tau_1 - 2})) \\ &\times (m(\tau_1 - 2, \tau_1; s_{\tau_1 - 2}) - d(\tau_1 - 2, \tau_1; s_{\tau_1 - 2})) \end{aligned}$$

$$n_1(\tau_1-2;s_{\tau_1-2})$$

$$= \left[\frac{x(\tau_1-1;s_{\tau_1-2}\mathrm{u})-x(\tau_1-1;s_{\tau_1-2}\mathrm{m})}{u(\tau_1-2,\tau_1;s_{\tau_1-2})-m(\tau_1-2,\tau_1;s_{\tau_1-2})}\right]\frac{1}{P(\tau_1-2,\tau_1;s_{\tau_1-2})}$$

$$-\frac{n_2(\tau_1-2;s_{\tau_1-2})P(\tau_1-2,\tau_2;s_{\tau_1-2})}{P(\tau_1-2,\tau_1;s_{\tau_1-2})} \tag{6.32b}$$

$$\times\left[\frac{u(\tau_1-2,\tau_2;s_{\tau_1-2})-m(\tau_1-2,\tau_2;s_{\tau_1-2})}{u(\tau_1-2,\tau_1;s_{\tau_1-2})-m(\tau_1-2,\tau_1;s_{\tau_1-2})}\right]$$

$$n_0(\tau_1-2;s_{\tau_1-2})$$

$$=\frac{x(\tau_1-1;s_{\tau_1-2}\mathrm{u})-n_1(\tau_1-2;s_{\tau_1-2})P(\tau_1-2,\tau_1;s_{\tau_1-2})u(\tau_1-2,\tau_1;s_{\tau_1-2})}{B(\tau_1-2;s_{\tau_1-3})r(\tau_1-2;s_{\tau_1-2})}$$

$$-\frac{n_2(\tau_1-2;s_{\tau_1-2})P(\tau_1-2,\tau_2;s_{\tau_1-2})u(\tau_1-2,\tau_2;s_{\tau_1-2})}{B(\tau_1-2;s_{\tau_1-3})r(\tau_1-2;s_{\tau_1-2})} \tag{6.32c}$$

DERIVATION OF EXPRESSION (6.32). To simplify the notation, define

$$\begin{aligned}
n_j(\tau_1-2;s_{\tau_1-2}) &\equiv n_j \qquad \text{for } j=0,1,2\\
B(\tau_1-2;s_{\tau_1-3}) &\equiv B\\
P(\tau_1-2,t_j;s_{\tau_1-2}) &\equiv P_j \qquad \text{for } j=1,2\\
r(\tau_1-2;s_{\tau_1-2}) &\equiv r\\
u(\tau_1-2,\tau_j;s_{\tau_1-2}) &\equiv u_j \qquad \text{for } j=1,2\\
m(\tau_1-2,\tau_j;s_{\tau_1-2}) &\equiv m_j \qquad \text{for } j=1,2\\
d(\tau_1-2,\tau_j;s_{\tau_1-2}) &\equiv d_j \qquad \text{for } j=1,2\\
x(\tau_1-1;s_{\tau_1-2}\mathrm{u}) &\equiv x_\mathrm{u}\\
x(\tau_1-1;s_{\tau_1-2}\mathrm{m}) &\equiv x_m\\
x(\tau_1-1;s_{\tau_1-2}\mathrm{d}) &\equiv x_\mathrm{d}
\end{aligned}$$

System (6.31) rewritten is

$$\begin{aligned}
n_0Br+n_1P_1u_1+n_2P_2u_2 &= x_\mathrm{u}\\
n_0Br+n_1P_1m_1+n_2P_2m_2 &= x_\mathrm{m}\\
n_0Br+n_1P_1d_1+n_2P_2d_2 &= x_\mathrm{d}
\end{aligned}$$

We derive the equations in reverse order. First, to obtain (6.32c), take the first equation, divide by Br, and rearrange terms to isolate n_0 on the left side.

Next, subtract the second equation from the first, and the third equation from the second, to get the new system:

$$\begin{aligned}
n_1P_1(u_1-m_1)+n_2P_2(u_2-m_2) &= x_\mathrm{u}-x_\mathrm{m}\\
n_1P_1(m_1-d_1)+n_2P_2(m_2-d_2) &= x_\mathrm{m}-x_\mathrm{d}
\end{aligned}$$

This is two equations in two unknowns. To obtain expression (6.32*b*), take the first equation, divide by $u_1 - m_1$, and rearrange terms. This gives

$$n_1 P_1 = \frac{x_u - x_m}{u_1 - m_1} - n_2 P_2 \frac{u_2 - m_2}{u_1 - m_1}$$

Substitution into the second equation gives

$$\frac{x_u - x_m}{u_1 - m_1}(m_1 - d_1) - n_2 P_2 \frac{u_2 - m_2}{u_1 - m_1}(m_1 - d_1) + n_2 P_2 (m_2 - d_2) = x_m - x_d$$

Algebra yields

$$\begin{aligned} &n_2 P_2((u_1 - m_1)(m_2 - d_2) - (u_2 - m_2)(m_1 - d_1)) \\ &= (x_m - x_d)(u_1 - m_1) - (x_u - x_m)(m_1 - d_1) \end{aligned}$$

Dividing by $P_2((u_1 - m_1)(m_2 - d_2) - (u_2 - m_2)(m_1 - d_1))$ gives the result (6.32*a*). This is nonzero since

$$\begin{bmatrix} 1 & u_1 & u_2 \\ 1 & m_1 & m_2 \\ 1 & d_1 & d_2 \end{bmatrix}$$

is nonsingular, so its determinant is nonzero. ■

The cost of constructing this portfolio at time $\tau_1 - 2$, denoted $x(\tau_1 - 2; s_{\tau_1 - 2})$, is

$$\begin{aligned} x(\tau_1 - 2; s_{\tau_1 - 2}) \equiv\ & n_0(\tau_1 - 2; s_{\tau_1 - 2}) B(\tau_1 - 2; s_{\tau_1 - 3}) \\ & + n_1(\tau_1 - 2; s_{\tau_1 - 2}) P(\tau_1 - 2, \tau_1; s_{\tau_1 - 2}) \\ & + n_2(\tau_1 - 2; s_{\tau_1 - 2}) P(\tau_1 - 2, \tau_2; s_{\tau_1 - 2}) \end{aligned} \tag{6.33}$$

Repeating the above procedure inductively backward gives for an arbitrary time t

$$\begin{aligned} n_2(t; s_t) = \ & \frac{1}{P(t, \tau_2; s_t)} \\ & \times [x(t+1; s_t\text{m}) - x(t+1; s_t\text{d}))(u(t, \tau_1; s_t) - m(t, \tau_1; s_t)) \\ & - (x(t+1; s_t\text{u}) - x(t+1; s_t\text{m}))(m(t, \tau_1; s_t) - d(t, \tau_1; s_t))] \\ & \div [(u(t, \tau_1; s_t) - m(t, \tau_1; s_t))(m(t, \tau_2; s_t) - d(t, \tau_2; s_t)) \\ & - (u(t, \tau_2; s_t) - m(t, \tau_2; s_t))(m(t, \tau_1; s_t) - d(t, \tau_1; s_t))] \end{aligned} \tag{6.34a}$$

$$\begin{aligned} n_1(t, s_t) = & \left[\frac{x(t+1; s_t\text{u}) - x(t+1; s_t\text{m})}{u(t, \tau_1; s_t) - m(t, \tau_1; s_t)} \right] \frac{1}{P(t, \tau_1; s_t)} \\ & - \frac{n_2(t; s_t) P(t, \tau_2; s_t)}{P(t, \tau_1; s_t)} \left[\frac{u(t, \tau_2; s_t) - m(t, \tau_2; s_t)}{u(t, \tau_1; s_t) - m(t, \tau_1; s_t)} \right] \end{aligned} \tag{6.34b}$$

$$n_0(t; s_t) = \frac{1}{B(t; s_{t-1})r(t; s_t)} \times [x(t+1; s_t\text{u}) - n_1(t; s_t)P(t, \tau_1; s_t)u(t, \tau_1; s_t) - n_2(t; s_t)P(t, \tau_2; s_t)u(t, \tau_2; s_t)] \tag{6.34c}$$

The cost of constructing this portfolio at time t is the arbitrage-free price, denoted $x(t; s_t)$, and it is given by

$$x(t; s_t) \equiv n_0(t; s_t)B(t; s_{t-1}) + n_1(t; s_t)P(t, \tau_1; s_t) + n_2(t; s_t)P(t, \tau_2; s_t) \tag{6.35}$$

This construction illustrates that the market is complete by showing that it is possible to generate an arbitrary simple contingent claim at time t using only the τ_1- and τ_2-maturity zero-coupon bonds and the money market account.

2 Risk-Neutral Probabilities

Arbitrage opportunities with respect to the trading strategy set Φ_2 are assumed to be nonexistent in this economy. This section analyzes the implication of this assumption for the stochastic processes exogenously imposed on the zero-coupon bond prices $P(t, \tau_1; s_t)$ and $P(t, \tau_2; s_t)$ and the spot rate process $r(t; s_t)$. This analysis is somewhat different from and more complicated than the analysis for the one-factor economy.

Given that the relevant trading strategies in Φ_2 only involve the money market account, the τ_1-maturity zero-coupon bond, and the τ_2-maturity zero-coupon bond, no arbitrage implies that no security dominates any of the others; i.e.,

$$u(t, \tau_1; s_t) > r(t; s_t) > d(t, \tau_1; s_t) \qquad \text{for all } s_t \text{ and } t < \tau_1 - 1 \tag{6.36a}$$

$$u(t, \tau_2; s_t) > r(t; s_t) > d(t, \tau_2; s_t) \qquad \text{for all } s_t \text{ and } t < \tau_2 - 1 \tag{6.36b}$$

It is not the case that $[u(t, \tau_i; s_t) \geq u(t, \tau_j; s_t)$, $m(t, \tau_i; s_t) \geq m(t, \tau_j; s_t)$, and $d(t, \tau_i; s_t) \geq d(t, \tau_j; s_t)$ for $i \neq j$, $i, j \in \{1, 2\}$, and for all s_t and $t < \tau_1 - 1$ with one inequality strict for some s_t and $t < \tau_1 - 1]$. (6.36c)

Condition (6.36*a*) states that the τ_1-maturity bond neither dominates nor is dominated by the money market account. Condition (6.36*b*) states that the τ_2-maturity bond neither dominates nor is dominated by the money market account. Finally, condition (6.36*c*) says that neither the τ_1-maturity or the τ_2-maturity zero-coupon bond dominates the other.

The proofs of these conditions are straightforward. If one is violated, an arbitrage opportunity in the trading strategy set Φ_2 is available. For example, suppose condition (6.36*c*) is violated; i.e., suppose the return on the τ_1-maturity zero-coupon bond dominates the τ_2-maturity zero-coupon bond at some time and state. The arbitrage opportunity in the trading strategy set Φ_2 is created as follows. Do nothing until the first time the return over the next period on the τ_1-maturity bond dominates that on the τ_2-maturity bond (i.e., the first time expression (6.36*c*) is violated). Then buy one τ_1-maturity bond and finance this position by shorting $P(t, \tau_1)/P(t, \tau_2)$ units of the τ_2-maturity bond. This initial position has zero value. Liquidate this portfolio at the end of the next time period. The value of the τ_1-maturity bond is always enough to cover the short position in the τ_2-maturity bond, generating an arbitrage opportunity. The proofs of conditions (6.36*a–b*) are similar (see expression (6.19) below).

These expressions, along with the nonsingularity condition (4.13), imply that there exists a unique pair of pseudo probabilities $[\pi^{\mathrm{u}}(t; s_t), \pi^{\mathrm{m}}(t; s_t)]$ whose sum is strictly between zero and one such that the following hold:[4]

$$\begin{aligned} r(t; s_t) &= \pi^{\mathrm{u}}(t; s_t)u(t, \tau_1; s_t) + \pi^{\mathrm{m}}(t; s_t)m(t, \tau_1; s_t) \\ &\quad + (1 - \pi^{\mathrm{u}}(t; s_t) - \pi^{\mathrm{m}}(t; s_t))d(t, \tau_1; s_t) \end{aligned} \tag{6.37a}$$

and

$$\begin{aligned} r(t; s_t) &= \pi^{\mathrm{u}}(t; s_t)u(t, \tau_2; s_t) + \pi^{\mathrm{m}}(t; s_t)m(t, \tau_2; s_t) \\ &\quad + (1 - \pi^{\mathrm{u}}(t; s_t) - \pi^{\mathrm{m}}(t; s_t))d(t, \tau_2; s_t) \end{aligned} \tag{6.37b}$$

for all s_t and $t < \tau_1 - 1$. To interpret expression (6.37), we perform some algebra. Dividing expression (6.37) by $r(t; s_t)$ and multiplying it by $P(t, \tau_1; s_t) \div B(t; s_{t-1})$ for (6.37*a*) and by $P(t, \tau_2; s_t)/B(t; s_{t-1})$ for (6.37*b*) give

$$\begin{aligned} \frac{P(t, \tau_i; s_t)}{B(t; s_{t-1})} &= \pi^{\mathrm{u}} \frac{P(t+1, \tau_i; s_t\mathrm{u})}{B(t+1; s_t)} + \pi^{\mathrm{m}}(t; s_t) \frac{P(t+1, \tau_i; s_t\mathrm{m})}{B(t+1; s_t)} \\ &\quad + \left(1 - \pi^{\mathrm{u}}(t; s_t) - \pi^{\mathrm{m}}(t; s_t)\right) \frac{P(t+1, \tau_i; s_t\mathrm{d})}{B(t+1; s_t)} \qquad \text{for } i = 1, 2 \end{aligned} \tag{6.38}$$

Using the expectations operator, we can rewrite this as

$$\frac{P(t, \tau_i; s_t)}{B(t; s_{t-1})} = \tilde{E}_t\left(\frac{P(t+1, \tau_i; s_{t+1})}{B(t+1; s_t)}\right) \qquad \text{for } i = 1, 2 \tag{6.39}$$

where $\tilde{E}_t(\bullet)$ is the time t expectation using the pseudo probabilities $\pi^{\mathrm{u}}(t; s_t)$ and $\pi^{\mathrm{m}}(t; s_t)$. This shows that the discounted τ_1-maturity zero-coupon bond price

[4]This is true since

$$\begin{bmatrix} 1 & u(t, \tau_1; s_t) & u(t, \tau_2; s_t) \\ 1 & m(t, \tau_1; s_t) & m(t, \tau_2; s_t) \\ 1 & d(t, \tau_1; s_t) & d(t, \tau_2; s_t) \end{bmatrix}$$

being nonsingular implies that

$$\begin{bmatrix} u(t, \tau_1; s_t) - d(t, \tau_1; s_t) & m(t, \tau_1; s_t) - d(t, \tau_1; s_t) \\ u(t, \tau_2; s_t) - d(t, \tau_2; s_t) & m(t, \tau_2; s_t) - d(t, \tau_2; s_t) \end{bmatrix}$$

is nonsingular. To see this, just calculate the determinant of each matrix.

is a martingale under the pseudo probabilities. For the τ_1-maturity bond this specializes to

$$P(t, \tau_1; s_t) = \tilde{E}_t\left(\frac{1}{\Pi_{j=t}^{\tau_1 - 1} r(j; s_j)}\right) \tag{6.40}$$

The proof of expression (6.40) is identical to that which generates expression (6.24) from (6.23) and is therefore left to the reader.

For future reference, we write explicit expressions for the pseudo probabilities.

$$\begin{aligned} \pi^{\mathrm{u}}(t; s_t) \\ &= [(r(t; s_t) - d(t, \tau_2; s_t))(m(t, \tau_1; s_t) - d(t, \tau_1; s_t)) \\ &\quad - (r(t; s_t) - d(t, \tau_1; s_t))(m(t, \tau_2; s_t) - d(t, \tau_2; s_t))] \\ &\quad \div [(u(t, \tau_2; s_t) - d(t, \tau_2; s_t))(m(t, \tau_1; s_t) - d(t, \tau_1; s_t)) \\ &\quad - (u(t, \tau_1; s_t) - d(t, \tau_1; s_t))(m(t, \tau_2; s_t) - d(t, \tau_2; s_t))] \end{aligned} \tag{6.41a}$$

$$\begin{aligned} \pi^{\mathrm{m}}(t; s_t) \\ &= [(u(t, \tau_2; s_t) - d(t, \tau_2; s_t))(r(t, \tau_1; s_t) - d(t, \tau_1; s_t)) \\ &\quad - (u(t, \tau_1; s_t) - d(t, \tau_1; s_t))(r(t; s_t) - d(t, \tau_2; s_t))] \\ &\quad \div [(u(t, \tau_2; s_t) - d(t, \tau_2; s_t))(m(t, \tau_1; s_t) - d(t, \tau_1; s_t)) \\ &\quad - (u(t, \tau_1; s_t) - d(t\tau_1; s_t))(m(t, \tau_2; s_t) - d(t, \tau_2; s_t))] \end{aligned} \tag{6.41b}$$

$$\begin{aligned} 1 - \pi^{\mathrm{u}}(t; s_t) - \pi^{\mathrm{m}}(t; s_t) \\ &= [(u(t, \tau_1; s_t) - r(t; s_t))(u(t, \tau_2; s_t) - m(t, \tau_2; s_t)) \\ &\quad - (u(t, \tau_2; s_t) - r(t; s_t))(u(t, \tau_1; s_t) - m(t, \tau_1; s_t))] \\ &\quad \div [(u(t, \tau_2; s_t) - d(t, \tau_2; s_t))(m(t, \tau_1; s_t) - d(t, \tau_1; s_t)) \\ &\quad - (u(t, \tau_1; s_t) - d(t, \tau_1; s_t))(m(t, \tau_2; s_t) - d(t, \tau_2; s_t))] \end{aligned} \tag{6.41c}$$

DERIVATION OF EXPRESSION (6.41). We use the abbreviated notation from the proof of expression (6.32) along with

$$\pi^{\mathrm{u}}(t; s_t) \equiv \pi^{\mathrm{u}}$$

$$\pi^{\mathrm{m}}(t; s_t) \equiv \pi^{\mathrm{m}}$$

The system of linear equations (6.37) can be written

$$r = \pi^{\mathrm{u}} u_1 + \pi^{\mathrm{m}} m_1 + (1 - \pi^{\mathrm{u}} - \pi^{\mathrm{m}}) d_1$$

$$r = \pi^{\mathrm{u}} u_2 + \pi^{\mathrm{m}} m_2 + (1 - \pi^{\mathrm{u}} - \pi^{\mathrm{m}}) d_2$$

Rewritten:

$$r - d_1 = \pi^{\mathrm{u}}(u_1 - d_1) + \pi^{\mathrm{m}}(m_1 - d_1)$$

$$r - d_2 = \pi^{\mathrm{u}}(u_2 - d_2) + \pi^{\mathrm{m}}(m_2 - d_2)$$

Solving the first equation for π^{m} gives

$$\pi^{\mathrm{m}} = \frac{r - d_1}{m_1 - d_1} - \pi^{\mathrm{u}} \frac{u_1 - d_1}{m_1 - d_1} \tag{$*$}$$

Substitution into the second equation and solving for π^{u} gives expression (6.41*a*), i.e.,

$$\pi^{\mathrm{u}} = \frac{(r - d_2)(m_1 - d_1) - (r - d_1)(m_2 - d_2)}{(u_2 - d_2)(m_1 - d_1) - (u_1 - d_1)(m_2 - d_2)}$$

Substitution of π^{u} into (*) and some algebra yield (6.23*b*), i.e.,

$$\pi^{\mathrm{m}} = \frac{(u_2 - d_2)(r - d_1) - (u_1 - d_1)(r - d_2)}{(u_2 - d_2)(m_1 - d_1) - (u_1 - d_1)(m_2 - d_2)}$$

Finally, substitution of π^{u} and π^{m} into $1 - \pi^{\mathrm{u}} - \pi^{\mathrm{m}}$ yields (6.23*c*), i.e.,

$$1 - \pi^{\mathrm{u}} - \pi^{\mathrm{m}} = \frac{(u_1 - r)(u_2 - m_2) - (u_2 - r)(u_1 - m_1)}{(u_2 - d_2)(m_1 - d_1) - (u_1 - d_1)(m_2 - d_2)}$$

■

In summary, no arbitrage with respect to the trading strategy set Φ_2 implies the existence of pseudo probabilities $\pi^{\mathrm{u}}(t; s_t), \pi^{\mathrm{m}}(t; s_t)$ satisfying expression (6.39). The converse of this statement is also true. Similar to the one-factor case, the existence of pseudo probabilities $\pi^{\mathrm{u}}(t; s_t), \pi^{\mathrm{m}}(t; s_t)$ satisfying expression (6.39) implies that there are no arbitrage opportunities with respect to the trading strategy set Φ_2. (The proof is identical to that presented in the appendix to Chapter 6 for the one-factor case and is therefore omitted.) This is an important observation, useful for constructing arbitrage-free evolutions of the zero-coupon bond price curve.

3 Risk-Neutral Valuation

Given a simple contingent claim $x(\mathcal{T}_1 - 1; s_{\mathcal{T}_1 - 1})$ with maturity date $\mathcal{T}_1 - 1$, its arbitrage-free price, denoted $x(0)$, is

$$x(0) \equiv n_0(0) + n_1(0)P(0, \mathcal{T}_1) + n_2(0)P(0, \mathcal{T}_2) \tag{6.42}$$

where $(n_0(t; s_t), n_1(t; s_t)n_2(t; s_t)) \in \Phi_2$ is the self-financing trading strategy that creates the synthetic contingent claim. Such a self-financing trading strategy was constructed in expression (6.34).

Using the risk-neutral probabilities as given in expression (6.31), it can now be shown that expression (6.43) holds:

$$x(0) = \tilde{E}_0\left(\frac{x(\mathcal{T}_1 - 1; s_{\mathcal{T}_1 - 1})}{B(\mathcal{T}_1 - 1; s_{\mathcal{T}_1 - 2})}\right)B(0) \tag{6.43}$$

where $\tilde{E}_0(\bullet)$ is the time 0 expected value using the pseudo probabilities $\pi^{\mathrm{u}}(t; s_t)$ and $\pi^{\mathrm{m}}(t; s_t)$. This is an alternate, but equivalent expression for the value of the contingent claim x. The time 0 value of the contingent claim is seen to be its discounted expected value using the pseudo probabilities. This is the *risk-neutral valuation* formula for calculating arbitrage free values.

DERIVATION OF EXPRESSION (6.43). This derivation uses matrix algebra and is easily generalized to $N \geq 3$ factors. Expression (6.31) can be written (using the notation from the derivation of expression (6.32)) as

$$\begin{bmatrix} r & u_1 & u_2 \\ r & m_1 & m_2 \\ r & d_1 & d_2 \end{bmatrix} \begin{bmatrix} n_0 B \\ n_1 P_1 \\ n_2 P_2 \end{bmatrix} = \begin{bmatrix} x_{\mathrm{u}} \\ x_{\mathrm{m}} \\ x_{\mathrm{d}} \end{bmatrix}$$

Similarly, expression (6.37) can be written as

$$[\pi^{\mathrm{u}} \quad \pi^{\mathrm{m}} \quad \pi^{\mathrm{d}}] \begin{bmatrix} r & u_1 & u_2 \\ r & m_1 & m_2 \\ r & d_1 & d_2 \end{bmatrix} = [r \quad r \quad r]$$

where $\pi^{\mathrm{d}} \equiv 1 - \pi^{\mathrm{u}} - \pi^{\mathrm{m}}$. Now, let

$$U \equiv \begin{bmatrix} r & u_1 & u_2 \\ r & m_1 & m_2 \\ r & d_1 & d_2 \end{bmatrix}$$

Then

$$[\pi^{\mathrm{u}} \quad \pi^{\mathrm{m}} \quad \pi^{\mathrm{d}}] = (r\ r\ r)U^{-1}$$

So

$$[\pi^{\mathrm{u}} \quad \pi^{\mathrm{m}} \quad \pi^{\mathrm{d}}] \begin{bmatrix} x_{\mathrm{u}} \\ x_{\mathrm{m}} \\ x_{\mathrm{d}} \end{bmatrix} = (r\ r\ r)U^{-1}U \begin{bmatrix} n_0 B \\ n_1 P_1 \\ n_2 P_2 \end{bmatrix} = [n_0 B + n_1 P_1 + n_2 P_2]r$$

That is, $(\pi^{\mathrm{u}} x^{\mathrm{u}} + \pi^{\mathrm{m}} x^{\mathrm{m}} + \pi^{\mathrm{d}} x^{\mathrm{d}})/r = n_0 B + n_1 P_1 + n_2 P_2$.

This gives expression (6.43) for time $\tau_1 - 2$. Using the backward-inductive procedure and the law of iterated expectations as in the derivation of expression (6.27) gives the result. ■

Note that the arbitrage-free price of the contingent claim x can be determined using only knowledge of $\{r(0), u(t, t+1; s_t)\}$, $\{P(0, \tau_1), (u(t, \tau_1; s_t), m(t, \tau_1; s_t), d(t, \tau_1; s_t))\}$, and $\{P(0, \tau_2), (u(t, \tau_2; s_t), m(t, \tau_2; s_t), d(t, \tau_2; s_t))\}$. No information regarding the stochastic processes of the other zero-coupon bonds is needed. The extension of expression (6.43) to multiple cash flows and American-type features is identical to that extension in the one-factor economy, and is therefore omitted.

4 Bond Trading Strategies

The purpose of this section is to price the entire zero-coupon bond price curve given (*i*) the prices of two zero-coupon bonds $P(0, \tau_1)$ and $P(0, \tau_2)$ and their stochastic processes $\{(u(t, \tau_1; s_t), m(t, \tau_1; s_t)), d(t, \tau_1); s_t), (u(t, \tau_2; s_t), m(t, \tau_2; s_t), d(t, \tau_2; s_t))\}$, (*ii*) the current spot rate $r(0)$ and its stochastic process $(u(t, t+1; s_t))$, and (*iii*) the assumption of no arbitrage opportunities in the trading strategy set Φ_2.

The distinct maturity discount bonds $T \leq \tau_1 - 1$ can all be viewed as contingent claims (of the simple, European type) and valued using expression (6.42) or (6.43). In this context, the value of a T-maturity zero-coupon bond is

$$P(t,T;s_t) = \tilde{E}_t\left(\frac{1}{\Pi_{j=t}^{T-1} r(j;s_j)}\right)$$

where $\tilde{E}_t(\bullet)$ is expectation using the pseudo probabilities $\pi^{\mathrm{u}}(t;s_t)$ and $\pi^{\mathrm{m}}(t;s_t)$ given in expression (6.41). If the price of the traded T-maturity bond differs from its arbitrage-free price in expression (6.44), an arbitrage opportunity exists.

SECTION C
$N \geq 3$ FACTOR ECONOMIES

The extension of the economy in Section 6.B to $N \geq 3$ factors is straightforward. As long as $N \leq \tau_1 - 1$, the markets are complete with respect to the trading strategy set Φ_N. For each additional factor added, however, one additional zero-coupon bond is needed to form the appropriate trading strategy. Equations (6.39), (6.40), (6.43), and (6.44) generalize to the $N \geq 3$ factor economy with little effort.

SECTION D
COMPUTER EXERCISES

This set of exercises using the Trees software (Chapter 16) should help the reader understand the construction of synthetic zero-coupon bonds.

Run the Trees software, which gives a different spot-rate evolution than in the book. Go to "display," select "term structure," and change the description to "pure discount bond prices." Then, at each node, one gets the vector of zero-coupon bond prices. We are interested in the four-period zero-coupon bond's price at each node.

a. Construct Fig. 6.1 for this bond process by reading the relevant four-period zero-coupon bond prices off the tree. Note that at time 1, the four-period zero-coupon bond only has three time periods remaining until maturity.

b. Construct Fig. 6.2 from the spot-rate tree.

c. Compute the synthetic two-period zero-coupon bond's price by replicating Fig. 6.3. Note that you can check the theoretical values by looking at the two-period zero-coupon bond's price on the vector at each node of the tree.

d. Repeat *(a)*–*(c)* with a downward-sloping initial term structure.

SECTION E
REFERENCES TO CHAPTER 6

[1] Cox, J., and M. Rubinstein, 1985. *Options Markets.* Prentice Hall, Englewood Cliffs, N.J.

[2] Harrison, J. M., and D. M. Kreps, 1970. "Martingales and Arbitrage in Multiperiod Securities Markets." *Journal of Economic Theory* 20, 381–408.

[3] Jarrow, R., and A. Rudd, 1983. *Option Pricing,* Richard D. Irwin, Homewood, Ill.

[4] Jarrow, R., 1995. "Pricing Interest Rate Options." *Finance: Handbook in Operations Research and Management Science*, eds. R. Jarrow, V. Maksimovic, and W. Ziemba. North Holland, Amsterdam.

SECTION F
APPENDIX TO CHAPTER 6

This appendix provides the proof that the existence of pseudo probabilities $\pi(t; s_t)$ satisfying expression (6.23) implies that there are no arbitrage opportunities with respect to the trading strategy set Φ_1.

First, note that $B(t; s_{t-1}) > 0$ for all t, s_{t-1} because

$$r(t; s_t) = \frac{1}{P(t, t+1; s_t)} > 0$$

for all t, s_t.

Suppose there exists $\pi(t; s_t)$ between 0 and 1 satisfying expression (6.23). Suppose also there exists an arbitrage opportunity $(n_0(t; s_t), n_1(t; s_t))$ in Φ_1. We search for a contradiction.

From expression (5.11*b*) and from the fact that $B(t; s_{t-1}) > 0$ for all t, s_{t-1}, we obtain

$$B(\tau_1 - 1; s_{\tau_1-2})\tilde{E}_{\tau_1-1}\left(\frac{1}{B(\tau_1; s_{\tau_1-1})}[n_0(\tau_1 - 1; s_{\tau_1-1})B(\tau_1; s_{\tau_1-1}) + \sum_{j=1}^{K} n_j(\tau_1 - 1; s_{\tau_1-1})P(\tau_1, \tau_j; s_{\tau_1})]\right) > 0$$

But by expression (6.23) this equals

$$n_0(\tau_1 - 1; s_{\tau_1-1})B(\tau_1 - 1; s_{\tau_1-2}) + \sum_{j=1}^{K} n_j(\tau_1 - 1; s_{\tau_1-1})P(\tau_1 - 1, \tau_j; s_{\tau_1-1}) > 0$$

Using the self-financing condition (5.9) gives

$$n_0(\tau_1 - 2; s_{\tau_1-2})B(\tau_1 - 1; s_{\tau_1-2}) + \sum_{j=1}^{K} n_j(\tau_1 - 2; s_{\tau_1-2})P(\tau_1 - 1, \tau_j; s_{\tau_1-1}) > 0$$

Repeating this procedure again by applying $B(\tau_1 - 2; s_{\tau_1-3})\tilde{E}_{\tau_1-2}(\bullet) \div B(\tau_1 - 1; s_{\tau_1-2})$ to the above inequality yields

$$n_0(\tau_1 - 3; s_{\tau_1-3})B(\tau_1 - 2; s_{\tau_1-3}) + \sum_{j=1}^{K} n_j(\tau_1 - 3; s_{\tau_1-3})P(\tau_1 - 2, \tau_j; s_{\tau_1-2}) > 0$$

Continuing backward to time 0 yields

$$n_0(0)B(0) + \sum_{j=1}^{K} n_j(0)P(0, \tau_j) > 0$$

This contradicts expression (5.11a). Therefore, there exist no arbitrage opportunities with respect to Φ_1.

CHAPTER 7

Contingent Claims Valuation—Theory

The previous chapter showed how to determine and take advantage of arbitrage opportunities within the yield curve. That procedure takes as given knowledge of the spot rate (and its evolution) and of the prices (and evolution) of only one bond in a one-factor economy, or two bonds in a two-factor economy, and so forth. This information is used to compute arbitrage-free prices for the entire zero-coupon bond price curve. If the market prices differ, arbitrage opportunities exist. The analysis of Chapter 6 provides the insights necessary to construct bond trading strategies for arbitraging the yield curve.

The purpose of this chapter is different. Its purpose is to price interest rate options given the market prices of the *entire* zero-coupon bond price curve and its stochastic evolution. We do not ascertain whether these zero-coupon bond prices are correct relative to each other, as in arbitraging the yield curve. Rather, the desire is to price options relative to the market prices for the entire zero-coupon bond price curve. We therefore need to impose conditions on the stochastic evolution of the bond price curve so that given the market prices, it is arbitrage-free. Options are priced relative to this evolution.

This change in perspective is dictated by the circumstances surrounding the application. If the initial zero-coupon bond price curve is not taken as given, mispricings observed in interest rate options could be due to mispriced zero-coupon bonds. Trading these zero-coupon bond mispricings using options is an indirect and highly levered strategy. A better approach is to trade these zero-coupon bond mispricings directly, using the bond trading strategies of Chapter 6. The techniques of this chapter, therefore, seek mispricings of interest rate options, relative to the market prices of the entire zero-coupon bond price curve (not just the prices of a few bonds). Arbitrage opportunities discovered in this setting are due to the options themselves.

This chapter emphasizes the theory underlying this methodology, which is decomposed into the one-factor case, the two-factor case, and the $N \geq 3$–factor case. The details of specific applications are postponed to subsequent chapters. For example, Chapter 8 studies coupon bonds and options, Chapter 9 studies forward and futures contracts, Chapter 10 studies swaps, caps, and floors, and Chapter 11 studies interest rate exotics.

SECTION A
THE ONE-FACTOR ECONOMY

Consider the one-factor economy as described in Chapter 4, Section 4.A. We assume that there are no arbitrage opportunities with respect to the largest class of self-financing trading strategies possible Φ_τ. This class of trading strategies uses all the available zero-coupon bonds and the money market account (see Chapter 5, Section 5.A).

Taken as given (exogenous) are the current prices and the stochastic processes for all the zero-coupon bonds, $\{P(0,T)$ for all $0 \leq T \leq \tau$ and $(u(t,T;s_t), d(t,T;s_t))$ for $0 \leq t \leq T \leq \tau$ and for all $s_t\}$. Because these processes are exogenously specified, we need to investigate the restrictions that must be imposed so that they are arbitrage-free. This analysis is pursued below.

1 Complete Markets

The one-factor economy is complete with respect to the trading strategy set Φ_τ. This follows directly from the observation in Chapter 6, Section 6.A.1, that the one-factor economy is complete with respect to the trading strategy set Φ_1. Indeed, if only one zero-coupon bond and the money market account are needed to synthetically construct any contingent claim using Φ_1, then adding more bonds to the trading strategy set (as in Φ_τ) does not alter this conclusion. The advantage of using the larger trading strategy set Φ_τ is that having all zero-coupon bonds trade simultaneously allows the possibility of constructing more complicated portfolios involving multiple zero-coupon bonds.

2 Risk-Neutral Probabilities

Arbitrage opportunities with respect to the trading strategy set Φ_τ are assumed to be nonexistent in this economy. This section analyzes the restrictions that this assumption imposes upon the stochastic processes for the evolution of the *entire* zero-coupon bond price curve. Recall that the assumption of no arbitrage opportunities with respect to the trading strategy set Φ_τ is more restrictive than the assumption of no arbitrage opportunities with respect to the trading strategy set Φ_1. Indeed, the set of self-financing trading strategies with respect to the larger trading strategy set Φ_τ allows the use of all the zero-coupon bonds rather than just the one with maturity τ_1. Consequently, the no-arbitrage restrictions proven earlier with respect to the trading strategy set Φ_1 still apply with respect to the trading strategy set Φ_τ.

Recalling that analysis from Chapter 6, Section 6.A.2, no arbitrage with respect to the trading strategy set Φ_1 (for a given τ_1-maturity zero-coupon bond) implies that there exists a unique pseudo probability $\pi(\text{t}, \tau_1; s_t)$ such that $P(t, \tau_1; s_t)/B(t; s_{t-1})$ is a martingale; i.e.,

$$\frac{P(t, \tau_1; s_t)}{B(t; s_{t-1})} = \pi(t, \tau_1; s_t)\frac{P(t+1, \tau_1; s_t\text{u})}{B(t+1; s_t)} + (1 - \pi(t, \tau_1; s_t))\frac{P(t+1, \tau_1; s_t\text{d})}{B(t+1; s_t)} \tag{7.1a}$$

The form of expression (7.1a) most useful for calculations is

$$P(t, \tau_1; s_t) = \frac{1}{r(t; s_t)}[\pi(t, \tau_1; s_t)P(t+1, \tau_1; s_t\text{u}) + (1 - \pi(t, \tau_1; s_t))P(t+1, \tau_1; s_t\text{d})] \tag{7.1b}$$

The pseudo probabilities are determined by expression (6.25) and are repeated here for convenience:

$$\pi(t, \tau_1; s_t) = \frac{r(t; s_t) - d(t, \tau_1; s_t)}{u(t, \tau_1; s_t) - d(t, \tau_1; s_t)} \tag{7.2a}$$

$$1 - \pi(t, \tau_1; s_t) = \frac{u(t, \tau_1; s_t) - r(t; s_t)}{u(t, \tau_1; s_t) - d(t, \tau_1; s_t)} \tag{7.2b}$$

In expression (7.2) we have made explicit in the notation the dependence of the pseudo probabilities upon the τ_1-maturity zero-coupon bond.

Because all the zero-coupon bonds are available for trade in the set Φ_τ, expression (7.2) must simultaneously hold for every possible τ_1-maturity zero-coupon bond selected, i.e., for all τ_1 such that $0 \le \tau_1 \le \tau$. This argument could not be made if we only used the smaller set of trading strategies Φ_1. Therefore, there exists a unique and potentially different pseudo probability for each zero-coupon bond that makes that zero-coupon bond a martingale (after division by the money market account's value). This condition ensures that there are no arbitrage opportunities between any single zero-coupon bond and the money market account, i.e., that neither of these securities dominates the other. This says nothing, however, about the absence of arbitrage opportunities across zero-coupon bonds of different maturities. These are the restrictions we now seek.

We know that since the market is complete with respect to the trading strategy set Φ_1, it is also complete with respect to the larger trading strategy set Φ_τ. Thus, given the τ-maturity bond and the money market account, we can create a synthetic T-maturity zero-coupon bond of any maturity. No arbitrage with respect to Φ_τ should imply that the traded T-maturity bond equals its arbitrage-free price[1] as defined in Chapter 5, Section 5.C.

To see this argument, let $(n_0(t; s_t), n_\tau(t; s_t) : 0 \leq t \leq \tau_1 - 1)$ be the self-financing trading strategy in the money market account and τ-maturity zero-coupon bond that duplicates the τ_1-maturity zero-coupon bond. The portfolio holdings are given (see expressions (6.11)–(6.18)) by

$$n_0(t; s_t) = \frac{x(t+1; s_t\text{d})u(t,\tau; s_t) - x(t+1; s_t\text{u})d(t,\tau; s_t)}{B(t; s_{t-1})r(t; s_t)[u(t,\tau; s_t) - d(t,\tau; s_t)]} \tag{7.3a}$$

$$n_\tau(t; s_t) = \frac{x(t+1; s_t\text{u}) - x(t+1; s_t\text{d})}{P(t,\tau; s_t)[u(t,\tau; s_t) - d(t,\tau; s_t)]} \tag{7.3b}$$

where

$$x(\tau_1; s_{\tau_1}) \equiv P(\tau_1, \tau_1; s_{\tau_1}) = 1 \qquad \text{for all } s_{\tau_1} \tag{7.3c}$$

and

$$x(t; s_t) = n_0(t; s_t)B(t; s_{t-1}) + n_\tau(t; s_t)P(t,\tau; s_t) \qquad \text{for } 0 \leq t \leq \tau_1 - 1 \tag{7.3d}$$

Given that there are no arbitrage opportunities with respect to Φ_τ, it must be the case that

$$P(t, \tau_1; s_t) = n_0(t; s_t)B(t; s_{t-1}) + n_\tau(t; s_t)P(t,\tau; s_t) \tag{7.4}$$

To prove expression (7.4), we use proof by contradiction. Proof by contradiction works by supposing the contrary to what you want to prove, and then showing that this supposition leads to a contradiction. The logical implication is that it is false to suppose the contrary, so the result is proven. Therefore, to prove expression (7.4), let us suppose the contrary: that is, suppose $P(t, \tau_1; s_t) > n_0(t; s_t)B(t; s_{t-1}) + n_\tau(t; s_t)P(t,\tau; s_t)$ for some t and s_t.

An arbitrage opportunity with respect to Φ_τ can now be constructed. The arbitrage opportunity is as follows. At time 0, start monitoring prices to determine when the violation of expression (7.4) occurs. When it occurs, sell the τ_1-maturity bond, buy $n_\tau(t; s_t)$ units of the τ-maturity bond, and buy $n_0(t; s_t)$ units of the money market account. This generates a strictly positive cash

---

[1]Recall that in Chapter 5, Section 5.C, trading strategies with respect to Φ_1 only involved the τ_1-maturity bond and the money market account. No other zero-coupon bond could be traded. Hence, we *defined* the arbitrage-free price to be expression (5.13). This section, however, uses the assumption of no arbitrage opportunities with respect to Φ_τ to *prove* that expression (5.13) holds.

inflow of $[P(t,\tau_1;s_t) - n_0(t;s_t)B(t;s_{t-1}) - n_\tau(t;s_t)P(t,\tau;s_t)]$ dollars. Invest this additional inflow in the money market account, and roll it over in the money market account until time τ_1. In addition, hold the portfolio that generated this time t cash inflow, expression (7.3), rebalancing $n_0(t;s_t)$ and $n_\tau(t;s_t)$ as required until time τ_1, when it is also liquidated. By construction, this strategy has zero cash flows at time t and a strictly positive cash flow of $[P(t,\tau_1;s_t) - n_0(t;s_t)B(t;s_{t-1}) - n_\tau(t;s_t)P(t,\tau;s_t)]B(\tau_1;s_{\tau-1}) > 0$ dollars at time τ_1. Hence, an arbitrage opportunity has been constructed. But this contradicts the assumption of no arbitrage opportunities. Therefore, $P(t,\tau_1;s_t) \le n_0(t;s_t)B(t;s_{t-1}) + n_\tau(t;s_t)P(t,\tau;s_t)$ must be true. The reverse inequality is proven in an equivalent fashion[2] and is left to the reader as an exercise.

From Chapter 6, Section 6.A.3, expression (6.27), we know that we can rewrite expression (7.4) as

$$\frac{P(t,\tau_1;s_t)}{B(t;s_{t-1})} = \pi(t,\tau;s_t)\frac{P(t+1,\tau_1;s_t\text{u})}{B(t+1;s_t)} + (1-\pi(t,\tau;s_t))\frac{P(t+1,\tau_1;s_t\text{d})}{B(t+1;s_t)} \tag{7.5a}$$

or equivalently,

$$P(t,\tau_1;s_t) = \frac{1}{r(t;s_t)}[\pi(t,\tau;s_t)P(t+1,\tau_1;s_t\text{u}) + (1-\pi(t,\tau;s_t))P(t+1,\tau_1;s_t\text{d})] \tag{7.5b}$$

where $\pi(t,\tau;s_t)$ are the *unique* pseudo probabilities associated with the τ-maturity bond. Expression (7.5) must hold for all $0 \le t < \tau_1 < \tau$ and s_t. But expression (7.1) is also valid. The uniqueness of the pseudo probabilities $\pi(t,\tau_1;s_t)$ in that expression implies that

$$\pi(t,\tau;s_t) = \pi(t,\tau_1;s_t) \qquad \text{for all } \tau_1, t, s_t \qquad \text{such that } 0 \le t \le \tau_1 - 1 \le \tau - 1 \tag{7.6}$$

In words, the pseudo probabilities must be independent of the particular τ_1-maturity bond selected. Consequently, under the assumption of no arbitrage opportunities with respect to Φ_τ, we can go back to our earlier notation $\pi(t;s_t)$ for the pseudo probabilities.

Expression (7.6) can be given an economic interpretation. From expression (7.2*b*), we see that $1-\pi(t,\tau;s_t)$ is a measure of the excess return per unit of risk

[2]This same argument could not have been made if we had used only the smaller set of trading strategies Φ_1. The set Φ_1 does not allow holdings in more than one zero-coupon bond.

provided by the τ-maturity zero-coupon bond. First, the numerator $u(t, \tau; s_t) - r(t; s_t)$ is the excess return provided by the τ-maturity bond above the spot rate in the good state of nature. This is the compensation for bearing the risk of the τ-maturity zero-coupon bond. Second, the denominator, $u(t, \tau; s_t) - d(t, \tau; s_t)$, is a measure of risk, since it measures the spread in returns possible from holding the τ-maturity bond.[3] The ratio, therefore, is a measure of excess return, per unit of risk, for the τ-maturity bond. Another, more analytic justification for this economic interpretation can be found in the appendix to this chapter.

The economic interpretation of condition (7.6) is that, to prevent arbitrage, all zero-coupon bonds must have the same excess return per unit of risk. Otherwise, those zero-coupon bonds with higher excess returns, per unit of risk, are good buys. Those zero-coupon bonds with lower excess returns, per unit of risk, are good sells. Combined, these differences imply that there can be no equilibrium and that these strategies should generate arbitrage profits.

Note that from expression (7.2), expression (7.6) implies that there are cross-restrictions on the parameters in the bond processes $(u(t, T; s_t), d(t, T; s_t))$ across different maturities T. The stochastic processes chosen for the evolution of the zero-coupon bond price curve are not arbitrary, given an initial zero-coupon bond price curve. Rather, the processes must be restricted so that expression (7.6) holds. Otherwise, they would not be arbitrage-free. It is this additional restriction that differentiates the bond-trading strategy techniques of Chapter 6 from the option pricing techniques of Chapter 7. These restrictions will be explored more fully in Chapter 12 below.

In summary, no arbitrage with respect to the trading strategy set Φ_τ for the one-factor economy implies the existence of unique pseudo probabilities $\pi(t, s_t)$ that are independent of any particular zero-coupon bond and are such that $P(t, T; s_t)/B(t, s_{t-1})$ is a martingale for all T-maturity zero-coupon bonds.

The converse of this statement is also true. The existence of pseudo probabilities $\pi(t; s_t)$ that are independent of any particular zero-coupon bond selected and are such that $P(t, T; s_t)/B(t; s_{t-1})$ is a martingale for all T-maturity bonds implies that there are no arbitrage opportunities with respect to the trading strategy set Φ_τ. The proof of this assertion is identical to that contained in the appendix to Chapter 6 and is therefore omitted.

EXAMPLE: ARBITRAGE-FREE ZERO-COUPON BOND PRICE CURVE EVOLUTION. A bond price process evolution that satisfies the restrictions of expression (7.6) is given in Fig. 4.4 of Chapter 4. Using expression (7.2) for an arbitrage

[3] Simple algebra shows that $E_t(P(t+1, \tau; s_{t+1})/P(t, \tau; s_t)) = q_t(s_t)u(t, \tau; s_t) + (1 - q(s_t))d(t, \tau; s_t)$ and $\text{Var}_t(P(t+1, \tau; s_{t+1})/P(t, \tau; s_t)) = q_t(s_t)(1 - q_t(s_t))[u(t, \tau; s_t) - d(t, \tau; s_t)]^2$. Thus, the spread in returns possible from holding the τ-maturity bond is proportional to the bond return's standard derivation. This is another justification for this spread as a risk measure.

maturity τ_1, we see that $\pi(t, \tau_1; s_t) = \frac{1}{2}$ for all $0 \leq t < \tau_1 - 1 \leq \tau - 1$. A sample calculation for $t = 1, s_t = \text{u}$ gives

$$\pi(1, 3; \text{u}) = \frac{1.017606 - 1.015426}{1.019785 - 1.015426} = 0.5 \qquad \text{for the three-period bond}$$

$$\pi(1, 4; \text{u}) = \frac{1.017606 - 1.013754}{1.021455 - 1.013754} = 0.5 \qquad \text{for the four-period bond}$$

The remaining calculations are left to the reader. The satisfaction of condition (7.6) implies that the stochastic process given in Fig. 4.4 is arbitrage-free. ■

3 Risk-Neutral Valuation

The pseudo probabilities given in expression (7.6) are used as in Chapter 6, Section 6.A.3, to price all interest rate–dependent contingent claims. The difference between this calculation and that given in Chapter 6 is that the pseudo probabilities in Chapter 6 depended upon the τ_1-maturity bond's specification and could differ from those given by the τ-maturity bond. Now, however, these probabilities must be identical (as given in expression (7.6)). Given this specification, contingent claims are priced and hedged in an identical fashion as using expression (6.27). This procedure is illustrated in subsequent chapters.

SECTION B
THE TWO-FACTOR ECONOMY

The case of the two-factor economy is almost identical to that of the one-factor economy, so the description of the methodology will be brief. Consider the two-factor economy as described in Chapter 4, Section 4.B. We assume that there are no arbitrage opportunities with respect to the trading strategy set Φ_τ. Taken as given (exogenous) is the stochastic process for all the zero-coupon bonds, $\{P(0, T)$ for all $0 \leq T \leq \tau$ and $(u(t, T; s_t), m(t, T; s_t), d(t, T; s_t))$ for all $0 \leq t \leq T \leq \tau$ and $s_t\}$. The purpose is to price interest rate–dependent contingent claims.

1 Complete Markets

Given that the two-factor economy is complete with respect to the trading strategy set Φ_2 (see Chapter 6, Section 6.A.2), the two-factor economy is complete with respect to the larger trading strategy set Φ_τ. Indeed, the trading strategy set Φ_τ allows the self-financing trading strategies to utilize more zero-coupon bonds, so if the market is complete with respect to the smaller trading strategy set Φ_2, it is complete with respect to the larger trading strategy set Φ_τ.

2 Risk-Neutral Probabilities

The assumption that there are no arbitrage opportunities with respect to the larger trading strategy set Φ_τ implies that there are no arbitrage opportunities with respect to the smaller trading strategy set Φ_2 for all possible pairs of τ_1-maturity and τ_2-maturity zero-coupon bonds selected.

From Chapter 6, Section 6.B.2, this implies that there exists unique pseudo probabilities $\pi^{\mathrm{u}}(t, \tau_1, \tau_2; s_t), \pi^{\mathrm{m}}(t, \tau_1, \tau_2; s_t)$ such that

$$\begin{aligned}\frac{P(t, \tau_i; s_t)}{B(t; s_{t-1})} &= \pi^{\mathrm{u}}(t, \tau_1, \tau_2; s_t)\frac{P(t+1, \tau_i; s_t\mathrm{u})}{B(t+1; s_t)} + \pi^{\mathrm{m}}(t, \tau_1, \tau_2; s_t)\frac{P(t+1, \tau_i; s_t\mathrm{m})}{B(t+1; s_t)} \\ &\quad + \left(1 - \pi^{\mathrm{u}}(t, \tau_1, \tau_2, s_t) - \pi^{\mathrm{m}}(t, \tau_1, \tau_2; s_t)\right)\frac{P(t+1, \tau_i; s_t\mathrm{d})}{B(t+1; s_t)}\end{aligned} \tag{7.7}$$

for $i = 1, 2$, where the dependence on the τ_1- and τ_2-maturity zero-coupon bonds selected is indicated in the notation for the pseudo probabilities. Expression (7.7) guarantees that none of the money market account, the τ_1-maturity zero-coupon bond, nor the τ_2-maturity zero-coupon bond dominates either of the others. But no arbitrage with respect to the larger trading strategy set Φ_τ is stronger.

Because the market is complete with respect to the smaller trading strategy set Φ_2, given the $\tau - 1$–maturity and τ-maturity bonds and the money market account, there exist different self-financing trading strategies that duplicate the τ_1-maturity zero-coupon bond and the τ_2-maturity zero-coupon bond. No arbitrage opportunities with respect to the larger trading strategy set Φ_τ implies that the initial cost of these synthetic zero-coupon bonds equals the market price. The proof is identical to the one used to prove expression (7.4). This, in turn, implies by expression (6.43) that

$$\begin{aligned}&\frac{P(t, \tau_i; s_t)}{B(t; s_{t-1})} \\ &\quad = \pi^{\mathrm{u}}(t, \tau - 1, \tau; s_t)\frac{P(t+1, \tau_i; s_t\mathrm{u})}{B(t+1; s_t)} + \pi^{\mathrm{m}}(t, \tau - 1, \tau; s_t)\frac{P(t+1, \tau_i; s_t\mathrm{m})}{B(t+1; s_t)} \\ &\qquad + \left(1 - \pi^{\mathrm{u}}(t, \tau - 1, \tau, s_t) - \pi^{\mathrm{m}}(t, \tau - 1, \tau; s_t)\right)\frac{P(t+1, \tau_i; s_t\mathrm{d})}{B(t+1; s_t)}\end{aligned} \tag{7.8}$$

for $i = 1, 2$. The distinction between this system and expression (7.7) is the replacement of the pseudo probabilities $\pi^{\mathrm{u}}(t, \tau_1, \tau_2; s_t)$ and $\pi^{\mathrm{m}}(t, \tau_1, \tau_2; s_t)$ by $\pi^{\mathrm{u}}(t, \tau - 1, \tau; s_t)$ and $\pi^{\mathrm{m}}(t, \tau - 1, \tau; s_t)$.

By the uniqueness of the pseudo probabilities $\pi^{\mathrm{u}}(t, \tau_1, \tau_2; s_t)$ and $\pi^{\mathrm{m}}(t, \tau_1, \tau_2; s_t)$ in expression (7.7), we get

$$\pi^{\mathrm{u}}(t, \tau - 1, \tau; s_t) = \pi^{\mathrm{u}}(t, \tau_1, \tau_2; s_t) \tag{7.9a}$$

$$\pi^{\mathrm{m}}(t, \tau - 1, \tau; s_t) = \pi^{\mathrm{m}}(t, \tau_1, \tau_2; s_t) \tag{7.9b}$$

for all s_t and $0 \leq t < \tau_1 - 1 < \tau_2 - 1 \leq \tau - 1$. That is, the pseudo probabilities must be independent of the particular pair of zero-coupon bonds with maturities τ_1 and τ_2 selected.

In summary, no arbitrage with respect to the larger trading strategy set Φ_τ for the two-factor economy implies the existence of unique pseudo probabilities $\pi^{\mathrm{u}}(t; s_t)$, $\pi^{\mathrm{m}}(t; s_t)$, independent of any pair of zero-coupon bonds selected, such that $P(t, T; s_t)/B(t; s_{t-1})$ is a martingale for all T-maturity zero-coupon bonds.

The converse of this statement is also true. The existence of pseudo probabilities $\pi^{\mathrm{u}}(t; s_t)$, $\pi^{\mathrm{m}}(t; s_t)$ independent of any pair of zero-coupon bonds selected, such that $P(t, T; s_t)/B(t; s_{t-1})$ is a martingale for all T-maturity zero-coupon bonds, implies that there are no arbitrage opportunities with respect to the trading strategy set Φ_τ. The proof of this statement mimics the proof contained in the appendix to Chapter 6 and is left to the reader as an exercise.

3 Risk-Neutral Valuation

The pseudo probabilities given in expression (7.9) are used as in Chapter 6, Section 6.B.3, expression (6.43), to price interest rate–dependent contingent claims. The difference between this calculation and that given in Chapter 6 is that the pseudo probabilities in Chapter 6 depended on the τ_1- and τ_2-maturity bonds selected, whereas these do not. The valuation procedure is otherwise identical, and it is illustrated in subsequent chapters.

SECTION C
$N \geq 3$–FACTOR ECONOMIES

The extension of Chapter 7, Section 7.B, to $N \geq 3$ factors is straightforward. Because of the results in Chapter 6, Section 6.C, the markets are complete with respect to the trading strategy set Φ_τ. Furthermore, the same analysis as that above guarantees that no arbitrage with respect to the trading strategy set Φ_τ implies the existence of unique pseudo probabilities, independent of any N-collection of different-maturity zero-coupon bonds selected, such that $P(t, T; s_t)/B(t; s_{t-1})$ is a martingale for all T. Risk-neutral valuation proceeds in the usual fashion.

SECTION D
APPENDIX TO CHAPTER 7

This appendix shows that $\pi(t, T; s_t)$ is a measure of the risk premium for a T-maturity, zero-coupon bond.

The standard measure for the risk premium on the T-maturity zero-coupon bond is given by

$$\phi(t,T;s_t) = \frac{E_t(P(t+1,T;s_t)/P(t,T;s_t)) - r(t;s_t)}{\sqrt{\mathrm{Var}_t}(P(t+1,T;s_T)/P(t,T;s_t))}$$

Simple algebra shows that

$$\frac{E_t(P(t+1,T;s_t))}{P(t,T;s_t)} = q_t(s_t)u(t,T;s_t) + (1-q_t(s_t))d(t,T;s_t)$$

and

$$\begin{aligned}\mathrm{Var}\left(\frac{P(t+1,T;s_t)}{P(t,T;s_t)}\right) &= E\left(\left[\frac{P(t+1,T;s_t)}{P(t,T;s_t)}\right]^2\right) - \left[E\left(\frac{P(t+1,T;s_t)}{P(t,T;s_t))}\right)\right]^2 \\ &= q_t(s_t)(1-q_t(s_t))[u(t,T;s_t) - d(t,T;s_t)]^2\end{aligned}$$

Thus,

$$\begin{aligned}\phi(t,T;s_t) &= \frac{q_t(s_t)u(t,T;s_t) + (1-q_t(s_t))d(t,T;s_t) - r(t;s_t)}{\sqrt{q_t(s_t)(1-q_t(s_t))}[u(t,T;s_t) - d(t,T;s_t)]} \\ &= \frac{\sqrt{q_t(s_t)}}{\sqrt{1-q_t(s_t)}} + \left(\frac{d(t,T;s_t) - r(t,s_t)}{u(t,T;s_t) - d(t,T;s_t)}\right)\left(\frac{1}{\sqrt{q_t(s_t)(1-q_t(s_t))}}\right) \\ &= \frac{\sqrt{q_t(s_t)}}{\sqrt{1-q_t(s_t)}} - \frac{\pi(t,T;s_t)}{\sqrt{q_t(s_t)(1-q_t(s_t))}}\end{aligned}$$

This last expression shows that $\pi(t,T;s_t)$ is linearly related to the risk premium, given that $q_t(s_t)$ is fixed.

Note that the equality of $\pi(t,T;s_t)$ across all T holds if and only if $\phi(t,T;s_t)$ is equal across all T. This completes the derivation.

CHAPTER 8

Coupon Bonds and Options

Chapter 7 presented the general theory for valuing contingent claims written against the term structure of interest rates. This chapter and the next three illustrate this procedure by valuing various contingent claims. In this chapter we study coupon bonds, bond options, and callable coupon bonds.

Section 8.A analyzes coupon bonds from the perspective of the arbitrage-free pricing methodology. Without specifying an evolution for the term structure of interest rates, it shows that a coupon bond is equivalent to a portfolio of zero-coupon bonds. Specifying a particular evolution for the term structure allows a more refined hedging analysis. It is shown that in a one-factor model a coupon bond can be hedged with one zero-coupon bond, in a two-factor model a coupon bond can be hedged with two zero-coupon bonds, and so forth. Examples are provided to illustrate these results.

Section 8.B studies the traditional coupon bond risk measures of duration (modified duration) and convexity. The limitations and shortcomings of these traditional measures relative to the arbitrage-free pricing methodology are presented herein. It is shown that modified duration is a valid risk measure for bonds only if the evolution of the yield curve for zero-coupon bonds experiences parallel shifts. Convexity is an incomplete adjustment for larger parallel shifts in the yield curve. The next two sections study various types of options on bonds. Section 8.C investigates European options, and Section 8.D analyzes American options. These financial securities illustrate the full power of the technology developed in Chapter 7. Examples are provided.

Finally, Section 8.E values coupon bonds with call provisions. All Treasury bonds issued prior to 1985 are callable in the last five years of their life (see Chapter 2). Without specifying an evolution for the term structure of interest rates, it is shown that a callable coupon bond is equivalent to an ordinary coupon bond plus a written American call option on the bond. Specifying a particular term-structure model allows for a complete hedging analysis.

SECTION A
COUPON BONDS

United States government notes and bonds are coupon-bearing (see Chapter 2), and some are callable. This section studies the arbitrage-free pricing of the noncallable coupon bonds. The valuation method presented is independent of the particular evolution of the term structure of interest rates selected; in particular, it does not depend on the number or specification of the factors in the economy, either one, two, or three factors.

We define a *coupon bond* to be a sequence of certain cash flows $C_1, C_2, \ldots, C_T$ at times $0 \leq 1 \leq 2 \leq \cdots \leq T \leq \tau$. Usually, the first $T - 1$ payments represent a coupon, and the last payment, at time T, represents a coupon plus principal.

Using risk-neutral valuation, the arbitrage-free price (see expression (6.28) in Chapter 6) of this coupon bond at time t under state s_t, denoted $\mathcal{B}(t; s_t)$, is

$$\mathcal{B}(t; s_t) = \sum_{i=t+1}^{T} \tilde{E}_t\left(\frac{C_i}{B(i, s_{i-1})}\right) B(t; s_{t-1}) \tag{8.1}$$

where $\tilde{E}_t(\bullet)$ is the time t expected value using the pseudo probabilities given by either expression (6.25) in the one-factor economy or expression (6.41) in the two-factor economy.

The summation index starts at $t + 1$, which is the first coupon payment occurring after time t. By construction, the price of the coupon bond, $\mathcal{B}(t; s_t)$, is forward-looking. It represents the present value of all future cash flows. $\mathcal{B}(t; s_t)$ is the bond's price ex-coupon. Its value does not include the coupon payment made at time t, C_t. Time t has the interpretation of being the coupon's ex-date.

Since the ith coupon payment C_i is nonrandom, using either expression (6.30) or (6.44) we can rewrite formula (8.1) as

$$\mathcal{B}(t; s_t) = \sum_{i=t+1}^{T} C_i P(t, i; s_t) \tag{8.2}$$

The coupon bond is seen to be equivalent to a portfolio of zero-coupon bonds; in particular it consists of C_i zero-coupon bonds maturing at times $i = t + 1, \ldots, T$. If the coupon bond's price differed from expression (8.2), an arbitrage opportunity with respect to the trading strategy set Φ_τ could be constructed. For example, if $\mathcal{B}(t; s_t)$ exceeded the right side of expression (8.2), one could sell

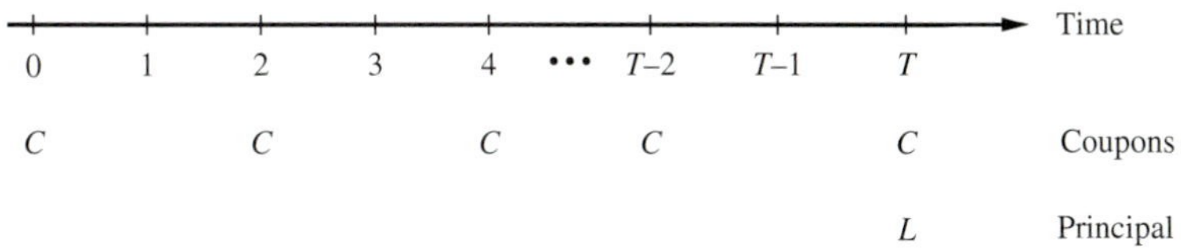

TABLE 8.1
The cash flow to a typical coupon bond.

the coupon bond short at time t and buy C_i zero-coupon bonds maturing at time i for each $i = t+1, \ldots, T$. Holding this portfolio until time T generates an arbitrage opportunity.

It is instructive to investigate a typical coupon bond with cash flows as given in Table 8.1. This typical bond has a coupon payment of C dollars paid every other period, at the times $t, t+2, t+4, \ldots, T-2, T$. For example, if each period corresponds to a quarter of a year, the coupons in Table 8.1 are paid semiannually for $(T-t)/4$ years. At the maturity date of the bond, time T, the principal of L dollars is also paid.

For the typical coupon bond, the bond's price in expression (8.2) can be rewritten in a simplified fashion as

$$\mathcal{B}(t; s_t) = \sum_{i=1}^{(T-t)/2} CP(t, t+2i; s_t) + LP(t, T; s_t) \tag{8.3}$$

This expression assumes that a coupon payment occurred at time t and it represents the bond's arbitrage-free price, ex-coupon, at time t.

Recall from Chapter 2 that the market convention in buying and selling bonds is to pay a quoted price plus accrued interest (because we are in frictionless markets, the ask price equals the bid price, which equals the quoted price). We next discuss how $\mathcal{B}(t; s_t)$ relates to the bond's quoted price. The relation is straightforward. To be arbitrage-free, the price paid for the coupon bond must equal $\mathcal{B}(t; s_t)$. That is, quoted price + accrued interest $= \mathcal{B}(t; s_t)$.

For a coupon-payment date t (the ex-date), accrued interest equals zero, so the quoted price equals $\mathcal{B}(t; s_t)$. For a date t between coupon payments, the accrued interest equals $C/2$ for the typical bond in Table 8.1,[1] so the quoted price $+C/2 = \mathcal{B}(t; s_t)$; i.e., quoted price $= \mathcal{B}(t; s_t) - C/2$. Of course, if more dates fall between the coupon payment dates than illustrated in Table 8.1, the accrued interest calculation must be modified accordingly (in a prorated fashion).[2]

[1]The coupon bond's ask yield as defined in Chapter 2 is based on $\mathcal{B}(t; s_t) - C/2$, the (ask) quoted price.

[2]For example, if there are two dates between coupon payments, the accrued interest is either $C/3$ (at the first noncoupon time) or $2C/3$ (at the second noncoupon time).

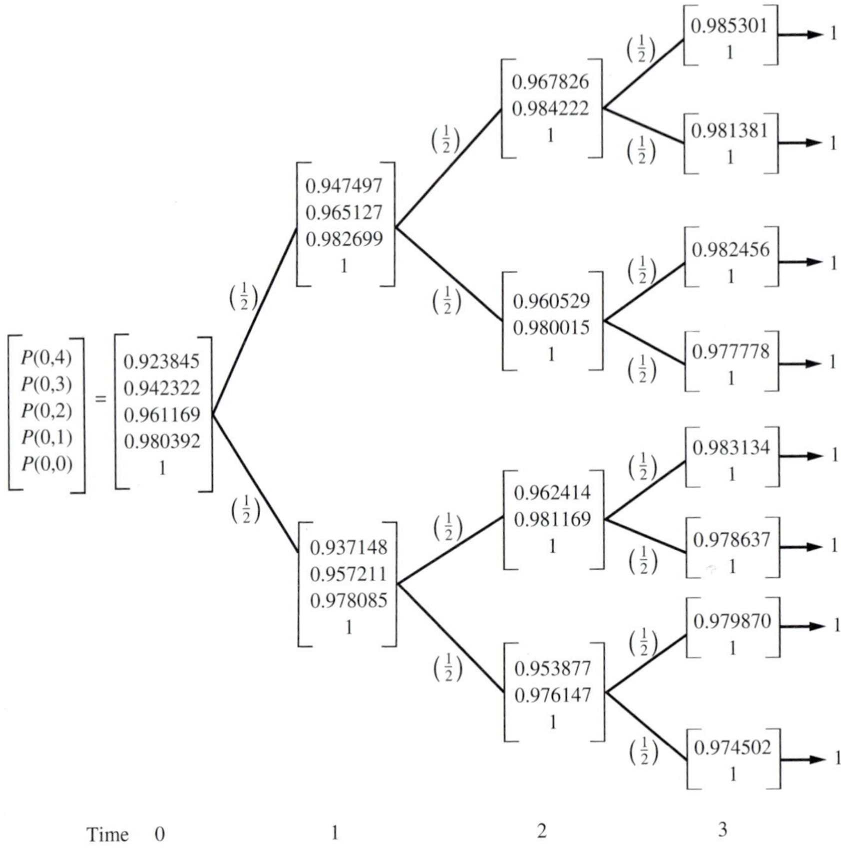

FIGURE 8.1
A one-factor bond price curve evolution; pseudo probabilities are in parentheses along the branches.

EXAMPLE: COUPON BOND CALCULATION. To illustrate this calculation, we use the zero-coupon bond price curve evolution of Fig. 4.4, repeated here for convenience as Fig. 8.1. This stochastic process is arbitrage-free because the pseudo probability calculated for each maturity zero-coupon bond equals $\frac{1}{2}$ and satisfies expression (7.6). These pseudo probabilities appear along the branches of the tree. In Fig. 8.2 are provided, for easy reference, the money market account process and the spot rate process.

Consider a coupon bond whose cash flows are as given in Table 8.2. This coupon bond pays five dollars every other period, with a principal amount of 100 dollars paid at time 4. Using expression (8.2), the value of this coupon bond at time 0, ex-coupon, is

$$\begin{aligned}\mathcal{B}(0) &= 5P(0,2) + 105P(0,4)\\ &= 5[0.961169] + 105[0.923845]\\ &= 101.8096\end{aligned}$$

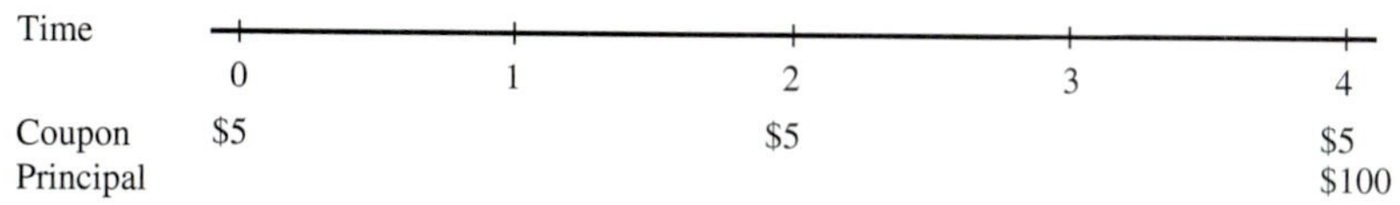

Time	0	1	2	3	4
Coupon	\$5		\$5		\$5
Principal					\$100

TABLE 8.2
An example of the cash flow to a coupon bond

If the market price for the coupon bond differed, an arbitrage opportunity would exist. For example, if the market price of this coupon bond were 102.000, then an arbitrage opportunity is represented by (*i*) shorting and holding until maturity the coupon bond, (*ii*) buying and holding until maturity five units of the two-period zero-coupon bond, and (*iii*) buying and holding until maturity 105 units of the four-period zero-coupon bond. The initial position brings in 102–101.8096 dollar. Subsequently, the cash flows to the short coupon bond are satisfied by the cash flows from the zero-coupon bond portfolio, leaving no further obligation.

The evolution of the coupon bond's value across time is provided in Fig. 8.3. The calculations for the remaining states in times 1 and 2 utilize expression (8.3), and they are left to the reader as an exercise. ■

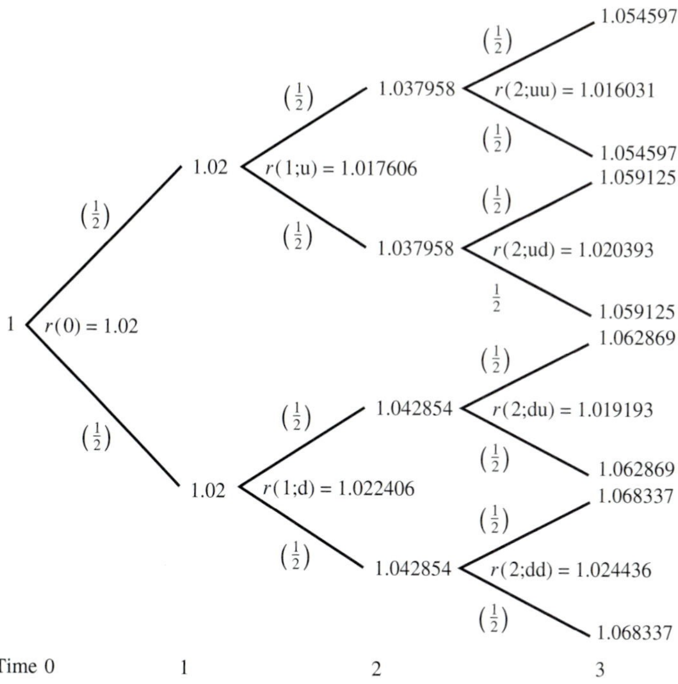

FIGURE 8.2
The money market account process and the spot rate process implied by Fig. 8.1; pseudo probabilities lie along the branches.

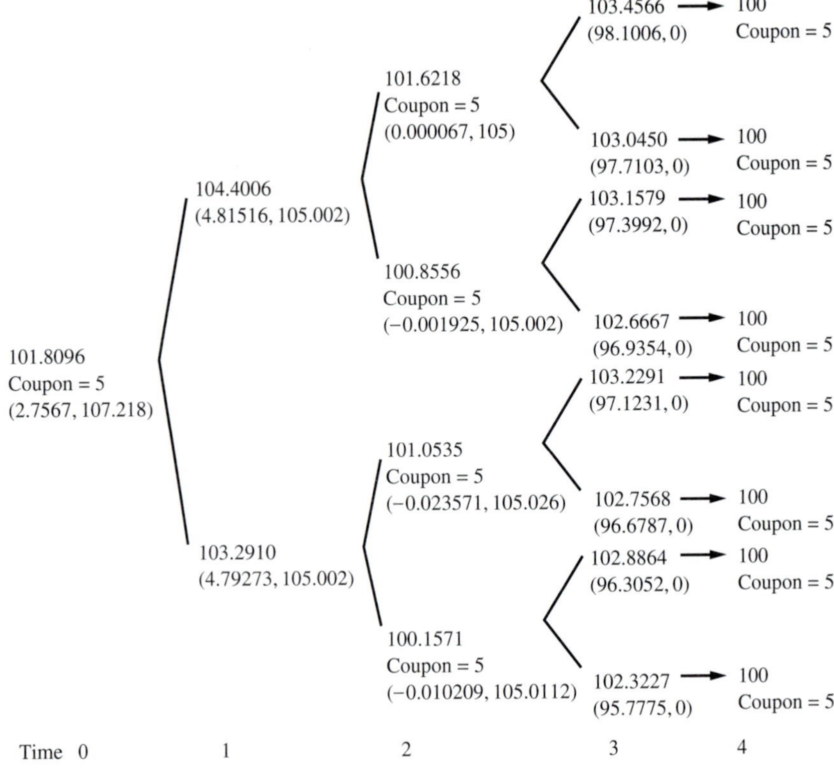

FIGURE 8.3
The evolution of the coupon bond's price for the example in the Table 8.2. The coupon payment at each date is indicated by the nodes. The synthetic coupon-bond portfolio positions $(n_0(t; s_t), n_1(t; s_t))$ in the money market account and four-period zero-coupon bond are given under each node.

The above arbitrage-free pricing technique did not depend on a particular evolution of the term structure of interest rates. A synthetic coupon bond is constructed via a buy and hold strategy involving a portfolio of zero-coupon bonds. Zero-coupon bonds are needed for each date on which a cash payment to the coupon bond is made. Given an explicit representation of the evolution of the term structure, however, fewer zero-coupon bonds can be used to construct a synthetic coupon bond. We illustrate this refinement through an example.

EXAMPLE: SYNTHETIC COUPON BOND CONSTRUCTION IN A ONE-FACTOR MODEL. To illustrate the synthetic construction of a coupon bond using only one zero-coupon bond, we consider the coupon bond in Table 8.2 under the one-factor term structure evolution given in Figs. 8.1 and 8.2.

We want to construct the coupon bond using a self-financing trading in the four-period zero-coupon bond $(n_1(t; s_t))$ and the money market account $(n_0(t; s_t))$.

We use expression (6.12) of Chapter 6 and the self-financing condition (6.13). The calculations are as follows.

At time 3 there is only one zero-coupon bond trading, the four-period zero. It is used to construct the money market account. Thus we can invest in either the four-period zero or the money market account (since both are identical). We choose, arbitrarily, the money market account:

Time 3, state uuu:

$$n_1(3; \text{uuu}) = 0$$

$$n_0(3; \text{uuu}) = \frac{\mathcal{B}(3; \text{uuu}) - n_1(3; \text{uuu})}{B(3; \text{uu})} = \frac{103.4566}{1.054697} = 98.1006$$

Time 3, state uud:

$$n_1(3; \text{uud}) = 0$$

$$n_0(3; \text{uud}) = \frac{\mathcal{B}(3; \text{uud}) - n_1(3; \text{uud})}{B(3; \text{uu})} = \frac{103.0450}{1.054597} = 97.7103$$

Time 3, state udu:

$$n_1(3; \text{udu}) = 0$$

$$n_0(3; \text{udu}) = \frac{\mathcal{B}(3; \text{udu}) - n_1(3; \text{udu})}{B(3; \text{ud})} = \frac{103.1579}{1.059125} = 97.3992$$

Time 3, state udd:

$$n_1(3; \text{udd}) = 0$$

$$n_0(3; \text{udd}) = \frac{\mathcal{B}(3; \text{udd}) - n_1(3; \text{udd})}{B(3; \text{ud})} = \frac{102.6667}{1.059125} = 96.9354$$

Time 3, state duu:

$$n_1(3; \text{duu}) = 0$$

$$n_0(3; \text{duu}) = \frac{\mathcal{B}(3; \text{duu}) - n_1(3; \text{duu})}{B(3; \text{du})} = \frac{103.2291}{1.062869} = 97.1231$$

Time 3, state dud:

$$n_1(3; \text{dud}) = 0$$

$$n_0(3; \text{dud}) = \frac{\mathcal{B}(3; \text{dud}) - n_1(3; \text{dud})}{B(3; \text{du})}$$

$$= \frac{102.7568}{1.062869} = 96.6787$$

Time 3, state ddu:

$$n_1(3; \text{ddu}) = 0$$

$$n_0(3; \text{ddu}) = \frac{\mathcal{B}(3; \text{ddu}) - n_1(3; \text{ddu})}{B(3; \text{dd})}$$

$$= \frac{102.8864}{1.068337} = 96.3052$$

Time 3, state ddd:

$$n_1(3; \text{ddd}) = 0$$

$$n_0(3; \text{ddd}) = \frac{\mathcal{B}(3; \text{ddd}) - n_1(3; \text{ddd})}{B(3; \text{dd})}$$

$$= \frac{102.3227}{1.068337} = 95.7775$$

Moving back to time 2, we choose the following:

Time 2, state uu

$$n_1(2; \text{uu}) = \frac{\mathcal{B}(3; \text{uuu}) - \mathcal{B}(3; \text{uud})}{P(3,4; \text{uuu}) - P(3,4; \text{uud})}$$

$$= \frac{103.4566 - 103.0450}{0.985301 - 0.981381} = 105$$

$$n_0(2; \text{uu}) = \frac{\mathcal{B}(2; \text{uu}) - n_1(2; \text{uu})P(2,4; \text{uu})}{B(2; \text{u})}$$

$$= \frac{101.6218 - (105)0.967826}{1.037958}$$

$$= 0.000067$$

Time 2, state ud:

$$n_1(2; \text{ud}) = \frac{\mathcal{B}(3; \text{udu}) - \mathcal{B}(3; \text{udd})}{P(3,4; \text{udu}) - P(3,4; \text{udd})}$$

$$= \frac{103.1579 - 102.6667}{0.982456 - 0.977778} = 105.002$$

$$n_0(2;\mathrm{ud}) = \frac{\mathcal{B}(2;\mathrm{ud}) - n_1(2;\mathrm{ud})P(2,4;\mathrm{ud})}{B(2;\mathrm{u})}$$

$$= \frac{100.8556 - 105.002(0.960529)}{1.037958}$$

$$= -0.001925$$

Time 2, state du:

$$n_1(2;\mathrm{du}) = \frac{\mathcal{B}(3;\mathrm{duu}) - \mathcal{B}(3;\mathrm{dud})}{P(3,4;\mathrm{duu}) - P(3,4;\mathrm{dud})}$$

$$= \frac{103.2291 - 102.7568}{0.983134 - 0.978637} = 105.026$$

$$n_0(2;\mathrm{du}) = \frac{\mathcal{B}(2;\mathrm{du}) - n_1(2;\mathrm{du})P(2,4;\mathrm{du})}{B(2;\mathrm{d})}$$

$$= \frac{101.0535 - 105.026(0.962414)}{1.042854}$$

$$= -0.023571$$

Time 2, state dd:

$$n_1(2;\mathrm{dd}) = \frac{\mathcal{B}(3;\mathrm{ddu}) - \mathcal{B}(3;\mathrm{ddd})}{P(3,4;\mathrm{ddu}) - P(3,4;\mathrm{ddd})}$$

$$= \frac{102.8864 - 102.3227}{0.979870 - 0.974502} = 105.0112$$

$$n_0(2;\mathrm{dd}) = \frac{\mathcal{B}(2;\mathrm{dd}) - n_1(2;\mathrm{dd})P(2,4;\mathrm{dd})}{B(2;\mathrm{d})}$$

$$= \frac{100.1571 - 105.0112(0.953877)}{1.042854}$$

$$= -0.010209$$

Moving back to time 1, we get

Time 1, state u:

$$n_1(1;\mathrm{u}) = \frac{[\mathcal{B}(2;\mathrm{uu}) + C] - [\mathcal{B}(2;\mathrm{ud}) + C]}{P(2,4;\mathrm{uu}) - P(2,4;\mathrm{ud})}$$

$$= \frac{(101.6218 + 5) - (100.8556 + 5)}{0.967826 - 0.960529} = 105.002$$

$$n_0(1;\mathrm{u}) = \frac{\mathcal{B}(1;\mathrm{u}) - n_1(1;\mathrm{u})P(1,4;\mathrm{u})}{B(1)}$$

$$= \frac{104.4006 - 105.002(0.947497)}{1.02}$$

$$= 4.81516$$

Note that we need to replicate the bond's price plus coupon at time 2 across the up and down states. The numerator in $n_1(1;\mathrm{u})$ reflects this joint cash flow.

Time 1, state d:

$$n_1(1;\mathrm{d}) = \frac{[\mathcal{B}(2;\mathrm{du}) + C] - [\mathcal{B}(2;\mathrm{dd}) + C]}{P(2,4;\mathrm{du}) - P(2,4;\mathrm{dd})}$$

$$= \frac{(101.0535 + 5) - (100.1571 + 5)}{0.962414 - 0.953877} = 105.002$$

$$n_0(1;\mathrm{d}) = \frac{\mathcal{B}(1;\mathrm{d}) - n_1(1;\mathrm{d})P(1,4;\mathrm{d})}{B(1)}$$

$$= \frac{103.291 - 105.002(0.937148)}{1.02}$$

$$= 4.79273$$

Finally, at time 0:

$$n_1(0) = \frac{\mathcal{B}(1;\mathrm{u}) - \mathcal{B}(1;\mathrm{d})}{P(1,4;\mathrm{u}) - P(1,4;\mathrm{d})}$$

$$= \frac{104.4006 - 103.291}{0.947497 - 0.937148} = \frac{1.1096}{0.010349} = 107.218$$

$$n_0(0) = \frac{\mathcal{B}(0) - n_1(0)P(0,4)}{B(0)}$$

$$= \frac{101.8096 - (107.218)(0.923845)}{1}$$

$$= 2.75670$$

The cost of constructing this synthetic coupon bond at time 0 is

$$n_0(0) + n_1(0)P(0,4) = 2.7567 + 107.218(0.923845) = 101.8096$$

which is the arbitrage-free price for the coupon bond at time 0.

This synthetic construction is more complicated than the buy and hold strategy discussed previously. This synthetic construction involving the four-period zero and the money market account involves rebalancing the portfolio across time. The rebalancing, however, is self-financing. For example, at time 0 we hold $n_0(0) = 2.7567$ units of the money market account and $n_1(0) = 107.218$ shares of the four-period zero. If at time 1 we move to the up state, we enter time 1, state u with $n_0(0)B(1;\mathrm{u}) + n_1(0)P(1;\mathrm{u}) = 2.7567(1.02) + 107.218(0.947497) = 104.4006$ dollars. We rebalance to $n_0(1;\mathrm{u}) = 4.81516$ units of the money market account and $n_1(1;\mathrm{u}) = 105.002$ shares of the four-period zero-coupon bond at a cost of $n_0(1;\mathrm{u})B(1;\mathrm{u}) + n_1(1;\mathrm{u})P(1,4;\mathrm{u}) = 4.81516(1.02) + 105.002(0.947497) = 104.4006$ dollars. This is exactly the value of our portfolio before rebalancing. Thus, the trading strategy is self-financing. ■

SECTION B
TRADITIONAL RISK MEASURES

This section studies the traditional techniques used to analyze and measure coupon bond risk: bond yields, duration (modified duration), and convexity. In doing so, it clarifies their shortcomings relative to the procedures presented in the previous section.

Consider the typical coupon bond of Table 8.1, whose coupon payment is C dollars every other period until time T, when it has a principal payment of L dollars. The time t value of this coupon bond is $\mathcal{B}(t; s_t)$. We point out that a zero-coupon bond is a special case of this definition. It is the case in which the coupon payment is set identically to zero ($C \equiv 0$) and the principal is set equal to unity ($L \equiv 1$).

Define the *bond's yield*, $Y(t; s_t)$, as one plus its percentage internal rate of return; i.e., $Y(t; s_t)$ is defined by the expression

$$\mathcal{B}(t; s_t) = \sum_{i=1}^{(T-t)/2} \frac{C}{Y(t; s_t)^{2i}} + \frac{L}{Y(t; s_t)^{(T-t)}} \tag{8.4}$$

This expression assumes that time t is a coupon payment date. We can think of the bond's yield, $Y(t; s_t)$, as a stochastic process changing randomly through time. To understand the percentage change in the bond's price for a small change in the bond's yield, we compute

$$\frac{1}{\mathcal{B}(t; s_t)} \frac{\partial \mathcal{B}(t; s_t)}{\partial Y(t; s_t)} = -\frac{\left(\sum_{i=1}^{(T-t)/2} 2iC/Y(t; s_t)^{2i} + (T-t)L/Y(t; s_t)^{(T-t)}\right)}{Y(t; s_t)\mathcal{B}(t; s_t)} \tag{8.5}$$

The coefficient on the right side is related to *duration*, denoted by Dur(t):

$$\text{Dur}(t) \equiv \frac{1}{\mathcal{B}(t; s_t)} \left[\sum_{i=1}^{(T-t)/2} \frac{2iC}{Y(t; s_t)^{2i}} + \frac{(T-t)L}{Y(t; s_t)^{T-t)}} \right] \tag{8.6}$$

Duration is a measure of the average life of the bond, such that the date of the ith payment is weighted by $(C/Y(t; s_t)^{2i})/\mathcal{B}(t; s_t)$, a number between 0 and 1. Another measure is also in common use, called *modified duration*. It is the duration divided by the coupon bond's yield, i.e.,

$$\text{MDur}(t) \equiv \frac{\text{Dur}(t)}{Y(t; s_t)} \tag{8.7}$$

Given a change in time $(t, t+1)$, the bond's yield changes by $\Delta Y(t; s_t) \equiv Y(t+1; s_{t+1}) - Y(t; s_t)$, and we can write the implied change in the bond's price $\Delta\mathcal{B}(t; s_t) \equiv \mathcal{B}(t+1; s_{t+1}) - \mathcal{B}(t; s_t)$ by

$$\Delta\mathcal{B}(t;s_t) \approx \frac{\partial\mathcal{B}(t;s_t)}{\partial t} + \frac{\partial\mathcal{B}(t;s_t)}{\partial Y(t;s_t)}\Delta Y(t;s_t)$$

$$= \frac{\partial\mathcal{B}(t;s_t)}{\partial t} - \text{MDur}(t)\mathcal{B}(t;s_t)\Delta Y(t;s_t) \tag{8.8}$$

The first term on the right side of expression (8.8) is the time decay, a known, deterministic change in the bond's price. The second term on the right side of expression (8.8) is random. As the bond's yield increases, the bond's price declines by the modified duration multiplied by the bond's price multiplied by the change in the bond's yield. This expression is an approximation involving only the first-order terms of the Taylor series expansion[3] of $\mathcal{B}(t;s_t)$ around t and $Y(t;s_t)$.

Consider a portfolio consisting of two coupon bonds, one denoted with a subscript a the other with a subscript b. Let the value of the portfolio be denoted

$$V(t;s_t) = \mathcal{B}_{\text{a}}(t;s_t) + n_b\mathcal{B}_{\text{b}}(t;s_t) \tag{8.9}$$

where $n_{\text{a}} = 1$ is the number of shares of bond a and n_{b} is the number of shares of bond b.

Over a change in time, the change in the portfolio's value,

$$\Delta V(t;s_t) \equiv V(t+1;s_{t+1}) - V(t;s_t)$$

is

$$\begin{aligned}\Delta V(t;s_t) &\approx \frac{\partial\mathcal{B}_{\text{a}}(t;s_t)}{\partial t} + n_{\text{b}}\frac{\partial\mathcal{B}_{\text{b}}(t;s_t)}{\partial t} \\ &\quad - \text{MDur}_{\text{a}}(t)\mathcal{B}_{\text{a}}(t;s_t)\Delta Y^{\text{a}}(t;s_t) - n_{\text{b}}\text{MDur}_{\text{b}}(t)\mathcal{B}_{\text{b}}(t;s_t)\Delta Y^{\text{b}}(t;s_t)\end{aligned} \tag{8.10}$$

Letting $n_{\text{b}} \equiv -\text{MDur}_{\text{a}}(t)\mathcal{B}_{\text{a}}(t;s_t)/\text{MDur}_{\text{b}}(t)\mathcal{B}_{\text{b}}(t;s_t)$, we have

$$\Delta V(t;s_t) \approx \frac{\partial\mathcal{B}_{\text{a}}(t;s_t)}{\partial t} + n_{\text{b}}\frac{\partial\mathcal{B}_{\text{b}}(t;s_t)}{\partial t}$$

for all s_{t+1} if and only if (8.11)

$$\Delta Y^{\text{a}}(t;s_t) = \Delta Y^{\text{b}}(t;s_t) \text{ for all } s_{t+1}$$

---

[3] Given a function $f(t,x)$ that is infinitely differentiable, the Taylor series expansion around t_0, x_0 is

$$\begin{aligned}f(t,x) &= f(t_0,x_0) + \frac{\partial f(t_0,x_0)}{\partial t}(t-t_0) + \frac{\partial f(t_0,x_0)}{\partial x}(x-x_0) \\ &\quad + \frac{1}{2}\frac{\partial^2 f(t_0,x_0)}{\partial x^2}(x-x_0)^2 + \frac{1}{2}\frac{\partial^2 f(t_0,x_0)}{\partial t^2}(t-t_0)^2 + \cdots\end{aligned}$$

Defining $1 \equiv t - t_0$ gives the expansion used in expression (8.8).

This says that a bond portfolio is hedged against random changes in yields using modified duration as a risk measure if and only if the change in the bond's yields is identical for all possible states s_{t+1}.

In summary, if expression (8.8) holds, modified duration is a valid risk measure only if bond yields shift in a parallel fashion for all possible pairs of bonds (a, b). However, because zero-coupon bonds are special cases of this result, we have shown that modified duration is a valid risk measure only if there is a parallel shift in the zero-coupon bond's yield curve, i.e., only if

$$\Delta y(t, T; s_t) = \Delta y(t, \tau; s_t) \qquad \text{for all } T, \tau, s_{t+1} \tag{8.12}$$

where $\Delta y(t, T; s_t) \equiv y(t+1, T; s_{t+1}) - y(t, T; s_t)$ and $y(t, T; s_t)$ is as defined in Chapter 3, expression (3.1).

Unfortunately, parallel shifts in the zero-coupon bond's yield curve are unlikely events, making modified duration a poor risk measure. In addition, even under parallel shifts, it is only valid given expression (8.8). Expression (8.8) is a good approximation only for *small changes in yields*, because expression (8.8) is generated by using the first-order terms of the Taylor series expansion. The omitted terms are small only if $\Delta Y(t; s_t)$ is small.

In contrast, the delta-approach construction of a synthetic coupon bond introduced in the previous section is correct given any prespecified evolution for the zero-coupon bond price curve. The evolution of the zero-coupon bond price curve can be selected to match the observed or actual evolution. To illustrate these facts, consider the following example, based on the term structure evolution given in Fig. 8.1.

EXAMPLE: ERROR IN MODIFIED DURATION HEDGING. Let the two bonds (a, b) in the portfolio be zero-coupon bonds of various maturities; i.e.,

$$\mathcal{B}_{\mathrm{a}}(0) = P(0, 2) = 0.961169$$

$$\mathcal{B}_{\mathrm{b}}(0) = P(0, 4) = 0.923845$$

From Chapter 6, Fig. 6.3 we know that a hedged portfolio involving these two zeros can only be obtained using

$$n_{\mathrm{a}} = 1$$

$$n_{\mathrm{b}} = -\left(\frac{P(1, 2; \mathrm{u}) - P(1, 2; \mathrm{d})}{P(1, 4; \mathrm{u}) - P(1, 4; \mathrm{d})}\right) = -0.445835$$

We now calculate the hedge based on modified duration. For this example it is easy to show that

$$\mathrm{Dur}_{\mathrm{a}}(0) = 2$$

$$\mathrm{Dur}_{\mathrm{b}}(0) = 4$$

A zero-coupon bond's duration is always equal to its time to maturity; see expression (8.6).

Given that the forward rate curve is flat at 1.02, we have $Y^{a}(0) = Y^{b}(0) = 1.02$. This follows from expression (3.1) in Chapter 3. Thus,

$$\text{MDur}_a(0) = \frac{2}{1.02}$$

$$\text{MDur}_b(0) = \frac{4}{1.02}$$

The modified-duration hedge determined from expression (8.10) is given by

$$n_a = 1$$

$$\begin{aligned} n_b &= \frac{-\text{MDur}_a(0)\mathcal{B}_a(0)}{\text{MDur}_b(t)\mathcal{B}_b(0)} \\ &= -\left[\frac{2(0.961169)}{1.02}\right] \Big/ \left[\frac{4(0.923845)}{1.02}\right] = -0.52020 \end{aligned}$$

This is the wrong hedge ratio. In this case the bond portfolio based on modified duration is *not riskless.* ■

Because hedging based on modified duration (or on duration) is not riskless, the second-order term in the Taylor series expansion underlying expression (8.8) involving larger changes in yields is usually introduced. This term is the coupon bond's *convexity*, denoted Conv(t), and it is defined by:

$$\begin{aligned} \text{Conv(t)} &\equiv \frac{\partial^2 \mathcal{B}(t; s_t)}{\partial Y(t; s_t)^2} \\ &= \sum_{i=1}^{(T-t)/2} \frac{2i(2i+1)C}{Y(t; s_t)^{2i+2}} + \frac{(T-t)(T-t+1)L}{Y(t; s_t)^{(T-t)+2}} > 0 \end{aligned} \tag{8.13}$$

The generalization of expression (8.8) using convexity is

$$\Delta\mathcal{B}(t; s_t) \approx \frac{\partial \mathcal{B}(t; s_t)}{\partial t} - \text{MDur}(t)\mathcal{B}(t; s_t)\Delta Y(t; s_t) + \left(\tfrac{1}{2}\right)\text{Conv}(t)(\Delta Y(t; s_t))^2 \tag{8.14}$$

The contribution to the bond's price due to convexity is always positive.

One can hedge a bond with respect to both modified duration and convexity. Consider three coupon bonds with indexes *a*, *b*, and *c*. The portfolio value is

$$V(t; s_t) = \mathcal{B}_a(t; s_t) + n_b\mathcal{B}_b(t; s_t) + n_c\mathcal{B}_c(t; s_t) \tag{8.15}$$

Over a change in time, the change in the portfolio's value is approximately

$$\begin{aligned} \Delta V(t; s_t) \approx\ & \frac{\partial \mathcal{B}_a(t)}{\partial(t)} + \frac{n_b \partial \mathcal{B}_b(t)}{\partial t} + n_c \frac{\partial \mathcal{B}_c(t)}{\partial t} \\ & - \text{MDur}_a(t)\mathcal{B}_a(t)\Delta Y(t)^a - n_b \text{MDur}_b(t)\mathcal{B}_b(t)\Delta Y(t)^b \\ & - n_c \text{MDur}_c(t)\mathcal{B}_c(t)\Delta Y(t)^c \end{aligned} \tag{8.16}$$

$$+ \tfrac{1}{2}\text{Conv}_{\text{a}}(t)(\Delta Y(t)^{\text{a}})^2$$
$$+ \tfrac{1}{2}n_{\text{b}}\text{Conv}_{\text{b}}(t)(\Delta Y(t)^{\text{b}})^2 + \tfrac{1}{2}n_{\text{c}}\text{Conv}(t)(\Delta Y(t)^{\text{c}})^2$$

To make this portfolio neutral with respect to parallel shifts in yields, choose n_{b} and n_{c} such that

$$\text{MDur}_{\text{a}}(t)\mathcal{B}_{\text{a}}(t) + n_{\text{b}}\text{MDur}_{\text{b}}(t)\mathcal{B}_{\text{b}}(t) + n_{\text{c}}\text{MDur}_{\text{c}}(t)\mathcal{B}_{\text{c}}(t) = 0 \quad (8.17a)$$

$$\text{Conv}_{\text{a}}(t) + n_{\text{b}}\text{Conv}_{\text{b}}(t) + n_{\text{c}}\text{Conv}_{\text{c}}(t) = 0 \quad (8.17b)$$

Standard linear algebra can be used to solve this system of two equations in two unknowns.

There are two problems with modified duration as a risk measure: first, it is valid only for small shifts in the yield curve, and second, it is valid only for parallel shifts in the yield curve. The convexity adjustment to the modified duration hedge is useful only for reducing the first of these biases, i.e., that due to small changes in yields. It does not remove the nonparallel shift bias. For this reason, we recommend the procedure based on the synthetic coupon bond construction.

SECTION C
EUROPEAN OPTIONS ON ZERO-COUPON BONDS

This section applies the theory developed in Chapter 7 to price a European call option on a zero-coupon bond. As this is an example of the more general analysis presented in Chapter 7, we illustrate the procedure with explicit calculations based on Figs. 8.1 and 8.2.

Let the European call option's exercise date be at time τ^* for $0 \le \tau^* \le \tau$, and let its exercise price be $K > 0$. We assume that the call is written on the zero-coupon bond that matures at time $T \ge \tau^*$.

Let the arbitrage-free value of the call option at time t under state s_t be denoted $C(t; s_t)$. By definition, the arbitrage-free value of the call option at the exercise date τ^* is

$$C(\tau^*; s_{\tau^*}) = \max(P(\tau^*, T; s_{\tau^*}) - K, 0) \quad (8.18)$$

If the T-maturity zero-coupon bond's price $P(\tau^*, T; s_{\tau^*})$ exceeds the exercise price K, the option is exercised. It is said to be in the money, and its value is the difference $P(\tau^*, T; s_{\tau^*}) - K > 0$. Otherwise, it ends up out of the money, unexercised, with zero value.

By the risk-neutral valuation procedure, its arbitrage-free value at time t is

$$C(t; s_t) = \tilde{E}\left(\frac{\max(P(\tau^*, T; s_{\tau^*}) - K, 0)}{B(\tau^*; s_{\tau^*-1})}\right)B(t; s_{t-1}) \quad (8.19)$$

A synthetic call option can be constructed using the procedure described in Chapter 7. We illustrate this risk-neutral valuation procedure and the construction of the synthetic call option with an example.

EXAMPLE: EUROPEAN CALL OPTION VALUATION. Consider a European call option on the four-period zero-coupon bond, with an exercise price $K =$ 0.961000 and an exercise date $\tau^* = 2$. The value of the call option at its maturity date is

$$C(2; s_2) = \max[P(2, 4; s_2) - 0.961000, 0]$$

Substituting in the values from Fig. 8.1 yields the following values:

$$\begin{aligned}
&\text{at } (2;\text{uu}): \quad \max[.967826 - 0.961000, 0] = 0.006826\\
&\text{at } (2;\text{ud}): \quad \max[.960529 - 0.961000, 0] = 0\\
&\text{at } (2;\text{du}): \quad \max[.962414 - 0.961000, 0] = 0.001414\\
&\text{at } (2;\text{dd}): \quad \max[.953877 - 0.961000, 0] = 0
\end{aligned}$$

These numbers are placed on the last node in Fig. 8.4. To deduce the arbitrage-free value at time 1, we use the risk-neutral valuation procedure.

At time 1, state u:

$$\begin{aligned}
C(1;\text{u}) &= \frac{\tilde{E}_1(C(2; s_2))}{r(1;\text{u})}\\
&= \left(\frac{1}{2}\right)\frac{0.006826 + 0}{1.017606} = 0.003354
\end{aligned}$$

At time 1, state d:

$$\begin{aligned}
C(1;\text{d}) &= \frac{\tilde{E}_1(C(2; s_2))}{r(1;\text{d})}\\
&= \left(\frac{1}{2}\right)\frac{0.001414 + 0}{1.022406} = 0.000692
\end{aligned}$$

Finally, at time 0:

$$\begin{aligned}
C(0) &= \frac{\tilde{E}_0(C(1; s_1))}{r(0)}\\
&= \left(\frac{1}{2}\right)\frac{0.003354 + 0.000692}{1.02} = 0.001983
\end{aligned}$$

These numbers appear at the nodes on Figure 8.4.

If the call's time 0 value differs from its arbitrage-free value 0.001983, an arbitrage opportunity exists. The arbitrage opportunity involves creating the synthetic call. If the market price for the call exceeds 0.001983, short the traded call and hold the synthetic. Conversely, if the market price for the call is less than 0.001983, buy the traded call and short the synthetic.

To calculate the synthetic-call portfolio holdings in the money market account ($n_0(t; s_t)$) and the four-period zero-coupon bond ($n_1(t; s_t)$), we use expression (6.12) of Chapter 6 and the self-financing condition (6.13). These calculations are as follows:

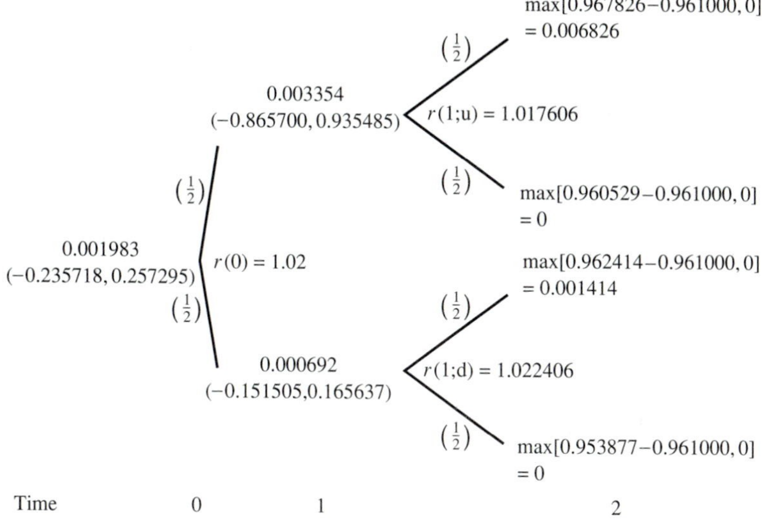

FIGURE 8.4
A European call option's value $C(t;s_t)$ on the four-period bond $P(t;4)$ with exercise price $K = 0.961000$ and exercise date 2, and the synthetic-call portfolio positions $(n_0(t;s_t),\ n_1(t;s_t))$; pseudo probabilities are in parentheses along the tree's branches.

At time 1, state u:

$$n_1(1;\mathrm{u}) = \frac{C(2;\mathrm{uu}) - C(2;\mathrm{ud})}{P(2,4;\mathrm{uu}) - P(2,4;\mathrm{ud})}$$

$$= \frac{0.006826 - 0}{0.967826 - 0.960529} = 0.935485$$

$$n_0(1;\mathrm{u}) = \frac{C(1;\mathrm{u}) - n_1(1;\mathrm{u})P(1,4;\mathrm{u})}{B(1)}$$

$$= \frac{0.003354 - (0.935485)0.947497}{1.02} = -0.865700$$

At time 1, state d:

$$n_1(1;\mathrm{d}) = \frac{C(2;\mathrm{du}) - C(2;\mathrm{dd})}{P(2,4;\mathrm{du}) - P(2,4;\mathrm{dd})} = \frac{0.001414 - 0}{0.9621414 - 0.953877}$$

$$= 0.165637$$

$$n_0(1;\mathrm{d}) = \frac{C(1;\mathrm{d}) - n_1(1;\mathrm{d})P(1,4;\mathrm{d})}{B(1)}$$

$$= \frac{0.000692 - (0.165637)0.937148}{1.02} = -0.151505$$

At time 0:

$$n_1(0) = \frac{C(1;\text{u}) - C(1;\text{d})}{P(1,4;\text{u}) - P(1,4;\text{d})} = \frac{0.003354 - 0.00692}{0.947497 - 0.937148} = 0.257295$$

$$\begin{aligned} n_0(0) &= C(0) - n_1(0)P(0,4) \\ &= 0.001983 - 0.257295(0.923845) = -0.235718 \end{aligned}$$

These portfolio holdings are given on Fig. 8.4 under each node in the tree.

We see that a synthetic call consists of a short position in the money market account and a long position in the four-period bond. These positions change across time and across states.

For this one-factor economy, it is also possible to create the synthetic call using the three-period bond, because any zero-coupon bond and the money market account complete the market (prior to the zero-coupon bond's maturity).

The calculations follow similarly and are briefly recorded. Let the synthetic call positions using the money market account and the three-period zero-coupon bond be denoted by $(\bar{n}_0(t;s_t), \bar{n}_1(t;s_t))$. They are calculated as follows:

At time 1, state u:

$$\begin{aligned} \bar{n}_1(1;\text{u}) &= \frac{C(2;\text{uu}) - C(2;\text{ud})}{P(2,3;\text{uu}) - P(2,3;\text{ud})} \\ &= \frac{0.006826 - 0}{0.984222 - 0.980015} = 1.622534 \\ \bar{n}_0(1;\text{u}) &= \frac{C(1;\text{u}) - \bar{n}_1(1;\text{u})P(1,3;\text{u})}{B(1)} \\ &= \frac{0.003354 - (1.622534)0.965127}{1.02} = -1.531958 \end{aligned}$$

At time 1, state d:

$$\begin{aligned} \bar{n}_1(1;\text{d}) &= \frac{C(2;\text{du}) - C(2;\text{dd})}{P(2,3;\text{du}) - P(2,3;\text{dd})} \\ &= \frac{0.001414 - 0}{0.981169 - 0.976147} = 0.281561 \\ \bar{n}_0(1;\text{d}) &= \frac{C(1;\text{d}) - \bar{n}_1(1;\text{d})P(1,3;\text{d})}{B(1)} \\ &= \frac{0.000692 - (0.281561)0.957211}{1.02} \\ &= -0.263550 \end{aligned}$$

At time 0:

$$\bar{n}_1(0) = \frac{C(1;\text{u}) - C(1;\text{d})}{P(1,3;\text{u}) - P(1,3;\text{d})} = \frac{0.003354 - 0.000692}{0.965127 - 0.957211} = 0.336281$$

$$\begin{aligned} \bar{n}_0(0) &= C(0) - \bar{n}_1(0)P(0,3) \\ &= 0.001983 - (0.336281)0.942322 = -0.314902 \end{aligned}$$

These holdings differ from those calculated for the four-period zero-coupon bond. In general, a larger number of the three-period bonds are needed to generate the synthetic call.

The calculation of the option's delta in terms of the three-period zero-coupon bond could have been done differently. Note that

$$\bar{n}_1(t; s_t) = n_1(t; s_t)\left(\frac{P(t+1, 4; s_t\text{u}) - P(t+1, 4; s_t\text{d})}{P(t+1, 3; s_t\text{u}) - P(t+1, 3; s_t\text{d})}\right) \tag{8.20}$$

In words, the option's delta in terms of the three-period bond equals the option's delta in terms of the four-period bond $n_1(0)$ multiplied by the delta of the four-period bond in terms of the three-period bond $[P(1,4;\text{u}) - P(1,4;\text{d})]/[P(1,3;\text{u}) - P(1,3;\text{d})]$.

For example,

$$\bar{n}_1(0) = n_1(0)\left(\frac{P(1,4;\text{u}) - P(1,4;\text{d})}{P(1,3;\text{u}) - P(1,3;\text{d})}\right)$$

$$= 0.257295\left(\frac{0.947497 - 0.937148}{0.965127 - 0.957211}\right) = 0.336281$$

■

The procedure for recalculating the option's delta in terms of a different underlying asset discussed in the previous example is generalizable. It can be used, for example, to hedge the call option using another traded option or a futures contract. The choice of the underlying asset for use in the hedge is often determined by liquidity considerations, which are not formally addressed in the frictionless market model above.

SECTION D
AMERICAN OPTIONS ON COUPON BONDS

This section illustrates the valuation procedure for American options by valuing an American call option on a coupon bond. Pricing an American call option on a zero-coupon bond would not be instructive, because both American and European call options on a zero-coupon bond have identical values. This follows from a general theorem of Merton's [2] that an American call option on an underlying asset with no cash flows will never be exercised early. We ask you to verify this result in exercise (*b*) at the end of this chapter.

Coupon bonds were analyzed in Section A. An arbitrary coupon bond has a sequence of known cash flows $C_1, C_2, \ldots, C_T$ at times $0 \leq 1 \leq 2 \leq \cdots \leq T \leq \tau$, with an arbitrage-free value given by expression (8.2), i.e.,

$$\mathcal{B}(t; s_t) = \sum_{i=t+1}^{T} C_i P(t, i; s_t) \tag{8.21}$$

By convention, the time t price of the coupon bond does not include the coupon payment made at time t, C_t. It represents the price ex-coupon.

Let the American call option on this bond have an exercise price of K_i dollars on each date i with $t \leq i \leq \tau^*$ and an expiration date of $\tau^* \leq T$. For this option the exercise price K_i changes across time according to a predetermined schedule. The American feature implies that the option can be exercised at any date prior to expiration. Because of the discrete nature of this model, we need to make an assumption concerning the timing of early exercise and the receipt of the bond's coupon. We assume that if the option is exercised at time t, the option holder receives the next coupon payment at time $t + 1$, C_{t+1}, not the time t payment, C_t. Any other convention concerning the timing of early exercise and the receipt of the coupon payment could be easily handled using an adjusted version of the following methodology.

The value of the American call at time t, under state s_t, will be denoted $A(t; s_t)$. To value this option, we start at the expiration date of the option, time τ^*, and work backward in time, valuing the option at each intermediate date until we reach time t. This procedure is known as backward induction. Let's begin.

At the expiration date τ^* its value, if not exercised before that date, is

$$A(\tau^*; s_{\tau^*}) = \max(\mathcal{B}(\tau^*; s_{\tau^*}) - K_{\tau^*}, 0) \tag{8.22}$$

At time $\tau^* - 1$, the value of the American option *if not exercised* is

$$\frac{\tilde{E}_{\tau^*-1}(A(\tau^*; s_{\tau^*}))}{r(\tau^* - 1; s_{\tau^*-1})}$$

This time $\tau^* - 1$ value does not include the coupon payment at time τ^*, since $\mathcal{B}(\tau^*; s_{\tau^*})$ is the ex-coupon price of the bond. *If it is exercised*, its value is

$$\mathcal{B}(\tau^* - 1; s_{\tau^*-1}) - K_{\tau^*-1}$$

This exercised value includes within the bond's price the present value of the coupon payment received at time τ^*, C_{τ^*}. The time $\tau^* - 1$ value of the option is the largest of these; i.e.,

$$A(\tau^* - 1; s_{\tau^*-1}) = \max\left[\frac{\tilde{E}_{\tau^*-1}(A(\tau^*; s_{\tau^*}))}{r(\tau^* - 1; s_{\tau^*-1})}, \mathcal{B}(\tau^* - 1; s_{\tau^*-1}) - K_{\tau^*-1}\right] \tag{8.23}$$

Continuing, moving backward to time $\tau^* - 2$, the value of the option is

$$A(\tau^* - 2; s_{\tau^*-2}) = \max\left[\frac{\tilde{E}_{\tau^*-2}(A(\tau^* - 1; s_{\tau^*-1}))}{r(\tau^* - 2; s_{\tau^*-2})}, \mathcal{B}(\tau^* - 2; s_{\tau^*-2}) - K_{\tau^*-2}\right] \tag{8.24}$$

By induction,

$$A(t; s_t) = \max\left[\frac{\tilde{E}_t(A(t + 1; s_{t+1})}{r(t; s_t)}, \mathcal{B}(t; s_t) - K_t\right] \tag{8.25}$$

The synthetic American call option is obtained by duplicating the optimal exercise value as implicitly indicated in expression (8.25).

The above procedure for valuing the American call option is called *stochastic dynamic programming*. It is the standard procedure used for solving the American option valuation problem discussed in Chapter 5, Section 5.C, and Chapter 6, Section 6.A.3 (see the discussion following expression (6.29)). Stochastic dynamic programming simultaneously determines both the optimal exercise policy and the maximum value of the option as indicated in the above derivation.[4] A good introductory reference to the mathematics underlying this technique can be found in Bertsekas and Shreve [1].

In the definition of the American call option given above, we allowed for an exercise price that changes across time, $\{K_i \text{ for } t \leq i \leq \tau^*\}$. This formulation includes two special cases worth mentioning. The first is the typical American call option, in which the exercise price is a fixed constant K for all times; i.e., $K_i = K$ for all i. We will study this case in the following example.

The second case is a delayed-exercise American call option, in which exercise cannot occur prior to some future date $T_m > t$. Exercise can only occur between time T_m and the expiration date of the option, at time τ^*. The exercise price between these dates can change and is given by the schedule $\{K_i$ for $T_m \leq i \leq \tau^*\}$. This delayed-exercise American call option is a special case of the previous formulation. Indeed, to see this, let the exercise schedule for the entire life of the option $\{K_i \text{ for } t \leq i \leq \tau^*\}$ be given by

$$\text{Delayed exercise schedule} = \begin{cases} K_i \equiv M & \text{for } t \leq i < T_m \\ K_i & \text{for } T_m \leq i \leq \tau^* \end{cases} \tag{8.26}$$

where M is selected to be a very large number, say $(10)^6 \times L$. Under this schedule we get the delayed-exercise American call. Technically, although the American call option under expression (8.26) allows exercise prior to time T_M, it will never be optimal to do so. This is seen by examining expression (8.25). The maximum on the right side of expression (8.25) is always $\tilde{E}_t(A(t+1; s_{t+1}))/r(t; s_t)$ prior to time T_m, because prior to time T_m, $\mathcal{B}(t; s_t) - M$ is a large negative number and $\tilde{E}_t(A(t+1; s_{t+1}))/r(t; s_t)$ is always nonnegative.

In summary, under the delayed exercise schedule (8.26), the American call option of expressions (8.22)–(8.25) is the delayed-exercise American call option. This delayed-exercise American call option is important in applications because it relates to the valuation of callable coupon bonds. This is discussed in the next section.

EXAMPLE: AMERICAN CALL OPTION VALUATION. Consider an American call option on the coupon bond in Table 8.2 with a constant strike price of 101 over the life of the option and expiration date 2. This coupon bond's arbitrage-free price is contained in Fig. 8.3.

---

[4]In the notation of Chapter 6, the stochastic dynamic programming technique jointly determines the maximum $a^* \in A$ and the value under this a^* of $\sum_{j=0}^{\tau^*} \tilde{E}(x(j, a^*; s_j)/B(j, s_{j-1}))B(0)$; see expression (6.29).

By the backward-valuation argument, at time 2, the American call's value is as follows:

$$
\begin{aligned}
A(2;\mathrm{uu}) &= \max(\mathcal{B}(2;\mathrm{uu}) - 101, 0)\\
&= \max(101.6218 - 101, 0) = 0.6218\\
A(2;\mathrm{ud}) &= \max(\mathcal{B}(2;\mathrm{ud}) - 101, 0)\\
&= \max(100.8557 - 101, 0) = 0\\
A(2;\mathrm{du}) &= \max(\mathcal{B}(2;\mathrm{du}) - 101, 0)\\
&= \max(101.0535 - 101, 0) = 0.0535\\
A(2;\mathrm{dd}) &= \max(\mathcal{B}(2;\mathrm{dd}) - 101, 0)\\
&= \max(100.1571 - 101, 0) = 0
\end{aligned}
$$

These numbers are tabulated in Fig. 8.5.

At time 1, state u:

$$
\begin{aligned}
A(1,\mathrm{u}) &= \max\left(\frac{[(1/2)A(2;\mathrm{uu}) + (1/2)A(2;\mathrm{ud})]}{r(1;\mathrm{u})}, \mathcal{B}(1;\mathrm{u}) - 101\right)\\
&= \max\left(\frac{[(1/2)0.6218 + (1/2)0]}{1.017606}, 104.4006 - 101\right)\\
&= \max(0.305506, 3.4006) = 3.4006
\end{aligned}
$$

This valuation implies that early exercise is optimal at time 1, state u giving a value of 3.4006. The synthetic call at time 1, state u, therefore, really does not exist, for it consists of zero unit of the money market account and one coupon bond. Note that if the American call is not exercised, it loses (significant) value by time 2. It goes from 3.4006 to either 0.6218 if u occurs or 0 if d occurs.

At time 1, state d:

$$
\begin{aligned}
A(1,\mathrm{d}) &= \max\left(\frac{[(1/2)A(2;\mathrm{du}) + (1/2)A(2;\mathrm{dd})]}{r(1;\mathrm{d})}, \mathcal{B}(1;\mathrm{d}) - 101\right)\\
&= \max\left(\frac{[(1/2)0.0535 + (1/2)0]}{1.022406}, 103.2910 - 101\right)\\
&= \max[0.026151, 2.2910] = 2.2910
\end{aligned}
$$

Again, early exercise is optimal at this node. The synthetic call at time 1, state d consists of zero unit of the money market account and one unit of the coupon bond purchased at $K = 101$ dollars. If the American call is not exercised, it loses (significant) value at time 2. It goes from 2.2910 to either 0.0535 if u occurs or 0 if d occurs.

Finally, at time 0:

$$
\begin{aligned}
A(0) &= \max\left(\frac{[(1/2)A(1;\mathrm{u}) + (1/2)A(1;\mathrm{d})]}{r(0)}, \mathcal{B}(0) - 101\right)\\
&= \max\left(\frac{[(1/2)3.4006 + (1/2)2.2910]}{1.02}, 101.8096 - 101\right)\\
&= \max(2.79, 0.8096) = 2.79
\end{aligned}
$$

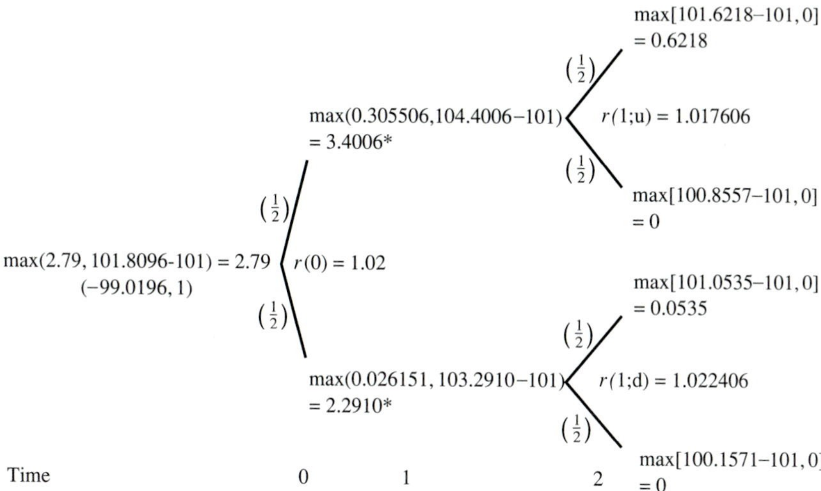

FIGURE 8.5
An American call option's values with constant strike price $K = 101$ and maturity date 2 on the coupon bond of Table 8.2. The synthetic American call option's portfolio positions in the money market account ($n_0(t; s_t)$) and in the coupon bond ($n_1(t; s_t)$) are given under the nodes where relevant. The asterisk means that it is optimal to exercise at the time and state identified.

Here it is optimal not to exercise the call, giving the call a value of 2.79.

To create the synthetic American call at time 0, we hold $n_0(0)$ units of the money market account and $n_1(0)$ units of the coupon bond determined as follows:

$$n_1(0) = \frac{A(1;\text{u}) - A(1;\text{d})}{\mathcal{B}(1;\text{u}) - \mathcal{B}(1;\text{d})}$$

$$= \frac{3.4006 - 2.2910}{104.4006 - 103.2910} = 1$$

$$n_0(0) = \frac{C(0) - n_1(0)\mathcal{B}(0)}{B(0)}$$

$$= \frac{2.79 - 1(101.8096)}{1} = -99.0196$$

One needs to purchase the coupon bond ($n_1(0) = 1$) and short -99.0196 units of the money market account. The reason one buys one unit of the coupon bond is that the option is exercised for sure at time 1.

Two observations about these calculations need to be made. First, the numerator in $n_1(0)$ contains the values for the option at time $t + 1$ under the *optimal decision selections*, which in this case is exercising in both the up and the down states. Second, the denominator in $n_1(0)$ is the difference in the value of the coupon bond at time 1. There is no coupon payment at time 1. ■

SECTION E
CALL PROVISIONS ON COUPON BONDS

This section studies the pricing and hedging of callable coupon bonds. Without specifying a particular evolution for the term structure of interest rates, it is first shown that a callable coupon bond is equivalent to an ordinary coupon bond plus a written *delayed-exercise* American call option on the ordinary coupon bond. Specifying a particular evolution, however, enables one to apply the techniques of Chapter 7.

We define a callable coupon bond to be a financial security issued by an entity (e.g., the United States government) with the following structure. It is like an ordinary coupon bond, but with an early retirement provision attached. It pays known cash flows of $C_1, C_2, \ldots, C_T$ dollars at times $0 \leq 1 \leq 2 \leq \cdots \leq T \leq \tau$, where T is the maturity date of the bond. However, each cash flow is paid only if the bond is not retired (called) earlier than the payment date. The bond can be retired (called) under the following conditions. First, it cannot be called prior to some time T_m. The bond is said to be *call protected* for T_m years. Second, between times T_m and the maturity, time T, it can be retired only at an additional cost of K_t dollars for $0 \leq t \leq T - 1$. The cost schedule is allowed to change with time. After the bond is retired, no future cash flows are paid. This completes the description.

Thus, at the discretion of the entity issuing the bond, the callable bond can be retired at any time t for $T_m \leq t \leq T - 1$ at a cost of K_t dollars. Retiring the bond at time t saves the entity the future cash flows of $C_{t+1}, C_{t+2}, \ldots, C_T$ dollars, and this may be optimal if interest rates fall (relative to the time the bond was issued). To value the callable coupon bond, we need to know the optimal call policy of the entity issuing the bond. To determine this, we assume that the objective of the entity issuing the bond is to minimize its liability; i.e., it desires to minimize the value of the callable coupon bond. Given this objective, we can use the stochastic dynamic programming approach introduced in the previous section to value and hedge this bond.

Prior to this demonstration, however, we need to define two other financial securities. First, consider an ordinary (noncallable) coupon bond with the identical cash flows $C_1, C_2, \ldots, C_T$ and maturity date T as the callable coupon bond. From Section 8.A, we know that the price of this coupon bond at time t is given by

$$\mathcal{B}(t; s_t) = \sum_{i=t+1}^{T} C_i P(t, i; s_t) \qquad (8.27a)$$

or

$$\mathcal{B}(t; s_t) = \frac{\tilde{E}_t(\mathcal{B}(t+1; s_{t+1}) + C_{t+1})}{r(t; s_t)} \qquad \text{where } \mathcal{B}(T; s_t) = 0 \quad (8.27b)$$

Second, consider a delayed-exercise American call option with expiration time $T-1$ on the ordinary coupon bond in expression (8.27). Let the exercise period start after time T_m, and let the exercise price schedule be $\{K_t \text{ for } T_m \leq t \leq T-1\}$. This delayed-exercise American call option was valued in Section 8.D (using (8.26)), and its value is given by

$$A(t; s_t) = \max\left(\frac{\tilde{E}_t(A(t+1; s_t))}{r(t; s_t)}, \mathcal{B}(T; s_t) - K_t\right) \tag{8.28}$$

where $A(T-1; s_{T-1}) = \max(\mathcal{B}(T-1; s_{T-1}) - K_{T-1}, 0)$.

In both expressions (8.27) and (8.28), the expectations are taken with respect to the pseudo probabilities from either a one-, two-, or $N \geq 3$–factor economy.

Let us denote the value of the callable coupon bond at time t under state s_t as $D(t; s_t)$. This bond's price is ex-coupon. Starting at time T, the value of the callable coupon bond, if not called earlier, equals its value after the last cash payment; i.e.,

$$D(T; s_T) = 0 \tag{8.29a}$$

Using expression (8.27b), we can rewrite this as

$$D(T; s_T) = \mathcal{B}(T; s_T) \tag{8.29b}$$

At time $T-1$, according to the risk-neutral valuation procedure, the value of the callable coupon bond is

$$D(T-1; s_{T-1}) = \min\left(\frac{\tilde{E}_{T-1}(D(T; s_T)) + C_T}{r(T-1; s_{T-1})}, K_{T-1}\right) \tag{8.30a}$$

This follows because the entity issuing the bond will retire it if K_{T-1} is less than the value of the future cash flows if not retired $(\tilde{E}_{T-1}(D(T; s_T) + C_T)/r(T-1; s_{T-1}))$. The coupon payment at time $T-1$ is already owed, and it is paid regardless of the retirement decision at time $T-1$. Thus it does not appear in this expression.

We perform some algebra on (8.30a). Substitution of (8.29a) gives

$$D(T-1; s_{T-1}) = \min\left(\frac{\tilde{E}_{T-1}(\mathcal{B}(T; s_T)) + C_T}{r(T-1; s_{T-1})}, K_{T-1}\right)$$

Next, using expression (8.27) yields

$$D(T-1; s_{T-1}) = \min(\mathcal{B}(T-1; s_{T-1}), K_{T-1})$$

But this can be written as

$$D(T-1; s_{T-1}) = \mathcal{B}(T-1; s_{T-1}) - \max(\mathcal{B}(T-1; s_{T-1}) - K_{T-1}, 0)$$

Finally, using expression (8.28) gives

$$D(T-1; s_{T-1}) = \mathcal{B}(T-1; s_{T-1}) - A(T-1; s_{T-1}) \tag{8.30b}$$

Expression (8.30b) shows that at time $T-1$, the callable coupon bond ($D(T-1; s_{T-1})$) is equivalent to an ordinary coupon bond ($\mathcal{B}(T-1; s_{T-1})$) less a delayed-exercise American call option on the ordinary coupon bond ($A(T-1; s_{T-1})$). Continuing backward to time $T-2$,

$$D(T-2; s_{T-2}) = \min\left(\frac{\tilde{E}_{T-2}(D(T-1; s_{T-1}) + C_{T-1})}{r(T-2; s_{T-2})}, K_{T-2}\right) \quad (8.31a)$$

We want to transform this expression to one similar to (8.30b). First, substitute (8.30b) into expression (8.31a) to obtain

$$D(T-2; s_{T-2}) = \min\left(\frac{\tilde{E}_{T-2}(\mathcal{B}(T-1; s_{T-1}) + C_{T-1})}{r(T-2; s_{T-2})} - \frac{\tilde{E}_{T-2}(A(T-1; s_{T-1}))}{r(T-2; s_{T-2})}, K_{T-2}\right)$$

Using expression (8.27) yields

$$D(T-2; s_{T-2}) = \min\left(\mathcal{B}(T-2; s_{T-2}) - \frac{\tilde{E}_{T-2}(A(T-1; s_{T-1}))}{r(T-2; s_{T-2})}, K_{T-2}\right)$$

Algebra gives

$$D(T-2; s_{T-2}) = \mathcal{B}(T-2; s_{T-2}) - \max\left(\mathcal{B}(T-2; s_{T-2}) - K_{T-2}, \frac{\tilde{E}_{T-2}(A(T-1; s_{T-1}))}{r(T-2; s_{T-2})}\right)$$

Finally, using expression (8.28) gives

$$D(T-2; s_{T-2}) = \mathcal{B}(T-2; s_{T-2}) - A(T-2; s_{T-2}) \quad (8.31b)$$

Continuing backward in a similar fashion, at time t we get

$$D(t; s_t) = \min\left(\frac{\tilde{E}_t(D(t+1; s_{t+1}) + C_{t+1})}{r(t; s_t)}, K_t\right) \quad (8.32a)$$

where $D(T; s_T) = 0$, or

$$D(t; s_t) = \mathcal{B}(t; s_t) - A(t; s_t) \quad (8.32b)$$

Expression (8.32b) shows that the callable coupon bond ($D(t; s_t)$) is equivalent to an ordinary coupon bond ($\mathcal{B}(t; s_t)$) less a delayed-exercise American call option on the ordinary coupon bond ($A(t; s_t)$). This result is independent of any particular evolution of the term structure of interest rates.

To construct a synthetic callable coupon bond, one needs to buy an ordinary (noncallable) coupon bond with the same characteristics and to short a delayed-exercise American call option on this ordinary coupon bond. If these do not trade, one can construct the synthetic callable coupon bond by synthetically constructing both the ordinary (noncallable) coupon bond as described in Section 8.A and the delayed-exercise American call option on this ordinary coupon bond as described in Section 8.D. These constructions require a specific model of the evolution of the term structure of interest rates. Because examples of these constructions have been provided in the text, no additional examples are provided here.

SECTION F
COMPUTER EXERCISES

This set of exercises using the Trees software should help the reader understand the calculations in Chapter 8.

Run the Trees software. It gives a different spot rate evolution from the one in the book, and this new evolution is the one used in the following exercises.

a. Go to the "claims" selection and choose "coupon bond." Generate a three-period zero-coupon bond by inserting a dollar cash flow only at time 3.

b. Keep the coupon bond from (*a*) and go to the "claims" selection and choose "European call." Enter strike price 0.980 and expiration 2. Choose "Display," then "on the tree," and then "European call" to display the European call options prices on the tree.

Next, repeat this construction, but this time create an American call with the same strike price and expiration date on the three-period zero-coupon bond from exercise (*a*). Do the European call and American call prices differ?

c. Go to the "claims" selection and choose "coupon bond." Enter the numbers from Table 8.2. This values the coupon bond. Display its prices by choosing "display" and "on the tree." Switch the display to "coupon bond prices." This is the analogue of Fig. 8.3. Check some calculations by hand using the zero-coupon bond price vectors at the nodes.

d. Keep the coupon bond entered from exercise (*c*). Go to the "claims" selection and choose "European call." Enter strike price 101 and expiration 2. Choose "display," then "on the tree," and then "European call" to display the European call option's prices on the tree. This is the analogue of Fig. 8.5 for a European call.

e. Repeat exercise (*d*) but replace "European call" with "American call." How do the two prices differ? Is there value to early exercise? What is the difference between this case and exercise (*b*)?

SECTION G
REFERENCES TO CHAPTER 8

1. Bertsekas, D., and S. Shreve, 1978. *Stochastic Optimal Control: The Discrete Time Case*. Academic, New York.
2. Merton, R., 1973. "Theory of Rational Option Pricing." *Bell Journal of Economics and Management Science* 4, 141–183.

CHAPTER 9

Forwards and Futures

This chapter applies the general contingent claims valuation theory to forward contracts, futures contracts, and options on futures. Under stochastic interest rates, we will show that forward and futures contracts are distinct securities and that forward and futures prices are (usually) different quantities. The material in this chapter was motivated by the original insights of Cox, Ingersoll, and Ross [2] and of Jarrow and Oldfield [6].

The futures contracts analyzed here are simplified versions of the exchange-traded futures contracts (see Chapter 2, Section 2.D). We simplified these contracts to facilitate understanding. References are provided for an analysis of the more complex exchange-traded Treasury futures contracts.

SECTION A
FORWARDS

We consider the forward contract defined in Chapter 3, Section 3.D, issued on a T_2-maturity zero-coupon bond with delivery date T_1. The time t forward price on this contract is denoted $F(t, T_1 : T_2)$. The purpose of this section is to use the contingent claim valuation methodology of Chapter 7 to give an alternative characterization of the forward price. Given the existence of the pseudo probabilities of Chapter 7, the subsequent analysis proceeds independently of the particular economy (with one, two, or $N \geq 3$ factors) studied.

Using the risk-neutral valuation approach, expression (6.27) or (6.43), the value of the forward contract *initiated* at time $t \leq T_1$ is zero:

$$0 = \tilde{E}_t\left(\frac{P(T_1, T_2) - F(t, T_1 : T_2)}{B(T_1)}\right)B(t) \tag{9.1}$$

Expression (9.1) holds because at the time the contract is initiated, no cash flows are exchanged and the forward contract has zero value. The right side is the present value of the cash flow received at the expiration date of the contract, time T_1. This cash flow is the bond's value $P(T_1, T_2)$ less the agreed-upon delivery price $F(t, T_1 : T_2)$; see Table 3.2. Expression (9.1) can be rewritten as

$$0 = \tilde{E}_t\left(\frac{P(T_1, T_2)}{B(T_1)}\right)B(t) - F(t, T_1 : T_2)\tilde{E}_t\left(\frac{1}{B(T_1)}\right)B(t) \tag{9.2}$$

Using expression (6.30) or (6.44) for the zero-coupon bond's price, this can be rewritten as

$$0 = P(t, T_2) - F(t, T_1 : T_2)P(t, T_1) \tag{9.3}$$

Rearranging terms gives the desired result:

$$F(t, T_1 : T_2) = \frac{P(t, T_2)}{P(t, T_1)} \tag{9.4}$$

The time t forward price of a T_1 expiration date contract on the T_2-maturity zero-coupon bond is the ratio of the two different zero-coupon bond prices.

This expression is easy to understand if one recognizes the ratio $1/P(t, T_1)$ as the future value of a dollar received at time T_1. Then expression (9.4) can be interpreted as the future value at time T_1 of the T_2-maturity zero-coupon bond—hence, a forward price.

From this expression we can obtain a relation between forward prices and forward rates:

$$F(t, T : T + 1) = \frac{P(t, T + 1)}{P(t, T)} = \frac{1}{f(t, T)}$$

The forward price of a zero-coupon bond that matures at time $T + 1$, one period after the forward contract's expiration date T, is the inverse of the time t forward rate for the same period $[T, T + 1]$.

The self-financing trading strategy that replicates a forward contract is easily determined from expression (9.3). It is given by *(i)* buying and holding until time T_1 the T_2-maturity zero-coupon bond and *(ii)* selling and holding until time T_1, the number $F(t, T_1 : T_2)$ of T_1-maturity zero-coupon bonds. At time t the value of this portfolio is zero because of expression (9.3). At time T_1 this portfolio gives the payoff to the forward contract. This is called a "cash and carry" strategy since one buys the spot (cash) commodity and carries (holds) it until the delivery date of the contract. This completes the proof.

Note that after the initiation date, the forward contract can have nonzero value. Indeed, at a subsequent date $t < m \leq T_1$, the forward contract's value, denoted $v(m; s_m)$, is

$$V(m;s_m) = \tilde{E}_m\left(\frac{P(T_1,T_2) - F(t,T_1{:}T_2)}{B(T_1)}\right)B(m;s_{m-1}) \tag{9.5}$$
$$= P(m,T_2;s_m) - F(t,T_1{:}T_2)P(m,T_1;s_m)$$

which can differ from zero.

EXAMPLE: FORWARD PRICE AND FORWARD CONTRACT VALUES. We illustrate the valuation equations (9.4) and (9.5) with an example by considering a forward contract with expiration date 2 on the three-period zero-coupon bond. The zero-coupon bond price evolution is that presented in Fig. 8.1. The implied money market account and spot rate process is given in Fig. 8.2.

Using expression (9.4), we compute the time 0 forward price to be

$$F(0,2{:}3) = \frac{P(0,3)}{P(0,2)} = \frac{0.942322}{0.961169} = 0.980392$$

The same formula generates forward prices at times 1 and 2 to be

$$F(1,2{:}3;\mathrm{u}) = \frac{P(1,3;\mathrm{u})}{P(1,2;\mathrm{u})} = \frac{0.965127}{0.982699} = 0.982119$$

$$F(1,2{:}3;\mathrm{d}) = \frac{P(1,3;\mathrm{d})}{P(1,2;\mathrm{d})} = \frac{0.957211}{0.978085} = 0.978658$$

$$F(2,2{:}3;\mathrm{uu}) = P(2,3;\mathrm{uu}) = 0.984222$$

$$F(2,2{:}3;\mathrm{ud}) = P(2,3;\mathrm{ud}) = 0.980015$$

$$F(2,2{:}3;\mathrm{du}) = P(2,3;\mathrm{du}) = 0.981169$$

$$F(2,2{:}3;\mathrm{dd}) = P(2,3;\mathrm{dd}) = 0.976147$$

These values are listed in Fig. 9.1.

The value of the forward contract at time 2 can now be determined.

$$v(2;\mathrm{uu}) = P(2,3;\mathrm{uu}) - F(0,2{:}3) = 0.984222 - 0.980392 = 0.003830$$

$$v(2;\mathrm{ud}) = P(2,3;\mathrm{ud}) - F(0,2{:}3) = 0.980015 - 0.980392 = -0.000377$$

$$v(2;\mathrm{du}) = P(2,3;\mathrm{du}) - F(0,2{:}3) = 0.981169 - 0.980392 = 0.000777$$

$$v(2;\mathrm{dd}) = P(2,3;\mathrm{dd}) - F(0,2{:}3) = 0.976147 - 0.980392 = -0.004245$$

These are the spot prices of the three-period zero-coupon bond at time 2 less the agreed-upon purchase price.

The value of the forward contract at time 1 is obtained via the risk-neutral valuation procedure:

$$v(1;\mathrm{u}) = \frac{\tilde{E}_1(v(2;s_2))}{r(1;\mathrm{u})}$$
$$= \frac{(1/2)0.003830 + (1/2)(-0.000377)}{1.017606} = 0.001696$$

$$v(1;\mathrm{d}) = \frac{\tilde{E}_1(v(2;s_2))}{r(1;\mathrm{d})}$$

$$= \frac{(1/2)0.000777 + (1/2)(-0.004245)}{1.022406} = -0.001696$$

Finally, at time 0:

$$v(0) = E_0\frac{(v(1;s_1))}{r(0)} = \frac{(1/2)0.001696 + (1/2)(-0.001696)}{1.02} = 0$$

The forward contract has zero value at initiation if the forward price satisfies expression (9.4), as it should. The reader can verify that the values for the forward contract in Fig. 9.1 satisfy the last equation in expression (9.5). Note also that in this example, the forward price changes over time and the forward contract's value changes over time with both positive and negative values.

Figure 9.2 illustrates these computations for a different forward contract initiated at time 0 with expiration date 3 on a four-period zero-coupon bond. These calculations are left to the reader as an exercise. This completes the example. ■

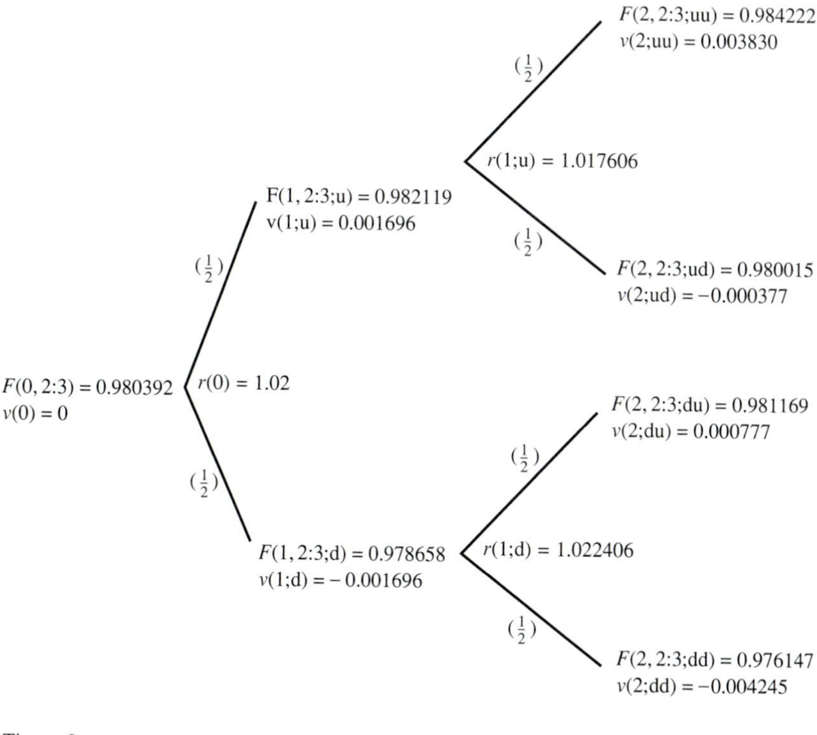

FIGURE 9.1
A forward contract initiated at time 0 on a three-period zero-coupon bond. The forward contract expires at time 2 with value $v(t; s_t)$ and forward price $F(t, 2 : 3; s_t)$.

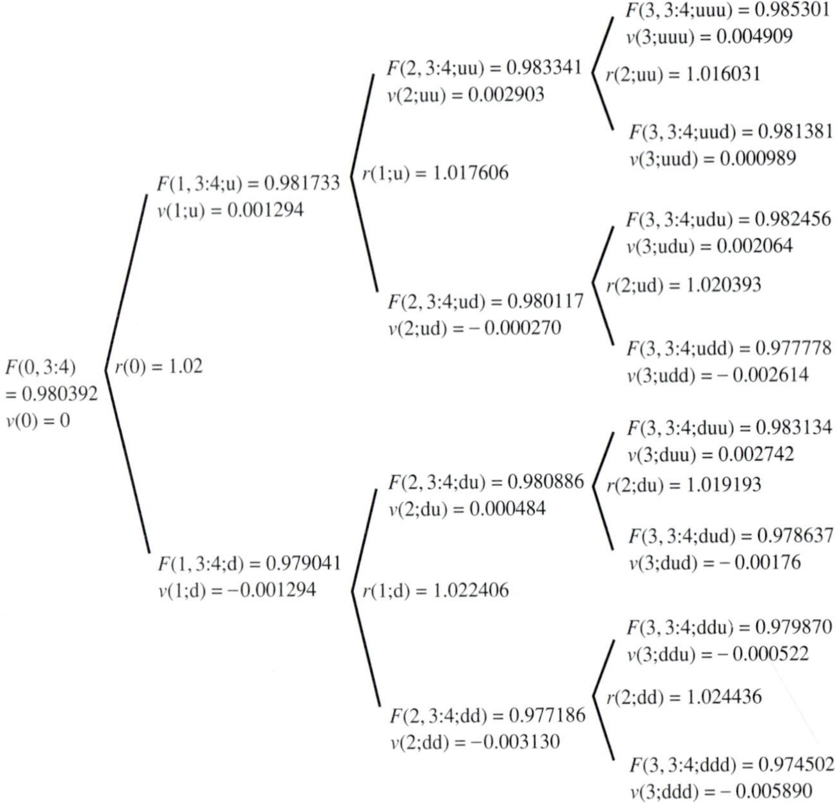

FIGURE 9.2
A forward contract initiated time 0 on a four-period zero-coupon bond. The forward contract expires at time 3 with value $v(t; s_t)$ and forward price $F(t, 3:4; s_t)$.

SECTION B
FUTURES

We consider the futures contracts defined in Chapter 3, Section 3.E, which are issued on a T_2-maturity zero-coupon bond with expiration date T_1. The futures price was denoted by $\mathcal{F}(t, T_1 : T_2)$. The purpose of this section is to use the contingent claim valuation methodology of Chapter 7 to give an alternative characterization for the futures price. Given the existence of the pseudo probabilities of Chapter 7, the subsequent analysis proceeds independently of the particular economy (with one, two, or $N \geq 3$ factors) studied.

To evaluate the futures price, we proceed in a backward-inductive fashion, using both the risk-neutral valuation procedure of expression (6.27) or (6.43) and the payoff structure in Table 3.2.

At time $T_1 - 1$ the value of the futures contract is zero, and it is given by expression (9.6):

$$0 = \tilde{E}_{T_1-1}\left(\frac{P(T_1, T_2) - \mathcal{F}(T_1 - 1, T_1{:}T_2)}{B(T_1)}\right)B(T_1 - 1) \tag{9.6}$$

Recognizing that the money market account's value $B(T_1)$ is known at time $T_1 - 1$ and that the futures price at expiration is the spot price, i.e., $\mathcal{F}(T_1, T_1{:}T_2) = P(T_1, T_2)$, we get

$$0 = \tilde{E}_{T_1-1}(\mathcal{F}(T_1, T_1{:}T_2) - \mathcal{F}(T_1 - 1, T_1{:}T_2)) \tag{9.7}$$

Simple algebra yields:

$$\mathcal{F}(T_1 - 1, T_1{:}T_2) = \tilde{E}_{T_1-1}(\mathcal{F}(T_1, T_1{:}T_2)) \tag{9.8}$$

The time $T_1 - 1$ futures price is the time $T_1 - 1$ expectation of its value at time T_1.

Next, at time $T_1 - 2$, using Table 3.1 we get

$$0 = \tilde{E}_{T_1-2}\left(\frac{\mathcal{F}(T_1 - 1, T_1{:}T_2) - \mathcal{F}(T_1 - 2, T_1{:}T_2)}{B(T_1 - 1)}\right)B(T_1 - 2) \tag{9.9}$$

Because the money market account's value $B(T_1 - 1)$ is known at time $T_1 - 2$, following the same algebra that obtained expression (9.8) yields

$$\mathcal{F}(T_1 - 2, T_1{:}T_2) = \tilde{E}_{T_1-2}(\mathcal{F}(T_1 - 1, T_1{:}T_2)) \tag{9.10}$$

Continuing the same argument inductively backward in time generates our final result:

$$\mathcal{F}(t, T_1{:}T_2) = \tilde{E}_t(\mathcal{F}(t + 1, T_1{:}T_2)) \tag{9.11}$$

This says that under the pseudo probabilities, *futures prices are martingales.* This is an important result. It facilitates computation of futures prices, and it gives the pseudo probabilities their fourth name: *futures price martingale* probabilities.[1]

Using the law of iterated expectations (backward substitution), this martingale property implies that

$$\mathcal{F}(t, T_1{:}T_2) = \tilde{E}_t(P(T_1, T_2)) \tag{9.12}$$

The futures price is the time t expectation of the underlying T_2-maturity zero-coupon bond's price trading at time T_1.

EXAMPLE: FUTURES PRICE COMPUTATIONS. To illustrate the determination of the futures price across time, consider a futures contract on a three-period

[1]Other names for these futures price martingale probabilities are risk-neutral probabilities, martingale probabilities, and pseudo probabilities.

zero-coupon bond with delivery date time 2. The zero-coupon bond price curve evolution and spot rate process are contained in Figs. 8.1 and 8.2.

By definition, at time 2, the futures price is the spot price: i.e.,

$$\mathcal{F}(2,2\colon 3;\mathrm{uu}) = P(2,3;\mathrm{uu}) = 0.984222$$

$$\mathcal{F}(2,2\colon 3;\mathrm{ud}) = P(2,3;\mathrm{ud}) = 0.980015$$

$$\mathcal{F}(2,2\colon 3;\mathrm{du}) = P(2,3;\mathrm{du}) = 0.981169$$

$$\mathcal{F}(2,2\colon 3;\mathrm{dd}) = P(2,3;\mathrm{dd}) = 0.976147$$

Using expression (9.11), we obtain

$$\mathcal{F}(1,2\colon 3;\mathrm{u}) = \left(\tfrac{1}{2}\right)0.984222 + \left(\tfrac{1}{2}\right)0.980015 = 0.982119$$

and

$$\mathcal{F}(1,2\colon 3;\mathrm{d}) = \left(\tfrac{1}{2}\right)0.981169 + \left(\tfrac{1}{2}\right)0.976147 = 0.978658$$

The time 0 futures price is

$$\mathcal{F}(0,2\colon 3) = \left(\tfrac{1}{2}\right)0.982119 + \left(\tfrac{1}{2}\right)0.978658 = 0.980388$$

The futures price is seen to change randomly over time. These values are depicted in Fig. 9.3. The futures contract has zero value at each time and state. The cash flow paid out each period, due to marking to market, is also indicated below each node. The cash flow at time t, state s_t is the change in the futures price, i.e.,

$$\mathcal{F}(t,2\colon 3;s_t) - \mathcal{F}(t-1,2\colon 3;s_{t-1})$$

For example, at time 2, state uu,

$$\text{cash flow} = \mathcal{F}(2,2\colon 3;\mathrm{uu}) - \mathcal{F}(1,2\colon 3;\mathrm{u}) = 0.984222 - 0.982119 = 0.002104$$

The cash flows at the up and down nodes should differ only in sign, because the expected value of the cash flow is zero.

To create a synthetic futures contract, we need to create the cash flows in Fig. 9.3. The only difference between this procedure and what was previously done is that here we are duplicating cash flows instead of values. Otherwise, it is the same.

At time 1, state u, we choose $n_0(1;\mathrm{u})$ units of the money market account and $n_1(1;\mathrm{u})$ units of the three-period zero-coupon bond so that

$$n_0(1;\mathrm{u})B(2;\mathrm{u}) + n_1(1;\mathrm{u})P(2,3;\mathrm{uu}) = n_0(1;\mathrm{u})1.037958 + n_1(1;\mathrm{u})0.984222 = 0.002104$$

$$n_0(1;\mathrm{u})B(2;\mathrm{u}) + n_1(1;\mathrm{u})P(2,3;\mathrm{ud}) = n_0(1;\mathrm{u})1.037958 + n_1(1;\mathrm{u})0.980015 = -0.002104$$

The solution is

$$n_0(1;\mathrm{u}) = -0.946203$$

$$n_1(1;\mathrm{u}) = 1$$

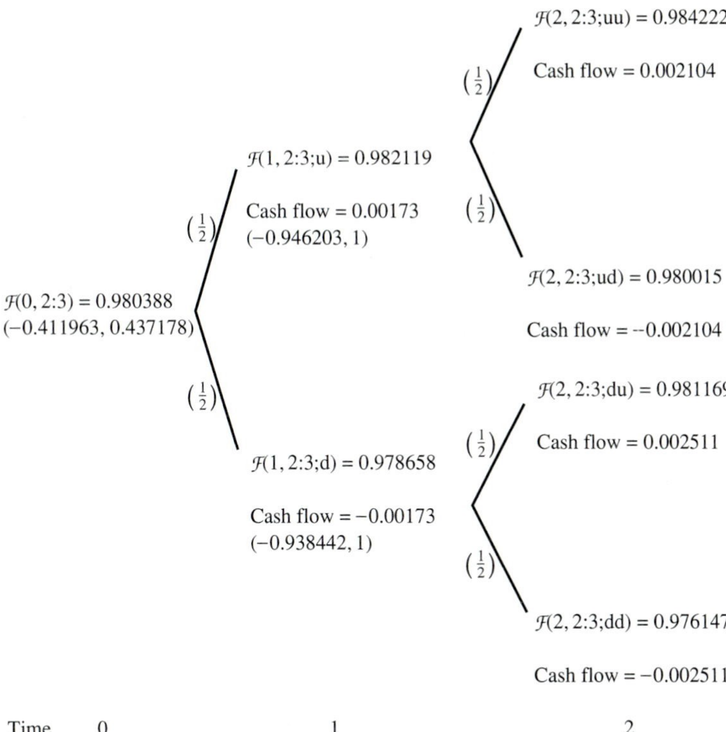

FIGURE 9.3
A futures contract with expiration date 2 on a three-period zero-coupon bond. Futures prices $\mathcal{F}(t, 2:3)$ are given at each node. Pseudo probabilities are on the branches of the tree. The synthetic futures contract positions $(n_0(t;s_t), n_1(t;s_t))$ in the money market account and the three-period bond are also provided.

That is, 0.946203 of a unit of the money market account is shorted (i.e., borrowed), and one three-period zero-coupon bond is held long. The cost of forming this portfolio is

$$n_0(1;\text{u})1.02 + n_1(1;\text{u})P(1,3;\text{u}) = -0.946203(1.02) + 1(0.965127) = 0$$

At time 1, state d we choose $n_0(1;\text{d})$, and $n_1(1;\text{d})$ so that

$$n_0(1;\text{d})B(2;\text{d}) + n_1(1;\text{d})P(2,3;\text{du})$$
$$= n_0(1;\text{d})1.042854 + n_1(1;\text{d})0.981169 = 0.002511$$

$$n_0(1;\text{d})B(2;\text{d}) + n_1(1;\text{d})P(2,3;\text{dd})$$
$$= n_0(1;\text{d})1.042854 + n_1(1;\text{d})0.976147 = -0.002511$$

The solution is

$$n_0(1;\mathrm{d}) = -0.938442$$
$$n_1(1;\mathrm{d}) = 1$$

That is, 0.938442 of a unit of the money market account is shorted, and one three-period zero-coupon bond is held long. The cost of forming this portfolio is

$$n_0(1;\mathrm{d})B(1) + n_1(1;\mathrm{d})P(1,3;\mathrm{d}) = -0.938442(1.02) + 1 \cdot (0.957211) = 0$$

Finally, at time 0, select $n_0(0)$ and $n_1(0)$ such that

$$n_0(0)B(1) + n_1(0)P(1,3;\mathrm{u}) = n_0(0)1.02 + n_1(0)0.965127 = 0.00173$$

$$n_0(0)B(1) + n_1(0)P(1,3;\mathrm{d}) = n_0(0)1.02 + n_1(0)0.957211 = -0.00173$$

The solution is:

$$n_0(0) = -0.411963$$
$$n_1(0) = 0.437178$$

The cost of forming this portfolio is

$$n_0(0)B(0) + n_1(0)P(0,3) = -0.411963(1) + 0.437178(0.942322) = 0$$

This is as it should be.

An alternative procedure for computing the synthetic futures contract is to use the delta approach. At time 1, state u we choose $n_1(1;\mathrm{u})$ units of the three-period zero-coupon bond via

$$n_1(1;\mathrm{u}) = \frac{\text{cash flow}(2;\mathrm{uu}) - \text{cash flow}(2;\mathrm{ud})}{P(2,3;\mathrm{uu}) - P(2,3;\mathrm{ud})}$$

$$= \frac{0.002104 - (-0.002104)}{0.984222 - 0.980015} = 1$$

and

$$n_0(1;\mathrm{u}) = \frac{0 - n_1(1;\mathrm{u})P(1,3;\mathrm{u})}{B(1)}$$

$$= \frac{-1(0.965127)}{1.02} = -0.946203$$

The first zero in the expression for $n_0(1;\mathrm{u})$ represents the value of the futures contract at time 1, state u.

Continuing, at time 1, state d,

$$n_1(1;\mathrm{d}) = \frac{\text{cash flow}(2;\mathrm{du}) - \text{cash flow}(2;\mathrm{dd})}{P(2,3;\mathrm{du}) - P(2,3;\mathrm{dd})}$$

$$= \frac{0.002511 - (-0.002511)}{0.981169 - 0.976147} = 1$$

and

$$
\begin{aligned}
n_0(1;\mathrm{d}) &= \frac{0 - n_1(1;\mathrm{d})P(1,3;\mathrm{d})}{B(1)} \\
&= \frac{-1(0.957211)}{1.02} = -0.938442
\end{aligned}
$$

Finally, at time 0,

$$
\begin{aligned}
n_1(0) &= \frac{\text{cash flow}(1;\mathrm{u}) - \text{cash flow}(1;\mathrm{d})}{P(1,3;\mathrm{u}) - P(1,3;\mathrm{d})} \\
&= \frac{0.00173 - (-0.00173)}{0.965127 - 0.957211} \\
&= 0.437178
\end{aligned}
$$

and

$$
\begin{aligned}
n_0(0) &= 0 - n_0(0)P(0,3) \\
&= 0 - (0.437178)(0.942322) \\
&= -0.411963
\end{aligned}
$$

This completes the alternative method for determining the synthetic futures contract.

The futures prices for a three-period futures contract on the four-period zero-coupon bond are provided in Fig. 9.4. The calculations are left to the reader as an exercise. ■

We can now use expression (9.12) to relate forward and futures prices. From expression (9.4), using expression (6.30) or (6.44) gives

$$
F(t,T_1\colon T_2) = \tilde{E}_t\left(\frac{P(T_1,T_2)}{B(T_1)}\right)\frac{B(t)}{P(t,T_1)} \tag{9.13}
$$

Consider the following property of expectations: if x and y are random variables,

$$
\tilde{E}(xy) = \tilde{E}(x)\tilde{E}(y) + \widetilde{\text{cov}}(x,y) \quad \text{where } \widetilde{\text{cov}}(x,y) \equiv \tilde{E}[(x - \tilde{E}(x))(y - \tilde{E}(y))]
$$

Using this property yields

$$
\begin{aligned}
&F(t,T_1\colon T_2) \\
&= \tilde{E}_t(P(T_1,T_2))\tilde{E}_t\left(\frac{1}{B(T_1)}\right)\frac{B(t)}{P(t,T_1)} + \widetilde{\text{cov}}_t\left(P(T_1,T_2), \frac{1}{B(T_1)}\right)\frac{B(t)}{P(t,T_1)}
\end{aligned} \tag{9.14}
$$

Finally, using expression (6.30) or (6.44) again and (9.12) gives

$$
F(t,T_1\colon T_2) = \mathcal{F}(t,T_1\colon T_2) + \widetilde{\text{cov}}_t\left(P(T_1,T_2), \frac{1}{r(t)\cdots r(T_1-1)}\right)\frac{1}{P(t,T_1)} \tag{9.15}
$$

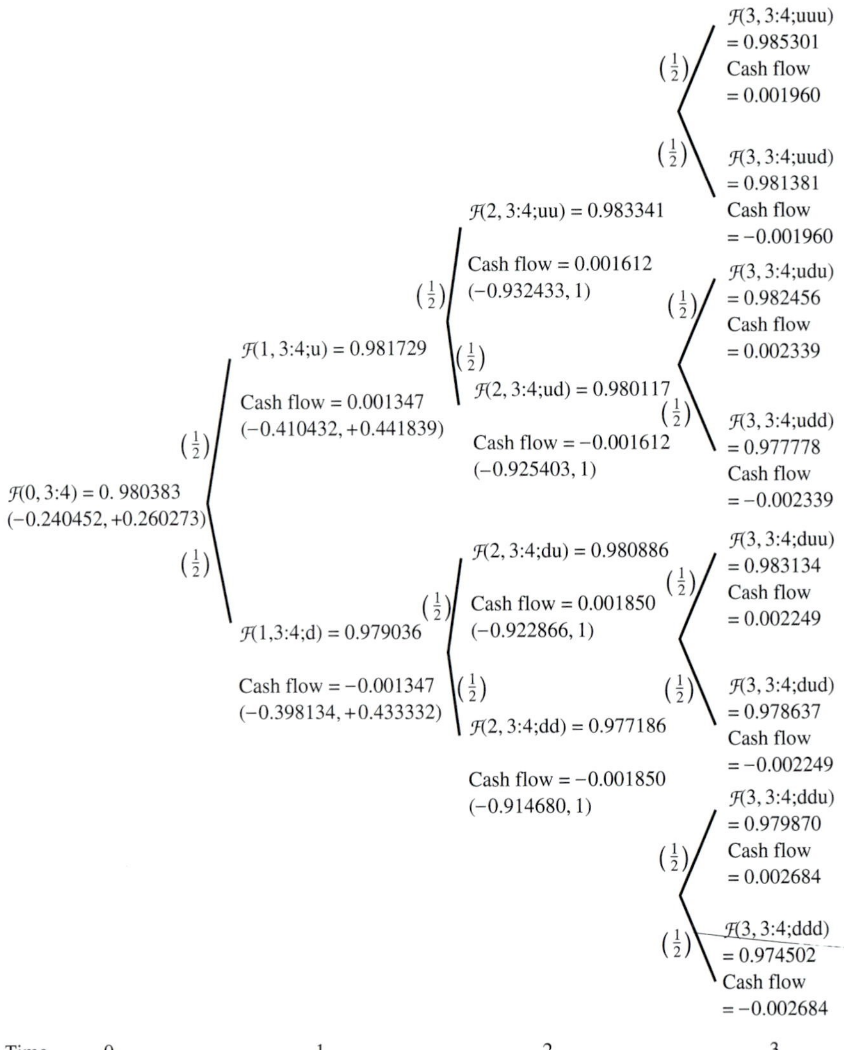

FIGURE 9.4
A futures contract with expiration date 3 on a four-period zero-coupon bond. Futures prices $\mathcal{F}(t, 3:4)$ are given at each node. Pseudo probabilities are along the branches of the tree. The synthetic futures contract positions $(n_0(t; s_t),\ n_1(t; s_t))$ in the money market account and four-period bond area also provided.

The forward price equals the futures price plus an adjustment term. The adjustment term reflects the covariance between the T_2-maturity zero-coupon bond's price and the spot rates over the time period $[t, T_1]$. When this covariance is zero, forward and futures prices are identical. In general, this occurs only at time $T_1 - 1$. At time $T_1 - 1$, expression (9.15) becomes

TABLE 9.1
A comparison of forward and future prices for a two-period contract on a three-period zero-coupon bond

(Time, state)	Forward price	Futures price	Spot price
0	0.980392	0.980388	0.942322
(1,u)	0.982119	0.982119	0.965127
(1,d)	0.978658	0.978658	0.957211
(2,uu)	0.984222	0.984222	0.984222
(2,ud)	0.980015	0.980015	0.980015
(2,du)	0.981169	0.981169	0.981169
(2,dd)	0.976147	0.976147	0.976147

$$F(T_1 - 1, T_1 : T_2)$$
$$= \mathcal{F}(T_1 - 1, T_1 : T_2) + \widetilde{\text{cov}}_{T_1 - 1}\left(P(T_1 - 1, T_2), \frac{1}{r(T_1 - 1)}\right)\frac{1}{P(T_1 - 1, T_1)} \tag{9.16}$$

This last term is zero because $1/r(T_1 - 1)$ is not random when viewed at time $T_1 - 1$. Thus, on the day before the forward and futures contracts expire, the forward price equals the futures price. This makes sense, because on this day alone, the two contracts have identical cash flows (see Table 3.2).

EXAMPLE: RELATIONSHIP BETWEEN FORWARD AND FUTURES PRICES. The forward and futures prices for contracts with a delivery date of time 2 on a three-period zero-coupon bond are given in Figs. 9.1 and 9.3. For comparison, these prices are listed in Table 9.1. We see that at the expiration date 2, forward prices, futures prices, and spot prices are equal. At time 1, forward prices equal futures prices (as indicated by expression (9.16)). Finally, at time 0, the forward price (0.980392) differs from the futures price (0.980388). The forward price exceeds the futures price, implying that the covariance term in expression (9.16) is positive.

Table 9.2 provides a comparison of forward and futures prices for contracts with expiration date 3 on the four-period zero-coupon bond given in Figs. 9.2 and 9.4. As before, both the time 2 and time 3 forward and futures prices are equal. These correspond to the day before expiration and the expiration date of the contracts. However, prior to that date, forward and futures prices differ. The differences at time 0 are greater than those at time 1. ■

SECTION C
OPTIONS ON FUTURES

This section analyzes the arbitrage-free valuation of options on futures. Let us consider a futures contract of expiration date T_1 on a T_2-maturity zero-coupon

TABLE 9.2

A comparison of forward and futures prices for a three-period contract on a four-period zero-coupon bond

(Time, state)	Forward price	Futures price	Spot price
0	0.980392	0.980383	0.923845
(1,u)	0.981733	0.981729	0.947497
(1,d)	0.979041	0.979036	0.937148
(2,uu)	0.983341	0.983341	0.967826
(2,ud)	0.980117	0.980117	0.960529
(2,du)	0.980886	0.980886	0.962414
(2,dd)	0.977186	0.977186	0.953877
(3,uuu)	0.985301	0.985301	0.985301
(3,uud)	0.981381	0.981381	0.981381
(3,udu)	0.982456	0.982456	0.982456
(3,udd)	0.977778	0.977778	0.977778
(3,duu)	0.983134	0.983134	0.983134
(3,dud)	0.978637	0.978637	0.978637
(3,ddu)	0.979870	0.979870	0.979870
(3,ddd)	0.974502	0.974502	0.974502

bond with $T_1 \le T_2$. Next, consider a European call option on the futures. Let the European call option have a maturity date of $\tau^* < T_1$ and an exercise price of $K > 0$. By definition, the payoff to the option contract at maturity is

$$\max(\mathcal{F}(\tau^*, T_1\!:\!T_2) - K, 0).$$

If it finishes in the money, the call owner pays K dollars and receives a cash payout equal to the futures price $\mathcal{F}(\tau^*, T_1\!:\!T_2)$. Otherwise, it has zero value.

Using the risk-neutral valuation procedure and denoting the call's value at time t, state s_t as $C(t; s_t)$, we obtain

$$C(t; s_t) = \tilde{E}_t\left(\frac{\max(\mathcal{F}(\tau^*, T_1\!:\!T_2; s_{\tau^*}) - K, 0)}{B(\tau^*; s_{\tau^*-1})}\right)B(t; s_{t-1}) \qquad (9.17)$$

This call can be created synthetically using any T-maturity bond with $T > \tau^*$ and the money market account. It can also be created synthetically using the underlying futures contract and the money market account. This procedure is illustrated through the following example.

EXAMPLE: OPTIONS ON FUTURES. Consider the futures contract of Fig. 9.4. This is a three-period futures contract on a four-period zero-coupon bond. Let us value a European call option on this futures price with maturity date 2 and strike price $K = 0.981000$.

The payoffs to the option at date 2 are

$$C(2; \text{uu}) = \max(0.983341 - 0.981000, 0) = 0.002341$$

$$C(2; \text{ud}) = \max(0.980117 - 0.981000, 0) = 0$$

$$C(2;\text{du}) = \max(0.980886 - 0.981000, 0) = 0$$
$$C(2;\text{dd}) = \max(0.977186 - 0.981000, 0) = 0$$

The values at time 1 are

$$C(1;\text{u}) = \frac{(1/2)0.002341 + (1/2)0}{1.017606} = 0.001150$$

$$C(1;\text{d}) = \frac{(1/2)0 + (1/2)0}{1.022406} = 0$$

Finally, its value at time 0 is

$$C(0) = \frac{(1/2)0.001150 + (1/2)0}{1.02} = 0.000564$$

The synthetic futures options can be generated by investing in the three-period zero-coupon bond ($n_1(t; s_t)$) and the money market account ($n_0(t; s_t)$) as follows:

$$n_1(1;\text{u}) = \frac{C(2;\text{uu}) - C(2;\text{ud})}{P(2,3;\text{uu}) - P(2,3;\text{ud})} = \frac{0.002341 - 0}{0.984222 - 0.980015} = 0.556460$$

$$\begin{aligned} n_0(1;\text{u}) &= \frac{C(1;\text{u}) - n_1(1;\text{u})P(1,3;\text{u})}{B(1)} \\ &= \frac{0.001150 - 0.556460(0.965127)}{1.02} \\ &= -0.525400 \end{aligned}$$

At time 1, state u, hold 0.556460 of a unit of the three-period zero-coupon bond and short 0.525400 of a unit of the money market account.

At time 1, state d, hold zero unit of both since the call has zero value.

At time 0,

$$n_1(0) = \frac{C(1;\text{u}) - C(1;\text{d})}{P(1,3;\text{u}) - P(1,3;\text{d})} = \frac{0.001150 - 0}{0.965127 - 0.957211} = 0.145324$$

$$\begin{aligned} n_0(0) &= C(0) - n_1(0)P(0,3) \\ &= 0.000564 - 0.145324(0.942322) = -0.136378 \end{aligned}$$

That is, hold 0.145324 of a unit of the three-period zero-coupon bond and short 0.136378 of a unit of the money market account.

Instead, we could have hedged this option using the underlying futures contract. The synthetic position in the futures contract ($\overline{n}_1(t; s_t)$) and the money market account ($\overline{n}_0(t; s_t)$) can be obtained as follows:

At time 1, state u,

$$\begin{aligned} \overline{n}_1(1;\text{u}) &= \frac{C(2;\text{uu}) - C(2;\text{ud})}{\text{cash flow}(2;\text{uu}) - \text{cash flow}(2;\text{ud})} \\ &= \frac{0.002341 - 0}{0.001612 - (-0.001612)} \\ &= 0.726117 \end{aligned}$$

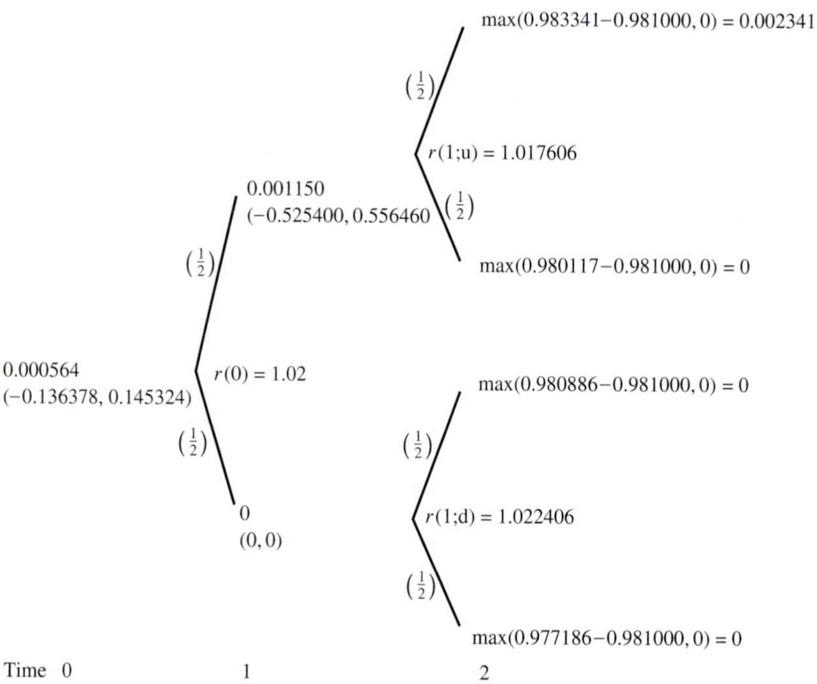

FIGURE 9.5
A European call option with maturity date 2 and exercise price $K = 0.981000$ on the futures price from Fig. 9.4. The synthetic call positions in the money market account $n_0(t; s_t)$ and in the three-period zero-coupon bond $n_1(t; s_t)$ are given under each node. Pseudo probabilities are along the branches of the tree.

and

$$\begin{aligned}\overline{n}_0(1;\text{u}) &= \frac{C(1;\text{u}) - \overline{n}(1;\text{u}) \cdot 0}{B(1)} \\ &= \frac{0.001150}{1.02} \\ &= 0.001127\end{aligned}$$

We hold 0.726117 of a unit of the futures contract and 0.001127 of a unit of the money market account; both are positive positions.

At time 1, state d, hold zero units of both assets.

At time 0,

$$\begin{aligned}\overline{n}_1(0) &= \frac{C(1;\text{u}) - C(1;\text{d})}{\text{cash flow}(1;\text{u}) - \text{cash flow}(1;\text{d})} \\ &= \frac{0.001150 - 0}{0.001347 - (-0.001347)} \\ &= 0.426875\end{aligned}$$

and

$$\overline{n}_0(0) = C(0) - \overline{n}_1(0) \cdot 0$$
$$= 0.000564$$

We hold 0.426875 of a unit of the futures contract and 0.000564 of a unit of the money market account.

This completes the synthetic construction using the futures contract. A general result appears in this construction. When futures contracts are being used as the hedging instrument, the dollar position in the money market account in the synthetic option is always equal to the value of the option being hedged. This is because the value of a futures contract is always zero.

The above calculations are summarized in Fig. 9.5. ∎

SECTION D
EXCHANGE-TRADED TREASURY FUTURES CONTRACTS

The futures contracts analyzed in this chapter are simplified versions of the Treasury futures contracts actually traded on organized exchanges (see Chapter 2, Section 2.D). Exchange-traded Treasury futures contracts have various imbedded options within them related to the delivery procedure. These imbedded options, known as *(i)* the delivery option, *(ii)* the wildcard option, and *(iii)* the quality option, can significantly influence the futures price. To value and hedge these futures contracts with their imbedded options, one can utilize the theory of Chapter 7 in conjunction with an explicit description of the exchange-traded Treasury futures contracts. This analysis is straightforward and is left to outside reading. For a description of the imbedded options, see Edwards and Ma [3] or Kolb [8]. For an analysis with respect to the influence of the imbedded options on the futures price, see Cohen [1], Gay and Manaster [4, 5], and Kane and Marcus [7].

SECTION E
COMPUTER EXERCISES

This set of exercises using the Trees software should help the reader understand the calculations in chapter 9.

Run the Trees software. It gives a different spot rate evolution from that presented in the book, and this new evolution is the one used in the following exercises.

a. Go to the "claims" selection and choose "coupon bond." Enter the cash flow for a zero-coupon bond maturing at date 3. Next, go to "claims" and choose "forward." Enter the delivery date 2. Go to "display" and then "on the tree" and choose "forwards." This gives the analogue of Fig. 9.1. Check some of these numbers by hand.

b. Keep the coupon bond from exercise *(a)*. Go to "claims," then "futures." Enter the delivery date 2. Go to "display," and then "on the tree" and choose "futures." This gives the analogue of Fig. 9.3. Do the futures prices differ from the forward prices at time 0?

c. Repeat *(a)* and *(b)* for a four-period zero-coupon bond and a forward and futures contract with delivery date 3.

d. Go in the "model" choice and select "sigma." Set all items in "sigma" to be zero. Keep "type of model" as constant. This gives a constant and nonrandom evolution of spot rates at 1.02. Repeat *(a)* and *(b)* for this tree. Show that forward prices and spot prices are identical.

SECTION F
REFERENCES TO CHAPTER 9

1. Cohen, H., 1995. "Isolating the Wild Card Option." *Mathematical Finance,* 5 (2), 155–166.
2. Cox, J., J. Ingersoll, and S. Ross, 1981. "The Relation between Forward Prices and Futures Prices." *Journal of Financial Economics* 9 (4), 321–346.
3. Edwards, F. R., and C. W. Ma, 1992. *Futures and Options.* McGraw-Hill, New York.
4. Gay, G., and S. Manaster, 1984. "The Quality Option Implicit in Futures Contracts." *Journal of Financial Economics* 13, 353–370.
5. Gay, G., and S. Manaster, 1986. "Implicit Delivery Options and Optimal Delivery Strategies for Financial Futures Contracts." *Journal of Financial Economics* 16, 41–72.
6. Jarrow, R., and G. Oldfield, 1981. "Forward Contracts and Futures Contracts." *Journal of Financial Economics* 9 (4), 373–382.
7. Kane, A., and A. Marcus, 1986. "Valuation and Optimal Exercise of the Wild Card Option in Treasury Bond Futures Markets." *Journal of Finance* 41 (1), 195–207.
8. Kolb, R., 1991. *Understanding Futures Markets,* 3d ed. Kolb, Miami.

CHAPTER 10

Swaps, Caps, Floors, and Swaptions

This chapter applies the contingent claims valuation theory developed in Chapter 7 to the pricing and hedging of interest rate swaps, caps, floors, and swaptions. Prior to this, however, it is necessary to understand fixed-rate and floating-rate loans. Fortunately for us, we have already studied fixed- and floating-rate loans in this book. At that time, however, they were analyzed from a different perspective and given different names. Fixed-rate loans correspond to (noncallable) coupon bonds, and floating-rate loans correspond to shorting the money market account.

The analysis in this chapter is presented from two related perspectives. The first perspective takes advantage of the simple structure of the swap contract and the previously stated analogy between fixed-rate loans/coupon bonds and floating-rate loans/money market accounts to derive the results quickly and efficiently. The second perspective is based on a detailed cash flow analysis, using the risk-neutral valuation procedure of Chapter 7 to obtain present values. The same results are obtained from both perspectives. This redundancy facilitates understanding. In addition, the detailed cash flow analysis is the method employed for analyzing the exotic interest rate swaps discussed in Chapter 11.

SECTION A
FIXED-RATE AND FLOATING-RATE LOANS

A *floating rate loan* of one dollar, in our frictionless and default-free setting, is equivalent to shorting the money market account, which involves paying the spot rate of interest every period. Paying this interest as a cash flow maintains the value of the short position in the money market account at one dollar at

TABLE 10.1
Cash flow from a floating-rate loan of one dollar (the principal) with a maturity date T

Time	0	1	2	...	T
Borrow	+1				
Pay interest		$-[r(0)-1]$	$-[r(1)-1]$	...	$-[r(T-1)-1]$
Pay principal					-1

the start of each period. A typical floating rate loan of one dollar is depicted in Table 10.1.

Examining Table 10.1, we see that the initial borrowing is one dollar. At the end of each period, the interest payment owed, $r(t) - 1$, is paid. The outstanding borrowing remains one dollar. At the termination date (time T), the interest plus principal is paid, and it is equal to $r(T - 1)$ dollars. To get a floating-rate loan of larger principal, say L dollars, one simultaneously enters into L of these unit-value floating-rate loans.

As the floating-rate is market determined, it costs 0 dollar to enter into a floating-rate loan contract. This is identical to saying that it costs 0 dollar to short the money market account in a frictionless and competitive economy. Note that after its initiation, the floating-rate loan is continually reset on the interest payment dates to have one-dollar value.

This same point can be made by computing the present value of the cash flows paid on a floating-rate loan. Let the value of the floating-rate loan at time t given state s_t be denoted by $V_r(t; s_t)$. Using the risk-neutral valuation procedure from Chapter 7,

$$V_r(t; s_t) = \tilde{E}_t\left(\sum_{j=t}^{T-1} \frac{r(j; s_j) - 1}{B(j+1; s_t)}\right)B(t; s_t) + \tilde{E}_t\left(\frac{1}{B(T; s_{T-1})}\right)B(t; s_t) = 1 \tag{10.1}$$

where the expectations are taken with respect to the pseudo probabilities in either the one-, two-, or $N \geq 3$-factor case. The derivation of expression (10.1) is contained below.

Expression (10.1) shows that the value of the cash flows from the floating-rate loan at time t equals one dollar, which is the amount borrowed. Thus, the floating-rate loan has a net present value of zero.

DERIVATION OF EXPRESSION (10.1). For simplicity of notation, we omit the s_t argument. Looking at the cash flows, we get

$$\text{cash flows} = \sum_{j=t}^{T-1} \frac{r(j) - 1}{B(j+1)} + \frac{1}{B(T)} = \sum_{j=t}^{T-2} \frac{r(j) - 1}{B(j+1)} + \frac{r(T-1)}{B(T)}$$

But $B(T) = B(T-1)r(T-1)$. So

$$\text{cash flows} = \sum_{j=t}^{T-2} \frac{r(j)-1}{B(j+1)} + \frac{1}{B(T-1)} = \sum_{j=t}^{T-3} \frac{r(j)-1}{B(j+1)} + \frac{r(T-2)}{B(T-1)}$$

Continuing backward in this fashion, one gets

$$\text{cash flows} = \frac{r(t)-1}{B(t+1)} + \frac{1}{B(t+1)} = \frac{r(t)}{B(t+1)} = \frac{1}{B(t)}$$

Thus,

$$V_r(t) = \tilde{E}_t(\text{cash flows})B(t) = \tilde{E}_t(1) = 1 \qquad \blacksquare$$

A *fixed-rate loan* of $\mathcal{B}(0)$ dollars, in our frictionless and default-free setting, is equivalent to shorting the coupon bond, described in Chapter 8, Section 8.A. Shorting the coupon bond as in Chapter 8 consists of receiving the value of the bond $\mathcal{B}(0)$ at time 0 (the loan) and paying out a sequence of equal and fixed coupon payments, $C_1 = C_2 = \cdots = C_{T-1} \equiv C$ at equally spaced times $0 \le 1 \le 2 \le \cdots \le T-1 \le \tau$. The last payment, C_T, represents an interest payment C plus the principal L. This cash flow is depicted in Table 10.2. The (coupon) rate on the loan is defined to be $1 + (C/L)$ per period.

The same point can be made by computing the present value of the cash flows paid on the fixed-rate loan. Let the value of the fixed-rate loan at time t given state s_t be denoted by $V_c(t; s_t)$. Using the risk-neutral valuation procedure from Chapter 7,

$$\begin{aligned} V_c(t; s_t) &= \tilde{E}_t\left(\sum_{j=t}^{T-1} \frac{C}{B(j+1; s_j)}\right)B(t; s_{t-1}) + \tilde{E}_t\left(\frac{L}{B(T; s_{T-1})}\right)B(t; s_{t-1}) \\ &= \sum_{j=t}^{T-1} CP(t, j+1; s_t) + LP(t, T; s_t) \qquad (10.2) \\ &= \mathcal{B}(t; s_t) \end{aligned}$$

where the expectations are taken with respect to the pseudo probabilities in the one-, two-, or $N \ge 3$–factor case.

TABLE 10.2
Cash flow to a fixed-rate loan with coupon C, principal L, and maturity date T

Time	0	1	2	...	T
Borrow	$\mathcal{B}(0)$				
Pay interest		$-C$	$-C$	...	$-C$
Pay principal					$-L$

The second equality in expression (10.2) follows from expression (6.24) of Chapter 6. The third equality in expression (10.2) follows from expression (8.1).

Expression (10.2) shows that the value of the cash flows to a fixed-rate loan at time t equals $\mathcal{B}(t; s_t)$, which is the amount borrowed. Thus, the fixed-rate loan has a net present value of zero.

The difference between floating- and fixed-rate loans can now be investigated. Floating-rate loans have a unit market value at each date, but randomly changing interest rate payments $r(t; s_t) - 1$. In contrast, the fixed-rate loan has changing market values $\mathcal{B}(t; s_t)$, but fixed interest rate payments of C. Thus, these two types of loans exhibit opposite and symmetric risks. Floating-rate loans have no capital gains risk, only interest rate payment risk. Conversely, fixed-rate loans have capital gains risk, but no interest rate payment risk.

SECTION B
INTEREST RATE SWAPS

An *interest rate swap* is a financial contract that obligates the holder to receive fixed-rate loan payments and pay floating-rate loan payments (or vice versa). We study interest rate swaps in this section. We first study the valuation of interest rate swaps, then the definition of the swap rate, and finally the construction of synthetic swaps.

1 Swap Valuation

Consider an investor who has a fixed-rate loan with a principal of L dollars and a maturity date T. The cash payment at every intermediate date t is C. The principal repaid at time T is L dollars. The investor wants to exchange this fixed-rate loan for a floating-rate loan with principal L dollars, maturity date T, and floating interest payments of $L(r(t-1; s_{t-1}) - 1)$ dollars per period. He does this by entering into a swap receiving fixed and paying floating.

Figure 10.1 illustrates the cash flow streams from this swap transaction. The cash flows from a swap receiving fixed and paying floating are depicted in Table 10.3. The swap holder receives fixed-rate payments C and pays floating at $(r(t-1) - 1)L$. The principals cancel. The swap contract, therefore, has the value $\mathcal{B}(0) - L$. Let $S(t; s_t)$ represent the value of the swap at time t given state s_t. Then the value of the swap at any period t is $S(t; s_t) = \mathcal{B}(t; s_t) - L$.

This same point can be made by computing the present value of the cash flows from the swap. Using the risk-neutral valuation procedure of Chapter 7,

$$S(t; s_t) = \tilde{E}_t\left(\sum_{j=t}^{T-1} \frac{C - (r(j; s_j) - 1)L}{B(j+1; s_j)}\right)B(t; s_{t-1}) \qquad (10.3)$$

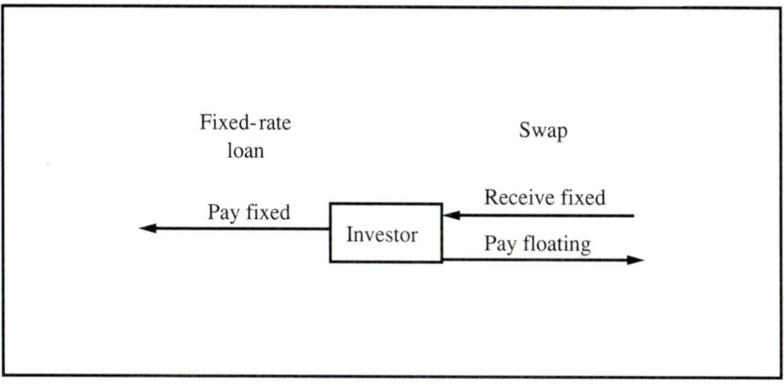

FIGURE 10.1
A swap that changes a fixed-rate loan into a floating-rate loan.

Defining $c \equiv 1 + C/L$ to be one plus the coupon rate on the fixed-rate loan, we can rewrite this as

$$\begin{aligned} S(t; s_t) &= \tilde{E}_t\left(\sum_{j=t}^{T-1} \frac{[c - r(j; s_j)]L}{B(j+1; s_j)}\right) B(t; s_{t-1}) \\ &= \mathcal{B}(t; s_t) - L \end{aligned} \tag{10.4}$$

The derivation of expression (10.4) is contained below.

Expression (10.4) shows that the swap's time 0 value is equal to the discounted expected cash flows from receiving fixed payments at rate c and paying floating payments at $r(t; s_t)$. The swap value as given in expression (10.4) is independent of any particular model for the evolution of the term structure of interest rates.

It is important to emphasize that the swap's value can be computed by using only the initial zero-coupon bond price curve (and expression (10.2)). This follows because this value equals $\mathcal{B}(t; s_t) - L$.

The derivation of expression (10.4) now follows for interested readers. Expression (10.4) will prove useful in the next chapter when we study exotic interest rate swaps.

DERIVATION OF EXPRESSION (10.4). For simplicity of notation, we omit the s_t argument. To get the first equality, substitute $C = (c - 1)L$ into expression (10.3) and simplify.

To get the second equality, write

$$\begin{aligned} &\tilde{E}_t\left(\sum_{j=t}^{T-1} \frac{C - (r(j) - 1)L}{B(j+1)}\right) B(t) \\ &= \tilde{E}_t\left(\sum_{j=t}^{T-1} \frac{C}{B(j+1)}\right) B(t) - \tilde{E}_t\left(\sum_{j=0}^{T-1} \frac{r(j) - 1}{B(j+1)}\right) B(t) L \end{aligned}$$

TABLE 10.3

The cash flows and values from a swap receiving fixed and paying floating

	0	1	2	...	$T-1$	T
Floating payments		$-[r(0)-1]L$	$-[r(1)-1]L$	...	$-[r(T-2)-1]L$	$-[r(T-1)-1]L-L$
Fixed payments		$+C$	$+C$	...	$+C$	$+C+L$
Net payments	0	$C-[r(0)-1]L$	$C-[r(1)-1]L$	...	$C-[r(T-2)-1]L$	$C-[r(T-1)-1]L$
Swap value	$\mathcal{B}(0)-L$	$\mathcal{B}(1)-L$	$\mathcal{B}(2)-L$	...	$\mathcal{B}(T-1)-L$	$\mathcal{B}(T)-L$

$$= \tilde{E}_t\left(\sum_{j=t}^{T-1} \frac{C}{B(j+1)} + \frac{L}{B(T)}\right)B(t) - \left[\tilde{E}_t\left(\sum_{j=t}^{T-1} \frac{r(j)-1}{B(j+1)} + \frac{1}{B(T)}\right)\right]B(t)L$$

This last inequality follows by adding and subtracting $\tilde{E}_t(1/B(T))B(t)L$. Finally, using expressions (10.1) and (10.2) gives the result. ■

2 The Swap Rate

The *swap rate* is defined to be that coupon rate C/L such that the swap has zero value at time 0, i.e., such that $S(0) = 0$ or $\mathcal{B}(0) = L$. In other words, this rate makes the time 0 coupon bond's value at par (at L), and the swap fairly priced at a zero dollar. It is important to emphasize that this determination of the swap rate is under the assumption of no default risk for either counterparty to the swap contract. Default risk and credit risk spreads are important elements in the actual application of these techniques to the swap market. These extensions require a generalization of the model presented, and they are available in Jarrow and Turnbull [1, 2].

The swap contract can be synthetically created by using the procedure described in Chapter 7. An example will illustrate these computations.

EXAMPLE: SWAP VALUATION. We use the evolution of the zero-coupon bond price curve given in Figs. 8.1 and 8.2. Consider a swap receiving fixed and paying floating with maturity date $T = 3$ and principal $L = 100$.

First, we need to determine the swap rate. To do this, we need to find the coupon payment C per period such that the value of the swap is zero, i.e., $S(0) = 0$. We first compute the swap's value for an arbitrary coupon payment of C:

$$\begin{aligned} S(0) &= \mathcal{B}(0) - 100 \\ &= CP(0,1) + CP(0,2) + (C + 100)P(0,3) - 100 \\ &= C[0.980392 + 0.961169 + 0.942322] + 100(0.942322) - 100 \\ &= C(2.8838) - 5.7678 \end{aligned}$$

Setting $S(0) = 0$ and solving for C yield

$$C = \frac{5.7678}{2.8838} = 2$$

The swap rate is $C/L = 2/100 = 0.02$.

The cash flows and values of this swap, with swap rate 0.02, are shown in Figure 10.2. We receive fixed and pay floating. The calculations are as follows. At time 3, for each possible state:

$$\begin{aligned} S(3;\text{uuu}) &= L - L = 100 - 100 = 0 \\ \text{cash flow}(3;\text{uuu}) &= C - (r(2;\text{uu}) - 1)L = 2 - 1.60307 = 0.39693 \\ S(3;\text{uud}) &= 100 - 100 = 0 \end{aligned}$$

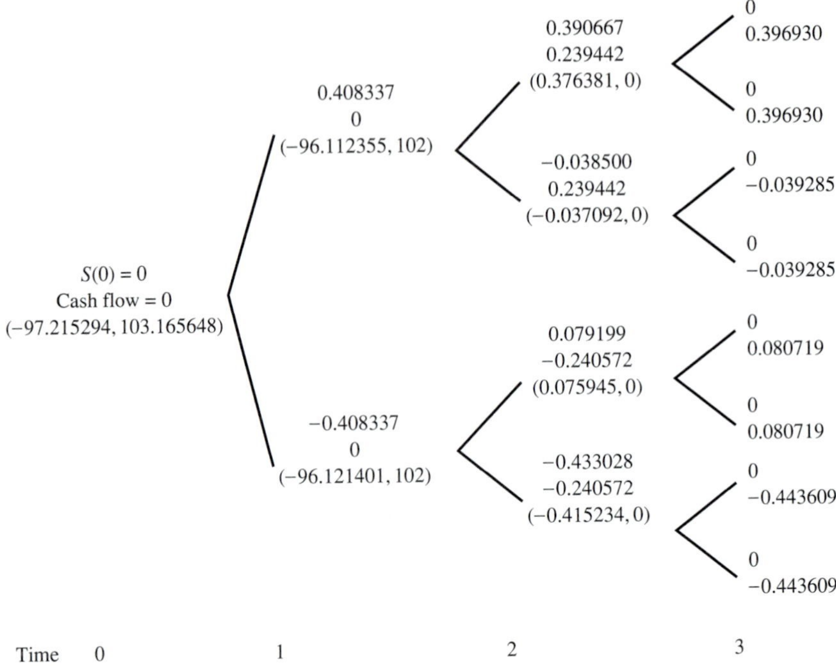

FIGURE 10.2
A swap receiving fixed and paying floating with maturity time 3, principal \$100, and swap rate 0.02. Given first is the swap's value, then the swap's cash flow. The synthetic swap portfolio positions in the money market account and in the three-period zero-coupon bond $(n_0(t; s_t), n_1(t; s_t))$ are given under each node.

$$\text{cash flow}(3; \text{uud}) = 2 - (r(2; \text{uu}) - 1)100 = 0.39693$$
$$S(3; \text{udu}) = 100 - 100 = 0$$
$$\text{cash flow}(3; \text{udu}) = 2 - (r(2; \text{ud}) - 1)100 = -0.039285$$
$$S(3; \text{udd}) = 100 - 100 = 0$$
$$\text{cash flow}(3; \text{udd}) = 2 - (r(2; \text{ud}) - 1)100 = -0.039285$$
$$S(3; \text{duu}) = 100 - 100 = 0$$
$$\text{cash flow}(3; \text{duu}) = 2 - (r(2; \text{du}) - 1)100 = 0.080719$$
$$S(3; \text{dud}) = 100 - 100 = 0$$
$$\text{cash flow}(3; \text{dud}) = 2 - (r(2; \text{du}) - 1)100 = 0.080719$$
$$S(3; \text{ddu}) = 100 - 100 = 0$$
$$\text{cash flow}(3; \text{ddu}) = 2 - (r(2; \text{dd}) - 1)100 = -0.443609$$
$$S(3; \text{ddd}) = 100 - 100 = 0$$
$$\text{cash flow}(3; \text{ddd}) = 2 - (r(2; \text{dd}) - 1)100 = -0.443609$$

Continuing backward through the tree:

$$S(2; \text{uu}) = \mathcal{B}(2; \text{uu}) - L = 102P(2,3; \text{uu}) - 100$$
$$= 102(0.984222) - 100 = 0.390667$$
$$\text{cash flow}(2; \text{uu}) = C - [r(1; u) - 1]L = 2 - 1.76056 = 0.239442$$
$$S(2; \text{ud}) = 102P(2,3; \text{ud}) - 100 = -0.038500$$
$$\text{cash flow}(2; \text{ud}) = 2 - (r(1; u) - 1)100 = 0.239442$$
$$S(2; \text{du}) = 102P(2,3; \text{du}) - 100 = 0.079199$$
$$\text{cash flow}(2; \text{du}) = 2 - (r(1; d) - 1)100 = -0.240572$$
$$S(2; \text{dd}) = 102P(2,3; \text{dd}) - 100 = -0.433028$$
$$\text{cash flow}(2; \text{dd}) = 2 - (r(1; d) - 1)100 = -0.240572$$

Finally, at time 1:

$$S(1; \text{u}) = \mathcal{B}(1; \text{u}) - L = 2P(1,2; \text{u}) + 102P(1,3; \text{u}) - 100$$
$$= 2(0.982699) + 102(0.965127) - 100 = 0.408337$$
$$\text{cash flow}(1; \text{u}) = C - [r(0) - 1]L = 2 - 2 = 0$$
$$S(1; \text{d}) = 2P(1,2; \text{d}) + 102P(1,3; \text{d}) - 100 = -0.408337$$
$$\text{cash flow}(1; \text{d}) = 2 - (r(0) - 1)100 = 0$$

From Fig. 10.2 we see that the cash flow from the swap can be positive or negative. Similarly, the value of the swap can be positive or negative as well, depending upon the movements of the spot rate of interest. ■

3 Synthetic Swaps

There are numerous ways of creating this swap synthetically. The first is to use a *buy and hold* strategy. This method is to short the money market account (pay floating) and to synthetically create the coupon bond with maturity $T = 3$, principal value of 100, and coupon payments of two dollars per period (receive fixed). This coupon bond can be synthetically created by purchasing two zero-coupon bonds maturing at dates 1 and 2, and 102 zero-coupon bonds maturing at date 3. The value of this combined position at each date and state will match the summed values of the swap and its cash flow. This synthetic swap is independent of any particular model of the evolution of the term structure of interest rates.

A second method for synthetically creating this swap is to use a dynamic portfolio consisting of the three-period zero-coupon bond and the money market account. This approach requires a specification of the evolution of the term structure of interest rates.

EXAMPLE: SYNTHETIC SWAP CONSTRUCTION. At time 2, state uu the value of the swap and its cash flow are known for sure; therefore, the swap can be synthetically created by holding none of the three-period zero-coupon bond,

$$n_1(2;\text{uu}) = 0$$

and the units of the money market account held are

$$\begin{aligned} n_0(2;\text{uu}) &= \frac{S(2;\text{uu}) - n_1(2;\text{uu})P(2,3;\text{uu})}{B(2;\text{u})} \\ &= \frac{0.390667}{1.037958} = 0.376381 \end{aligned}$$

The calculations for the remaining states are similar:

$$\begin{aligned} n_1(2;\text{ud}) &= 0 \\ n_0(2;\text{ud}) &= \frac{-0.038500}{1.037958} = -0.037092 \\ n_1(2;\text{du}) &= 0 \\ n_0(2;\text{du}) &= \frac{0.079199}{1.042854} = 0.075945 \\ n_1(2;\text{dd}) &= 0 \\ n_0(2;\text{dd}) &= \frac{-0.433028}{1.042854} = -0.415234 \end{aligned}$$

At time 1, state u the number of three-period zero-coupon bonds held is

$$\begin{aligned} n_1(1;\text{u}) &= \frac{(S(2;\text{uu}) + \text{cash flow}(2;\text{uu})) - (S(2;\text{ud}) + \text{cash flow}(2;\text{ud}))}{\text{P}(2,3;\text{uu}) - \text{P}(2,3;\text{ud})} \\ &= \frac{0.630109 - 0.200942}{0.984222 - 0.980015} = 102 \end{aligned}$$

The number of units of the money market account held is

$$\begin{aligned} n_0(1;\text{u}) &= \frac{S(1;\text{u}) - n_1(1;\text{u})P(1,3;\text{u})}{B(1)} \\ &= \frac{0.408337 - 102(0.965127)}{1.02} = -96.112355 \end{aligned}$$

At time 1, state d the calculations are

$$\begin{aligned} n_1(1;\text{d}) &= \frac{(S(2;\text{du}) + \text{cash flow}(2;\text{du})) - (S(2;\text{dd}) + \text{cash flow}(2;\text{dd}))}{\text{P}(2,3;\text{du}) - \text{P}(2,3;\text{dd})} \\ &= \frac{-0.161373 - (-0.6736)}{0.981169 - 0.976149} = 102 \\ n_0(1;\text{d}) &= \frac{S(1;\text{d}) - n_1(1;\text{d})P(1,3;\text{d})}{B(1)} \\ &= \frac{-0.408337 - 102(0.957211)}{1.02} = -96.121401 \end{aligned}$$

At time 0,

$$n_1(0) = \frac{(S(1;\text{u}) + \text{cash flow}(1;\text{u})) - (S(1;\text{d}) + \text{cash flow}(1;\text{d}))}{\text{P}(1,3;\text{u}) - \text{P}(1,3;\text{d})}$$

$$= \frac{0.408337 - (-0.408337)}{0.965127 - 0.957211} = 103.165648$$

$$n_0(0) = S(0) - n_1(0)P(0,3)$$

$$= 0 - 103.165648(0.942322) = -97.215294$$

The time 0 synthetic swap consists of a long position of 103.165 three-period zero-coupon bonds and short -97.215 units of the money market account. This makes sense since this swap is long fixed borrowing and short floating. ■

SECTION C
INTEREST RATE CAPS

This section values interest rate caps. A simple *interest rate cap* is a provision often attached to a floating-rate loan that limits the interest paid per period to a maximum amount, $k - 1$, where k is 1 plus a percentage. For example, if $r(t) > k$ occurs, the holder of the floating-rate loan with an interest rate cap pays only k dollars (not $r(t)$). Obviously, if the floating-rate loan in Table 10.1 has zero value, a floating-rate loan with an interest rate cap attached may have positive value. That is, the holder of a floating-rate loan with an interest rate cap may be willing to pay a positive amount to enter into the contract, because the interest rate cap potentially saves on interest payments in future periods. The purpose of this section is to value simple interest rate caps.

The interest rate cap on the floating-rate loan of Table 10.1 with maturity date τ^* can be decomposed into the sum of τ^* caplets. A *caplet* is an interest rate cap specific to only a single time period. It is a European call on the spot interest rate. For example, a caplet with maturity T and a strike k is a simple contingent claim with a time T cash flow of

$$\max(r(T-1; s_{T-1}) - k, 0)$$

This cash flow is known at time $T - 1$ because the spot rate is known at time $T - 1$.

The arbitrage-free value of the T-maturity caplet at time t, denoted $c(t, T; s_t)$, is obtained using the risk-neutral valuation procedure:

$$c(t, T; s_t) = \tilde{E}_t\left(\frac{\max(r(T-1; s_{T-1}) - k, 0)}{B(T; s_{T-1})}\right)B(t; s_{t-1}) \qquad (10.5)$$

An interest rate cap on the floating-rate loan in Table 10.1 is then the sum of the values of the caplets from which it is composed. Let $I(t, \tau^*; s_t)$ denote the value of an interest rate cap at time t with strike k and expiration date τ^*; then

$$I(t, \tau^*; s_t) = \sum_{j=1}^{\tau^*} c(t, j; s_t) \tag{10.6}$$

The interest rate cap can be created synthetically by using the procedure described in Chapter 7.

EXAMPLE: CAP VALUATION. To illustrate this computation, we utilize the spot rate process given in Fig. 8.2. Consider an interest rate cap with maturity date $\tau^* = 3$ and a strike of $k = 1.02$. This interest rate cap can be decomposed into three caplets: one at time 1, one at time 2, and one at time 3. We value and discuss the synthetic construction of each caplet in turn.

From Fig. 8.2 we see that the caplet at time 1, $c(0, 1)$, has zero value. Formally,

$$\begin{aligned} c(0, 1) &= \frac{\tilde{E}_0(\max(r(0) - 1.02, 0))}{r(0)} \\ &= \frac{(1/2)(0) + (1/2)(0)}{1.02} = 0 \end{aligned}$$

Hence, this caplet can be excluded from further consideration.

Next, consider the caplet with maturity at time 2. By expression (10.5), at time 2 its value under each state is as follows:

$$\begin{aligned} c(2, 2; \text{uu}) &= \max(r(1; \text{u}) - 1.02, 0) = \max(1.017606 - 1.02, 0) = 0 \\ c(2, 2; \text{ud}) &= \max(r(1; \text{u}) - 1.02, 0) = 0 \\ c(2, 2; \text{du}) &= \max(r(1; \text{d}) - 1.02, 0) = \max(1.022406 - 1.02, 0) = 0.002406 \\ c(2, 2; \text{dd}) &= \max(r(1; \text{d}) - 1.02, 0) = 0.002406 \end{aligned}$$

These numbers can be found in Fig. 10.3. Continuing backward through the tree,

$$\begin{aligned} c(1, 2; \text{u}) &= \frac{(1/2)0 + (1/2)0}{r(1; \text{u})} = 0 \\ c(1, 2; \text{d}) &= \frac{(1/2)0.002406 + (1/2)0.002406}{1.022406} = 0.002353 \end{aligned}$$

The denominator in the calculation of $c(1, 2; \text{d})$ is $r(1; \text{d}) = 1.022406$.

Finally, at time 0, the caplet's value is

$$\begin{aligned} c(0, 2) &= \frac{(1/2)0 + (1/2)0.002353}{1.02} \\ &= 0.001153 \end{aligned}$$

These numbers appear in Fig. 10.3.

We can synthetically create this two-period caplet with the money market account and a three-period zero-coupon bond. At time 1, state u no position is required. At time 1, state d the number of three-period zero-coupon bonds is

$$n_1(1; \text{d}) = \frac{c(2, 2; \text{du}) - c(2, 2; \text{dd})}{P(2, 3; \text{du}) - P(2, 3; \text{dd})} = \frac{0.002406 - 0.002406}{0.981169 - 0.976147} = 0$$

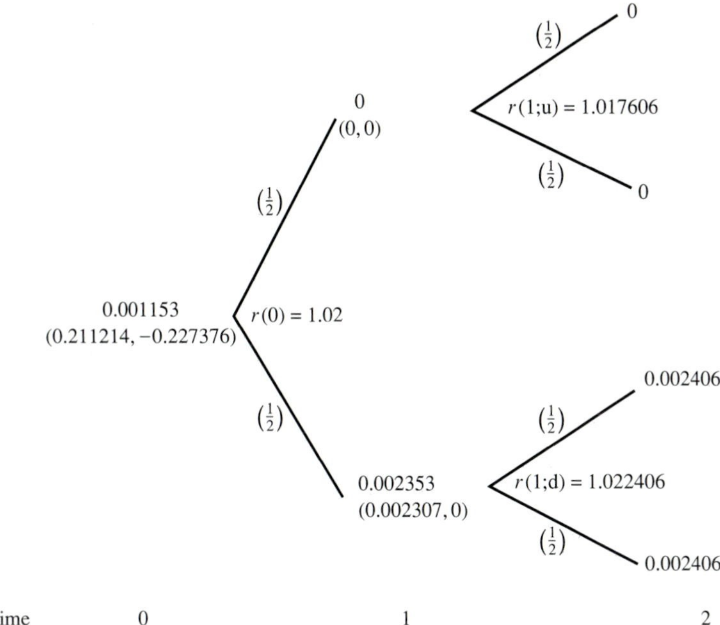

FIGURE 10.3
A two-period caplet with a 1.02 strike. The synthetic caplet portfolio positions in the money market account and in the three-period zero-coupon bond $(n_0(t; s_t), n_1(t; s_t))$ are given under each node.

The number of units of the money market account held is:

$$\begin{aligned} n_0(1; \mathrm{d}) &= \frac{c(1, 2; \mathrm{d}) - n_1(1; \mathrm{d})P(1, 3; \mathrm{d})}{B(1)} \\ &= \frac{0.002353 - 0(0.957211)}{1.02} \\ &= 0.002307 \end{aligned}$$

At time 0, the calculations are

$$n_1(0) = \frac{c(1, 2; \mathrm{u}) - c(1, 2; \mathrm{d})}{P(1, 3; \mathrm{u}) - P(1, 3; \mathrm{d})} = \frac{0 - 0.002353}{0.965127 - 0.957211} = -0.227376$$

and

$$\begin{aligned} n_0(0) &= c(0, 2) - n_1(0)P(0, 3) \\ &= 0.001153 + 0.227376(0.942322) \\ &= 0.211214 \end{aligned}$$

The time 0 synthetic two-period caplet consists of 0.211214 of a unit of the money market account and *short* 0.227376 of the three-period zero-coupon bond. This makes sense since the three-period zero-coupon bond declines as interest

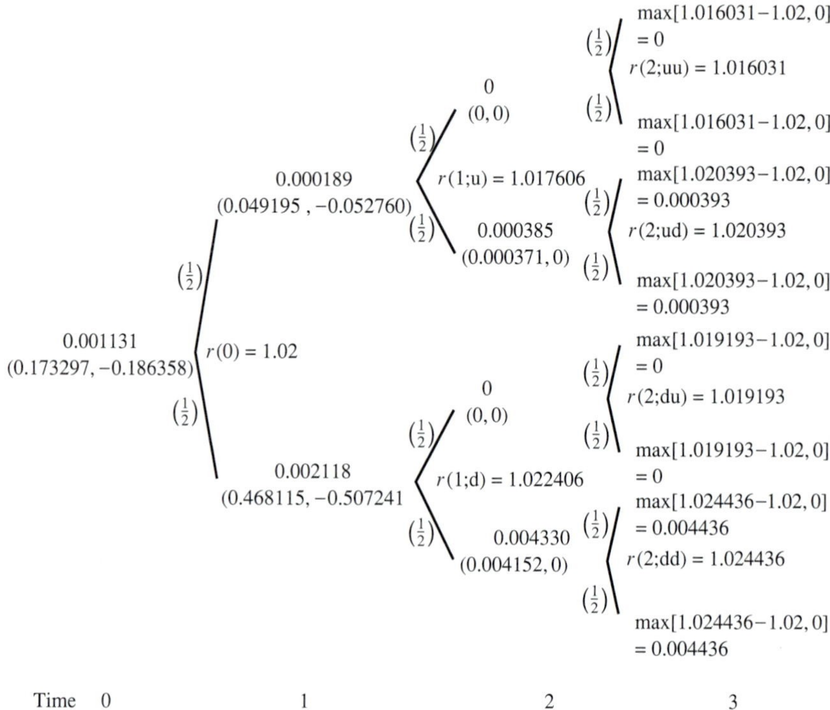

FIGURE 10.4
A three-period caplet with a 1.02 strike. The synthetic caplet portfolio positions in the money market account and in the four-period zero-coupon bond $(n_0(t; s_t), n_1(t; s_t))$ are given under each node.

rates rise. This inverse price movement necessitates a short position in the three-period zero-coupon bond to duplicate the caplet.

The calculations for the value of the three-period caplet and the synthetic three-period caplet positions in the money market account and the four-period zero-coupon bond are presented in Fig. 10.4. These calculations are similar to those described above, and they are left to the reader to verify as an exercise.

The interest rate cap's value is the sum of the three separate caplets' values, i.e.,

$$\begin{aligned} I(0,3) &= c(0,1) + c(0,2) + c(0,3) \\ &= 0 + 0.001153 + 0.001131 = 0.002284 \quad \text{dollar} \end{aligned}$$

Thus, for this example, to enter into a floating-rate loan of three periods plus an interest rate cap with strike 1.02, the holder must pay out 0.002284 dollar.

The synthetic interest rate cap can be obtained as the sum of the three separate synthetic caplets. These positions are easily read off Figs. 10.3 and 10.4, and they are left to the reader to aggregate. The position involves the money market account, the three-period bond, and the four-period bond. ■

SECTION D
INTEREST RATE FLOORS

This section values interest rate floors. An *interest rate floor* is a provision associated with a floating-rate loan that guarantees that a minimum interest payment of $k - 1$ is made, where k is 1 plus a percentage. Unlike an interest rate cap, this provision benefits the lender. It therefore reduces the value of a floating-rate loan below zero. That is, the holder of a floating-rate loan plus a floor must be paid to enter into the contract. The purpose of this section is to value interest rate floors.

An interest rate floor on the floating-rate loan of Table 10.1 with maturity date τ^* can be decomposed into the sum of τ^* floorlets. A *floorlet* is an interest rate floor specific to only a single time period. A floorlet is a European put on the spot interest rate. For example, a floorlet with maturity T and strike k is a simple contingent claim with a time T cash flow of

$$\max(k - r(T-1; s_{T-1}), 0)$$

This cash flow is known at time $T - 1$ because the spot rate is known at time $T - 1$.

The arbitrage-free value of the T-maturity floorlet at time t, denoted $d(t, T; s_t)$, is obtained using the risk-neutral valuation procedure:

$$d(t, T; s_t) = \tilde{E}_t\left(\frac{\max(k - r(T-1; s_{T-1}), 0)}{B(T; s_{T-1})}\right)B(t; s_{t-1}) \qquad (10.7)$$

An interest rate floor on the floating-rate loan in Table 10.1 equals the sum of the values of the floorlets of which it is composed. Let $J(t, \tau^*; s_t)$ denote the value of an interest rate floor at time t with strike k and expiration date τ^*; then

$$J(t, \tau^*; s_t) = \sum_{j=1}^{\tau^*} d(t, j; s_t) \qquad (10.8)$$

The interest rate floor can be synthetically created by using the procedure described in Chapter 7.

EXAMPLE: FLOOR VALUATION. To illustrate this computation, we utilize the spot rate process given in Fig. 8.2. Consider an interest rate floor with maturity date $\tau^* = 3$ and strike $k = 1.0175$. This interest rate floor can be decomposed into three floorlets: one at time 1, one at time 2, and one at time 3. We value and discuss the synthetic construction of each floorlet in turn.

From Fig. 8.2 we see that the floorlet at time 1, $d(0, 1)$, has zero value. Formally,

$$d(0,1) = \frac{\tilde{E}_0(\max(1.0175 - r(0), 0))}{r(0)}$$

$$= \frac{(1/2)0 + (1/2)0}{1.02} = 0$$

Hence, this floorlet can be excluded from further consideration.

Next, consider the floorlet with maturity at time 2. By expression (10.7) its value at time 2 is zero under all states; i.e.,

$$\begin{aligned}
d(2,2;\mathrm{uu}) &= \max(1.0175 - r(1;\mathrm{u}), 0) = \max(1.0175 - 1.017606, 0) = 0\\
d(2,2;\mathrm{ud}) &= \max(1.0175 - r(1;\mathrm{u}), 0) = 0\\
d(2,2;\mathrm{du}) &= \max(1.0175 - r(1;\mathrm{d}), 0) = \max(1.0175 - 1.022406, 0) = 0\\
d(2,2;\mathrm{dd}) &= \max(1.0175 - r(1;\mathrm{d}), 0) = 0
\end{aligned}$$

Hence, at time 1 its value is also zero under each state:

$$d(1,2;\mathrm{u}) = \frac{(1/2)0 + (1/2)0}{r(1;\mathrm{u})} = 0$$

$$d(1,2;\mathrm{d}) = \frac{(1/2)0 + (1/2)0}{r(1;\mathrm{d})} = 0$$

This is also true at time 0:

$$d(0,2) = \frac{(1/2)0 + (1/2)0}{r(0)} = 0$$

So this floorlet can also be excluded from future consideration.

The calculations for the three-period floorlet are contained in Fig. 10.5. The time 3 payoffs to the floorlet, using (10.7), are

$$\begin{aligned}
d(3,3;\mathrm{uuu}) &= \max(1.0175 - r(1;\mathrm{uu}), 0) = \max(1.0175 - 1.016031, 0)\\
&= 0.001469\\
d(3,3;\mathrm{uud}) &= \max(1.0175 - r(1;\mathrm{uu}), 0) = 0.001469\\
d(3,3;\mathrm{udu}) &= \max(1.0175 - r(1;\mathrm{ud}), 0) = \max(1.0175 - 1.020393, 0) = 0\\
d(3,3;\mathrm{udd}) &= \max(1.0175 - r(1;\mathrm{ud}), 0) = 0\\
d(3,3;\mathrm{duu}) &= \max(1.0175 - r(1;\mathrm{du}), 0) = \max(1.0175 - 1.019193, 0) = 0\\
d(3,3;\mathrm{dud}) &= \max(1.0175 - r(1;\mathrm{du}), 0) = 0\\
d(3,3;\mathrm{ddu}) &= \max(1.0175 - r(1;\mathrm{dd}), 0) = \max(1.0175 - 1.024436, 0) = 0\\
d(3,3;\mathrm{ddd}) &= \max(1.0175 - r(1;\mathrm{dd}), 0) = 0
\end{aligned}$$

The floorlet has a positive value only at time 2, state uu. Its value is

$$d(2;\mathrm{uu}) = \frac{(1/2)0.001469 + (1/2)0.001469}{1.016031} = 0.001446$$

Continuing backward in the tree, the floorlet has a positive value only at time 1, state u:

$$d(1;\mathrm{u}) = \frac{(1/2)0.001446 + (1/2)0}{1.017606} = 0.000711$$

Finally, its time 0 value is

$$d(0) = \frac{(1/2)0.000711 + (1/2)0}{1.02} = 0.000348.$$

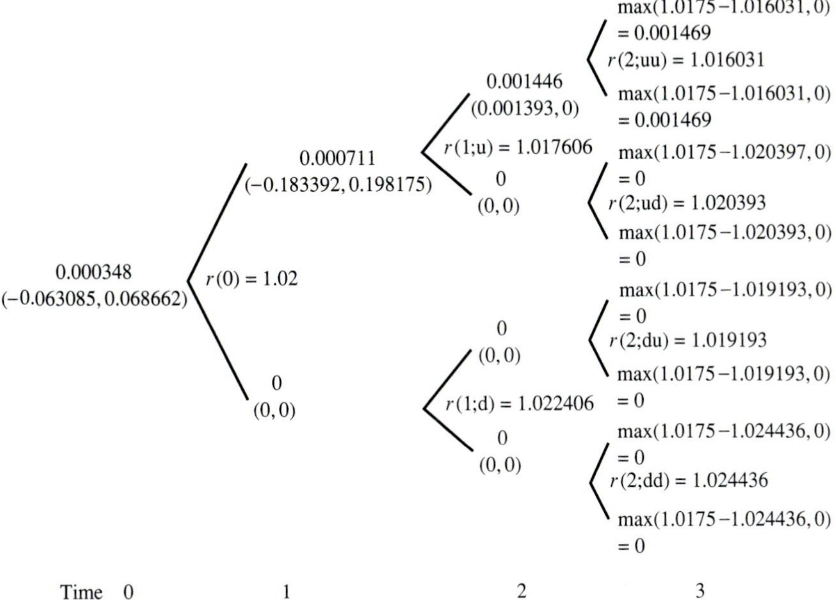

FIGURE 10.5
A three-period floorlet with a 1.0175 strike. The synthetic floorlet portfolio positions in the money market account and in the four-period zero-coupon bond $(n_0(t; s_t), n_1(t; s_t))$ are given under each node.

To synthetically create the floorlet, we use the four-period zero-coupon bond and the money market account. The calculations are as follows:

At time 2, state uu,

$$n_1(2; \text{uu}) = \frac{d(3, 3; \text{uuu}) - d(3, 3; \text{uud})}{P(3, 4; \text{uuu}) - P(3, 4; \text{uud})} = \frac{0.001469 - 0.001469}{0.985301 - 0.981381} = 0$$

$$n_0(2; \text{uu}) = \frac{d(2; \text{uu}) - n_1(2; \text{uu})P(2, 4; \text{uu})}{B(2; \text{uu})}$$

$$= \frac{0.001446 - 0(0.984222)}{1.037958} = 0.001393$$

At time 1, state u,

$$n_1(1; \text{u}) = \frac{d(2, 3; \text{uu}) - d(2, 3; \text{ud})}{P(2, 4; \text{uu}) - P(2, 4; \text{ud})} = \frac{0.001446 - 0}{0.967826 - 0.960529} = 0.198175$$

$$n_0(1; \text{u}) = \frac{d(1; \text{u}) - n_1(1; \text{u})P(1, 4; \text{u})}{B(1; \text{u})}$$

$$= \frac{0.000711 - (0.198175)0.947497}{1.02}$$

$$= -0.183392$$

Finally, at time 0,

$$n_1(0) = \frac{d(1,3;\mathrm{u}) - d(1,3;\mathrm{d})}{P(1,4;\mathrm{u}) - P(1,4;\mathrm{d})} = \frac{0.000711 - 0}{0.947497 - 0.937148} = 0.068662$$

$$n_0(0) = d(0,1) - n_1(0)P(0,4)$$
$$= 0.000348 - 0.068662(0.923845) = -0.063085$$

To duplicate the three-period floorlet at time 0, one must go long 0.068662 of a unit of the four-period zero-coupon bond and go short 0.063085 of a unit of the money market account.

The interest rate floor's value is the sum of the three separate floorlets' values; i.e.,

$$J(0,3) = d(0,1) + d(0,2) + d(0,3)$$
$$= 0 + 0 + 0.000348 = 0.000348 \quad \text{dollar}$$

Thus, for this example, to enter into a floating-rate loan of three periods plus an interest rate floor with strike 1.0175, the holder must receive 0.000348 of a dollar.

The synthetic interest rate floor can be obtained by summing the positions in the three synthetic floorlets. ■

SECTION E SWAPTIONS

This section values swaptions, which are options issued on interest rate swaps. Consider the swap receiving fixed and paying floating discussed in Section 10.B. This swap has a swap rate C/L, a maturity date T, and a principal equal to L dollars. Its time t, state s_t value is denoted by $S(t; s_t)$ and is given in expression (10.4).

A *European call option* on the swap $S(t; s_t)$ with an expiration date $T^* \le T$ and a strike price of K dollars has a payoff at time T^* equal to $\max[S(T^*; s_{T^*}) - K, 0]$. The arbitrage-free value of the swaption, denoted $O(t; s_t)$, is obtained using the risk-neutral valuation procedure; i.e.,

$$O(t; s_t) = \tilde{E}_t\left(\frac{\max[S(T^*; s_{T^*}) - K, 0]}{B(T^*; s_{T^*-1})}\right)B(t; s_{t-1}) \tag{10.9}$$

The European call option can be synthetically created by using the procedure described in Chapter 7.

Substitution of expression (10.4) into expression (10.9) generates a significant relation:

$$O(t; s_t) = \tilde{E}_t\left(\frac{\max[\mathcal{B}(T^*; s_{T^*}) - (L + K), 0]}{B(T^*; s_{T^*-1})}\right)B(t; s_t) \tag{10.10}$$

Expression (10.10) shows that a European call option with strike K and expiration T^* on a swap receiving fixed and paying floating with maturity T, principal L, and swap rate C/L is equivalent to a European call option with a strike $L + K$ and an expiration date of T^* on a (noncallable) coupon bond $\mathcal{B}(t; s_t)$ with maturity T, coupon C, and principal L. The pricing and synthetic construction of these bond options are discussed in Chapter 8. Thus, we have already studied the pricing and synthetic construction of swaptions. Nonetheless, for completeness, we give an example based on expression (10.9).

EXAMPLE: EUROPEAN CALL OPTION ON A SWAP. We illustrate the calculation of the swaption value in expression (10.9) using the swap example in Section 10.A, which is based on Figs. 8.1 and 8.2. Recall that the swap in the example of Section 10.B.2 is receiving fixed and paying floating, and it has a swap rate $C/L = 0.02$, a maturity date $T = 3$, and a principal $L = 100$. The valuation of the swap is contained in Fig. 10.2.

Consider a European call option on this swap. Let the maturity date of the option be $T^* = 1$, and let the strike price be $K = 0$. Using the risk-neutral valuation procedure, the value of the swaption is as follows:

Time 1, state u:

$$O(1; \mathrm{u}) = \max[0.408337, 0] = 0.408337$$

Time 1, state d:

$$O(1; \mathrm{d}) = \max[-0.408337, 0] = 0$$

Time 0:

$$O(0) = \frac{(1/2)O(1; \mathrm{u}) + (1/2)O(1; \mathrm{d})}{r(0)}$$

$$= \frac{(1/2)(0.408337) + (1/2)0}{1.02} = 0.200165$$

We can synthetically create this swaption with the money market account and a three-period zero-coupon bond. At time 0 the calculations are as follows:

$$n_1(0) = \frac{O(1; \mathrm{u}) - O(1; \mathrm{d})}{P(1, 3; \mathrm{u}) - P(1, 3; \mathrm{d})} = \frac{0.408337 - 0}{0.965127 - 0.957211} = 51.5838$$

$$n_0(0) = \frac{O(0) - n_1(0)P(0, 3)}{B(0)}$$

$$= 0.200165 - (51.5838)0.942322 = -48.4083$$

The synthetic option consists of 51.5838 units of the three-period zero-coupon bond, and it is short 48.4083 units of the money market account. The swaption's value is 0.200165. These numbers are presented in Fig. 10.6. ■

American swaptions (calls and puts) can be valued and hedged by using the stochastic dynamic programming approach illustrated previously in Chapter 8.

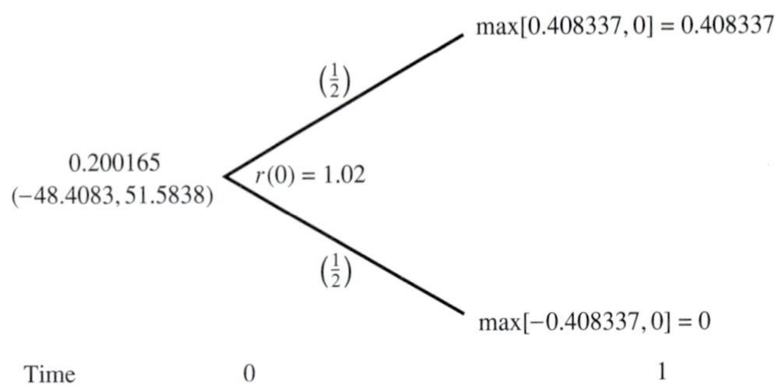

FIGURE 10.6
A European call option with strike 0 and expiration date 1 on the swap in Fig. 10.2. The synthetic swaption positions in the money market account and three-period zero-coupon bond $(n_0(t; s_t), n_1(t; s_t))$ are given under each node.

SECTION F
COMPUTER EXERCISES

This set of exercises using the Trees software should help the reader understand the pricing of swaps and swaptions.

Run the Trees software. It gives a different spot rate evolution from the one in the book, and this new evolution is the one used in the following exercises.

a. This exercise shows how to value an *existing* swap. Consider a swap receiving fixed and paying floating with swap rate 0.03, maturity time 3, and principal \$100 dollars. To value this swap we use expression (10.4).

First, go to the "claims" selection and choose "coupon bond." Enter a cash flow of \$3 at times 1 and 2 and a cash flow of \$103 at time 3. This values the coupon bond $\mathcal{B}(0)$. Display its prices by choosing "display" and "on the tree." Switch the display to "coupon bond prices."

To get the value of the swap, subtract L from each node in the tree.

b. Next, we find the swap rate on a *newly* issued swap. Let the swap receive fixed and pay floating, with maturity 3 years and principal 100 dollars. We want to find C such that

$$\mathcal{B}(0: C) = 100$$

The second argument in $\mathcal{B}(0 : C)$ is new, and it represents the coupon payment. Since this a linear equation in C, we need two points on this curve to uniquely determine its value.

From exercise (a) we compute x:

$$\mathcal{B}(0: 3) = x$$

where $x = 3\sum_{j=1}^{3} P(0, j) + 100P(0, 3)$. Repeat exercise (*a*), but change the swap rate to 0.04. Then we compute y, i.e.,

$$\mathcal{B}(0\colon 4) = y$$

where $y = 4\sum_{j=1}^{3} P(0, j) + 100P(0, 3)$.

Given x and y, we can determine $\sum_{j=1}^{3} P(0, j)$ and $100P(0, 3)$. Indeed, $\sum_{j=1}^{3} \times P(0, j) = y - x$, and $100P(0, 3) = y - 4(y - x)$. Then

$$\mathcal{B}(0\colon C) = C\sum_{j=1}^{3} P(0, j) + 100P(0, 3) - 100 = 0$$

implies that

$$C = \frac{100 - 100P(0, 3)}{\sum_{j=1}^{3} P(0, j)}$$

$$= \frac{100 - (y - x)}{y - 4(y - x)}$$

The swap rate is $C/100$. Compute $C/100$ using the x and y obtained above.

c. Repeat the above exercise, but compute $\sum_{j=1}^{3} P(0, j)$ and $100P(0, 3)$ directly using the zero-coupon bond prices.

d. For the swap in exercise (*a*), this problem values a European call option on it by using expression (10.10).

Consider a European call option with maturity date 2 and strike price 0 on the swap of exercise (*a*). To value this option, repeat the coupon-bond construction in exercise (*a*). Go to the "claims" selection and choose "European call." Enter strike $L + K = 100 + 0 = 100$ and expiration 2. Choose "display," then "on the tree," and then "European call" to display the European call option's prices on the tree. This is the answer.

SECTION G
REFERENCES TO CHAPTER 10

[1] Jarrow, R., and S. Turnbull, 1995. "Pricing Derivatives on Financial Securities Subject to Credit Risk." *Journal of Finance,* 50 (1), 53–86.

[2] Jarrow, R., and S. Turnbull, 1995. *Derivative Securities.* Southwestern Publishers, Cleveland.

CHAPTER 11

Interest Rate Exotics

This chapter applies the theory from Chapter 7 to price and hedge various interest rate exotic options. In particular, we study digital options, range notes, and index-amortizing swaps. These options are called exotic because they are more complex than ordinary call and put options. To study exotic options, we must first define the notion of a simple interest rate.

SECTION A
SIMPLE INTEREST RATES

This section defines simple interest rates. A *simple interest rate of maturity* $T - t$, denoted $R(t, T)$, is defined in terms of the price $P(t, T)$ as

$$R(t, T) \equiv \frac{1}{(T - t)}\left(\frac{1}{P(t, T)} - 1\right) \tag{11.1}$$

Alternatively,

$$P(t, T) = \frac{1}{1 + R(t, T)(T - t)} \tag{11.2}$$

Unlike the other rates in this book, $R(t, T)$ represents a *percentage*: it is a number between -1 and 1. Recall that all other rates in this book are defined to be one plus a percentage.

Simple interest rates measure the holding-period return on a zero-coupon bond. In this sense they are similar to the yield on a zero-coupon bond, except that yields include compounding, while simple interest rates do not.[1]

[1]Recall that the yield $y(t, T)$ is defined in Chapter 3 by expression (3.2), $P(t, T) = 1/[y(t, T)]^{(T-t)}$. This expression explicitly incorporates compounding of interest (interest earned on interest).

EXAMPLE: SIMPLE INTEREST RATES. Using the zero-coupon bond prices from Fig. 8.1, the time 0 simple interest rates are

$$R(0,1) = \frac{1}{P(0,1)} - 1 = \frac{1}{0.980392} - 1 = 0.020000$$

$$R(0,2) = \frac{1}{2}\left(\frac{1}{P(0,2)} - 1\right) = \frac{1}{2}\left(\frac{1}{0.961169} - 1\right) = 0.020200$$

$$R(0,3) = \frac{1}{3}\left(\frac{1}{P(0,3)} - 1\right) = \frac{1}{3}\left(\frac{1}{0.942322} - 1\right) = 0.020403$$

$$R(0,4) = \frac{1}{4}\left(\frac{1}{P(0,4)} - 1\right) = \frac{1}{4}\left(\frac{1}{0.923845} - 1\right) = 0.020608$$

Note that the simple interest rate of maturity one is $R(0,1) = r(0) - 1 = 0.02$. ■

By their definitions, we see that the spot rate at time t equals one plus the simple interest rate with unit maturity; i.e.,

$$r(t) = \frac{1}{P(t, t+1)} = 1 + R(t, t+1) \tag{11.3}$$

Digital options and range notes are typically written on simple interest rates.

SECTION B DIGITAL OPTIONS

A *European call digital option* with expiration date T and strike price k on the simple interest rate with time to maturity T^* is defined by its payoff at expiration. Denote the digital's time t value under state s_t as $D(t; s_t)$. Then the digital's time T payoff is

$$D(T; s_T) = \begin{cases} 1 & \text{if } R(T, T+T^*; s_T) > k \\ 0 & \text{if } R(T, T+T^*; s_T) \leq k \end{cases} \tag{11.4}$$

The digital call option pays a dollar if the simple interest rate with time to maturity T^* exceeds the strike rate k. Otherwise, it pays nothing.

Using the risk-neutral valuation procedure of Chapter 7, we find the value of the digital option at time t to be

$$D(t; s_t) = \tilde{E}_t\left(\frac{D(T; s_T)}{B(T; s_{T-1})}\right) B(t; s_{t-1}) \tag{11.5}$$

It is interesting to rewrite expression (11.4) using expression (11.1). Note that

$$R(T, T+T^*; s_T) > k \qquad \text{if and only if} \qquad \frac{1}{P(T, T+T^*)} > 1 + kT^*$$

and that this holds if and only if $P(T, T + T^*) < \dfrac{1}{1 + kT^*}$

This allows us to rewrite expression (11.4) as

$$D(T; s_T) = \begin{cases} 1 & \text{if } P(T, T + T^*) < \dfrac{1}{1 + kT^*} \\ 0 & \text{if } P(T, T + T^*) \geq \dfrac{1}{1 + kT^*} \end{cases} \tag{11.6}$$

Thus, a European digital *call* option on the simple interest rate is equivalent to a European digital *put* option on the zero-coupon bond with maturity date $T + T^*$.

A synthetic digital option can be constructed by using the techniques of Chapter 7.

EXAMPLE: DIGITAL CALL VALUATION. This example is based on Figs. 8.1 and 8.2. Consider a European call digital option with expiration date $T = 2$ and strike price $k = 0.02$ on the simple interest rate with time to maturity $T^* = 2$.

To value this option, we use expression (11.6). The calculations are as follows. The modified strike is

$$\frac{1}{1 + kT^*} = \frac{1}{1 + 0.02(2)} = 0.961538$$

The payoffs are

Time 2, state uu:

$$D(2; \text{uu}) = 0 \qquad \text{because } P(2, 4; \text{uu}) = 0.967826 > 0.961538$$

Time 2, state ud:

$$D(2; \text{ud}) = 1 \qquad \text{because } P(2, 4; \text{ud}) = 0.960529 < 0.961538$$

Time 2, state du:

$$D(2; \text{du}) = 0 \qquad \text{because } P(2, 4; \text{du}) = 0.962414 > 0.961538$$

Time 2, state dd:

$$D(2; \text{dd}) = 1 \qquad \text{because } P(2, 4; \text{dd}) = 0.953877 > 0.961538$$

Time 1, state u:

$$D(1; \text{u}) = \frac{(1/2)(0) + (1/2)1}{1.017606} = 0.049135$$

The synthetic digital in the four-period zero-coupon bond and the money market account is

$$n_1(1; \text{u}) = \frac{D(2, \text{uu}) - D(2; \text{ud})}{P(2, 4; \text{uu}) - P(2, 4; \text{ud})} = \frac{0 - 1}{0.967826 - 0.960529} = -137.0426$$

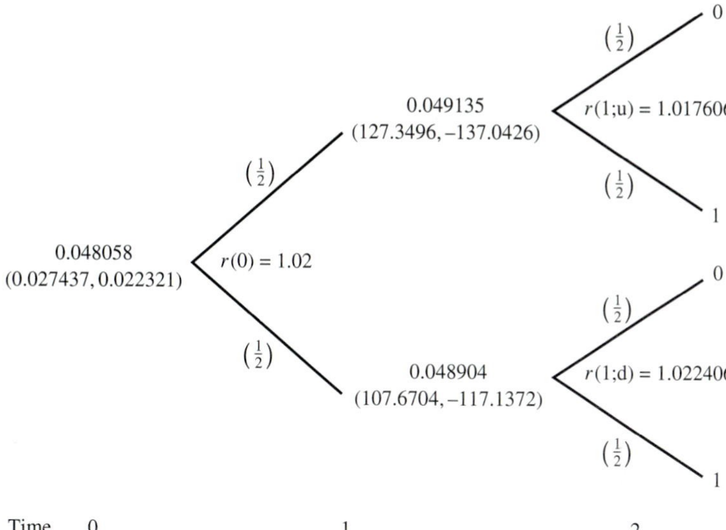

FIGURE 11.1
A European digital call option's values with strike $k = 0.02$ and expiration date $T = 2$ on the simple interest rate with time to maturity $T^* = 2$. The synthetic option portfolio position in the money market account and four-period zero-coupon bond $(n_0(t; s_t),\ n_1(t; s_t))$ is given under each node.

$$n_0(1;\text{u}) = \frac{D(1;\text{u}) - n_1(1;\text{u})P(1,4;\text{u})}{B(1)}$$
$$= \frac{0.049135 + (137.0426)0.947497}{1.02} = 127.3496$$

Time 1, state d:

$$D(1;\text{d}) = \frac{(1/2)(0) + (1/2)1}{1.022406} = 0.048904$$

The synthetic digital in the four-period zero-coupon bond and the money market account is

$$n_1(1;\text{d}) = \frac{D(2;\text{du}) - D(2;\text{dd})}{P(2,4;\text{du}) - P(2,4;\text{dd})} = \frac{0-1}{0.962414 - 0.953877} = -117.1372$$

$$n_0(1;\text{d}) = \frac{D(1;\text{d}) - n_1(1;\text{d})P(1,4;\text{d})}{B(1)}$$
$$= \frac{0.048904 + (117.1372)0.937148}{1.02} = 107.6704$$

Time 0:

$$D(0) = \frac{(1/2)0.049135 + (1/2)0.048904}{1.02}$$
$$= 0.048058$$

The synthetic digital in the four-period zero-coupon bond and the money market account is

$$n_1(0) = \frac{D(1;\mathrm{u}) - D(1;\mathrm{d})}{P(1,4;\mathrm{u}) - P(1,4;\mathrm{d})} = \frac{0.049135 - 0.048904}{0.947497 - 0.937148} = 0.022321$$

$$\begin{aligned} n_0(0) &= D(0) - n_1(0)P(0,4) \\ &= 0.048058 - 0.022321(0.923845) = 0.027437 \end{aligned}$$

These numbers are contained in Figure 11.1. The synthetic digital construction shows the difficulty in replicating the option (considering transaction costs). As the expiration date approaches, the delta in the four-period zero becomes quite large. It goes from +0.022321 of a unit at time 0 to either −137.0426 at time 1 in the up state or −117.1372 at time 1 in the down state. ■

The above techniques can be extended to European digital *put* options. *American* digital options can be valued using the stochastic dynamic programming technique discussed in Chapter 8.

SECTION C
RANGE NOTES

This section studies range notes. A *range note* is a financial security with a principal of L dollars and a maturity date T that pays the spot rate[2] of interest $r(t) - 1$ times L on any date t over the life of the contract where the simple interest rate with maturity T^*, $R(t, t + T^*)$, lies within the range k_l, k_u. The range limits k_l and k_u are called the lower and upper bound, respectively. The cash flow is paid at time $t + 1$.

This description is clarified by introducing the notation for an *index function:*

$$l_{\{k_l < R(t,t+T^*;s_t) < k_u\}} = \begin{cases} 1 & \text{if } k_l < R(t, t + T^*; s_t) < k_u \\ 0 & \text{otherwise} \end{cases} \tag{11.7}$$

Using this new index function, we can write the cash flows to a range note from time $t + 1$ until maturity as

$$\text{cash flows from } t + 1 \text{ to } T = \sum_{j=t}^{T-1} [r(j; s_j) - 1] L l_{\{k_l < R(j,j+T^*;s_j) < k_u\}} \tag{11.8}$$

Expression (11.8) has the first cash flow at time $t+1$, $[r(t)-1]Ll_{\{k_l < R(t,t+T^*) < k_u\}}$. The last payment is made at time T, and it is determined by the simple interest rate at time $T - 1$.

---

[2]A generalization is to allow the note to pay based on a second simple interest rate of maturity T^* instead of the spot rate of interest; see Turnbull [3].

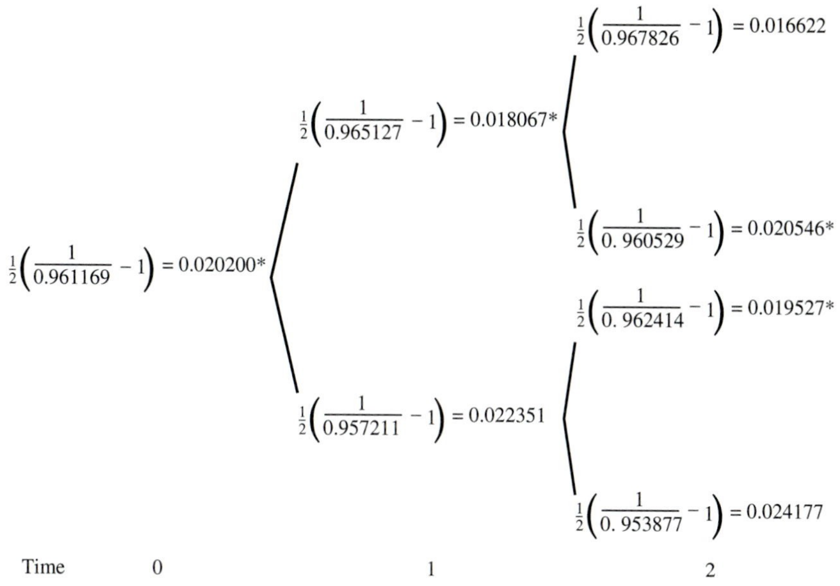

$\frac{1}{2}\left(\frac{1}{0.967826} - 1\right) = 0.016622$

$\frac{1}{2}\left(\frac{1}{0.965127} - 1\right) = 0.018067*$

$\frac{1}{2}\left(\frac{1}{0.960529} - 1\right) = 0.020546*$

$\frac{1}{2}\left(\frac{1}{0.961169} - 1\right) = 0.020200*$

$\frac{1}{2}\left(\frac{1}{0.962414} - 1\right) = 0.019527*$

$\frac{1}{2}\left(\frac{1}{0.957211} - 1\right) = 0.022351$

$\frac{1}{2}\left(\frac{1}{0.953877} - 1\right) = 0.024177$

Time 0 1 2

FIGURE 11.2
The evolution of a simple interest rate of maturity 2. An asterisk indicates that the simple interest rate lies between $k_l = 0.018$ and $k_u = 0.022$.

Let $N(t; s_t)$ denote the value of the range note at time t under state s_t. Then using the risk-neutral valuation procedure gives

$$N(t; s_t) = \tilde{E}_t\left(\sum_{j=t}^{T-1} \frac{[r(j; s_j) - 1]LI_{\{k_l < R(j, j+T*;\ s_j) < k_u\}}}{B(j+1; s_j)}\right)B(t; s_{t-1}) \quad (11.9)$$

A synthetic range note can be constructed by using the techniques of Chapter 7.

EXAMPLE: **RANGE NOTE VALUATION.** This example is based on Figs. 8.1 and 8.2. Consider a range note with the following provisions. Its maturity is $T = 3$ with principal $L = 100$. Let the lower bound be $k_l = 0.018$ and the upper bound be $k_u = 0.022$ on the simple interest rate with maturity $T^* = 2$.

To value this range note, we first compute the evolution of the simple interest rate $R(t, 2) = [1/P(t, t+2) - 1]/2$. This evolution is given in Fig. 11.2. We only need the evolution up to time 2 because the time 3 payment is based on the simple interest rate at time 2. A sample calculation, at time 2, state uu, is

$$R(2, 2; \text{uu}) = \frac{1}{2}\left[\frac{1}{P(2, 4; \text{uu})} - 1\right]$$
$$= \frac{1}{2}\left[\frac{1}{0.967826} - 1\right] = 0.016622$$

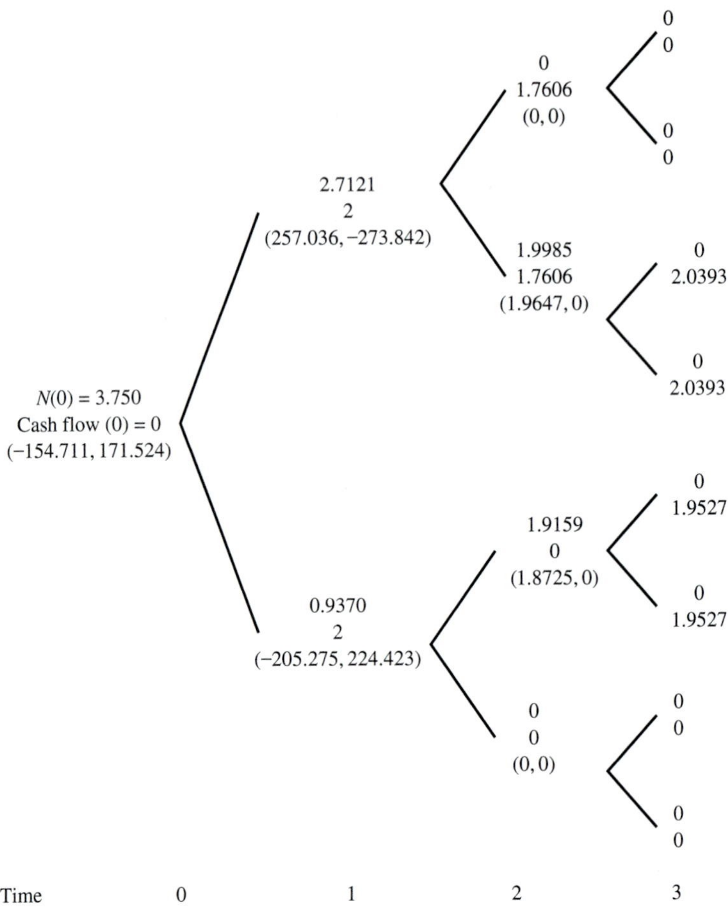

FIGURE 11.3
A range note with maturity $T = 3$, principle $L = 100$, and lower bound $k_l = 0.018$ and upper bound $k_u = 0.022$ on the simple interest rate with maturity $T^* = 2$. At each node, the first number is the value $(N(t; s_t))$ and the second number is the cash flow (cash flow $(t; s_t)$). The synthetic range note positions in the money market account and the four-period zero-coupon bond $(n_0(t; s_t), n_1(t; s_t))$ are given under each node.

From this evolution, we can compute the cash flows to the range note at each time and state. Sample calculations for time 3 are

$$\text{cash flow(3;uuu)} = 100[r(2;\text{uu}) - 1]l_{\{0.018<R(2,2;\text{uu})<0.02\}} = 0$$

because $R(2, 2; \text{uu}) = 0.016622$ is below the lower bound, and

$$\begin{aligned}\text{cash flow(3;udu)} &= 100[r(2;\text{ud}) - 1]l_{\{0.018<R(2,2;\text{ud})<0.02\}} \\ &= 100(1.020393 - 1) = 2.0393\end{aligned}$$

because $R(2, 2; \text{ud}) = 0.020546$ is between the lower and upper bounds. The remaining calculations are left as exercises for the reader. The results are presented in Fig. 11.3.

Using the risk-neutral valuation procedure, we can compute the value of the range note at time t from these cash flows as follows:

$$N(t; s_t) = \frac{1}{r(t; s_t)}\left(\frac{1}{2}[N(t+1; s_t\text{u}) + \text{cash flow}(t+1; s_t\text{u})] + \frac{1}{2}[N(t+1; s_t\text{d}) + \text{cash flow}(t+1; s_t\text{d})]\right) \tag{11.10}$$

where $N(3; s_3) \equiv 0$ for all s_3. A sample calculation for time 1, state u is

$$N(1; u) = \frac{1}{1.017606}\left[\frac{1}{2}(0 + 1.7606) + \frac{1}{2}(1.9985 + 1.7606)\right] = 2.7121$$

This occurs because $N(2; \text{uu}) = 0$, cash flow$(2; \text{uu}) = 1.7606$, $N(2; \text{ud}) = 1.9985$, cash flow$(2; \text{ud}) = 1.7606$, and $r(1; \text{u}) = 1.017606$. The remaining calculations are left as exercises for the reader. The results are contained in Fig. 11.3.

Finally, we can construct this range note synthetically using the money market account and the four-period zero-coupon bond via the equations

$$n_1(t; s_t) = \frac{[N(t+1; s_t\text{u}) + \text{cash flow}(t+1; s_t\text{u})] - [N(t+1; s_t\text{d}) + \text{cash flow}(t+1; s_t\text{d})]}{P(t+1, 4; s_t\text{u}) - P(t+1, 4; s_t\text{d})} \tag{11.11a}$$

and

$$n_0(t; s_t) = \frac{N(t; s_t) - n_1(t; s_t)P(t, 4; s_t)}{B(t; s_{t-1})} \tag{11.11b}$$

A sample calculation for time 1, state u is

$$n_1(1; \text{u}) = \frac{(0 + 1.7606) - (1.9985 + 1.7606)}{0.967827 - 0.960529} = -273.842$$

and

$$n_0(1; \text{u}) = \frac{2.7121 + 273.842(0.947497)}{1.02} = 257.036$$

This follows because

$$N(2; \text{uu}) = 0$$
$$\text{cash flow}(2; \text{uu}) = 1.7606$$
$$N(2; \text{ud}) = 1.9985$$
$$\text{cash flow}(2; \text{ud}) = 1.7606$$
$$P(2, 4; \text{uu}) = 0.967827$$

$$P(2,4;\text{ud}) = 0.960529$$

$$N(1;\text{u}) = 2.7121$$

$$P(1,4;\text{u}) = 0.947497$$

$$B(1) = 1.02$$

The remaining calculations are left as exercises for the reader. The results are given in Fig. 11.3.

It is interesting to observe that the range note goes from being long the four-period zero-coupon bond at time 0 (171.524 units) to short the four-period zero-coupon bond at time 1, state u (−273.842 units). This whiplash effect makes hedging range notes very difficult (considering transaction costs). ■

SECTION D INDEX-AMORTIZING SWAPS

Index-amortizing swaps are interest rate swaps in which the principal declines (amortizes) when interest rates decline. Consequently, these instruments are useful as (partial) hedges against prepayment risk in mortgage-backed securities.[3] Unlike the "plain vanilla" swaps discussed in Chapter 10, these exotic swaps are difficult to value because their cash flows (in general) depend on the entire history of spot interest rates.

Formally, an *index-amortizing swap* is a swap (say, receive fixed and pay floating) in which the principal is reduced by an amortizing schedule based on the spot rate of interest. The amortizing schedule does not apply until after a prespecified *lockout period* has passed.

In symbols, let T be the maturity of the index-amortizing swap with initial principal L_0 receiving fixed at rate c and paying floating at $r(t)$. Let the lockout period be T^* years. For $t \leq T^*$ the principal is fixed at L_0. For $t > T^*$ the following change in the principal occurs:

$$L(t;s_t) = L(t-1;s_{t-1})[1 - a(t;s_t)] \quad \text{for } t > T^* \tag{11.12}$$

where $L(T^*;s_{T^*}) = L_0$ and $a(t;s_t)$ is the amortizing amount. This expression states that the principal remaining at time t, $L(t;s_t)$, equals the principal at time $t-1$, $L(t-1;s_{t-1})$, reduced by the amortizing schedule amount $a(t;s_t)$.

[3]Mortgages are sometimes prepaid when the level of interest rates declines. This prepayment of a mortgage's principal is similar to the reduction in the principal on an index-amortizing swap. Mortgage-backed securities and prepayment risk are not discussed further in this textbook. Two useful references are McConnell and Singh [1] and Titman and Torous [2].

A typical amortizing schedule would look like the following:

$$a(t; s_t) \equiv \begin{cases} 0 & \text{if } r(t; s_t) > k_0 \\ b_0 & \text{if } k_0 \geq r(t; s_t) > k_1 \\ b_1 & \text{if } k_1 \geq r(t; s_t) > k_2 \\ b_2 & \text{if } k_2 \geq r(t; s_t) > k_3 \\ b_3 & \text{if } k_3 \geq r(t; s_t) > k_4 \\ b_4 & \text{if } k_4 \geq r(t; s_t) > k_5 \\ 1 & \text{if } k_5 \geq r(t; s_t) \end{cases} \tag{11.13}$$

where $k_0 > k_1 > k_2 > k_3 > k_4 > k_5$ and $0 < b_0 < b_1 < b_2 < b_3 < b_4 < 1$ are positive constants determined at the initiation of the swap.

The amortizing schedule in expression (11.13) depends on the spot interest rate at time t. If the spot interest rate is larger than k_0, no reduction in principal occurs: $a(t; s_t) = 0$. If the spot interest rate lies between k_0 and k_1, a reduction of $a(t; s_t) = b_0$ percent of the principal occurs; if the spot interest rate lies between k_1 and k_2, a reduction of $a(t; s_t) = b_1$ percent of the principal occurs; and so forth down the schedule. Although we have only written seven different levels for the amortization, it is easy to augment this schedule to accommodate an arbitrary number of levels.

EXAMPLE: AMORTIZING SCHEDULE. An example of an amortizing schedule is

$$a(t; s_t) \equiv \begin{cases} 0 & \text{if } r(t; s_t) > 1.01 \\ 0.25 & \text{if } 1.01 \geq r(t; s_t) > 1.0075 \\ 0.5 & \text{if } 1.0075 \geq r(t; s_t) > 1.005 \\ 0.75 & \text{if } 1.005 \geq r(t; s_t) > 1.0025 \\ 1 & \text{if } 1.0025 > r(t; s_t) \end{cases}$$

This completes the example. ■

The time t cash flow to the (receive fixed, pay floating) index-amortizing swap can be written as

$$\text{cash flow}(t; s_{t-1}) = [c - r(t-1; s_{t-1})]L(t-1; s_{t-1}) \tag{11.14}$$

The cash flow at time t is determined at time $t-1$. The cash flow is the sum of receiving fixed $(c-1)L(t-1; s_{t-1})$ and paying floating $[r(t-1; s_{t-1}) - 1] \times L(t-1; s_{t-1})$. The principal on which the one-dollar interest payments are based is determined according to expressions (11.12) and (11.13).

Let $\text{IA}(t; s_t)$ denote the time t value of the index-amortizing swap given state s_t. Using the risk-neutral valuation procedure of Chapter 7, we have that

$$\text{IA}(t; s_t) = \tilde{E}_t\left(\sum_{j=t+1}^{T} \frac{[c - r(j-1; s_{j-1})]L(j-1; s_{j-1})}{B(j; s_{j-1})}\right)B(t; s_{t-1}) \tag{11.15}$$

Expression (11.15) represents the present value of the cash flows to the index-amortizing swap from time $t + 1$ until its maturity at time T. This value differs from the plain vanilla swap of expression (10.4) only by the replacement of a constant principal L with the amortizing principal $L(j-1; s_{j-1})$. The complexity in valuation occurs because of this small difference. Note that the principal $L(j-1; s_{j-1})$ and spot interest rate $r(j-1; s_{j-1})$ are correlated. Furthermore, the principal depends (in general) on the history of the interest rate process prior to time $j-1$ (through s_{j-1}). This implies, for example, that the principal at time $T-1$ will also be correlated with the spot interest rate occurring earlier at time t. Consequently, valuation becomes complex. We illustrate this procedure through an example.

EXAMPLE: INDEX-AMORTIZING SWAP VALUATION. This example is based on Figs 8.1 and 8.2.

To illustrate the computations, we consider a very simple index amortizing swap. Let the swap receive fixed at rate $c = 1.02$ and pay floating. Let the swap's maturity be $T = 3$ years, and let the initial principal be $L_0 = 100$. Let the lockout period be $T^* = 1$ year. Let the amortizing schedule be given by

$$a(t; s_t) = \begin{cases} 0 & \text{if } r(t; s_t) \geq 1.018 \\ 0.5 & \text{if } r(t; s_t) < 1.018 \end{cases}$$

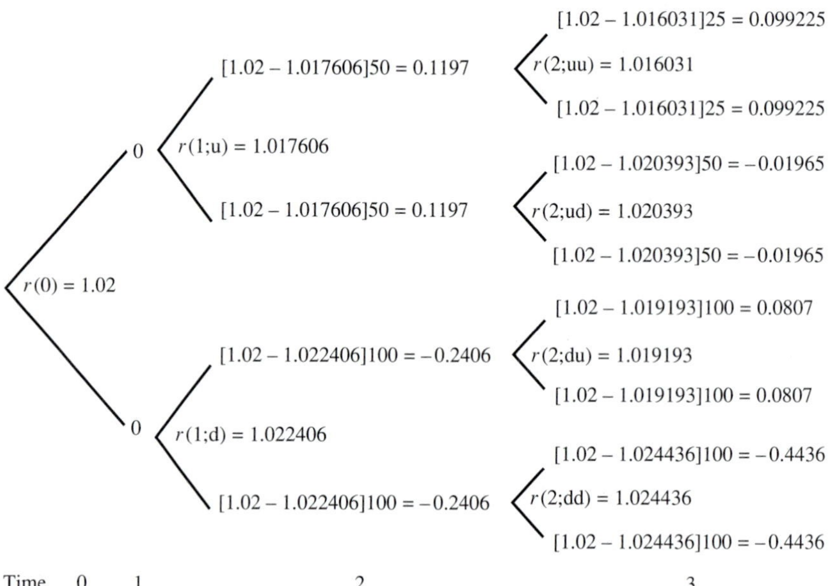

FIGURE 11.4
The cash flows from an index-amortizing swap with maturity $T = 3$, initial principal $L_0 = 100$, and lockout period $T^* = 1$ that amortizes 50 percent of the principal if $r(t; s_t) < 1.018$.

That is, the swap amortizes 50 percent of its principal each date the spot interest rate lies below 1.018.

This example is identical to the plain vanilla swap example studied in Chapter 10, Section 10.B, with the exception of the amortizing principal. Recall that the plain vanilla swap had zero value at time 0. We see below that the index-amortizing swap has a negative value at time 0.

We first compute the cash flows to the index-amortizing swap. These are given in Fig. 11.4. A sample set of calculations is as follows:

At time 1, state u the cash flow is

$$[c - r(0)]L_0 = [1.02 - 1.02]100 = 0$$

At time 2, state uu the cash flow is

$$[c - r(1;\text{u})]L_1 = [1.02 - 1.017606]50 = 0.1197$$

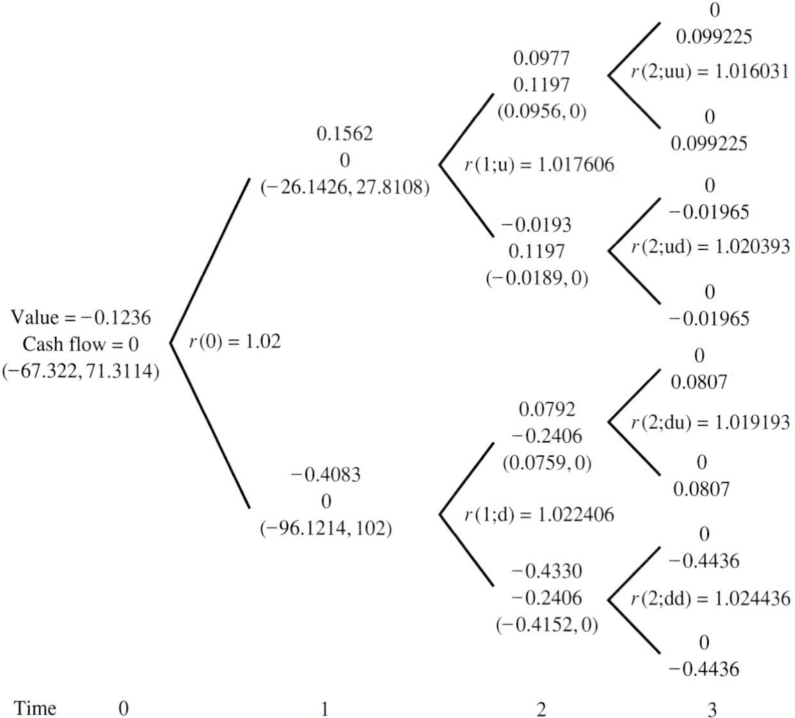

FIGURE 11.5

An index-amortizing swap with maturity $T = 3$, initial principal $L_0 = 100$, and lockout period $T* = 1$ that amortizes 50 percent of the principal if $r(t; s_t) <$ 1.018. The first number is the value, and the second is the cash flow. The synthetic index amortizing swap portfolio positions in the money market account and in the three-period zero-coupon bond $(n_0(t; s_t), n_1(t; s_t))$ are given under each node.

because $r(1;\text{u}) = 1.017606 < 1.018$ gives $a(1;\text{u}) = 0.5$, and therefore

$$L_1 = L_0[1 - a(1;\text{u})] = 100[1 - 0.5] = 50$$

At time 3, state uuu the cash flow is

$$[c - r(2;\text{uu})]L_2 = [1.02 - 1.016031]25 = 0.099225$$

because

$$L_2 = L_1[1 - a(2;\text{uu})] = 50[1 - 0.5] = 25$$

as $a(2;\text{u}) = 0.5$ since $r(2;\text{uu}) = 1.016031 < 1.018$.

The remaining calculations are left as exercises for the reader. Note that the lower branches of this tree are identical to those in Fig. 10.2 of Chapter 10 for the plain vanilla swap.

To value the index-amortizing swap, we use the risk-neutral valuation procedure. The value at time t is computed as follows:

$$\begin{aligned}\text{IA}(t;s_t) = \frac{1}{r(t;s_t)}\Bigg[&\frac{1}{2}(\text{IA}(t+1;s_t u) + \text{cash flow}(t+1;s_t\text{u})) \\ &+ \frac{1}{2}(\text{IA}(t+1;s_t\text{d}) + \text{cash flow}(t+1;s_t\text{d}))\Bigg]\end{aligned} \tag{11.16}$$

where

$$\text{IA}(3;s_3) \equiv 0 \qquad \text{for all } s_3$$

For example, at time 2, state uu:

$$\begin{aligned}\text{IA}(2;\text{uu}) &= \frac{1}{1.016031}\left[\frac{1}{2}(0 + 0.099225) + \frac{1}{2}(0 + 0.099225)\right] \\ &= 0.097659\end{aligned}$$

and at time 1, state u:

$$\begin{aligned}\text{IA}(1;\text{u}) &= \frac{1}{1.017606}\left[\frac{1}{2}(0.0977 + 0.1197) + \frac{1}{2}(-0.0193 + 0.1197)\right] \\ &= 0.1562\end{aligned}$$

The remaining calculations are similar and are left as exercises for the reader. They are contained in Fig. 11.5. Notice that the index amortizing swap's value at time 0, $\text{IA}(0) = -.1236$. This is less than the plain vanilla swap's value at time 0 which is zero.

Finally, we compute the synthetic index-amortizing swap portfolio using the money market account and the three-period bond via the equations

$$\begin{aligned}&n_1(t;s_t) \\ &= \frac{(\text{IA}(t+1;s_t\text{u}) + \text{cash flow}(t+1;s_t\text{u})) - (\text{IA}(t+1;s_t\text{d}) + \text{cash flow}(t+1;s_t\text{d}))}{P(t+1,3;s_t\text{u}) - P(t+1,3;s_t\text{d})}\end{aligned} \tag{11.17}$$

and

$$n_0(t;s_t) = \frac{\text{IA}(t;s_t) - n_1(t;s_t)P(t,3;s_t)}{B(t)}$$

for $t = 0$ and 1.

For time 2, since the money market account and the three-period bond are identical, we arbitrarily place all the investment in the money market account. Some sample calculations are as follows:

Time 2, state uu:

$$n_1(2;\text{uu}) = 0$$

$$n_0(2;\text{uu}) = \frac{\text{IA}(2;\text{uu})}{B(2;\text{u})} = \frac{0.099225}{1.037958}$$

$$= 0.0956$$

Time 1, state u:

$$n_1(1;\text{u}) = \frac{(\text{IA}(2;\text{uu}) + \text{cash flow}(2;\text{uu})) - (\text{IA}(2;\text{ud}) + \text{cash flow}(2;\text{ud}))}{P(2,3;\text{uu}) - P(2,3;\text{ud})}$$

$$= \frac{(0.0977 + 0.1197) - (-0.0193 + 0.1197)}{0.984222 - 0.980015} = 27.8108$$

$$n_0(1;\text{u}) = \frac{\text{IA}(1;\text{u}) - n_1(1;\text{u})P(1,3;\text{u})}{B(1)}$$

$$= \frac{0.1562 - (27.7908)0.965127}{1.02}$$

$$= -26.1426$$

The remaining calculations are left as exercises for the reader. All calculations are presented in Fig. 11.5. This completes the example. ■

The above techniques for valuing exotic interest rate options are easily modified to incorporate more complexities, such as early exercise considerations. The procedure requires a detailed specification of the interest rate option's cash flows given an evolution of the term structure of interest rates. Once this is understood, the procedures of Chapter 7 are easily applied.

SECTION E REFERENCES TO CHAPTER 11

1. McConnell, J., and M. Singh, 1994. "Rational Prepayments and the Valuation of Collateralized Mortgage Obligations." *Journal of Finance* 49, 891–921.
2. Titman, S., and W. Torous, 1989. "Valuing Commercial Mortgages: An Empirical Investigation of the Contingent Claims Approach to Valuing Risky Debt." *Journal of Finance* 44, 345–373.
3. Turnbull, S., 1994. "Interest Rate Digital Options and Range Notes." Unpublished manuscript, Queen's University, Kingston, Canada.

CHAPTER 12

Continuous-Time Limits

This chapter discusses the empirical implementation of the interest rate option models developed in the previous chapters. As a discrete-time model, its approximation to reality is expected to be good when the number of periods (τ) is quite large. In that case the discrete-time model is an approximation to the continuous trading limit. In fact, for purposes of empirical estimation, it is convenient to reparameterize the discrete-time model in terms of its continuous-time limit. Actual implementation of computer code is then done under this reparameterization (see Chapter 17). The primary purpose of this chapter is to study this reparameterization and the resulting continuous-time limit. A secondary purpose is to demonstrate how to construct arbitrage-free zero-curve evolutions such as that given in Fig. 4.4.

To parameterize the forward rate process[1,2] in terms of its continuous limit, we change the time scale in the discrete-time model. As it is currently constructed, there are τ time periods $t = 0, 1, 2, \ldots, \tau$. These time periods are arbitrarily specified. In order to take limits, let us fix a future date $\overline{\tau}$ (say, January $1, 2030$), and divide the time horizon 0 to $\overline{\tau}$ into subperiods of equal length Δ. Thus, in terms of calendar time, the discrete periods $0, 1, 2, \ldots, \tau$ correspond to the dates 0, Δ, 2Δ, $3\Delta, \ldots, \tau\Delta \equiv \overline{\tau}$. We are interested in studying the various discrete-time economies when the number of trading dates becomes large (i.e., $\tau \to \infty$) or, equivalently, when the time between trades becomes small (i.e., $\Delta \to 0$).

---

[1]For the bond trading models of Chapter 6, one could estimate the parameters of the bond process directly using expression (4.3). This estimation is problematic, however, because the parameters of the bond process are (in general) nonstationary.

[2]This chapter's analysis follows Heath, Jarrow, and Morton [7].

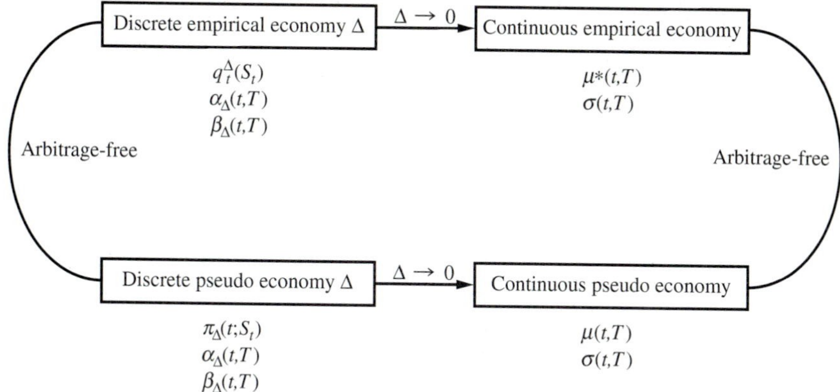

FIGURE 12.1
Discrete approximation system to the continuous empirical and continuous pseudo economies.

From the continuous-time perspective, the evolution of *observed* zero-coupon bond prices and forward rates (as in Fig. 2.1) are generated by a *continuous empirical economy* with parameters[3] *(i)* $\mu^*(t, T)$, the expected change in (the logarithm of) the forward rates per unit time, and *(ii)* $\sigma(t, T)$, the standard deviation of changes in (the logarithm of) the forward rates per unit time.

We would like to construct an approximating discrete-time empirical economy such that as the step size shrinks ($\Delta \to 0$), the discrete-time economy approaches the continuous-time economy. This is illustrated in Fig. 12.1 at the top of the diagram. A discrete-time empirical economy is characterized by *(i)* the probability of movements of forward rates $q_t^\Delta(s_t)$ and *(ii)* the (one plus) percentage changes in forward rates across the various states ($\alpha_\Delta(t, T; s_t)$, $\beta_\Delta(t, T; s_t)$ for the one-factor case). It is a fact from probability theory (see He [6]) that under mild technical conditions, this approximation can be obtained by choosing

$$\frac{E_t\{\log f_\Delta(t+\Delta, T) - \log f_\Delta(t, T)\}}{\Delta} \to \mu^*(t, T) \qquad \text{as } \Delta \to 0$$

and

$$\frac{\mathrm{Var}_t\{\log f_\Delta(t+\Delta, T) - \log f_\Delta(t, T)\}}{\Delta} \to \sigma(t, T)^2 \qquad \text{as } \Delta \to 0$$

where the expectations and variance are obtained using $q_t^\Delta(s_t)$. Under these conditions, for small Δ, the two economies will be similar, and the discrete-time economy will be a good approximation to the limit economy (and conversely).

Given the discrete-time empirical economy constructed above, as in Chapter 7, the assumption of no arbitrage gives the existence of *unique* pseudo

[3]In mathematical notation, to be defined later, $d\tilde{f}(t, T) = \mu*(t, T)dt + \sigma(t, T)dW(t)$ where both $\sigma(t, T)$ and $dW(t)$ can be vector-valued processes for multiple-factor economies.

probabilities $\pi_\Delta(t; s_t)$, which are used for the valuation of contingent claims. The discrete-time pseudo economy is characterized by *(i)* the probability of movements of forward rates $\pi_\Delta(t; s_t)$ and *(ii)* the (one plus) percentage changes in forward rates across the various states ($\alpha_\Delta(t, T; s_t)$, $\beta_\Delta(t, T; s_t)$ for the one-factor case). The percentage changes in forward rates are *identical* across the two discrete-time economies; only the likelihoods of the movements differ. However, we need $\pi_\Delta(t; s_t) > 0$ if and only if $q_t^\Delta(s_t) > 0$. Those states with positive probability in the pseudo economy must have positive probability in the empirical economy, and conversely. This is called the *equivalent probability* condition. The arbitrage-free link between the two discrete-time economies is depicted on the left side of Fig. 12.1.

Analogous to the discrete-time case, the assumption of no arbitrage in the continuous-time model gives the existence of unique pseudo probabilities, which are used for the valuation of contingent claims.[4] These no-arbitrage restrictions imply that the limit pseudo economy has parameters *(i)* $\mu(t, T)$, the expected change in (the logarithm of) the forward rates per unit time, and *(ii)* $\sigma(t, T)$, the standard deviation of changes in (the logarithm of) the forward rates per unit time. The standard deviations of changes in forward rates are identical across the two limit economies; only the likelihoods (and, therefore, the expected changes of forward rates) can differ.[5] This arbitrage-free link between the two limit economies is depicted on the right side of Fig.12.1.

The construction is complete if the discrete-time pseudo economy also converges to the limit pseudo economy, because then for small Δ, contingent claim values as computed in the discrete-time model will be good approximations to contingent claim values as computed in the continuous-time model (and conversely). This is illustrated in the bottom part of Fig.12.1. This construction can be obtained if we choose

$$\frac{\tilde{E}_t\{\log f_\Delta(t+\Delta, T) - \log f_\Delta(t, T)\}}{\Delta} \longrightarrow \mu(t, T) \qquad \text{as } \Delta \longrightarrow 0$$

and

$$\frac{\widetilde{\text{Var}}_t\{\log f_\Delta(t+\Delta, T) - \log f_\Delta(t, T)\}}{\Delta} \longrightarrow \sigma(t, T)^2 \qquad \text{as } \Delta \longrightarrow 0$$

where the expectation and variance are obtained using $\pi_\Delta(t; s_t)$.

There are numerous ways of constructing the discrete-time economies such that Fig.12.1 is satisfied. This follows because we require only that the limiting systems match as $\Delta \to 0$. From among these constructions, we would like to select one that makes the computation of contingent claim values as simple as possible. This simplicity of computation occurs, for example, if the

[4]Heath, Jarrow, and Morton [8] provide the technical details. Also see Section 12.A.3.

[5]It can be shown that $\mu^*(t, T) = \mu(t, T) - \sigma(t, T)\phi(t)$ where $\phi(t)$ is a risk premium. This is discussed further in Section 12.A.3 below. The probability measures are equivalent (agree on zero probability events) because $\sigma(t, T)$ is identical across the two economies.

pseudo probabilities satisfy $\pi_\Delta(t; s_t) \equiv \frac{1}{2}$ for all Δ, t, and s_t. This identification has been used throughout this text. We show below that such a construction is always possible.

In summary, the purpose of this chapter is to construct a system of discrete-time and limit economies satisfying Fig. 12.1 and such that the pseudo probabilities satisfy $\pi_\Delta(t; s_t) \equiv \frac{1}{2}$. This is the task to which we now turn.

SECTION A
ONE-FACTOR ECONOMY

Consider the one-factor economy as described in Chapter 6, Section 6.A. The forward rate process can be characterized as in Chapter 4, Section 4.A, expression (4.5):

$$f_\Delta(t+\Delta, T; s_{t+\Delta}) = \begin{cases} \alpha_\Delta(t,T;s_t) f_\Delta(t,T;s_t) & \text{if } s_{t+\Delta} = s_t u \\ \quad \text{(with probability } q_t^\Delta(s_t) > 0) & \\ \beta_\Delta(t,T;s_t) f_\Delta(t,T;s_t) & \text{if } s_{t+\Delta} = s_t d \\ \quad \text{(with probability } 1 - q_t^\Delta(s_t) > 0) & \end{cases} \tag{12.1}$$

where $\tau\Delta - \Delta \geq T \geq t + \Delta$, and both t and T are integer multiples of Δ. The forward rates and the actual probabilities are indexed by Δ. If u occurs, forward rates change proportionately by $\alpha_\Delta(t, T; s_t)$, and if d occurs, forward rates change proportionately by $\beta_\Delta(t, T; s_t)$. The actual probabilities of the up and down movements are given by $q_t^\Delta(s_t)$ and $1 - q_t^\Delta(s_t)$, respectively. Expression (12.1) is expression (4.5) rewritten to include the new time notation.

Let us now reparameterize expression (12.1) in terms of three new stochastic processes, $\mu(t, T; s_t)$, $\sigma(t, T; s_t)$, and $\phi(t; s_t)$, implicitly defined as follows:

$$\alpha_\Delta(t,T;s_t) \equiv \exp\left[\mu(t,T;s_t)\Delta - \sigma(t,T;s_t)\sqrt{\Delta}\right] \tag{12.2a}$$

$$\beta_\Delta(t,T;s_t) \equiv \exp\left[\mu(t,T;s_t)\Delta + \sigma(t,T;s_t)\sqrt{\Delta}\right] \tag{12.2b}$$

$$q_t^\Delta(s_t) \equiv \tfrac{1}{2} + \tfrac{1}{2}\phi(t;s_t)\sqrt{\Delta} \tag{12.2c}$$

This parameterization was selected with Fig. 12.1 in mind. To explain, substitution into expression (12.1) gives

$$f_\Delta(t+\Delta, T; s_{t+\Delta}) =$$

$$\begin{cases} f_\Delta(t,T;s_t)\exp\left[\mu(t,T;s_t)\Delta - \sigma(t,T;s_t)\sqrt{\Delta}\right] & \text{if } s_{t+\Delta} = s_t u \\ \quad \text{(with probability } \frac{1}{2} + \frac{1}{2}\phi(t;s_t)\sqrt{\Delta} > 0) & \\ f_\Delta(t,T;s_t)\exp\left[\mu(t,T;s_t)\Delta + \sigma(t,T;s_t)\sqrt{\Delta}\right] & \text{if } s_{t+\Delta} = s_t d \\ \quad \text{(with probability } \frac{1}{2} - \frac{1}{2}\phi(t;s_t)\sqrt{\Delta} > 0) & \end{cases} \tag{12.3}$$

Next, take natural logarithms of both sides of expression (12.3) to obtain

$$\log f_\Delta(t+\Delta, T; s_{t+\Delta}) - \log f_\Delta(t, T; s_t)$$
$$= \begin{cases} \mu(t,T;s_t)\Delta - \sigma(t,T;s_t)\sqrt{\Delta} & \text{with probability } \frac{1}{2} + \frac{1}{2}\phi(t;s_t)\sqrt{\Delta} \\ \mu(t,T;s_t)\Delta + \sigma(t,T;s_t)\sqrt{\Delta} & \text{with probability } \frac{1}{2} - \frac{1}{2}\phi(t;s_t)\sqrt{\Delta} \end{cases} \quad (12.4)$$

The mean and variance of the changes in the logarithms of forward rates can be computed to be

$$E_t\{\log f_\Delta(t+\Delta, T) - \log f_\Delta(t,T)\} = [\mu(t,T) - \phi(t)\sigma(t,T)]\Delta \quad (12.5a)$$

and

$$\text{Var}_t\{\log f_\Delta(t+\Delta, T) - \log f_\Delta(t,T)\} = \sigma(t,T)^2\Delta - \phi(t)^2\sigma(t,T)^2\Delta^2 \quad (12.5b)$$

DERIVATION OF EXPRESSION(12.5). For simplicity of notation, define $\Delta \log f_\Delta(t,T) \equiv \log f_\Delta(t+\Delta,T) - \log f_\Delta(t,T)$. Using expression (12.4),

$$\begin{aligned} E_t(\Delta \log f_\Delta(t,T)) &= \left(\tfrac{1}{2} + \tfrac{1}{2}\phi(t)\sqrt{\Delta}\right)\left(\mu(t,T)\Delta - \sigma(t,T)\sqrt{\Delta}\right) \\ &\quad + \left(\tfrac{1}{2} - \tfrac{1}{2}\phi(t)\sqrt{\Delta}\right)\left(\mu(t,T)\Delta + \sigma(t,T)\sqrt{\Delta}\right) \\ &= \mu(t,T)\Delta - \phi(t)\sigma(t,T)\Delta \end{aligned}$$

$$\begin{aligned} \text{Var}_t(\Delta \log f_\Delta(t,T)) &= E_t(\Delta \log f_\Delta(t,T)^2) - [E_t(\Delta \log f_\Delta(t,T))]^2 \\ &= (\mu(t,T)\Delta - \sigma(t,T)\sqrt{\Delta})^2\left(\tfrac{1}{2} + \tfrac{1}{2}\phi(t)\sqrt{\Delta}\right) \\ &\quad + (\mu(t,T)\Delta + \sigma(t,T)\sqrt{\Delta})^2\left(\tfrac{1}{2} - \tfrac{1}{2}\phi(t)\sqrt{\Delta}\right) \\ &\quad - (\mu(t,T)\Delta - \phi(t)\sigma(t,T)\Delta)^2 \\ &= [\mu(t,T)^2\Delta^2 - 2\mu(t,T)\Delta\sigma(t,T)\sqrt{\Delta} + \sigma(t,T)^2\Delta]\left(\tfrac{1}{2} + \tfrac{1}{2}\phi(t)\sqrt{\Delta}\right) \\ &\quad + [\mu(t,T)^2\Delta^2 + 2\mu(t,T)\Delta\sigma(t,T)\sqrt{\Delta} + \sigma(t,T)^2\Delta]\left(\tfrac{1}{2} - \tfrac{1}{2}\phi(t)\sqrt{\Delta}\right) \\ &\quad - [\mu(t,T)^2\Delta^2 - 2\mu(t,T)\Delta\phi(t)\sigma(t,T)\Delta + \phi(t)^2\sigma(t,T)^2\Delta^2] \end{aligned}$$

Canceling like terms gives

$$\begin{aligned} \text{Var}_t(\Delta \log f_\Delta(t,T)) &= -\tfrac{1}{2}2\mu(t,T)\Delta\sigma(t,T)\sqrt{\Delta}\phi(t)\sqrt{\Delta} \\ &\quad - \tfrac{1}{2}2\mu(t,T)\Delta\sigma(t,T)\sqrt{\Delta}\phi(t)\sqrt{\Delta} \\ &\quad + 2\mu(t,T)\Delta\phi(t)\sigma(t,T)\Delta \\ &\quad + \sigma(t,T)^2\Delta - \phi(t)^2\sigma(t,T)^2\Delta^2 \\ &= \sigma(t,T)^2\Delta - \phi(t)^2\sigma(t,T)^2\Delta^2 \end{aligned}$$

■

Dividing by Δ and taking limits of these quantities as $\Delta \to 0$ give

$$\lim_{\Delta \to 0} E_t\{\log f_\Delta(t+\Delta, T) - \log f_\Delta(t,T)\}/\Delta = \mu(t,T) - \phi(t)\sigma(t,T) \quad (12.6a)$$

and

$$\lim_{\Delta \to 0} \mathrm{Var}_t\{\log f_\Delta(t+\Delta, T) - \log f_\Delta(t,T)\}/\Delta = \sigma(t,T)^2 \quad (12.6b)$$

Expression (12.6a) represents the drift $\mu^*(t,T) \equiv \mu(t,T) - \phi(t)\sigma(t,T)$ of the empirical process and $\sigma(t,T)$ represents the volatility of the empirical process. Both $\mu^*(t,T)$ and $\sigma(t,T)$ can in principle be estimated from past observations of forward rates. The stochastic process $\phi(t)$ is interpreted in Section 12.A.3 as a risk premium, i.e., a measure of the excess expected return (above the spot rate) per unit of standard deviation for the zero-coupon bonds.

The parameterization of the empirical discrete-time process as given in expression (12.2), therefore, is an approximation to the empirical continuous economy with drift $\mu^*(t,T) \equiv \mu(t,T) - \phi(t)\sigma(t,T)$ and volatility $\sigma(t,T)$. This identification corresponds to the top right of Fig. 12.1.

We next investigate the discrete-time pseudo economy implied by expression (12.2) and the assumption of no arbitrage.

1 Arbitrage-Free Restrictions

This section studies the restrictions implied by no arbitrage on the above system. From Chapters 6 and 7, expressions (6.25) and (7.6), this system is arbitrage-free if and only if there exist unique pseudo probabilities $\pi_\Delta(t; s_t)$ such that

$$\pi_\Delta(t; s_t) = \frac{r_\Delta(t; s_t) - d_\Delta(t, T; s_t)}{u_\Delta(t, T; s_t) - d_\Delta(t, T; s_t)} \quad (12.7)$$

for all $s_t, 0 \le t < T - \Delta$, and $T \le \tau\Delta$, where both t and T are integer multiples of Δ. Using expression (12.2) in expression (4.10) we get:[6]

$$u_\Delta(t, T; s_t) = r_\Delta(t; s_t) \exp\left\{ - \sum_{j=t+\Delta}^{T-\Delta} \mu(t, j; s_t)\Delta + \sum_{j=t+\Delta}^{T-\Delta} \sigma(t, j; s_t)\sqrt{\Delta} \right\} \quad (12.8a)$$

and

$$d_\Delta(t, T; s_t) = r_\Delta(t; s_t) \exp\left\{ - \sum_{j=t+\Delta}^{T-\Delta} \mu(t, j; s_t)\Delta - \sum_{j=t+\Delta}^{T-\Delta} \sigma(t, j; s_t)\sqrt{\Delta} \right\} \quad (12.8b)$$

[6]The summations in expression (12.8) are for steps of size Δ, so $j = t + \Delta, t + 2\Delta, \ldots, T - \Delta$.

Substitution of these expressions into (12.7) and simplification yield

$$\pi_\Delta(t;s_t) = \left[1 - \exp\left\{-\sum_{j=t+\Delta}^{T-\Delta}\mu(t,j;s_t)\Delta - \sum_{j=t+\Delta}^{T-\Delta}\sigma(t,j;s_t)\sqrt{\Delta}\right\}\right]$$
$$\div\left[\exp\left\{-\sum_{j=t+\Delta}^{T-\Delta}\mu(t,j;s_t)\Delta + \sum_{j=t+\Delta}^{T-\Delta}\sigma(t,j;s_t)\sqrt{\Delta}\right\}\right.$$
$$\left. - \exp\left\{-\sum_{j=t+\Delta}^{T-\Delta}\mu(t,j;s_t)\Delta - \sum_{j=t+\Delta}^{T-\Delta}\sigma(t,j;s_t)\sqrt{\Delta}\right\}\right] \tag{12.9}$$

for all s_t and $0 \leq t < T - \Delta$ and $T \leq \tau\Delta$, where both t and T are integer multiples of Δ.

Expression (12.9) gives the cross-restrictions on the drifts and volatilities of the forward rate process that are both necessary and sufficient for the existence of the pseudo probabilities.

Under these pseudo probabilities the change in the logarithm of forward rates is represented as

$$\log f_\Delta(t+\Delta,T;s_{t+\Delta}) - \log f_\Delta(t,T;s_t) =$$
$$\begin{cases} \mu(t,T;s_t)\Delta - \sigma(t,T;s_t)\sqrt{\Delta} & \text{with probability } \pi_\Delta(t;s_t) \\ \mu(t,T;s_t)\Delta + \sigma(t,T;s_t)\sqrt{\Delta} & \text{with probability } 1 - \pi_\Delta(t;s_t) \end{cases} \tag{12.10}$$

The mean and the variance of the changes in forward rates can be computed:

$$\tilde{E}_t\{\log f_\Delta(t+\Delta,T) - \log f_\Delta(t,T)\} = \mu(t,T)\Delta + (1 - 2\pi_\Delta(t))\sigma(t,T)\sqrt{\Delta} \tag{12.11a}$$

and

$$\widetilde{\mathrm{Var}}_t\{\log f_\Delta(t+\Delta,T) - \log f_\Delta(t,T)\} = 4\sigma(t,T)^2\Delta\pi_\Delta(t)(1 - \pi_\Delta(t)) \tag{12.11b}$$

DERIVATION OF EXPRESSION (12.11). For simplicity of notation, define $\Delta\log f_\Delta(t,T) \equiv \log f_\Delta(t+\Delta,T) - \log f_\Delta(t,T)$. Using expression (12.10),

$$\tilde{E}_t(\Delta\log f_\Delta(t,T))$$
$$= \pi_\Delta(t)(\mu(t,T)\Delta - \sigma(t,T)\sqrt{\Delta}) + (1 - \pi_\Delta(t))(\mu(t,T)\Delta + \sigma(t,T)\sqrt{\Delta})$$
$$= \mu(t,T)\Delta + (1 - 2\pi_\Delta(t))\sigma(t,T)\sqrt{\Delta}$$

$$\widetilde{\mathrm{Var}}_t(\Delta\log f_\Delta(t,T))$$
$$= E_t(\Delta\log f_\Delta(t,T)^2) - [\tilde{E}_t(\Delta\log f_\Delta(t,T))]^2$$
$$= (\mu(t,T)\Delta - \sigma(t,T)\sqrt{\Delta})^2\pi_\Delta(t) + (\mu(t,T)\Delta + \sigma(t,T)\sqrt{\Delta})^2(1 - \pi_\Delta(t))$$
$$- [\mu(t,T)\Delta + (1 - 2\pi_\Delta(t))\sigma(t,T)\sqrt{\Delta}]^2$$

Expanding the squares gives

$$\begin{aligned}
&\tilde{\text{Var}}_t(\Delta \log f_\Delta(t,T)) \\
&\quad = [\mu(t,T)^2\Delta^2 - 2\mu(t,T)\sigma(t,T)\sqrt{\Delta} + \sigma(t,T)^2\Delta]\pi_\Delta(t) \\
&\qquad + [\mu(t,T)^2\Delta^2 + 2\mu(t,T)\sigma(t,T)\sqrt{\Delta} + \sigma(t,T)^2\Delta](1 - \pi_\Delta(t)) \\
&\qquad - [\mu(t,T)^2\Delta^2 + 2\mu(t,T)(1 - 2\pi_\Delta(t))\sigma(t,T)\sqrt{\Delta} + \sigma(t,T)^2\Delta(1 - 2\pi_\Delta(t))^2]
\end{aligned}$$

Canceling like terms and simplifying yield

$$\widetilde{\text{Var}}_t(\Delta \log f_\Delta(t,T)) = 4\sigma(t,T)^2\Delta\pi_\Delta(t)(1 - \pi_\Delta(t))$$ ■

To construct Fig.12.1, we also require that as $\Delta \to 0$

$$\lim_{\Delta \to 0} \frac{\tilde{E}_t\{\log f_\Delta(t+\Delta,T) - \log f_\Delta(t,T)\}}{\Delta} = \mu(t,T) \qquad (12.12a)$$

and

$$\lim_{\Delta \to 0} \frac{\widetilde{\text{Var}}_t\{\log f_\Delta(t+\Delta,T) - \log f_\Delta(t,T)\}}{\Delta} = \sigma(t,T)^2 \qquad (12.12b)$$

This implies the added restriction that

$$\pi_\Delta(t;s_t) = \tfrac{1}{2} + 0(\sqrt{\Delta}) \qquad (12.13)$$

where $\lim_{\Delta \to 0} \frac{0(\sqrt{\Delta})}{\sqrt{\Delta}} = 0$

DERIVATION OF EXPRESSION (12.13). From expressions (12.11) and (12.12) one obtains

$$\lim_{\Delta \to 0} \frac{(1 - 2\pi_\Delta(t))\sigma(t,T)}{\sqrt{\Delta}} = 0$$

and

$$\lim_{\Delta \to 0} 4\pi_\Delta(t)(1 - \pi_\Delta(t)) = 1$$

The first of these gives (12.13), since it implies that

$$\lim_{\Delta \to 0} \frac{(\frac{1}{2} - \pi_\Delta(t))}{\sqrt{\Delta}} = 0$$

The second inequality is also satisfied by (12.13). ■

In summary, expressions (12.9) and (12.13) give the no-arbitrage restrictions such that the construction of the approximating economies as in Fig. 12.1 holds.

For computational efficiency, it is convenient to set the pseudo probabilities to $\frac{1}{2}$: $\pi(t;s_t) \equiv \frac{1}{2}$ for all t and s_t. This is a special case of expression (12.13).

With this restriction, we get from expression (12.9) that

$$\frac{1}{2}\left[\exp\left\{-\sum_{j=t+\Delta}^{T-\Delta}\mu(t,j;s_t)\Delta+\sum_{j=t+\Delta}^{T-\Delta}\sigma(t,j;s_t)\sqrt{\Delta}\right\}\right.$$
$$\left.-\exp\left\{-\sum_{j=t+\Delta}^{T-\Delta}\mu(t,j;s_t)\Delta-\sum_{j=t+\Delta}^{T-\Delta}\sigma(t,j;s_t)\sqrt{\Delta}\right\}\right] \tag{12.14}$$
$$=1-\exp\left\{-\sum_{j=t+\Delta}^{T-\Delta}\mu(t,j;s_t)\Delta-\sum_{j=t+\Delta}^{T-\Delta}\sigma(t,j;s_t)\sqrt{\Delta}\right\}$$

This is true if and only if

$$\exp\left\{\sum_{j=t+\Delta}^{T-\Delta}\mu(t,j;s_t)\Delta\right\}$$
$$=\frac{1}{2}\left[\exp\left\{+\sum_{j=t+\Delta}^{T-\Delta}\sigma(t,j;s_t)\sqrt{\Delta}\right\}+\exp\left\{-\sum_{j=t+\Delta}^{T-\Delta}\sigma(t,j;s_t)\sqrt{\Delta}\right\}\right]$$
$$\equiv\cosh\left(\sum_{j=t+\Delta}^{T-\Delta}\sigma(t,j;s_t)\sqrt{\Delta}\right) \tag{12.15}$$

where $\cosh x\equiv\frac{1}{2}(e^x+e^{-x})$.

The next subsection shows how to use this information to build trees similar to those used in the book's examples.

2 Computation of the Arbitrage-Free Term Structure Evolutions

This section shows how to use the previous expressions to compute an arbitrage-free term structure evolution. First, we compute the evolution of the zero-coupon bond prices. Substitution of expression (12.15) into expression (12.8) gives

$$u_\Delta(t,T;s_t)=r_\Delta(t;s_t)\left[\cosh\left(\sum_{j=t+\Delta}^{T-\Delta}\sigma(t,j;s_t)\sqrt{\Delta}\right)\right]^{-1}\exp\left\{\sum_{j=t+\Delta}^{T-\Delta}\sigma(t,j;s_t)\sqrt{\Delta}\right\} \tag{12.16a}$$

and

$$d_\Delta(t,T;s_t)$$
$$=r_\Delta(t;s_t)\left[\cosh\left(\sum_{j=t+\Delta}^{T-\Delta}\sigma(t,j;s_t)\sqrt{\Delta}\right)\right]^{-1}\exp\left\{-\sum_{j=t+\Delta}^{T-\Delta}\sigma(t,j;s_t)\sqrt{\Delta}\right\} \tag{12.16b}$$

Using expression (4.3) of Chapter 4, substitution of expression (12.16) yields

$$P_\Delta(t+\Delta, T; s_{t+\Delta}) = \begin{cases} P_\Delta(t,T;s_t) r_\Delta(t;s_t) \left[\cosh\left(\sum_{j=t+\Delta}^{T-\Delta} \sigma(t,j;s_t)\sqrt{\Delta}\right)\right]^{-1} \\ \quad \times \exp\left\{\sum_{j=t+\Delta}^{T-\Delta} \sigma(t,j;s_t)\sqrt{\Delta}\right\} & \text{if } s_{t+\Delta} = s_t\text{u} \\ P_\Delta(t,T;s_t) r_\Delta(t;s_t) \left[\cosh\left(\sum_{j=t+\Delta}^{T-\Delta} \sigma(t,j;s_t)\sqrt{\Delta}\right)\right]^{-1} \\ \quad \times \exp\left\{-\sum_{j=t+\Delta}^{T-\Delta} \sigma(t,j;s_t)\sqrt{\Delta}\right\} & \text{if } s_{t+\Delta} = s_t\text{d} \end{cases} \tag{12.17}$$

for $t < T - \Delta$ and $T \leq \tau\Delta$, where both t and T are integer multiples of Δ.

Expression (12.17) gives the realization of the discrete-time bond price process for the approximation as in Fig. 12.1. *Under the empirical probabilities* $\frac{1}{2} + \frac{1}{2}\phi(t; s_t)$, this bond price process converges to the limiting empirical process for the bond's price. *Under the pseudo probabilities* $\frac{1}{2}$, this converges to the limiting pseudo process for the bond's price. Because the pseudo economies are all that are relevant to application of the contingent claim valuation theory of Chapter 7, we never have to estimate the stochastic process $\phi(t; s_t)$. It is shown later, Section 12.A.3, that $\phi(t; s_t)$ can be interpreted as a risk premium, i.e., as a measure of the excess expected return (above the spot rate) per unit of standard deviation for the zero-coupon bonds. Therefore, to apply this technology to price contingent claims, one never has to estimate a zero-coupon bond's risk premium. This is an important characteristic of the model.

To construct the forward rate process evolution, from expression (12.15) we get

$$\begin{aligned} e^{\mu(t,t+\Delta;s_t)\Delta} &= \cosh(\sigma(t,t+\Delta;s_t)\sqrt{\Delta}) \qquad \text{and} \\ e^{\mu(t,T;s_t)\Delta} &= \frac{\cosh\left(\sum_{j=t+\Delta}^{T} \sigma(t,j;s_t)\sqrt{\Delta}\right)}{\cosh\left(\sum_{j=t+\Delta}^{T-\Delta} \sigma(t,j;s_t)\sqrt{\Delta}\right)} \end{aligned} \tag{12.18}$$

for $T \geq t + 2\Delta$ where both t and T are integer multiples of Δ. Substitution into expression (12.3) yields

$$f_\Delta(t+\Delta, T; s_{t+\Delta}) = \begin{cases} f_\Delta(t,T;s_t) \left[\dfrac{\cosh\left(\sum_{j=t+\Delta}^{T} \sigma(t,j;s_t)\sqrt{\Delta}\right)}{\cosh\left(\sum_{j=t+\Delta}^{T-\Delta} \sigma(t,j;s_t)\sqrt{\Delta}\right)}\right] e^{-\sigma(t,T;s_t)\sqrt{\Delta}} & \text{if } s_{t+\Delta} = s_t\text{u} \\ f_\Delta(t,T;s_t) \left[\dfrac{\cosh\left(\sum_{j=t+\Delta}^{T} \sigma(t,j;s_t)\sqrt{\Delta}\right)}{\cosh\left(\sum_{j=t+\Delta}^{T-\Delta} \sigma(t,j;s_t)\sqrt{\Delta}\right)}\right] e^{+\sigma(t,T;s_t)\sqrt{\Delta}} & \text{if } s_{t+\Delta} = s_t\text{d} \end{cases} \tag{12.19}$$

for $\tau\Delta \geq T + \Delta$ and $T - \Delta \geq t$ where both t and T are integer multiples of Δ, and where as a notational convenience we define

$$\cosh\left(\sum_{j=t+\Delta}^{t} \sigma(t, j; s_t)\sqrt{\Delta}\right) \equiv 1$$

We include this last identity so that expression (12.19) can be written in one line. Otherwise, because of the denominator involving the cosh function, we would have to write out two expressions: one when $T = t + \Delta$ and one when $T \geq t + 2\Delta$.

Thus, expression (12.19) gives the evolution of the discrete-time forward rate curve as in Fig. 12.1. Under the empirical probabilities $\frac{1}{2} + \frac{1}{2}\phi(t; s_t)$, this converges to the limiting empirical process for the forward rates. Under the pseudo probabilities $\frac{1}{2}$, this converges to the limiting pseudo process for the forward rates. The computation of contingent claims values is done using the pseudo probabilities.

Note that under the pseudo probabilities, a specification of the volatility structure of forward rates,

$$\begin{bmatrix} \sigma(t, t + \Delta; s_t) \\ \sigma(t, t + 2\Delta; s_t) \\ \vdots \\ \sigma(t, \tau\Delta - \Delta; s_t) \end{bmatrix}$$

for all $0 \leq t \leq \tau - \Delta$ and s_t is sufficient to determine the evolution of the forward rate curve. The risk premium process $\phi(t, T; s_t)$ does not appear in expression (12.19). Again, this is an important attribute of the model, which makes its implementation practical.

Two functional forms of the volatility function $\sigma(t, T; s_t)$ have received special attention in the literature.

Case 1: Deterministic volatility function

The first case is that in which the volatility $\sigma(t, T; s_t)$ is a deterministic function, independent of the state s_t. This restriction on the volatility function implies that forward rates can go negative. This is shown in the exercises at the end of this chapter. This case includes as special cases Ho and Lee's [10] model ($\sigma(t, T; s_t)$ is a constant) and a discrete-time approximation in the HJM framework to Vasicek's [17] and Hull and White's [11] models ($\sigma(t, T; s_t) = \xi e^{-\eta(T-t)}$ for $\xi, \eta > 0$ constants).

Case 2: Nearly proportional volatility function

The volatility is $\sigma(t, T; s_t) = \eta(t, T)\min(f(t, T) - 1, M)$, where $\eta(t, T)$ is a deterministic function and $M > 0$ is a large positive constant. In other words, in the second case $\sigma(t, T; s_t)$ is approximately proportional to the current value of the forward rate $f(t, T)$ less one. The proportionality factor is $\eta(t, T)$. This proportionality implies that forward rates are always nonnegative. Nonnegativity of forward rates is a condition usually required in models, because negative interest rates for zero-coupon bonds are inconsistent with the existence of cash currency, which can be stored costlessly at zero interest rates.

In case 2, the larger the forward rate, the larger the volatility. If the forward rate becomes too large, however, the volatility is bounded by $\eta(t, T)M$. This upper bound guarantees that forward rates do not explode with positive probability as $\Delta \to 0$. This is a necessary technical condition based on the limit economies in Fig 12.1; see Heath, Jarrow, and Morton [8] for details.

EXAMPLE: CONSTRUCTION OF FIG. 4.6. To construct Fig. 4.6, we used expression (12.19), with $\Delta \equiv 1$ and the following forward rates:

$$f(0,0) = f(0,1) = f(0,2) = f(0,3) = 1.02$$

We used the volatility function given in case 2 with the proportionality coefficient $\eta(t, T) \equiv \eta(T - t)$ depending only on time to maturity and having the values

$$\eta(0) = 0.11765$$

$$\eta(1) = 0.08825$$

$$\eta(2) = 0.06865$$

We set $M = 1{,}000{,}000$. The reader is asked to verify this construction in the computer exercises at the end of the chapter. ■

3 The Continuous-Time Limit

For purposes of empirical estimation and computation, we have constructed the discrete-time economies to converge to a continuous-time limit. It is instructive to study the continuous-time limits of the one-factor economy analyzed in the previous sections. This section is more abstract than the remainder of the text, and it can be skipped on a first reading.

The first step in analyzing the continuous-time economy is to study continuous compounding as the limit of the discretely compounded rates used in the previous sections. Intuitively, the *continuously compounded forward rate*, $\tilde{f}(t, T)$, is that rate such that for small time intervals Δ, the following condition holds:

$$f_\Delta(t, T) \approx e^{\tilde{f}(t,T)\Delta} \tag{12.20}$$

The left side of expression (12.20) is the forward rate over $[T, T + \Delta]$ as seen at time t. This forward rate is one plus a percentage. The right side gives the appreciation obtained from the time t continuously compounded forward rate $\tilde{f}(t, T)$ per unit time, compounding for the Δ units of time from T to $T + \Delta$. The continuously compounded forward rate $\tilde{f}(t, T)$ is a percentage, expressed as a number between 0 and 1. Expression (12.20) is only an approximation.

Formally, the continuously compounded forward rate is defined by

$$\tilde{f}(t,T) \equiv \lim_{\Delta \to 0} \frac{\log(f_\Delta(t,T))}{\Delta} \qquad \text{for } 0 \leq t \leq T \leq \tau \tag{12.21}$$

Expression (12.21) implies that

$$f_\Delta(t,T) = \exp\left\{\int_T^{T+\Delta} \tilde{f}(t,v)\,dv\right\} \tag{12.22}$$

Expression (12.22) is the formal version of expression (12.20). When the time interval Δ is small, expression (12.20) is approximately true.

In the computer implementation of the model in Chapter 17, only the continuously compounded forward rates are reported.

We can rewrite the zero-coupon bond prices in terms of the continuously compounded forward rates. Indeed, it can be shown that

$$P_\Delta(t,T) = \exp\left\{-\int_t^T \tilde{f}(t,v)\,dv\right\} \tag{12.23}$$

This expression will prove useful in Chapter 13.

DERIVATION OF EXPRESSION (12.23). Choose T so that T/Δ is an integer. From expression (3.4) of Chapter 3, we have

$$\begin{aligned} P_\Delta(t,T) &= \left[\prod_{j=t}^{T/\Delta-1} f_\Delta(t, j\Delta)\right]^{-1} \\ &= \left[\prod_{j=t}^{T/\Delta-1} \exp\left\{\int_j^{j+\Delta} \tilde{f}(t,v)\,dv\right\}\right]^{-1} \end{aligned}$$

by the definition of $\tilde{f}(t,v)$ in expression (12.22). Therefore,

$$P_\Delta(t,T) = \exp\left\{-\sum_{j=t}^{T/\Delta-1}\left[\int_j^{j+\Delta} \tilde{f}(t,v)\,dv\right]\right\} = \exp\left\{-\int_t^T \tilde{f}(t,v)\,dv\right\} \qquad \blacksquare$$

In the one-factor case under expressions (12.2) and (12.15), given suitable restrictions upon $\mu(t,T), \sigma(t,T)$, and $\phi(t)$, the random process

$$\frac{\log(f_\Delta(t+\Delta,T)) - \log(f_\Delta(t,T))}{\Delta} \tag{12.24}$$

converges[7] as the time step $\Delta \to 0$ to the random process given by the following:

$$\tilde{f}(t,T) - \tilde{f}(0,T) = \int_0^t \mu^*(v,T)\,dv + \int_0^t \sigma(v,T)\,dW^*(v) \tag{12.25a}$$

[7]Formally, the random process given in (12.24) converges weakly to that in expression (12.25). The defintion of weak convergence is rather technical and can be found in Billingsley[2].

under the empirical probabilities, where $\{W^*(t): t\varepsilon[0,\tau]\}$ is a Brownian motion, initialized at zero, and

$$\tilde{f}(t,T) - \tilde{f}(0,T) = \int_0^t \mu(v,T)\,dv + \int_0^t \sigma(v,T)\,dW(v) \qquad (12.25b)$$

under the pseudo-probabilities, where $\{W(t): t\varepsilon[0,\tau]\}$ is a Brownian motion, initialized at zero. Further, it can be shown (see Heath, Jarrow, and Morton [8]) that

$$dW(v) \equiv dW^*(v) - \phi(v)\,dv \qquad (12.25c)$$

and

$$\int_0^t \mu(v,T)dv = -\int_0^t \sigma(v,T)\left[\int_v^T \sigma(v,y)\,dy\right]dv \qquad (12.25d)$$

The first term on the right side of expression (12.25*a*) is an ordinary integral from first-year calculus. The second term is a stochastic integral, whose definition we leave for outside reading (see Protter [14]). A complete understanding of these integrals is not necessary for an understanding of the remainder of the text.

Expressions (12.25*a*) and (12.25*b*) are the direct result of expressions (12.6) and (12.12), respectively. They give the limiting processes, which are characterized by their drifts and volatilities.

Expression (12.25*c*) in conjunction with the two previous expressions shows that

$$\mu^*(t,T) = \mu(t,T) - \sigma(t,T)\phi(t) \qquad (12.26)$$

This relates the drift of forward rates in the empirical economy ($\mu^*(t,T)$) to the drift of forward rates in the pseudo economy ($\mu(t,T)$).

Expression (12.25*d*) is the limiting form of expression (12.15). It is the no-arbitrage restriction written in terms of the volatilities of the forward rates process in the pseudo economy (the proof is in Heath, Jarrow, and Morton [8]). Combined with expression (12.26), the no-arbitrage restriction expression (12.25*d*) is equivalent to

$$\frac{E_t(dP(t,T)/P(t,T)) - r(t)\,dt}{\sqrt{\text{Var}_t}(dP(t,T)/P(t,T))} = \phi(t)\,dt \qquad (12.27)$$

for all t, T, where $dP(t,T)$ is the instantaneous change in the T-maturity zero-coupon bond's price over $[t, t+dt]$.

The proof of this is contained in Heath, Jarrow, and Morton [8]. This result gives $\phi(t)$ the interpretation of being a *risk premium*, i.e., the excess expected return (above the spot rate) per unit of standard deviation for the zero-coupon bonds. The arbitrage-free restriction is therefore equivalent to the statement that all zero-coupon bonds must have the same excess expected return per unit of risk. This is the continuous-time analogue of the no-arbitrage condition expression (7.6) of Chapter 7.

Two examples of expression (12.25) are useful in applications.

Case 1: Deterministic volatility functions

The first example is that in which the volatility function is a deterministic function, i.e.,

$$\sigma(t,T) \text{ is nonrandom} \tag{12.28}$$

In this case, the limiting random variable $\tilde{f}(t,T) - \tilde{f}(0,T)$, can be shown to be normally distributed with

$$\text{mean} = \int_0^t \mu(v,T)\,dv \qquad \text{and} \qquad \text{variance} = \int_0^t \sigma^2(v,T)\,dv$$

This implies, from expression (12.25), that the zero-coupon bond's price $P(t,T)$ is log-normally distributed. This log-normality enables one to compute analytic expressions for various types of options (see Heath, Jarrow, and Morton [8]). Expression (12.25) with the restriction (12.28) is called a *Gaussian economy.*

When $\sigma(t,T)$ is a constant, independent of t and T, we get a continuous-time limit of the Ho and Lee model [10]. When $\sigma(t,T) = \xi e^{-\eta(T-t)}$ for ξ, η constants, we get in the HJM framework a version of Vasicek [17] and Hull and White [11].

Case 2: Nearly proportional volatility functions

A second example useful in applications is that in which the volatility function satisfies the condition

$$\sigma(t,T) = \eta(t,T)\min(\tilde{f}(t,T), M) \tag{12.29}$$

where $\eta(t,T)$ is a deterministic function and M is a large, positive constant. In this case it can be shown that the limiting process for $\tilde{f}(t,T)$ is positive for sure. The bound M is included to keep the forward rate process from exploding in finite time; see Heath, Jarrow, and Morton [8] for details. No known distribution for $\tilde{f}(t,T)$ is available, and the limiting random variable is best approximated via expression (12.19).

Cases 1 and 2 are the limiting forms of the two cases discussed in Section 12.A.2.

SECTION B
TWO-FACTOR ECONOMY

This section extends the previous analysis to a two-factor economy. Because we are interested in computing contingent claim values as in Chapter 7, we give only the characterization for the pseudo economies. This corresponds to the lower part of Fig. 12.1.

Consider the two-factor economy as described in Chapter 6, Section 6.B. The forward rate process can be characterized as in Chapter 4, Section 4.B, expression (4.17):

$$f_\Delta(t, +\Delta, T; s_{t+\Delta}) = \begin{cases} \alpha_\Delta(t,T;s_t) f_\Delta(t,T;s_t) & \text{if } s_{t+\Delta} = s_t\text{u} \left(\text{with pseudo probability } \tfrac{1}{4}\right) \\ \gamma_\Delta(t,T;s_t) f_\Delta(t,T;s_t) & \text{if } s_{t+\Delta} = s_t\text{m} \left(\text{with pseudo probability } \tfrac{1}{4}\right) \\ \beta_\Delta(t,T;s_t) f_\Delta(t,T;s_t) & \text{if } s_{t+\Delta} = s_t\text{d} \left(\text{with pseudo probability } \tfrac{1}{2}\right) \end{cases} \tag{12.30}$$

where $\tau\Delta - \Delta \geq T \geq t + \Delta$, and where t and T are integer multiples of Δ. Let us reparameterize expression (12.30) in terms of three new stochastic processes $\mu(t,T;s_t)$, $\sigma_1(t,T;s_t)$, and $\sigma_2(t,T;s_t)$ as follows:

$$\alpha_\Delta(t,T;s_t) = \exp\left\{ \mu(t,T;s_t)\Delta - \sigma_1(t,T;s_t)\sqrt{\Delta} - \sqrt{2}\,\sigma_2(t,T;s_t)\sqrt{\Delta} \right\} \tag{12.31a}$$

$$\gamma_\Delta(t,T;s_t) = \exp\left\{ \mu(t,T;s_t)\Delta - \sigma_1(t,T;s_t)\sqrt{\Delta} + \sqrt{2}\,\sigma_2(t,T;s_t)\sqrt{\Delta} \right\} \tag{12.31b}$$

$$\beta_\Delta(t,T;s_t) = \exp\{\mu(t,T;s_t)\Delta + \sigma_1(t,T;s_t)\sqrt{\Delta}\} \tag{12.31c}$$

Substitution into expression (12.30) gives

$$f_\Delta(t + \Delta, T; s_{t+\Delta}) = \begin{cases} f_\Delta(t,T;s_t) \exp\left\{ \mu(t,T;s_t)\Delta - \sigma_1(t,T;s_t)\sqrt{\Delta} - \sqrt{2}\,\sigma_2(t,T;s_t)\sqrt{\Delta} \right\} \\ \qquad \text{if } s_{t+\Delta} = s_t u \text{ (with probability } \tfrac{1}{4}) \\ f_\Delta(t,T;s_t) \exp\left\{ \mu(t,T;s_t)\Delta - \sigma_1(t,T;s_t)\sqrt{\Delta} + \sqrt{2}\,\sigma_2(t,T;s_t)\sqrt{\Delta} \right\} \\ \qquad \text{if } s_{t+\Delta} = s_t m \text{ (with probability } \tfrac{1}{4}) \\ f_\Delta(t,T;s_t) \exp\left\{ \mu(t,T;s_t)\Delta + \sigma_1(t,T;s_t)\sqrt{\Delta} \right\} \\ \qquad \text{if } s_{t+\Delta} = s_t d \text{ (with probability } \tfrac{1}{2}) \end{cases} \tag{12.32}$$

Thus, the stochastic processes $\mu(t,T;s_t)$, $\sigma_1(t,T;s_t)$, and $\sigma_2(t,T;s_t)$ can be interpreted as the drift and the volatilities $(\sigma_1(t,T;s_t), \sigma_2(t,T;s_t))$ for the process $\log f_\Delta(t+\Delta,T;s_{t+\Delta}) - \log f_\Delta(t,T;s_t)$ with $\sigma_i(t,T;s_t)$ for $i = 1,2$ being the volatilities for the first and second factors. Indeed, a straightforward calculation shows that

$$\tilde{E}_t\{\log f_\Delta(t+\Delta,T) - \log f_\Delta(t,T)\} = \mu(t,T)\Delta \tag{12.33a}$$

$$\widetilde{\text{Var}}_t\{\log f_\Delta(t+\Delta,T) - \log f_\Delta(t,T)\} = \sigma_1^2(t,T)\Delta + \sigma_2^2(t,T)\Delta \quad (12.33b)$$

under the pseudo probabilities given in expression (12.32).

1 Arbitrage-Free Restrictions

We next study the restrictions that the existence of the pseudo probabilities implies about the reparameterization. For computational efficiency, we set the pseudo probabilities in expression (12.32) equal to the following:

$$\begin{aligned} \pi_\Delta^u(t;s_t) &\equiv \tfrac{1}{4} \\ \pi_\Delta^m(t;s_t) &\equiv \tfrac{1}{4} \\ 1 - \pi_\Delta^u(t;s_t) - \pi_\Delta^m(t;s_t) &\equiv \tfrac{1}{2} \end{aligned} \quad (12.34)$$

for all s_t and t. From expression (4.19) we get

$$u_\Delta(t,T;s_t) = r_\Delta(t;s_t)\exp\left\{-\sum_{j=t+\Delta}^{T-\Delta}\mu(t,j;s_t)\Delta + \sum_{j=t+\Delta}^{T-\Delta}\sigma_1(t,j;s_t)\sqrt{\Delta} + \sqrt{2}\sum_{j=t+\Delta}^{T-\Delta}\sigma_2(t,j;s_t)\sqrt{\Delta}\right\} \quad (12.35a)$$

$$m_\Delta(t,T;s_t) = r_\Delta(t;s_t)\exp\left\{-\sum_{j=t+\Delta}^{T-\Delta}\mu(t,j;s_t)\Delta + \sum_{j=t+\Delta}^{T-\Delta}\sigma_1(t,j;s_t)\sqrt{\Delta} - \sqrt{2}\sum_{j=t+\Delta}^{T-\Delta}\sigma_2(t,j;s_t)\sqrt{\Delta}\right\} \quad (12.35b)$$

$$d_\Delta(t,T;s_t) = r_\Delta(t;s_t)\exp\left\{-\sum_{j=t+\Delta}^{T-\Delta}\mu(t,j;s_t)\Delta - \sum_{j=t+\Delta}^{T-\Delta}\sigma_1(t,j;s_t)\sqrt{\Delta}\right\} \quad (12.35c)$$

Recall the martingale condition (6.39):

$$\frac{P_\Delta(t,T;s_t)}{B_\Delta(t;s_{t-1})} = \frac{P_\Delta(t,T;s_t)}{B_\Delta(t;s_{t-1})r_\Delta(t;s_t)}\left[\left(\tfrac{1}{4}\right)\mu_\Delta(t,T;s_t) + \left(\tfrac{1}{4}\right)m_\Delta(t,T;s_t) + \left(\tfrac{1}{2}\right)d_\Delta(t,T;s_t)\right] \quad (12.36)$$

Substitution of expression (12.35) into (12.36) gives, after some algebra, the no-arbitrage restriction:

$$\exp\left\{\sum_{j=t+\Delta}^{T-\Delta} \mu(t,j;s_t)\Delta\right\}$$
$$= \frac{1}{2}\exp\left\{-\sum_{j=t+\Delta}^{T-\Delta} \sigma_1(t,j;s_t)\sqrt{\Delta}\right\} + \frac{1}{2}\exp\left\{\sum_{j=t+\Delta}^{T-\Delta} \sigma_1(t,j;s_t)\sqrt{\Delta}\right\}$$
$$\times\left(\frac{1}{2}\exp\left\{\sqrt{2}\sum_{j=t+\Delta}^{T-\Delta} \sigma_2(t,j;s_t)\sqrt{\Delta}\right\} + \frac{1}{2}\exp\left\{-\sqrt{2}\sum_{j=t+\Delta}^{T-\Delta} \sigma_2(t,j;s_t)\sqrt{\Delta}\right\}\right) \tag{12.37}$$

for $t \leq T + 2\Delta$ and $T \leq \tau\Delta - \Delta$, where t and T are integer multiples of Δ.

2 Computation of the Arbitrage-Free Term Structure Evolutions

We show how to compute the arbitrage-free evolution of the forward rate curve. Using expression (12.37), we get

$$\sum_{j=t+\Delta}^{T-\Delta} \mu(t,j)\Delta$$
$$= \log\left(\frac{1}{2}\exp\left\{-\sum_{j=t+\Delta}^{T-\Delta} \sigma_1(t,j)\sqrt{\Delta}\right\} + \frac{1}{2}\exp\left\{\sum_{j=t+\Delta}^{T-\Delta} \sigma_1(t,j)\sqrt{\Delta}\right\}\right.$$
$$\left.\times\left[\frac{1}{2}\exp\left\{\sqrt{2}\sum_{j=t+\Delta}^{T-\Delta} \sigma_2(t,j)\sqrt{\Delta}\right\} + \frac{1}{2}\exp\left\{-\sqrt{2}\sum_{j=t+\Delta}^{T-\Delta} \sigma_2(t,j)\sqrt{\Delta}\right\}\right]\right) \tag{12.38}$$

This system can be solved recursively, as

$$\mu(t,t+\Delta)\Delta$$
$$= \log\left(\frac{1}{2}\exp\left\{-\sigma_1(t,t+\Delta)\sqrt{\Delta}\right\} + \frac{1}{2}\exp\left\{\sigma_1(t,t+\Delta)\sqrt{\Delta}\right\}\right.$$
$$\left.\times\left[\frac{1}{2}\exp\left\{\sqrt{2}\sigma_2(t,t+\Delta)\sqrt{\Delta}\right\} + \frac{1}{2}\exp\left\{-\sqrt{2}\sigma_2(t,t+\Delta)\sqrt{\Delta}\right\}\right]\right) \tag{12.39a}$$

and

$$\mu(t,K)\Delta = -\mu(t,K-\Delta)\Delta$$
$$+\log\left(\frac{1}{2}\exp\left\{-\sum_{j=t+\Delta}^{K}\sigma_1(t,j)\sqrt{\Delta}\right\}+\frac{1}{2}\exp\left\{\sum_{j=t+\Delta}^{K}\sigma_1(t,j)\sqrt{\Delta}\right\}\right.$$
$$\left.\times\left[\frac{1}{2}\exp\left\{\sqrt{2}\sum_{j=t+\Delta}^{K}\sigma_2(t,j)\sqrt{\Delta}\right\}+\frac{1}{2}\exp\left\{-\sqrt{2}\sum_{j=t+\Delta}^{K}\sigma_2(t,j)\sqrt{\Delta}\right\}\right]\right)$$
$$\text{for } \tau\Delta-\Delta \geq K \geq t+2\Delta \tag{12.39b}$$

Given two vectors of volatilities:

$$\begin{bmatrix}\sigma_1(t,t+\Delta;s_t)\\ \sigma_1(t,t+2\Delta;s_t)\\ \vdots\\ \sigma_1(t,\tau\Delta-\Delta;s_t)\end{bmatrix} \quad\text{and}\quad \begin{bmatrix}\sigma_2(t,t+\Delta;s_t)\\ \sigma_2(t,t+2\Delta;s_t)\\ \vdots\\ \sigma_2(t,\tau\Delta-\Delta;s_t)\end{bmatrix}$$

expressions (12.39*a*) and (12.39*b*) can be used in conjunction with expression (12.32) to generate an evolution of forward rates for the pseudo economy.

To get the evolution of the zero-coupon bond price process, one uses the evolution of the forward rates just computed plus the definition of a bond's price as given in expression (3.4) of Chapter 3. These evolutions are all that are needed to compute contingent claim values as in Chapter 7.

SECTION C
$N \geq 3$–FACTOR ECONOMIES

The previous analysis is easily extended to $N \geq 3$–factor economies. The basic equations (12.30) are augmented to include additional states, with additional volatilities. Generalized versions of (12.31)–(12.37) follow through the existence of the pseudo probabilities. As before, the forward rate curve evolution can be determined by using knowledge of the volatility parameters alone and not the drifts. This is a key attribute of the model.

To illustrate the basic pattern for $N \geq 3$, we give the relevant equations for the three-factor case. As we are only interested in computing contingent claim values as in Chapter 7, we only provide the equations for the discrete-time pseudo economy. This is the lower part of Fig. 12.1.

First, the forward rate process, under the pseudo probabilities, evolves according to expression (12.40):

$$f_\Delta(t+\Delta,T;s_{t+\Delta}) = f_\Delta(t,T;s_t)e^{\mu(t,T;s_t)} \times \begin{cases} \exp\{-\sigma_1(t,T;s_t)\sqrt{\Delta} - \sqrt{2}\sigma_2(t,T;s_t)\sqrt{\Delta} - 2\sigma_3(t,T;s_t)\sqrt{\Delta}\} \\ \quad \text{(with probability } \tfrac{1}{8}) \\ \exp\{-\sigma_1(t,T;s_t)\sqrt{\Delta} - \sqrt{2}\sigma_2(t,T;s_t)\sqrt{\Delta} + 2\sigma_3(t,T;s_t)\sqrt{\Delta}\} \\ \quad \text{(with probability } \tfrac{1}{8}) \\ \exp\{-\sigma_1(t,T;s_t)\sqrt{\Delta} + \sqrt{2}\sigma_2(t,T;s_t)\sqrt{\Delta}\} \\ \quad \text{(with probability } \tfrac{1}{4}) \\ \exp\{+\sigma_1(t,T;s_t)\sqrt{\Delta}\} \\ \quad \text{(with probability } \tfrac{1}{2}) \end{cases} \tag{12.40}$$

where $\tau\Delta - \Delta \geq T \geq t + \Delta$, and where t and T are integer multiples of Δ. Under the pseudo probabilities, a straightforward calculation shows that

$$\tilde{E}_t\{\log f_\Delta(t+\Delta,T) - \log f_\Delta(t,T)\} = \mu(t,T)\Delta \tag{12.41a}$$

$$\widetilde{\text{Var}}_t\{\log f_\Delta(t+\Delta,T) - \log f_\Delta(t,T)\} = \sigma_1(t,T)^2\Delta + \sigma_2(t,T)^2\Delta + \sigma_3(t,T)^2\Delta \tag{12.41b}$$

Under (12.40), the no-arbitrage condition (6.39) is

$$\exp\left\{\sum_{j=t+\Delta}^{T-\Delta} \mu(t,j;s_t)\Delta\right\} = \frac{1}{2}e^{\Sigma_1}\left(\frac{1}{2}e^{\Sigma_2}\left(\frac{1}{2}e^{\Sigma_3} + \frac{1}{2}e^{-\Sigma_3}\right) + \frac{1}{2}e^{-\Sigma_2}\right) + \frac{1}{2}e^{-\Sigma_1} \tag{12.42}$$

where

$$\Sigma_1 \equiv \sum_{j=t+\Delta}^{T-t} \sigma_1(t,j;s_t)\sqrt{\Delta}$$

$$\Sigma_2 \equiv \sqrt{2}\sum_{j=t+\Delta}^{T-t} \sigma_2(t,j;s_t)\sqrt{\Delta}$$

$$\Sigma_3 \equiv 2\sum_{j=t+\Delta}^{T-t} \sigma_3(t,j;s_t)\sqrt{\Delta}$$

for $t \leq T + 2\Delta$ and $T \leq \tau\Delta - \Delta$, where t and T are integer multiples of Δ.

Expression (12.42) can be solved recursively, just as in expression (12.39) for $\mu(t,T;s_t)$. Given this value, expression (12.40) provides the equations for computing the arbitrage-free evolution of the forward rate curve. The inputs needed are the vectors of volatilities:

$$\begin{bmatrix} \sigma_1(t, t+\Delta; s_t) \\ \vdots \\ \sigma_1(t, \tau\Delta - \Delta; s_t) \end{bmatrix} \quad \begin{bmatrix} \sigma_2(t, t+\Delta; s_t) \\ \vdots \\ \sigma_2(t, \tau\Delta - \Delta; s_t) \end{bmatrix} \quad \begin{bmatrix} \sigma_3(t, t+\Delta; s_t) \\ \vdots \\ \sigma_3(t, \tau\Delta - \Delta; s_t) \end{bmatrix}$$

SECTION D
COMPUTATIONAL ISSUES

This section briefly discusses the computational issues involved in implementing the one-, two-, or three-factor model on a computer. Four techniques are discussed, and references are provided: *(i)* bushy trees, *(ii)* lattice computations, *(iii)* partial differential equations, and *(iv)* Monte Carlo simulation.

1 Bushy Trees

The procedure provided for computing forward rate curve evolutions in expression (12.19) for the one-factor case, expression (12.39) for the two-factor case, or expression (12.42) for the three-factor case is often called a *bushy tree*. It is called a bushy tree because the number of branches on the tree expands exponentially as the number of time steps increases. For example, in the one-factor case, the number of branches (nodes) at time t equals 2^t. For the two-factor case, the number of nodes at time t equals 3^t, and so forth.

For large numbers of time steps (say $t \geq 14$), depending upon what computational tricks are employed, the computing time becomes excessive. For this reason it is often incorrectly believed that contingent claim valuation cannot be done using bushy trees. This belief is incorrect because a large number of time steps is not always essential for obtaining good approximations.

For European options or American options with six or seven decision nodes (of economic importance), bushy trees provide very accurate values with step sizes of only 10–12. This is because the branches spread out very quickly, giving a fine grid of values at the last date in the tree. From a numerical integration perspective (recall valuation is equivalent to computing an expected value), the approximating grid at the last date will be quite accurate.

For exotic options with multiple cash flow times (say ≥ 12) or long-dated American options with many decision nodes of economic importance (say ≥ 12), bushy trees provide a less attractive, time-intensive computational procedure.

Of course, as the computing technology improves, these concerns with bushy trees become less and less of a problem. For path-dependent options, such as index-amortizing swaps, bushy trees and Monte Carlo simulation appear to be the preferred approaches. This occurs because each path through the tree must be recorded to determine a value, and the lattice or partial differential equation approach does not record this information. For a more complete discussion of these issues, see Heath, Jarrow, and Morton [9].

2 Lattices

Special cases of the one-factor model allow for more efficient computation. These are the cases in which the tree recombines at various nodes; for example, the values of forward rates after an up followed by a down are the same as after a down followed by up.

For the one-factor economy, the tree recombines when the volatility function $\sigma(t, T)$ is a constant, independent of either time or the maturity date. We ask the reader to verify this fact in the computer exercises at the end of this chapter. Furthermore, under a time transformation, case 1 (the deterministic volatility function), can also be shown to recombine; see Amin [1].

Given the pseudo probabilities, the spot rate process itself is sufficient to determine the zero-coupon bond prices and therefore forward rates. The spot rate process can be made to recombine under various transformations; see Nelson and Ramaswamy [13]. These transformations work well for the one-factor case. More research is needed for the multifactor case from a lattice approach.

One-factor lattice approaches work well for most contingent claims, except those that are path dependent, e.g., index-amortizing swaps. This is because a lattice does not remember the path taken through the tree, but only the current node. For path-dependent options, bushy trees and Monte Carlo simulation appear to be better approaches.

3 Partial Differential Equations

Numerical techniques are quite refined for solving partial differential equations, by either implicit or explicit difference techniques; see Kincaid and Cheney [12]. These techniques can be applied to price interest rate options when the spot rate process is (strong) Markov in a finite number of state variables. When the spot rate process is (strong) Markov, the use of Ito's lemma (from stochastic calculus) enables one to transform the expected value relation to a partial differential equation subject to boundary conditions. Papers providing various conditions for characterizing the spot rate evolution as a Markov process include Caverhill [3] and Ritchken and Sankarasubramanian [15]. A limitation of this approach is that it cannot easily handle path-dependent options, such as index-amortizing swaps.

4 Monte Carlo Simulation

As stated earlier, contingent claims valuation reduces to calculating an expected value given the arbitrage-free evolution of the term structure of interest rates. Monte Carlo techniques are well suited for such computations. These techniques appear to be especially well suited for multiple-factor models, in which computations using bushy trees are time-consuming. Good references for these techniques are Clewlow and Caverhill [4] and Duanmu [5]. Because Monte Carlo simulation is a forward-looking technique, it has some difficulty handling American options. More research is needed along these lines; see Tilley [16].

SECTION E
COMPUTER EXERCISES

This set of exercises using the Trees software is designed to clarify the computations in expression (12.19) using the different volatilities: case 1 (constant), and case 2 (proportional).

> ***Construction of Fig. 4.6.*** Run the Trees software, select "model,"and then select "sigma." This is the volatility function for a one-factor model. There are two choices: *(i)* "constant," which corresponds to case 1 with $\sigma(t,T) = \sigma(T-t)$, a constant that depends only on the time to maturity; and *(ii)* "proportional," which corresponds to case 2 with $\eta(t,T) = \eta(T-t)$, a constant that depends only on the time to maturity.
>
> Choose "proportional" and change $\eta(0) = 0.11765, \eta(1) = 0.08825, \eta(2) = 0.06865$. Leave all other entries unchanged. Compare the spot rates to those in Fig. 4.8. They are the same up to rounding errors. Compare the forward rates with those in Fig. 4.6.

a. Go to "model" and then "sigma." Change the sigma to "constant," and input 0.05 for each maturity in the vector. Run the software. Do you get any negative interest rates? What does this do to the zero-coupon bond prices? Show that the tree recombines in this circumstance.

b. Repeat *(a)*, but use "proportional" instead of "constant." Do you still get negative spot rates?

SECTION F
REFERENCES TO CHAPTER 12

1. Amin, K., 1991. "On the Computation of Continuous Time Options Prices Using Discrete Approximations." *Journal of Financial and Quantitative Analysis* 26, 477–496.
2. Billingsley, P., 1968. *Convergence of Probability Measures.* John Wiley & Sons, New York.
3. Caverhill, A., 1994. "When Is the Short Rate Markovian?" *Mathematical Finance* 4 (4), 305–312.
4. Clewlow, L., and A. Caverhill, 1994. "On the Simulation of Contingent Claims." *Journal of Derivatives* 2 (2), 66–74.

5. Duanmu, Z., 1994. *First Passage Time Density Approach to Pricing Barrier Options and Monte Carlo Simulation of the HJM Interest Rate Model.* Ph.D. dissertation, Cornell University.
6. He, Hua, 1990. "Convergence from Discrete-to-Continuous-Time Contingent Claims Prices." *Review of Financial Studies* 3 (4), 523–546.
7. Heath, D., R. Jarrow, and A. Morton, 1991. "Contingent Claim Valuation with a Random Evolution of Interest Rates." *Review of Futures Markets* 54–76.
8. Heath, D., R. Jarrow, and A. Morton, 1992. "Bond Pricing and the Term Structure of Interest Rates: A New Methodology for Contingent Claims Valuation." *Econometrica* 60 (1), 77–105.
9. Heath, D., R. Jarrow, and A. Morton, 1992. "Easier Done Than Said." *Risk Magazine* 5 (9), 77–80.
10. Ho, T.S., and S. Lee, 1986. "Term Structure Movements and Pricing Interest Rate Contingent Claims." *Journal of Finance* 41, 1011–1028.
11. Hull, J., and A. White, 1990. "Pricing Interest Rate Derivative Securities." *Review of Financial Studies* 3 (4), 573–592.
12. Kincaid, D., and W. Cheney, 1991. *Numerical Analysis.* Brooks/Cole, Pacific Grove, Calif.
13. Nelson, D., and K. Ramaswamy, 1990. "Simple Binomial Processes as Diffusion Approximations in Financial Models." *Review of Financial Studies* 3 (1), 393–430.
14. Protter, P., 1990. *Stochastic Integration and Differential Equations.* Springer-Verlag, New York.
15. Ritchken, P., and L. Sankarasubramanian, 1995. "Volatility Structures of Forward Rates and the Dynamics of the Term Structure." *Mathematical Finance,* 5(1), 55–72.
16. Tilley, J., 1993. "Valuing American Options in a Path Simulation Model." *Transactions* 45, 83–104.
17. Vasicek, O., 1977. "An Equilibrium Characterization of the Term Structure." *Journal of Financial Economics* 5, 177–188.

CHAPTER 13

Parameter Estimation

The previous chapters take the input parameters, the initial forward rate curve, and the volatility function(s) as given. This chapter studies how to obtain these inputs from observable market prices of zero-coupon bonds and various interest rate options. This chapter does not exhaust the possible approaches to this problem. Rather, it provides a first-pass analysis constructed to illustrate the issues involved. In any particular implementation, these techniques will almost certainly need to be modified, refined, and extended. Studies that use related but different techniques are Flesaker [3] and Zhao [6].

This chapter is divided into two sections. The first shows how to obtain the initial forward rate curve, and the second analyzes volatility function estimation.

SECTION A
THE INITIAL FORWARD RATE CURVE

This section studies estimation of the initial forward rate curve: $f_\Delta(0, j\Delta)$ for $j \in \{0, 1, \ldots, N-1\}$ where $N\Delta = \tau$. For concreteness, we choose $\Delta = 1/365$, so we are estimating daily rates on a *per-year* basis.

The data available for estimating the initial forward rate curve are daily observations of zero-coupon bond prices, as illustrated in Fig. 2.1 of Chapter 2. They are time-series data. Depending on the day of the week, we observe zero-coupon bond prices with maturities spaced approximately seven days apart. The only difference across weekdays is the time to maturity of the zero-coupon bond of shortest maturity. It can be anywhere from one to seven days. For simplicity, suppose we start our observations on Thursday, so that the shortest-maturity T-bill matures in seven days. The modification necessary for the other weekdays is obvious.

Let us represent the price observations on this date by the $m \times 1$ vector

$$\begin{bmatrix} P(0,7\Delta) \\ P(0,14\Delta) \\ \vdots \\ P(0,7m\Delta) \end{bmatrix}$$

where $7m\Delta = N\Delta = \tau$.

The first difficulty encountered is that the number of observed zero-coupon bond prices each day (m) are insufficient to determine the number of forward rates desired ($N - 1 = 7m - 1$). There are missing zero-coupon bond price observations. We will discuss two different methods for getting around the missing zero-coupon bond price observations. The first method is to fill in the missing zero-coupon prices by linear interpolation and then to compute the desired forward rates from those. The second method is to estimate the seven-day forward rates from the available bond prices and then to compute the desired daily forward rates from those.

Let us discuss the first approach. To fill in the missing zero-coupon bond price observations, one can use linear interpolation (spline techniques are also possible). The general formula is

$$P(0, j\Delta) = \left(\frac{7-j}{7}\right)P(0,0) + \left(\frac{j}{7}\right)P(0,7\Delta) \qquad \text{for } j = 0, 1, \ldots, 7 \tag{13.1}$$

$$P(0, j\Delta) = \left(\frac{7(k+1)-j}{7}\right)P(0,7k\Delta) + \left(\frac{j-7k}{7}\right)P(0,7(k+1)\Delta)$$
$$\text{for } 7k \leq j \leq 7(k+1) \text{ and } 1 < k \leq m-1 \tag{13.2}$$

Then, it is easy to compute the desired forward rates from these as

$$f_\Delta(0, j\Delta) = \frac{P(0, j\Delta)}{P(0,(j+1)\Delta)} \qquad \text{for } j = 0, \ldots, N-1 \tag{13.3}$$

The second approach computes

$$f_{7\Delta}(0, 7j\Delta) = \frac{P(0,7j\Delta)}{P(0,7(j+1)\Delta)} \qquad \text{for } j = 0, \ldots, m-1 \tag{13.4}$$

and then assumes constant forward rates over the daily subintervals,[1] or

---

[1] Another approximation, which includes compounding, is

$$f_\Delta(0, j\Delta) = f_{7\Delta}(0, 7k\Delta)^{1/7} \qquad \text{for } 7k \leq j < 7(k+1) \text{ and } 1 < k$$

$$f_\Delta(0, j\Delta) = 1 + \left(\frac{f_{7\Delta}(0, 7k\Delta) - 1}{7}\right) \quad \text{for } 7k \le j < 7(k+1) \text{ and } 0 \le k \le m-1 \tag{13.5}$$

This approximates the forward rate curve with a step function. This completes the estimation of the initial forward rate curve $f_\Delta(t, j\Delta)$ for $j = 0, \ldots, N-1$.

To transform these into continuously compounded forward rates, one can then use expression (12.20). This gives

$$\tilde{f}(t, T) = \frac{\log f_\Delta(t, j\Delta)}{\Delta} \qquad \text{for } j\Delta \le T < (j+1)\Delta \tag{13.6}$$

The continuously compounded forward rates are assumed to be constant over each step of size Δ.

In some applications one may want to modify these forward rates so that a particular set of computed prices for interest rate derivatives match market prices. For example, in the pricing of call provisions on Treasury bonds, one may want to adjust the forward rates so that computed noncallable Treasury bond prices match market prices. This matching will in turn provide better prices for the call provisions that are options on the noncallable Treasury bonds (see Heath, Jarrow, and Morton [4]). Alternatively, if one is pricing options on Treasury futures and the computed Treasury futures prices differ from market Treasury futures prices, the forward rates can be adjusted so that computed Treasury futures prices equal their market prices (see Amin and Morton [1]). In turn, this equality will provide better prices for Treasury bond futures options.

SECTION B
VOLATILITY FUNCTION ESTIMATION

This section studies two distinct approaches for estimating the volatility function(s)[2] $\sigma_j(t, T)$ for $j = 1, \ldots, N$: (*i*) historic volatility estimation and (*ii*) implicit volatility estimation. Historic volatility estimation uses time-series observations of past forward rates (generated in the last section) to estimate these volatility functions. Implicit volatility estimation uses current market prices of various interest rate derivatives, and it inverts the computed price formulas to obtain the volatility functions such that the computed prices match the market prices. For this reason, implicit volatility estimation is sometimes called *curve-fitting*. Since the techniques discussed are independent of the number of factors selected, we analyze the general case of N factors.

---

[2]This method allows up to N factors given N forward rates. The hope, of course, is that only a small number of factors can explain most of the variation in forward rates.

The basic $(N \times 1)$ vector equation for forward rates that underlies the volatility estimation procedure is expression $(12.25a)$, rewritten here as

$$\begin{bmatrix} \log f_\Delta(t+\Delta, t+\Delta) \\ \vdots \\ \log f_\Delta(t+\Delta, t+N\Delta) \end{bmatrix} \approx \begin{bmatrix} \log f_\Delta(t, t+\Delta) \\ \vdots \\ \log f_\Delta(t, t+N\Delta) \end{bmatrix} + \begin{bmatrix} \mu^*(t, t+\Delta) \\ \vdots \\ \mu^*(t, t+N\Delta) \end{bmatrix} \Delta$$

$$+ \begin{bmatrix} \sum_{j=1}^{N} \sigma_j(t, t+\Delta)\Delta W_j(t) \\ \vdots \\ \sum_{j=1}^{N} \sigma_j(t, t+N\Delta)\Delta W_j(t) \end{bmatrix} \tag{13.7}$$

where

$$\begin{bmatrix} \Delta W_1(t) \\ \vdots \\ \Delta W_N(t) \end{bmatrix}$$

is an $N \times 1$ vector that is approximately normally distributed with mean 0 and covariance matrix $I\Delta$ where I is the $N \times N$ identity matrix. It is important to stress that this evolution is under the actual or empirical probabilities. This is a discrete-time approximation to the continuous-time process of expression $(12.25a)$.

The previous section (expression (13.5)) provides the estimates for the forward rates $f_\Delta(t, t + j\Delta)$ in expression (13.7).

1 Historic Volatilities

We illustrate the historic estimation procedure for the two cases of volatility functions studied in Chapter 12.

Case 1: Deterministic volatility functions:

$\sigma_j(t,T) = \sigma_j(T-t)$ is a deterministic function of $T-t$ for all $j = 1, \ldots, N$.

$\mu^*(t,T) = \mu^*(T-t)$ is a deterministic function of $T-t$.

Case 2: (Nearly) proportional volatility functions:[3]

$\sigma_j(t,T) = \sigma_j(T-t)\min\left(\tilde{f}(t,T), M\right)$ where $\sigma_j(T-t)$ is a deterministic function of $T-t$ for $j = 1, \ldots, N$.

$\mu*(t,T) = \mu*(T-t)\min\left(\tilde{f}(t,T), M\right)$ where $\mu*(T-t)$ is a deterministic function of $T-t$ and M is a large, positive constant.

---

[3]In Chapter 12 we used $\eta_j(T-t)$ instead of $\sigma_j(T-t)$ in case 2. We change the notation in this chapter to facilitate the subsequent exposition.

The function $\tilde{f}(t, T)$ is given in expression (13.6).

For case 1, define the vector stochastic process $x(t)$, an $N \times 1$ vector, as

$$\begin{bmatrix} x_1(t) \\ \vdots \\ x_N(t) \end{bmatrix} = \begin{bmatrix} [\log f_\Delta(t + \Delta, t + \Delta) - \log f_\Delta(t, t + \Delta)]/\Delta \\ \vdots \\ [\log f_\Delta(t + \Delta, t + N\Delta) - \log f_\Delta(t, t + N\Delta)]/\Delta \end{bmatrix} \tag{13.8a}$$

and for case 2, define the vector stochastic process $x(t)$, an $N \times 1$ vector, by

$$x_j(t) = \begin{cases} \dfrac{\log f_\Delta(t + \Delta, t + j\Delta) - \log f_\Delta(t, t + j\Delta)}{\log f_\Delta(t, t + j\Delta)\Delta} & \text{if } f_\Delta(t, t + j\Delta) \leq M \\ \dfrac{\log f_\Delta(t + \Delta, t + j\Delta) - \log f_\Delta(t, t + j\Delta)}{M\Delta} & \text{if } f_\Delta(t, t + j\Delta) > M \end{cases} \tag{13.8b}$$

for $j = 1, \ldots, N$. In both cases, $x(t)$ is a time-homogenous normally distributed random process with an $N \times 1$ mean vector

$$\mu * = \begin{pmatrix} \mu^*(\Delta) \\ \vdots \\ \mu^*(N\Delta) \end{pmatrix}$$

and an $N \times N$ covariance matrix Σ whose (i, j)-th element is

$$\sum_{k=1}^{N} \sigma_k(\Delta i)\sigma_k(\Delta j)$$

The additional restrictions in cases 1 and 2 were imposed in order to obtain this time-homogenous normally distributed random process. This structure enables us to apply standard principal component analysis (see Jolliffe [5]) to estimate the unknown volatility functions (vectors). Using a time-series of K observations of $x(t)$ (using either expression (13.8a) or (13.8b)), we can obtain the $N \times N$ sample covariance matrix $\hat{\Sigma}$. This matrix can be decomposed as

$$\hat{\Sigma} = ALA' \tag{13.9}$$

where the $N \times N$ matrix $A = (a_1, \ldots, a_N)$ gives the N eigenvectors a_i for $i = 1, \ldots, N$ of $\hat{\Sigma}$ and the $N \times N$ diagonal matrix $L = \text{diag}(\ell_1, \ldots, \ell_N)$ provides the N eigenvalues ℓ_i for $i = 1, \ldots, N$. The prime denotes transpose. This decomposition gives the estimates of the N volatility functions as

$$\begin{bmatrix} \sigma_i(\Delta) \\ \vdots \\ \sigma_i(N\Delta) \end{bmatrix} = a_i\sqrt{\ell_i} \qquad \text{for } i = 1, \ldots, N \tag{13.10}$$

A demonstration that this identification yields expression (13.7) is presented in the appendix to this chapter. Sampling distributions are available for these estimates (see Jolliffe [5, chapter 3]). For a one-factor model, we set $N = 1$ and use (13.10) for the volatility function (vector). Sample estimates of these volatility vectors can be found in Heath, Jarrow, and Morton [4] for the first two factors.

2 Implicit Volatilities

The idea behind implicit volatility estimation is to use market prices from traded interest rate derivatives to estimate the volatility vectors. This is done by finding those volatility vectors such that a collection of computed interest rate derivative prices match observed market prices. This technique is sometimes called curve-fitting. We discuss two methods for this estimation.

The first method imposes no restrictions on the $N \times N$ volatility matrix

$$\begin{bmatrix} \sigma_1(t, t+\Delta; s_t) & \ldots & \sigma_N(t, t+\Delta; s_t) \\ \vdots & & \vdots \\ \sigma_1(t, t+N\Delta; s_t) & & \sigma_N(t, t+N\Delta; s_t) \end{bmatrix}$$

This matrix can depend on the time t and history s_t. The procedure finds those $N \times N$ values of this matrix that match market prices.

The second method reduces the number of parameters to be estimated by imposing restricted functional forms on the volatility functions, e.g.,

$$\sigma_j(t, T) = \sigma_j e^{-\lambda_j (T-t)}$$

Then only the parameters in these functional forms (σ_j, λ_j) for $j = 1, \ldots, N$ need to be determined implicitly from market prices. In this case, there are only $2N$ parameters to estimate. For a study using this second approach, see Amin and Morton [1]. It is also possible to combine both historic and implicit estimation in creative ways; see Cohen [2].

SECTION C
APPENDIX: MATHEMATICAL DEMONSTRATION THAT THE PRINCIPAL COMPONENTS DECOMPOSITION YIELDS EXPRESSION (13.7)

This demonstration comes from Joliffe [5, chapters 1–3].

Define

$$\underset{N \times K}{X} \equiv [\underset{N \times 1}{x(1)} \quad \ldots \quad \underset{N \times 1}{x(K)}]$$

where K is the number of time-series observations. Principal components analysis finds the $N \times N$ orthogonal matrix A (orthogonal means that $A'A = AA' = I$) such that

$$\underset{K\times N}{X'} = \underset{K\times N}{Z'} \times \underset{N\times N}{A}$$

where $Z' \equiv [z(1), \ldots, z(K)]'$, $z(j)$ is an $N \times 1$ vector, and the sample covariance matrix satisfies

$$\hat{\text{cov}}(X) = \hat{\Sigma} = ALA'$$

But $X'A' = Z'AA'$ implies that $Z' = X'A'$, where

$$\begin{aligned}\hat{\text{cov}}(Z) &= A'\hat{\text{cov}}(X)A \\ &= A'ALA'A \\ &= L\end{aligned}$$

Define

$$\underset{N\times 1}{w(t)} \equiv \underset{N\times N}{\begin{pmatrix} 1/\sqrt{\ell_1} & & \\ & \ddots & \\ & & 1/\sqrt{\ell_N} \end{pmatrix}} z(t)$$

and

$$\underset{N\times K}{W} \equiv [w(1) \quad \ldots \quad w(K)]$$

Then

$$\underset{N\times 1}{z(t)} \equiv \begin{pmatrix} \sqrt{\ell_1} & & \\ & \ddots & \\ & & \sqrt{\ell_N} \end{pmatrix} w(t)$$

$$\begin{aligned}\hat{\text{cov}}(W) &= \begin{pmatrix} 1/\sqrt{\ell_1} & & \\ & \ddots & \\ & & 1/\sqrt{\ell_N} \end{pmatrix} \hat{\text{cov}}(Z) \begin{pmatrix} 1/\sqrt{\ell_1} & & \\ & \ddots & \\ & & 1/\sqrt{\ell_N} \end{pmatrix} \\ &= \begin{pmatrix} 1/\sqrt{\ell_1} & & \\ & \ddots & \\ & & 1/\sqrt{\ell_N} \end{pmatrix} L \begin{pmatrix} 1/\sqrt{\ell_1} & & \\ & \ddots & \\ & & 1/\sqrt{\ell_N} \end{pmatrix} \\ &= I\end{aligned}$$

Thus,

$$\underset{K\times N}{X'} = \underset{K\times N}{W'} \begin{pmatrix} \sqrt{\ell_1} & & \\ & \ddots & \\ & & \sqrt{\ell_N} \end{pmatrix} A$$

$$\underset{N\times K}{X} = A' \begin{pmatrix} \sqrt{\ell_1} & & \\ & \ddots & \\ & & \sqrt{\ell_N} \end{pmatrix} \underset{N\times K}{W}$$

$$x(t) = A' \begin{pmatrix} \sqrt{\ell_1} & & \\ & \ddots & \\ & & \sqrt{\ell_N} \end{pmatrix} w(t)$$

because $\hat{\text{cov}}(W) = I$

This last expression is the matrix form of expression (13.7). The vector $w(t)$ has a nonzero mean vector. This completes the demonstration.

SECTION D
REFERENCES TO CHAPTER 13

1. Amin, K., and A. Morton, 1995. "Implied Volatility Functions in Arbitrage Free Term Structure Models." *Journal of Financial Economics* forthcoming.
2. Cohen, H., 1991. *Testing Pricing Models for the Treasury Bond Futures Contract.* Ph.D. dissertation, Cornell University.
3. Flesaker, B., 1993. "Testing the Heath-Jarrow-Morton/Ho-Lee Model of Interest Rate Contingent Claims Pricing." *Journal of Financial and Quantitative Analysis* 28 (4), 483–496.
4. Heath, D., R. Jarrow, and A. Morton, 1991. "Contingent Claim Valuation with a Random Evolution of Interest Rates." *Review of Futures Markets,* 54–76.
5. Jolliffe, I. T., 1986. *Principal Component Analysis.* Springer-Verlag, New York.
6. Zhao, J., 1994. *Investigating Term Structure Models for Contingent Claim Valuation in the Eurodollar Market.* Ph.D. dissertation, Cornell University.

CHAPTER 14

Spot Rate Models

The purpose of this chapter is to provide a brief explanation of an alternative approach to Heath, Jarrow, and Morton [3] for pricing interest rate options. This approach is based on an exogenous specification of the spot rate process, examples of which include Cox, Ingersoll, and Ross [2], Black, Derman, and Toy [1], Hull and White [4], and Vasicek [6].

This chapter is divided into two sections. The first section discusses bond pricing (the analogue of Chapter 6), and the second section discusses contingent claims valuation (the analogue of Chapter 7).

SECTION A
BOND PRICING

This section studies the spot rate model approach to pricing bonds. This section is the analogue of Chapter 6.

1 One-Factor Economy

Given exogenously is the evolution of the spot interest rate process as in Fig. 4.7. In the notation of Chapter 4, expression (4.11), this is written as

$$r(t+1; s_{t+1}) = \begin{cases} u(t+1, t+2; s_t\text{u}) & \text{with probability } q_t(s_t) > 0 \\ d(t+1, t+2; s_t\text{d}) & \text{with probability } 1 - q_t(s_t) > 0 \end{cases} \tag{14.1}$$

To perform this analysis, we reparameterize this process as

$$r(t+1; s_{t+1}) = \begin{cases} r(t; s_t)a(t; s_t) & \text{if } s_{t+1} = s_t\text{u} \\ r(t; s_t)b(t; s_t) & \text{if } s_{t+1} = s_t\text{d} \end{cases} \tag{14.2}$$

In addition, this approach also *assumes* that we are given the unique pseudo probabilities $\pi(t; s_t)$ for all t, s_t such that[1]

$$P(t,T; s_t) = \tilde{E}_t\left(\frac{1}{\prod_{j=t}^{T-1} r(j; s_t)}\right) \qquad \text{for all } s_t \text{ and } 0 \le t \le T \le \tau \tag{14.3}$$

where $\tilde{E}_t(\bullet)$ is expectation under the given pseudo probabilities.

For convenience, the pseudo probabilities can be set equal to $\frac{1}{2}$:

$$\pi(t; s_t) \equiv \tfrac{1}{2} \qquad \text{for all } s_t \text{ and } 0 \le t \le T \le \tau - 1$$

This is done, for example, in Black, Derman, and Toy [1].

Because the pseudo probabilities are independent of any particular zero-coupon bond, from Chapter 7 we know that there are no arbitrage opportunities with respect to the largest trading strategy set Φ_τ; see expression (7.6).

The evolution of the zero-coupon bond price curve is given by expression (14.3). Given this evolution, the same analysis as in Chapter 7, Section 7.A.1, shows that the market is complete with respect to Φ_τ. Recall from Chapter 7 that if the market is complete with respect to Φ_1, it is also complete with respect to the largest set of trading strategies Φ_τ.

EXAMPLE: BOND PRICE VALUATION. This example uses the spot rate process given in Fig. 4.8. Let the pseudo probabilities be $\pi(t; s_t) = \frac{1}{2}$ for all s_t and $0 \le t \le T \le \tau - 1$. The risk-neutral valuation analysis in Chapter 7 shows that the implied time 0 zero-coupon bond prices are

$$\begin{aligned} P(0,4) &= 0.923845 \\ P(0,3) &= 0.942322 \\ P(0,2) &= 0.961169 \\ P(0,1) &= 0.980392 \end{aligned}$$

This structure also implies the bond price evolution given in Fig. 4.4.

2 Two-Factor and $N \geq 3$–Factor Economies

The extension of the spot rate model to two or more factors is straightforward. In expression (14.2), an additional outcome for the spot rate at time $t+1$ is added for each additional factor.

---

[1] This is in contrast to the method of Chapter 7, where the $\pi(t; s_t)$ are determined via a specification of the zero-coupon bond price curve evolution.

The pseudo-probabilities assumption is augmented to include the additional outcomes for the spot rate at time $t + 1$. This additional structure implies that there are no arbitrage opportunities with respect to the largest trading strategy set Φ_τ and that the market is complete with respect to Φ_τ, just as in Chapter 7.

The zero-coupon bond price process satisfies expression (14.3), and its evolution is completely determined by the given structure. Thus, the identical analysis as in Chapter 7 can be applied to the evolution of the zero-coupon bond prices implied by expression (14.3).

SECTION B
CONTINGENT CLAIMS VALUATION

The analysis in Section 14.A is useful for pricing zero-coupon bonds and arbitraging the yield curve. This section studies the pricing of interest rate options given the initial zero-coupon bond price curve. This is the analogue of Chapter 7.

Given for this analysis are the specification of the spot rate process as in expression (14.2) and a specification of the unique pseudo probabilities such that expression (14.3) holds for all zero-coupon bonds. These pseudo probabilities are often arbitrarily set equal to $\frac{1}{2}$. This is the same structure as in Section 14.A.

As before, since the pseudo probabilities are independent of any particular zero-coupon bond, the analysis in Chapter 7 shows that there are no arbitrage opportunities with respect to the largest trading strategy set Φ_τ.

Since expression (14.3) determines the evolution of the zero-coupon bonds, the analysis in Chapter 7 also shows that the market is complete with respect to the largest trading strategy set Φ_τ.

In addition, this section also takes as given the initial zero-coupon bond price curve:

$$\{P(0, T) \text{ for } 0 \leq T \leq \tau\} \tag{14.4}$$

To incorporate this additional information, the spot rate model approach determines the parameters for the evolution of the spot rate process so that the theoretical prices in expression (14.3) match the observed prices in expression (14.4). For example, in the one-factor economy, the spot rate process parameters $a(t; s_t)$ and $b(t; s_t)$ are chosen such that expression (14.3) for $t = 0$ matches the given initial curve. Usually, a solution exists (in fact, it is often nonunique).[2] This procedure is known as *curve-fitting*. An example will help clarify this procedure.

---

[2]In the nonunique case, additional contingent claim values can be matched, or a particular limiting form of the spot rate processes can be obtained.

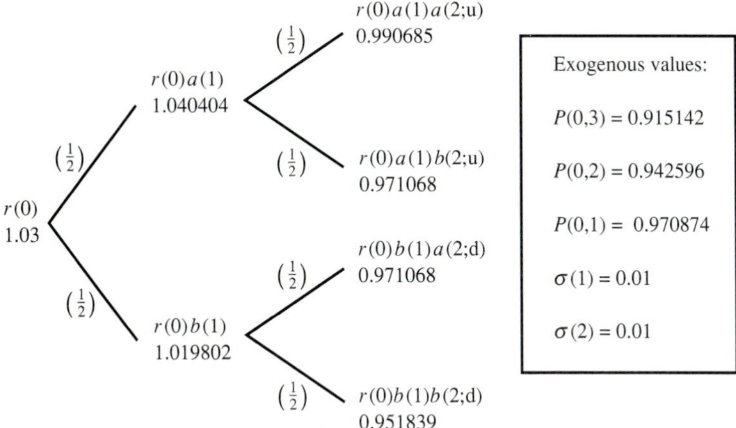

FIGURE 14.1
A spot rate process evolution. The pseudo probabilities are given on the branches of the tree. The numbers under the nodes are the values of the spot rates that match the exogenous values.

EXAMPLE: MATCHING THE INITIAL CURVE. We consider a three-period economy with $t = 0, 1, 2$. Let the spot rate process $\{r(t) : t = 0, 1, 2\}$ be as given in Fig. 14.1. We let the pseudo probabilities be $\pi(t; s_t) \equiv \frac{1}{2}$ for all s_t and $t = 0, 1, 2$. Also given is the following initial zero-coupon bond price curve:

$$\begin{aligned} P(0,3) &= 0.915142 \\ P(0,2) &= 0.942596 \\ P(0,1) &= 0.970874 \end{aligned}$$

We want to determine the values $\{r(0), a(1), b(1), a(2;\mathrm{u}), b(2;\mathrm{u}), a(2;\mathrm{d}), b(2;\mathrm{d})\}$ such that expression (14.3) gives back the initial bond price curve. The analysis is by forward induction. We start at time 1. Expression (14.3) states that

$$0.970874 = P(0,1) = \frac{1}{r(0)}$$

Thus,

$$r(0) = \frac{1}{0.970874} = 1.03$$

Next, at time 2, expression (14.3) states that

$$0.942596 = P(0,2) = \frac{1}{2}\left(\frac{1}{r(0)a(1)r(0)}\right) + \frac{1}{2}\left(\frac{1}{r(0)b(1)r(0)}\right)$$

Using $r(0) = 1.03$, which is determined from the previous step at time 0, gives

$$0.942596 = \frac{1}{2(1.03)^2}\left[\frac{1}{a(1)} + \frac{1}{b(1)}\right]$$

$$2 = \frac{1}{a(1)} + \frac{1}{b(1)}$$

or

$$b(1) = \frac{a(1)}{2a(1) - 1}$$

We see here that there is not a unique solution for $a(1)$ and $b(1)$.

To uniquely determine $a(1)$ and $b(1)$, we need to add another condition. Standard practice is to select $a(1)$ and $b(1)$ such that the time 0 variance of the spot rate process matches some observed value, i.e.,

$$\widetilde{\text{Var}}_0\{\log r(1) - \log r(0)\} = \sigma(1)$$

where $\sigma(1)$ is given exogenously. Algebra gives

$$\tilde{E}_0\{\log r(1) - \log r(0)\} = \tfrac{1}{2}\log a(1) + \tfrac{1}{2}\log b(1)$$

and

$$\widetilde{\text{Var}}_0\{\log r(1) - \log r(0)\} = \frac{\log a(1) - \log b(1)}{2}$$

Letting $\sigma(1) = 0.01$,

$$0.01 = \sigma(1) = \tfrac{1}{2}[\log a(1) - \log b(1)]$$

Algebra gives

$$a(1) = b(1)e^{0.02}$$

Substitution into the previous equation for $a(1)$ and $b(1)$ gives

$$2 = \frac{1}{b(1)e^{0.02}} + \frac{1}{b(1)}$$

or

$$b(1) = \tfrac{1}{2}\left(e^{-0.02} + 1\right) = 0.990099$$

$$a(1) = (0.990099)e^{0.02} = 1.010101$$

This implies that the spot interest rates at time 1 are

$$r(1; \text{u}) = r(0)a(1) = 1.03(1.010101) = 1.040404$$

$$r(1; \text{d}) = r(0)b(1) = 1.03(0.990099) = 1.019802$$

Interest rates move approximately ± 1 percent. These numbers are given in Fig. 14.1.

Finally, at time 3, expression (14.3) states that

$$\begin{aligned} 0.915142 &= P(0,3) \\ &= \left(\frac{1}{4}\right)\frac{1}{r(0)a(1)a(2;\text{u})r(0)a(1)r(0)} + \left(\frac{1}{4}\right)\frac{1}{r(0)a(1)b(2;\text{u})r(0)a(1)r(0)} \\ &\quad + \left(\frac{1}{4}\right)\frac{1}{r(0)b(1)a(2;\text{d})r(0)b(1)r(0)} + \left(\frac{1}{4}\right)\frac{1}{r(0)b(1)b(2;\text{d})r(0)b(1)r(0)} \end{aligned}$$

Substituting in the previous values and simplifying yield

$$4 = \frac{1}{(1.040404)^2}\left(\frac{1}{a(2;\mathrm{u})} + \frac{1}{b(2;\mathrm{u})}\right) + \frac{1}{(1.019802)^2}\left(\frac{1}{a(2;\mathrm{d})} + \frac{1}{b(2;\mathrm{d})}\right)$$

Again, a unique solution is not obtainable. To obtain a unique solution, we first set $a(1)b(2;\mathrm{u}) = b(1)a(2;\mathrm{d})$. This condition makes the tree recombine: it gives a *lattice*. Second, we make the variance at time 1 independent of the state u or d and equal to some observable constant, $\sigma(2)$; i.e.,

$$\widetilde{\mathrm{Var}}_{1;\mathrm{u}}(\log r(2) - \log r(1)) = \widetilde{\mathrm{Var}}_{1;\mathrm{d}}(\log r(2) - \log r(1)) = \sigma(2)$$

We let $\sigma(2) = 0.01$. Then

$$\widetilde{\mathrm{Var}}_{1;\mathrm{u}}(\log r(2) - \log r(1)) = \tfrac{1}{2}(\log a(2;\mathrm{u}) - \log b(2;\mathrm{u})) = 0.01$$

$$\widetilde{\mathrm{Var}}_{1;\mathrm{d}}(\log r(2) - \log r(1)) = \tfrac{1}{2}(\log a(2;\mathrm{d}) - \log b(2;\mathrm{d})) = 0.01$$

Combined, these additional restrictions give us four equations in four unknowns. First, the conditional variance restrictions imply that

$$a(2;\mathrm{u}) = b(2;\mathrm{u})e^{0.02} \qquad \text{and} \qquad a(2;\mathrm{d}) = b(2;\mathrm{d})e^{0.02}$$

The lattice condition implies that $b(2;\mathrm{u}) = b(1)a(2;\mathrm{d})/a(1)$. Using the values computed from the previous step at time 1 yields

$$b(2;\mathrm{u}) = \frac{(0.990099)a(2;\mathrm{d})}{1.010101} = (0.980198)a(2;\mathrm{d})$$

Combining these last three equations:

$$a(2;\mathrm{u}) = (0.980198)b(2;\mathrm{d})e^{0.02}e^{0.02} = (1.020201)b(2;\mathrm{d})$$

$$a(2;\mathrm{d}) = b(2;\mathrm{d})e^{0.02} = (1.020201)b(2;\mathrm{d})$$

$$b(2;\mathrm{u}) = (0.980198)b(2;\mathrm{d})e^{0.02} = b(2;\mathrm{d})$$

Thus, substitution into the determining equation gives

$$4 = \frac{1}{(1.040404)^2}\left(\frac{1}{(1.020201)b(2;\mathrm{d})} + \frac{1}{b(2;\mathrm{d})}\right) + \frac{1}{(1.019802)^2}\left(\frac{1}{(1.020201)b(2;\mathrm{d})} + \frac{1}{b(2;\mathrm{d})}\right)$$

which implies

$$b(2;\mathrm{d}) = \frac{1}{4}\left(1 + \frac{1}{1.020201}\right)\left(\frac{1}{(1.040404)^2} + \frac{1}{(1.019802)^2}\right) = 0.933357$$

Thus, $b(2;\mathrm{u}) = 0.933357$ and $a(2;\mathrm{d}) = (1.020201)0.933357 = 0.952212 = a(2;\mathrm{u})$. The spot interest rates at time 2 are

$$r(2;\mathrm{uu}) = r(0)a(1)a(2;\mathrm{u}) = 1.040404(0.952212) = 0.990685$$

$$r(2;\mathrm{ud}) = r(0)a(1)b(2;\mathrm{u}) = 1.040404(0.933357) = 0.971068$$

$$r(2; \text{du}) = r(0)b(1)a(2; \text{d}) = 1.019802(0.952212) = 0.971068$$

$$r(2; \text{dd}) = r(0)b(1)b(2; \text{d}) = 1.019802(0.933357) = 0.951839$$

In this example we get negative interest rates at time 2. This illustrates a common problem with the spot rate approach: the curve fitting procedure often leads to implications in the evolution of the spot interest rate process that are not desired.

Given this structure and an evolution of the spot rate process that matches the initial zero-coupon bond price curve, we can value contingent claims exactly as in Chapter 7, and as illustrated in Chapters 8–11.

SECTION C LIMIT ECONOMIES

Using the notation of Chapter 12, Section 12.A., we can investigate reparameterizations of the discrete-time economy in order to approximate a continuous-time limit economy. We do the reparameterization only under the pseudo probabilities $\pi(t; s_t) \equiv \frac{1}{2}$ for all s_t and t. We also do the analysis only for the one-factor economy. Multiple factors are handled analogously by adding additional branches on the tree and additional Brownian motions in the limit economy.

We reparameterize expression (14.2) in terms of two new stochastic processes $\mu(t; s_t)$ and $\sigma(t; s_t)$:

$$r_\Delta(t + \Delta; s_{t+\Delta}) = \begin{cases} r_\Delta(t; s_t)e^{\{\mu(t;s_t)\Delta + \sigma(t;s_t)\sqrt{\Delta}\}} & \text{with pseudo probability } \frac{1}{2} \\ r_\Delta(t; s_t)e^{\{\mu(t;s_t)\Delta - \sigma(t;s_t)\sqrt{\Delta}\}} & \text{with pseudo probability } \frac{1}{2} \end{cases} \tag{14.5}$$

This implies that

$$\tilde{E}_t\{\log r_\Delta(t + \Delta) - \log r_\Delta(t)\} = \mu(t)\Delta \tag{14.6a}$$

$$\widetilde{\text{Var}}_t\{\log r_\Delta(t + \Delta) - \log r_\Delta(t)\} = \sigma^2(t)\Delta \tag{14.6b}$$

Define the continuously compounded spot rate[3] as

$$\tilde{r}(t) = \lim_{\Delta \to 0} \frac{\log(r_\Delta(t))}{\Delta} \tag{14.7}$$

Under suitable restrictions[4] upon $\mu(t)$ and $\sigma(t)$, $[\log r_\Delta(t + \Delta) - \log r_\Delta(t)]/\Delta$ converges (in distribution) to

$$d\tilde{r}(t) = \mu(t)\, dt + \sigma(t)\, dW(t) \tag{14.8}$$

---

[3]Note that expression (14.7) implies that $e^{\tilde{r}(t)\Delta} \approx r_\Delta(t)$.

[4]See Nelson and Ramaswamy [5].

under the pseudo probabilities where $\{W(t) : t \in [0, \tau]\}$ is a Brownian motion initialized at zero.

The following two restrictions upon the stochastic processes $\mu(t)$ and $\sigma(t)$ appear in the literature.

Case A: A normal distribution with mean reversion

In this case,

$\sigma(t)$ is nonrandom.
$\mu(t) \equiv \theta(t)[K(t) - \tilde{r}(t)]$ where both $\theta(t)$ and $K(t)$ are nonrandom.

The function $K(t)$ is the long-run spot rate at time t to which the process tends. The speed of adjustment to the long-run rate is measured by $\theta(t)$. The discrete-time approximation replaces $\tilde{r}(t)$ with $[\log r_\Delta(t)]/\Delta$, as suggested by expression (14.7).

This is the model of Vasicek [6] and Hull and White [4].

Case B: A log-normal distribution with mean reversion

In this case,

$\sigma(t) \equiv \eta(t)\tilde{r}(t)$ where $\eta(t)$ is nonrandom.
$\mu(t) \equiv \theta(t)[K(t) - \log \tilde{r}(t)]\tilde{r}(t)$ where both $\theta(t)$ and $K(t)$ are nonrandom.

The function $K(t)$ is the long-run $\log \tilde{r}(t)$, and $\theta(t)$ gives the speed of adjustment to the long-run logarithm of the spot rate.[5] The discrete-time approximation replaces $\tilde{r}(t)$ with $[\log r_\Delta(t)]/\Delta$, as suggested by expression (14.7).

This is the model of Black, Derman, and Toy [1].

To match the initial zero-coupon price curve, the function $\mu(t)$ is determined using forward induction as in the previous example. The volatility parameter $\sigma(t)$ can be determined by historical estimation or by implicit estimation (curve-fitting).[6]

SECTION D
REFERENCES TO CHAPTER 14

1. Black, F., E. Derman, and W. Toy, 1990. "A One-Factor Model of Interest Rates and Its Application to Treasury Bond Options." *Financial Analyst Journal* 46, 33–39.

---

[5]The process can be rewritten in natural logarithms as

$$d \log \tilde{r}(t) = \theta(t)[K(t) - \log \tilde{r}(t)]\, dt - \tfrac{1}{2}\sigma^2(t)\, dt + \sigma(t)\, dW(t)$$

This follows from Ito's lemma.

[6]Recall from Chapter 12, Fig. 12.1, that the volatility of the limit economy is the same under both the pseudo and the actual probabilities.

2. Cox, J., S. Ross, and J. Ingersoll, 1985. "A Theory of the Term Structure of Interest Rates." *Econometrica* 53, 385–407.
3. Heath, D., R. Jarrow, and A. Morton, 1992. "Bond Pricing and the Term Structure of Interest Rates: A New Methodology for Contingent Claims Valuation." *Econometrica* 60 (1), 77–105.
4. Hull, J., and A. White, 1990. "Pricing Interest Rate Derivative Securities." *Review of Financial Studies* 3 (4), 573–592.
5. Nelson, D., and K. Ramaswamy, 1990. "Simple Binomial Processes as Diffusion Approximations in Financial Models." *Review of Financial Studies* 3 (1), 393–430.
6. Vasicek, O., 1977. "An Equilibrium Characterization of the Term Structure." *Journal of Financial Economics* 5, 177–188.

CHAPTER 15

Extensions

A major advantage of the term structure model presented in this textbook is that it is easily extended to incorporate additional term structures. The introduction of additional term structures is the generalization needed to price and hedge foreign-currency derivatives, credit derivatives, and commodity options. This chapter briefly discusses each of these generalizations, providing references for subsequent reading.

SECTION A
FOREIGN-CURRENCY DERIVATIVES

To price and hedge foreign-currency derivatives, one needs a spot exchange rate of foreign into domestic currency and two zero-coupon bond price curves: *(i)* one for the domestic currency and *(ii)* one for the foreign currency.

The method for building an arbitrage-free evolution of these term structures proceeds in a fashion identical to that given in Chapters 4–7. The only complication is that in constructing the tree, two price vectors are included at each node. One vector is for the domestic-currency zero-coupon curve (just as before), and one vector is for the foreign-currency zero-coupon curve with the spot exchange rate appended. The arbitrage-free conditions correspond to the existence of pseudo probabilities, which make all dollar-denominated and dollar-translated securities (foreign zero-coupon bonds) martingales after normalization by the domestic money market account. Market completeness corresponds to the uniqueness of these pseudo probabilities. Pricing and hedging is done via the risk-neutral valuation procedure.

The only difficulty in applying these extensions in practice is that the computation time increases as more term structures are introduced into the model. Efficient numerical procedures become an important issue. References for this extension include Amin and Jarrow [2] and Amin and Bodurtha [1].

SECTION B
CREDIT DERIVATIVES AND COUNTERPARTY RISK

An important extension of the default-free term structure model to multiple term structures is when one includes securities with different levels of bankruptcy risk. The pricing and hedging of corporate debt and the pricing and hedging of swaps with counterparty risk are two prime examples.

The easiest way to analyze this pricing problem is to transform it into a foreign-currency derivative problem and then to use the methods for pricing and hedging foreign currency derivatives (with obvious modifications).

To see the foreign-currency analogy, consider two term structures of zero-coupon bonds: *(i)* the default-free term structure and *(ii)* the term structure for a risky firm. Call the risky firm XYZ. XYZ's zero-coupon bonds provide only a *promised dollar* payoff at future dates. The promised dollar is paid only if XYZ is not bankrupt at the payoff date.

One can think of XYZ zero-coupon debt differently. Consider XYZ zero-coupon bonds as first paying off in a hypothetical (foreign) currency, called XYZ dollars. That is, each XYZ zero-coupon bond pays one XYZ dollar for sure at its maturity. In XYZ dollars, XYZ debt can be considered default-free. But XYZ dollars need to be converted into actual dollars for analysis. The conversion rate (or spot exchange rate from XYZ dollars to dollars) is the payoff ratio at the zero-coupon bond's maturity. If XYZ is not bankrupt, the payoff ratio is unity. If it is bankrupt, less than the promised dollar is received.

Given this foreign-currency analogy, the pricing and hedging problem for foreign-currency derivatives can now be applied. This analogy also applies to counterparty risk as well. A counterparty to a contract only *promises* to make a payment, and when the contract provisions come due, payment is made only if the counterparty is not in default. Thus, this problem is identical to the one already discussed. Recommended references are Jarrow and Turnbull [4], Jarrow, Lando, and Turnbull [5], and Lando [6].

SECTION C
COMMODITY DERIVATIVES

The final extension studied is the pricing of commodity derivatives. Examples include oil futures, options on oil futures, precious metal futures, and options on precious metals.

Again, this pricing and hedging problem has two term structures. The first is the same as that already studied, the term structure of default-free zero-coupon bonds. The second term structure is the term structure of commodity futures prices for future delivery. Given these two term structures, the analysis proceeds in a fashion similar to that of Chapters 4–7. The only difference is that in constructing the tree, two price vectors are included at each node. One is for the default-free zero-coupon bond prices, and the second is for the commodity futures prices for future delivery.

The arbitrage-free conditions correspond to the existence of pseudo probabilities, which make the zero-coupon bond prices normalized by the money market account martingales and make the futures prices martingales (see Chapter 9 for the motivation of this last condition). Market completeness corresponds to the uniqueness of these pseudo probabilities. Pricing and hedging is done using the risk-neutral valuation procedure. This extension can be found in Carr and Jarrow [3].

SECTION D
REFERENCES TO CHAPTER 15

1. Amin, K., and J. Bodurtha, 1995. "Discrete Time Valuation of American Options with Stochastic Interest Rates." *Review of Financial Studies* 8 (1), 193–234.
2. Amin, K., and R. Jarrow, 1991. "Pricing Foreign Currency Options under Stochastic Interest Rates." *Journal of International Money and Finance* 10, 310–329.
3. Carr, P., and R. Jarrow, 1995. "A Discrete Time Synthesis of Derivative Security Valuation Using a Term Structure of Futures Prices." In W. Ziemba, R. Jarrow, and V. Maksimovic, eds., *Finance: Handbook in Operations Research and Management Science.* North Holland, Amsterdam.
4. Jarrow, R., and S. Turnbull, 1995. "Pricing Derivatives on Financial Securities Subject to Credit Risk." *Journal of Finance* 50 (1), 53–85.
5. Jarrow, R., D. Lando, and S. Turnbull, 1993. "A Markov Model for the Term Structure of Credit Risk Spreads." Unpublished manuscript, Cornell University.
6. Lando, D., 1994. *Three Essays on Contingent Claims Pricing.* Ph.D. dissertation, Cornell University.

PART II

The Computer Software

CHAPTER 16

Trees Software

To facilitate learning, we provided software to compute prices for many of the fixed-income securities and interest rate options studied in this book. The use of this software was illustrated at the end of each relevant chapter.

To access this software, click on the "Trees" icon. What then appears is a screen labeled "discrete HJM models" with three menu items, (*i*) model, (*ii*) claims, and (*iii*) display, and a tree with nodes labeled u, d, uu, ud, du, dd, etc. A number appears next to each node. These are the spot interest rates for each node; see Fig. 16.1.

SECTION A
MODEL

Under the "model" choice, there are three menu selections: sigma, initial term structure, and tree depth.

Sigma. The selection "sigma" gives Fig. 16.2, labeled "change sigma function." The "sigma" function corresponds to case 2, proportional volatility functions, from Chapter 12.

Initial term structure. The selection "initial term structures" gives Fig. 16.3. One can input various initial forward rate curves.

Tree depth. This selection enables the user to change the tree depth.

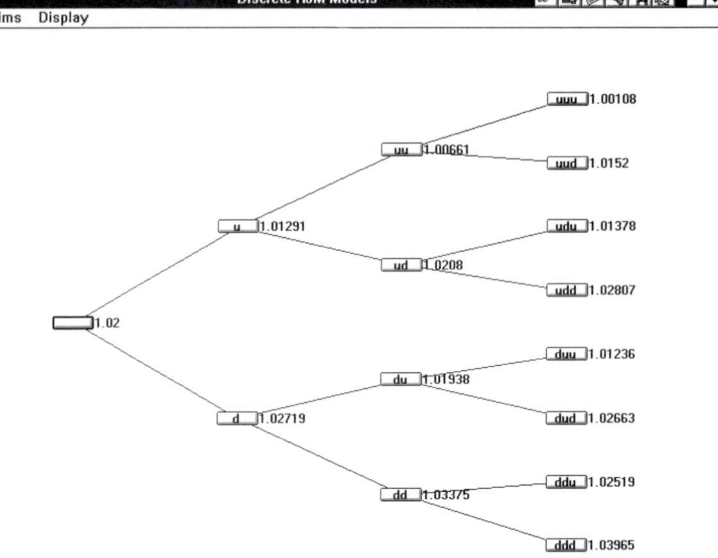

FIGURE 16.1
Discrete HJM models Screen.

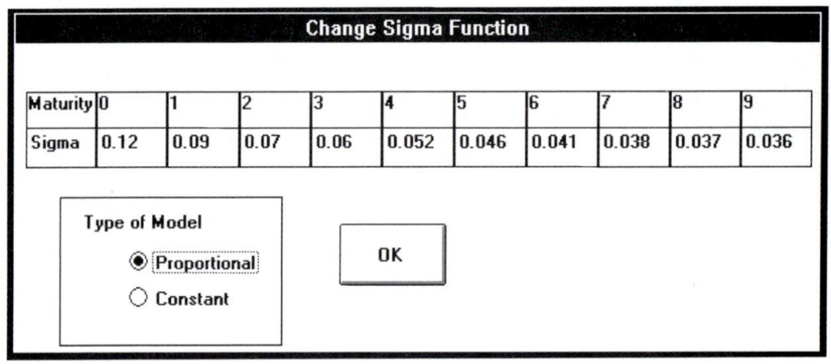

FIGURE 16.2
Change sigma function screen.

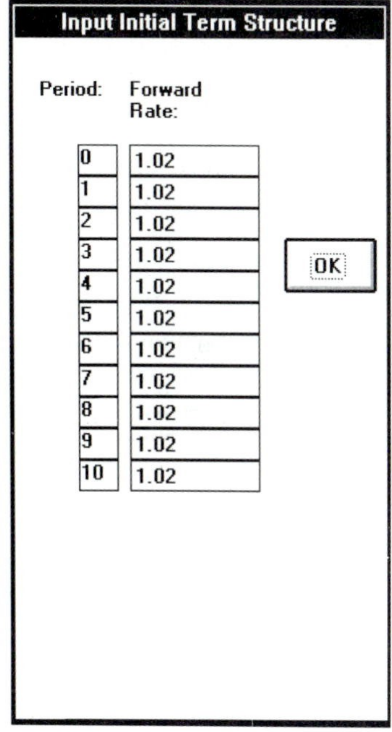

FIGURE 16.3
Input initial term structure screen.

SECTION B CLAIMS

Under the menu selection "claims" are six submenu items: coupon bonds, cap, forward, futures, European call, and American call. Selecting any one of these submenu items enables one to construct such a security.

Coupon bonds. Selecting "coupon bonds" requires the user to define a coupon bond; see Chapter 8.

Cap. Selecting "cap" requires the user to define a cap; see Chapter 10.

Forward. Selecting "forward" requires the user to define a forward contract; see Chapter 9. The underlying coupon bond must first be specified.

Futures. Selecting "futures" requires the user to define a futures contract; see Chapter 9. The underlying coupon bond must first be specified.

European call. Selecting "European call" requires the user to define a European call option; see Chapter 8. The underlying bond must first be selected.

American call. Selecting "American call" requires the user to define an American call option; see Chapter 8. The underlying bond must first be selected.

SECTION C DISPLAY

Display has two submenu items: on the tree, and term structure.

On the tree. Selecting "on the tree" changes the numbers that appear at the nodes of the tree. The selections are spot rates, coupon bond prices, cap, forward, futures, European call, and American call prices. The default selection is spot rates.

Term structure. Selecting "term structure" yields a screen labeled "choose description for term structure." Three choices are provided: forward rates, pure discount bond prices, and pure discount bond yields. The default selection is forward rates. Choosing one of these selections determines the term structure that appears on the screen when a node is clicked on. For example, clicking on node du gives the forward rate term structure at that date and time.

CHAPTER 17

HJM Demonstration Software

The computer examples in Chapters 3–11 and the Trees software provided were designed to illustrate the underlying theory in as simple a fashion as possible. Therefore, a four-period example based on only a single factor was employed. As a result, the Trees computer code provided is too simple to be useful for valuing actual traded securities.

The purpose of this chapter is to provide both more realistic examples[1] of the previous theory and more useful computer software. The examples are generated using a studentized version of a professionally written computer code, developed from the theory presented in Chapter 12. This code is useful for pricing actually traded securities with multiple factors. With this purpose in mind, we will now briefly revisit, this time with more realism, many of the examples studied in Chapters 3–11.

SECTION A INTRODUCTION

To run the HJM demonstration software, enter Windows and click on the "HJM demo" icon.

The "scenario" screen will appear; see Fig. 17.1. The basic inputs to the HJM valuation model appear on this screen: *(i)* the continuously compounded

[1]In the examples computed in this chapter, the start date for all the securities is the current date. Different starting days could generate small differences in some of the resulting numbers because of differences in day counts.

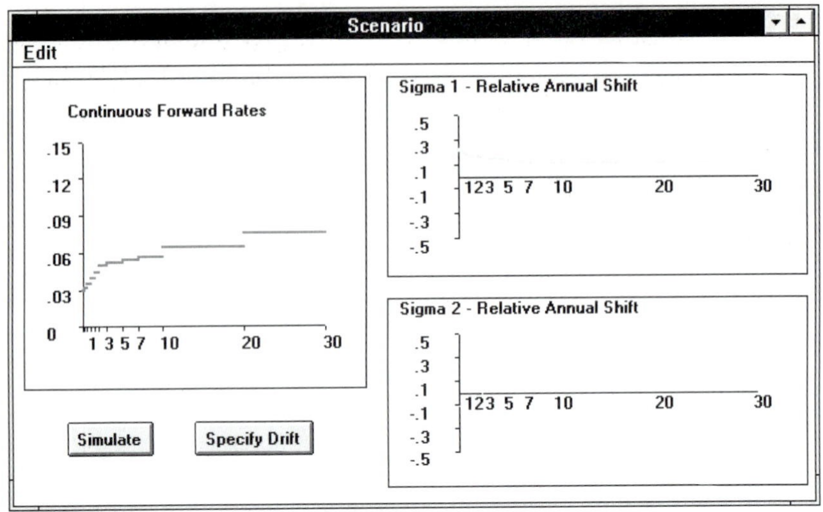

FIGURE 17.1
Scenario screen.

initial forward rates per year and *(ii)* the volatility functions for a one- or two-factor model.

1 Initial Forward Rates

The square box on the left of the scenario screen (Fig. 17.1) is labeled "continuous forward rates." This is a graph of the initial continuously compounded forward rates $\{\tilde{f}(0, T) \text{ for } 0 \leq T \leq 30\}$ on a per-year basis; see expression (12.21). The curve is piecewise flat.

To change the initial forward rate curve, click on "edit," in the upper left corner. Two choices, "rates" and "sigmas," appear. Click on "rates." A screen labeled "edit rates" appears; see Fig. 17.2.

Two columns of numbers appear on this screen. The first is labeled "time"; the second is labeled "rate." The first forward rate, 0.03, applies to the time period 0–0.25 year. The second forward rate, 0.0321, applies to the time period 0.25–0.5 year. The same pattern applies for the remaining forward rates and time periods.

In this demonstration version, only three forward rates can be changed: the forward rates for the periods 0–0.25 year, 2–3 years, and 20–30 years. The software linearly interpolates the remaining forward rates from these numbers. To change one of these forward rates, just click on the number, delete the current number, and type in the desired one.

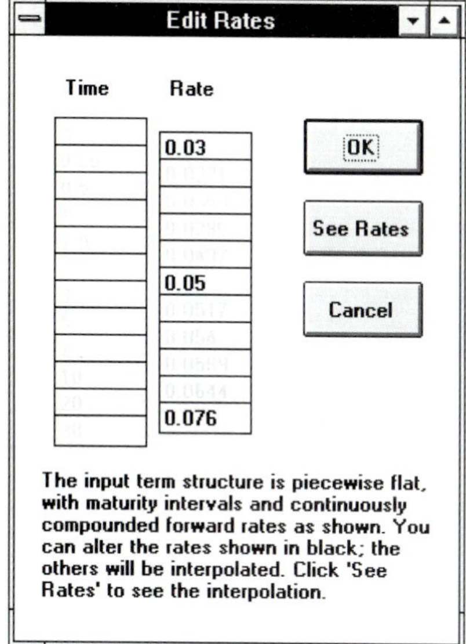

FIGURE 17.2
Edit rates screen.

2 Volatility Functions

The two rectangular boxes on the right of the scenario screen (Fig. 17.1) are labeled "sigma 1—relative annual shift" (the upper box) and "sigma 2—relative annual shift" (the lower box). These represent the volatility functions for, at most, a two-factor model. The volatility functions are given by the (nearly) proportional volatility functions in expression (12.29),

$$\sigma_i(T - t) = \eta_i(T - t)\min(\tilde{f}(t, T), M) \qquad \text{for } i = 1, 2 \qquad (17.1)$$

where the volatility functions are assumed to depend only on time to maturity $(T - t)$. The term "relative" corresponds to "proportional." The graph of $\eta_1(T-t)$ for $0 \leq T-t \leq 30$ is labeled "sigma 1," and the graph of $\eta_2(T-t)$ is labeled "sigma 2."

The first volatility function, $\eta_1(T - t)$, is downward sloping, and the graph's line is dark. The second volatility function, $\eta_2(T - t)$, is upward sloping, and the graph's line is dotted. This indicates that only sigma 1 is being used and that we are modeling a one-factor model. If both graph lines were dark, a two-factor model would be operational.

Modify sigma 1 or sigma 2

To modify the volatility functions, sigma 1 and sigma 2, click on "edit" in the upper left corner. Two choices, "rates" and "sigmas," appear. Click on "sigmas." A screen labeled "edit sigma functions" appears; see Fig. 17.3.

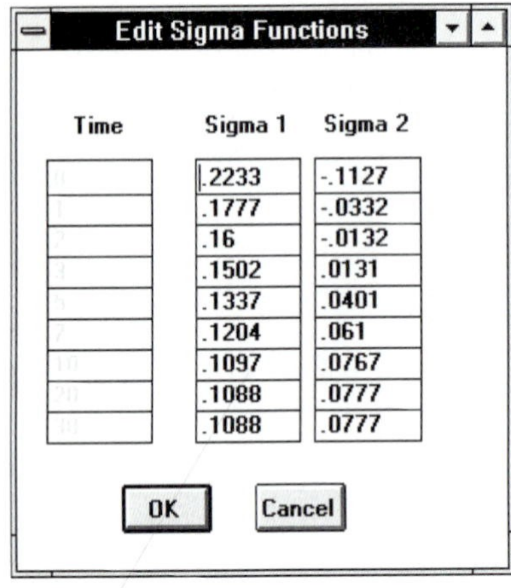

FIGURE 17.3
Edit sigma functions screen.

There are three columns. The first is labeled "time"; the second, "sigma 1"; the third, "sigma 2." The elements in the sigma 1 column represent $\eta_1(0) = 0.2233$, $\eta_1(1) = 0.1777$, $\eta_1(2) = 0.16$, $\ldots$, $\eta_1(30) = 0.1088$. The elements in the sigma 2 column represent $\eta_2(0) = -0.1127$, $\eta_2(1) = -0.0332$, $\eta_2(2) = -0.0132$, $\ldots$, $\eta_2(30) = 0.0777$. Values on the graph between these elements are linearly interpolated.

To change any of these values, just click on the desired entry, delete, and input the desired number.

Modify 1 or 2 factors

To change between one and two factors, click on "parameters" in the top menu bar. Two choices appear, "reset" and "set." Click on "set." A "set parameters" screen appears; see Fig. 17.4. The first row of instructions is labeled "number of factors." To have one factor, click on "one." To have two factors, click on "two."

3 Tree Construction

The software builds trees similar to those used in the text, using expression (12.19) or (12.30), with the initial forward rates $f_\Delta(t + \Delta, T)$ determined via expression (12.21) and given $\tilde{f}(t, T)$ as input above, and with the initial volatilities $\sigma_i(t, T)$ for $i = 1, 2$ determined via expression (17.1) with $\eta_i(T - t)$ as input above.

The only choice for the user allowed in the tree construction is the number of time steps. For a one-factor model the time to compute approximately doubles for each additional time step. Recall that for one time step there are two nodes at the last step in the tree. For two time steps there are 2^2 nodes at

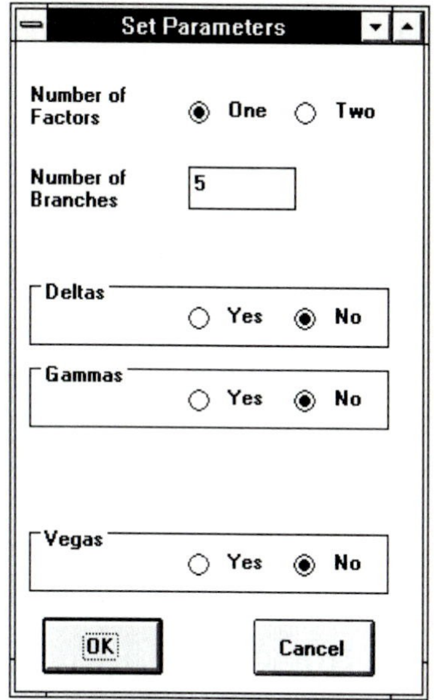

FIGURE 17.4
Set parameters screen.

the last step in the tree, and so forth. The default setting is five time steps. The maximum number of time steps is nine.

To modify the number of time steps, click on "parameters" in the top menu bar. Two choices appear, "reset" and "set." Click on "set." The "set parameters" screen appears; see Fig. 17.4.

The second row is labeled "number of branches." Click on this box, and insert the desired step size. *Warning: keep the step size small, or the computing time will be large.* The maximum number of time steps allowed is nine.

4 Simulate

The lower left corner of the "scenario" screen, Fig. 17.1, has two choices: one labeled "simulate" and the second labeled "specify drift."

The choice "simulate" will simulate *one possible evolution* of forward interest rates for the model selected. The evolution can be observed as it evolves for 20 years. It leaves a history of spot rates as it evolves. The evolution is determined via random sampling from a forward rate process determined via expression (12.25a); i.e.,

$$df(t, T) = \mu^*(t, T)\, dt + \sigma(t, T)\, dW(t) \tag{17.2}$$

where $\sigma(t, T)$ and $dW(t)$ can be vector-valued processes. Each time "simulate" is selected, a different sampling is made and a different 20-year evolution of forward rates appears.

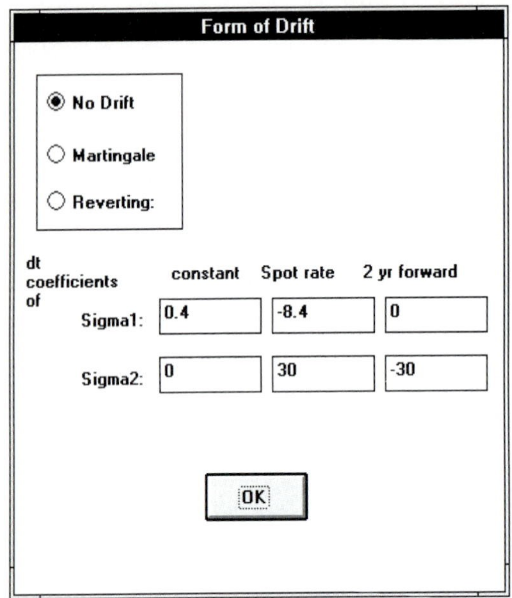

FIGURE 17.5
Form of drift screen.

The choice "specify drift" enables one to modify the forward rate process evolution in this equation in various ways. Clicking on "specify drift" obtains the "form of drift" screen, Fig. 17.5.

Three types of drifts can be selected: "no drift," "martingale," or "reverting." The "no drift" selection sets $\mu^*(t, T) \equiv 0$ in expression (17.2). The "martingale" selection sets

$$\mu^*(t, T) = -\sum_{i=1}^{2} \sigma_i(t, T) \int_t^T \sigma_i(t, v)\, dv$$

as in Chapter 12, expression (12.25*d*). This case gives the evolution of expression (12.25*b*) under the pseudo probabilities. The "reverting" selection sets

$$\mu^*(t, T) = -\sum_{i=1}^{2} \sigma_i(t, T) \int_t^T \sigma_i(t, v)\, dv - \sum_{i=1}^{2} \phi_i(t)\sigma_i(t, T)$$

where $\phi_i(t) \equiv \text{constant}_i + k_i r(t) + k_i^* f(t, 2)$ for $i = 1, 2$. This is expression (12.26), which gives the evolution of expression (12.25*a*) where the risk premium is a function of $r(t)$ and $f(t, 2)$. The coefficients constant_i, k_i, and k_i^* for $i = 1, 2$ are specified by changing the numbers in the boxes to the right of "sigma 1" and "sigma 2."

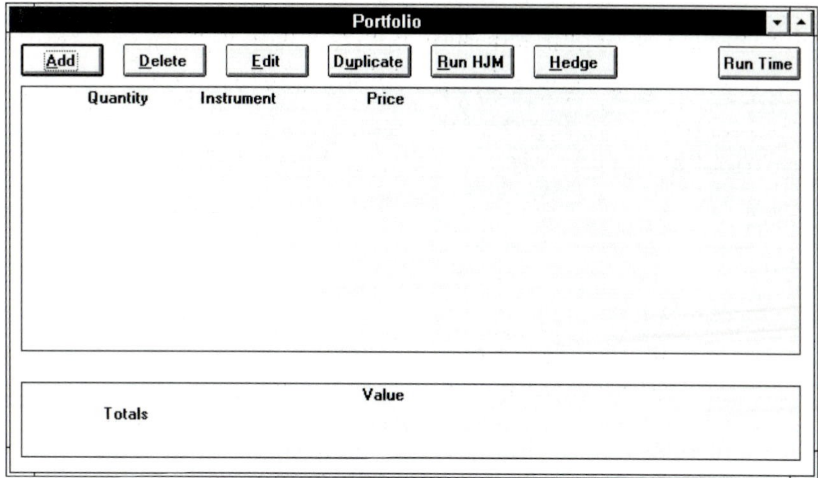

FIGURE 17.6
Portfolio screen.

5 Valuation of Fixed-Income Securities and Interest Rate Options

To price and hedge various securities using this software, one needs to click on the "Windows" choice in the upper menu bar. Two choices will appear: "portfolio" and "scenario." Clicking on "scenario" gives Fig. 17.1. Clicking on "portfolio" takes one to the valuation portion of the computer code.

Selecting "portfolio" generates the "portfolio" screen, Fig. 17.6. When this screen appears, it will be almost blank, with the exception of numerous menu selections. These are at the top of the screen, below the word "portfolio," and are entitled: "add," "delete," "edit," "duplicate," "run HJM," "hedge," and "run time."

The most important of these selections, at the start, is the first choice, "add."

Add

Clicking on "add" gives the "choose an instrument type" screen, Fig. 17.7. In the "choose an instrument type" screen, seven types of instruments can be selected for analysis. They are (1) bonds, (2) cap/floor, (3) periodic cap, (4) fixed-rate note, (5) floating-rate note, (6) swap, and (7) option. In subsequent sections we will discuss how to use each of these.

Modify computation of deltas

To speed up computation time, the software allows one to compute prices alone or prices plus deltas (or prices plus deltas, gammas, and vegas, defined

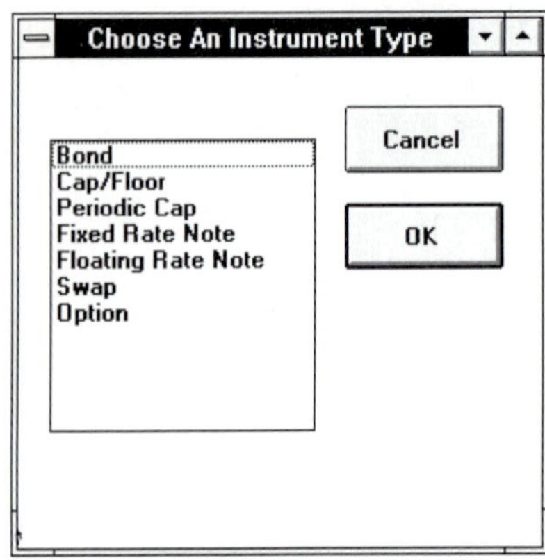

FIGURE 17.7
Choose an instrument type screen.

below). To modify these, click on the "parameters" choice in the upper menu bar. Two choices appear: "reset" and "set." Click on "set." The screen "set parameters" appears, Fig. 17.4. To compute deltas, click on "yes" in the delta box. To not compute deltas, click on "no."

To define the delta, the gamma, and the vega, we first need to introduce some different notation from that used in the text. Let f denote the *entire initial forward rate curve* (a continuous function). Let $V(f)$ represent the value of a contingent claim given the initial forward rate curve f. Let g denote another possible forward rate curve. Let $\varepsilon > 0$ be a small real number. Then εg represents a scalar multiple of the forward rate curve g. Further, $f + \varepsilon g$ represents the initial forward rate curve f shifted by adding the curve εg to it.

The *derivative of V in the direction of g,* if it exists, is defined by

$$D_g V(f) \equiv \lim_{\varepsilon \to 0} \frac{V(f + \varepsilon g) - V(f)}{\varepsilon} \tag{17.3}$$

The "delta" (or "delta1") is $D_{\sigma_1} V(f)$, where σ_1 is the first volatility function. "Delta2" is $D_{\sigma_1} V(f)$, where σ_2 is the second volatility function. The derivative in expression (17.3) is approximated by choosing $\varepsilon = 1$ so that $f + \varepsilon\sigma_i$ for $i = 1, 2$ represents a one-year standard deviation move caused by the ith factor in the forward rate curve. Recall that the volatility functions are measured on a per-year basis.

Gammas are defined as derivatives of derivatives. So

$$\text{gamma11} \equiv D_{\sigma_1}(D_{\sigma_1} V(f))$$

$$\text{gamma12} \equiv D_{\sigma_2}(D_{\sigma_1} V(f))$$

$$\text{gamma22} \equiv D_{\sigma_2}(D_{\sigma_2} V(f))$$

The approximation sets $\varepsilon = 1$ in expression (17.3).

The vega is defined as the derivative of the contingent claim value with respect to the volatility function, computed as

$$\text{vega} \equiv D_{(0.1\sigma_1)}V(\sigma_1, \sigma_2) + D_{(0.1\sigma_2)}V(\sigma_1, \sigma_2)$$

where V is a function of the curves σ_1 and σ_2. The perturbation functions are 0.1 of σ_1 and 0.1 of σ_2. In the approximation of the derivative, $\varepsilon = 1$.

SECTION B BONDS

To value and hedge various bonds, make sure that deltas are being computed. To do this, click on "parameters" and then click on "set," to obtain Fig. 17.4. Set deltas to "yes."

Next, click on "Windows," click on "portfolio," and then click on "add." Fig. 17.7, the "choose an instrument type" screen, appears.

Select "bond." The "bond" screen appears, Fig. 17.8. The "bond" screen enables you to construct and add to your portfolio various types of bonds. A bond is completely specified by *(i)* its length in years, *(ii)* the frequency of coupon payments (quarterly, semiannually, annually), *(iii)* the start date (when the last coupon was paid), *(iv)* the annual rate (coupon rate), and *(v)* the principal. The start date on this screen is today's date.

To illustrate the code, you will first value and hedge various zero-coupon bonds.

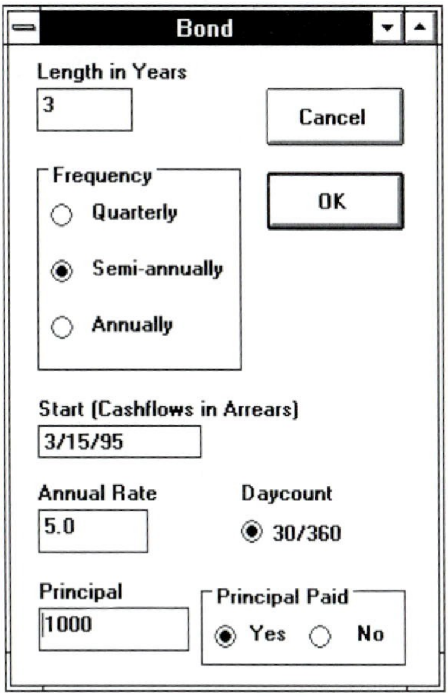

FIGURE 17.8
Bond screen.

1 Zero-Coupon Bonds

Choose "portfolio" and select "add." We are going to consider two different zero-coupon bonds, which mature at years 2 and 5, each paying $1000.

To obtain the first of these, select "bond" to obtain the bond screen, Fig. 17.8. Choose

Length in years = 2
Annual rate = 0
Principal = 1,000

Ignore all the other choices. When this selection is made, it will appear in the portfolio as

Quantity	0.00
Instrument	0 percent bond

No price will appear. To get a price, click on "run HJM." A price of $927.92 appears with a delta of −$0.66.

To obtain the five-year zero-coupon bond, you repeat the above procedure. Click on "add," and then add a bond with

Length in years = 5
Annual rate = 0
Principal = 1,000

Ignore all the other choices. When included, this will appear as the second 0 percent bond, with a quantity 0.00. Click on "run HJM." A price of $795.99 appears for this bond, with a delta of −$1.50.

We want to hold the five-year zero-coupon bond and hedge it with the two-year zero-coupon bond. To form this portfolio, first click on the 0.00 quantity for the second 0 percent bond. A "quantity" screen, Fig. 17.9, appears. Change the quantity to one. At the bottom of the screen the total value of your portfolio now appears as $795.99 with a delta of −$1.50.

To hedge this portfolio with the two-year zero, click on the "hedge" choice. The "hedging" screen appears, Fig. 17.10. In the "what to hedge?" box, click on "deltas." The box will adjust and say "choose one hedging instrument." This is because there is only one factor in the default settings. Choose the first 0 percent bond; recall that it has maturity of two years. Click on "compute hedge." The box says that −2.2628 units of the two-year zero-coupon bond are needed to hedge the five-year zero-coupon bond.

To do the hedge, click on "do hedge." The portfolio will automatically adjust to include the hedge with the two-year zero-coupon bond. The total portfolio value is now −$1,303.71 with a delta of zero. This means that the portfolio is insensitive to changes in the forward rate curve. This completes the zero-coupon bond illustration.

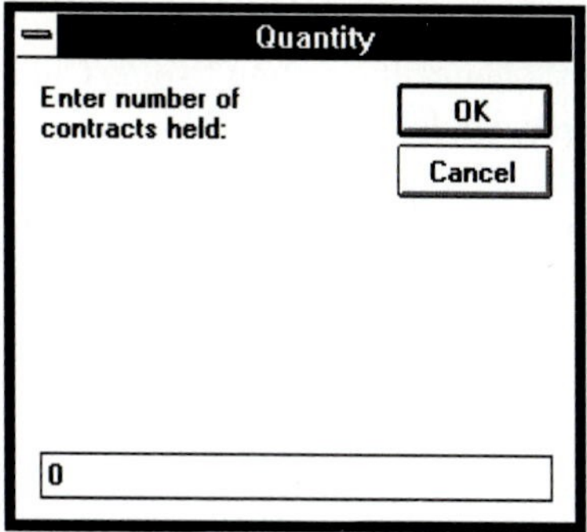

FIGURE 17.9
Quantity screen.

2 Coupon Bonds

To illustrate how to compute and hedge coupon bonds, go to the "add" choice. Use the following bond:

Length in years = 3
Semiannual payments
Annual rate = 5.0
Principal = 1,000

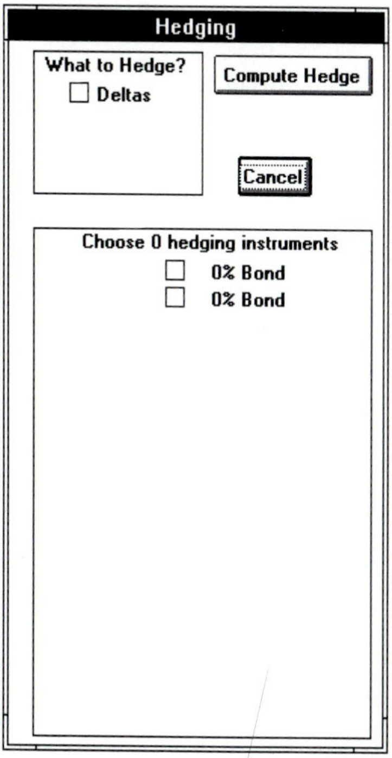

Hedging
What to Hedge?
Deltas
Compute Hedge
Cancel
Choose 0 hedging instruments
0% Bond
0% Bond

FIGURE 17.10
Hedging screen.

You add one unit of it to your portfolio by clicking on 0.00 unit under quantity. When the quantity screen, Fig. 17.9, appears, change the setting to one. Click on "run HJM" to obtain a price of $1,023.09 and a delta of −$1.07.

Let us consider hedging this bond with a two-year zero-coupon bond. You need to add the two-year zero-coupon bond to your set of securities. Choose "add," choose "bond," and then change the settings to

Length in years = 2
Annual rate = 0
Principal = 1,000

Ignore all the other choices. This bond enters your portfolio with quantities of zero. Run HJM to get a price of $927.92 and a delta of −$0.66.

To hedge the coupon bond with the two-year zero-coupon bond, select "hedge." Select "deltas" under "what to hedge?" Choose the 0 percent bond as your hedging instrument. Then select "compute hedge." The software says to short −1.6219 of the two-year zero-coupon bond.

Select "do hedge." The final portfolio has value −$481.92 and a delta of 0.00.

SECTION C EUROPEAN OPTIONS

We now show how to value and hedge European options on zero-coupon bonds and coupon bonds using the software.

1 European Option on a Zero-Coupon Bond

To value and hedge a European call option on a zero-coupon bond, you first need to create a zero-coupon bond.

Construct a five-year zero-coupon bond. Select "add" and then "bond." Then choose

Length in years = 5
Annual rate = 0
Principal = 1,000

Ignore all the other choices. Select "run HJM" to get a price of $795.99 and a delta of −$1.50.

Now you will construct the European call option. Again select "add." Go to the "option" row and select it. The "general option" screen appears, Fig. 17.11. On this screen there are various choices: *(i)* European/American, *(ii)* call/put, *(iii)* end date, *(iv)* strike, and *(v)* underlying asset. The start date is always the current date. Select

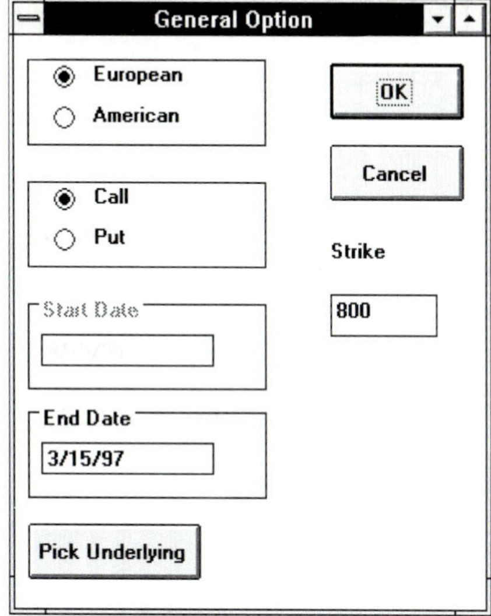

FIGURE 17.11
General option screen.

European
Call
End date two years from today
Strike = 800

Next you need to specify the underlying asset. Select "pick underlying." What appears is the 0 percent bond you created earlier. Choose it. When you return to the portfolio screen, the European call appears as your second security with 0.00 quantity. Run HJM to get the call price of $54.23 with a delta of −$0.90.

To hedge this option, first form a portfolio holding one unit of the option. Click on 0.00 quantity in the EuCall row, and add one unit of it to our portfolio. Next, select "hedge." Select "deltas" under "what to hedge?" Then select the 0 percent bond as the hedging instrument. Select "computed hedge" to get −0.6037 unit of the five-year zero. Select "do hedge" to get a portfolio value of −$426.31 with a delta of zero.

2 European Option on a Coupon Bond

To value and hedge a American option on a coupon bond, you need to create the coupon bond. Select "add" and then "bond." Keep the sample bond as given: three-year maturity, semiannual coupons, annual rate 5.0, principal 1,000. Select "run HJM" to get a price of $1,023.09 and delta of −$1.07.

Next create the option. Again select "add." Go to "option" and choose

European
Call
Strike 1010
End date one year from today

Then select "pick underlying" and select the 5 percent bond. Return to the portfolio and "run HJM." The call's price is \$4.49 with a delta of −\$0.26.

To hedge this option, form a portfolio of one unit of the option by clicking on the 0.00 under quantity for EuCall. Add one unit. Next select "hedge." Choose "deltas" in the "what to hedge?" box. Choose the 5 percent bond as the hedging instrument, and select "compute hedge" to get −0.2393 unit. Select "do hedge" to get a portfolio with −\$240.33 value and a delta of zero.

SECTION D
AMERICAN OPTIONS

This section shows how to price and hedge American options on zero-coupon bonds and coupon bonds using the software.

1 American Options on a Zero-Coupon Bond

To value and hedge an American call option on a five-year zero-coupon bond, you first need to create the zero-coupon bond. Select "add" and then "bond." Choose

Length in years = 5
Annual rate = 0
Principal = 1,000

Ignore all the other choices. Select "run HJM" to get a price of \$795.99 and a delta of −\$1.50.

To create the option, again select "add" and "option." Choose

American
Call
End date two years from today
Strike 800

Select "pick underlying," and choose the 0 percent bond. Press "run HJM" to get an American call option price of \$54.23 and a delta of −\$0.90. This is the same as the European call's value obtained earlier. This is as discussed in Chapter 8.

To hedge the option, first form a portfolio holding one unit of the option. Click on 0.00 under "quantity" in the AmCall row, and change it to 1. Next, select "hedge." Select "deltas," and select "0% bond" as the hedging instrument. Press "compute hedge" to get −0.6037 unit of the five-year zero. Press "do hedge" to get a portfolio value of −\$426.31 and a delta of zero. Again, this is the same as for the European call.

2 American Options on a Coupon Bond

To value and hedge an American option on a coupon bond, we need to create the coupon bond. Select "add" and then "bond." Keep the sample bond indicated: three-year maturity, semiannual coupons, annual rate 5.0, principal 1,000. Press "run HJM" to get a price of \$1,023.09 and a delta of −\$1.07.

To create the option, again select "add." Go to "option" and choose

American
Call
Strike 1010
End date one year from today

Select "pick underlying," and select the 5 percent bond. Return to the portfolio and select "run HJM." The call's price is \$13.10 with a delta of −\$1.07. This implies that immediate exercise is optimal. Indeed, the price of the bond less the strike price is \$1,023.09 − 1,010 = \$13.09. The delta is the same as the delta of the bond. The value is seen to be significantly greater than that of the corresponding European call, which was only \$4.49. This completes the illustration on option valuation.

SECTION E
SWAPS

This section shows how to value and hedge a swap. First, you need to create the swap. Select "add" and then "swap." What appears is the "swap" screen, Fig. 17.12. You will value a swap in which you receive fixed and pay floating.

To see what the underlying fixed note is, select "edit" under "receive." What appears is the "fixed rate note" screen, Fig. 17.13. This is the screen that would have appeared if under "add" you had selected "fixed rate note." This fixed-rate note has a maturity of three years, semiannual payments, an annual rate of 4 percent, and a principal of \$1,000,000.

To see what the underlying floating-rate note is, select "edit" under "pay." What appears is the "floating rate note" screen, Fig. 17.14. This is the screen that would have appeared if under "add" you had selected "floating rate note." This floating-rate note has a maturity of three years and semiannual payments; the maturity of the underlying floating rate is six months, and the principal is \$1,000,000.

Press "run HJM" to get the value of this swap as \$10,375.00 with a delta of −\$886.81.

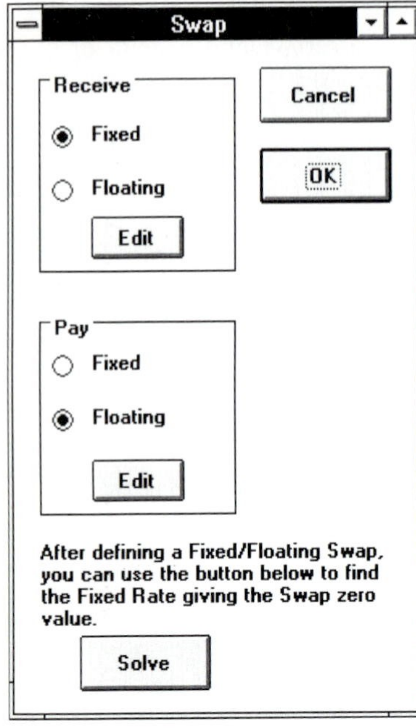

FIGURE 17.12
Swap screen.

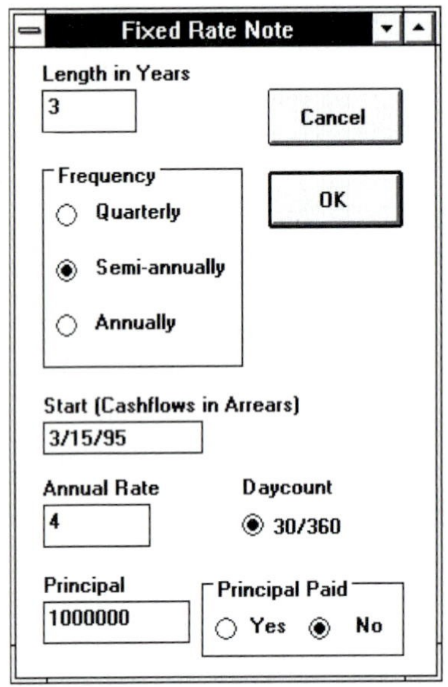

FIGURE 17.13
Fixed-rate note screen.

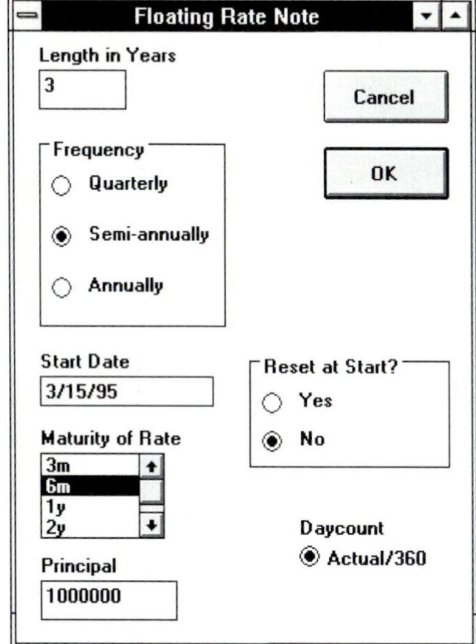

FIGURE 17.14
Floating-rate note screen.

If you want, you could solve for the fixed rate to give this swap zero value. To do this, return to "add," select "swap," and then select "solve." You get a rate of 3.630535 percent.

To hedge this swap, you need a hedging instrument. We will illustrate the procedure with a two-year zero-coupon bond. Select "add" and then "bond," and then choose two-year maturity, annual rate 0.0, principal 1,000. Ignore all the other selections. This is a two-year zero-coupon bond. Press "run HJM" to get a price of \$927.92 and a delta of −\$0.66.

Next, form a portfolio consisting of the swap. Go to quantity 0.00 for swap, click on 0.00, and change to 1.

To hedge the swap, press "hedge." Choose "deltas" in "what to hedge?" Choose the 0 percent bond as the hedging instrument, and press "compute hedge" to get −1,340.552 units of the two-year zero-coupon bond. Press "do hedge" to get a portfolio value of −\$1,233,556 with a delta of zero. This completes the illustration.

SECTION F
CAPS AND FLOORS

This section shows how to value and hedge caps and floors. First, you need to create a cap. Select "add" and then "cap." What appears is the "cap or floor" screen, Fig. 17.15. A cap or floor is defined by *(i)* its length in years, *(ii)* the frequency of payment, *(iii)* the strike, *(iv)* the first reset date, and *(v)* the principal. Keep the example as given, with length three years, quarterly frequency,

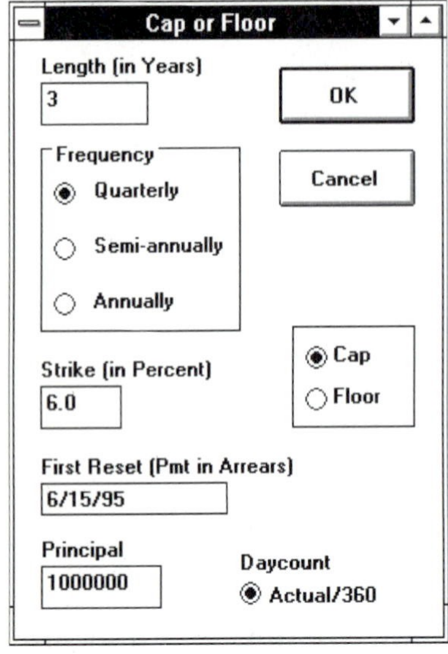

FIGURE 17.15
Cap or floor screen.

6 percent strike, and principal $1,000,000. Press "run HJM" to get a cap value of $2,197.80 and a delta of $151.55.

To hedge this swap, you need a hedging instrument. We will illustrate this procedure with a two-year zero-coupon bond. Select "add" and then "bond," and then choose two-year maturity, annual rate 0.0, and principal 1,000. Ignore all the other selections. This is a two-year zero-coupon bond. Press "run HJM" to get a price of $927.92 and a delta of −$0.66.

Next, form a portfolio consisting of the cap. Go to quantity 0.00 for cap, click on 0.00, and change to 1.

To hedge the cap, press "hedge." Choose "deltas" in "what to hedge?" Choose the 0 percent bond as the hedging instrument, and press "compute hedge" to get 229.0897 units of the two-year zero-coupon bond. Press "do hedge" to get a portfolio value of $214,775.70 with a delta of zero. This completes the example.

A floor is valued in the same way as a cap, except that in the "cap or floor" screen, you must choose "floor." This security is left as an exercise.

SECTION G SUMMARY

This chapter demonstrates how to use the HJM demonstration software included with the book. We have only illustrated the most straightforward calculations under a one-factor model. The software allows any instrument to be used as a hedge against any other instrument with either one or two factors. You are encouraged to play with the software and learn the relations among the various fixed-income securities and interest rate options.

INDEX